CADILLAC

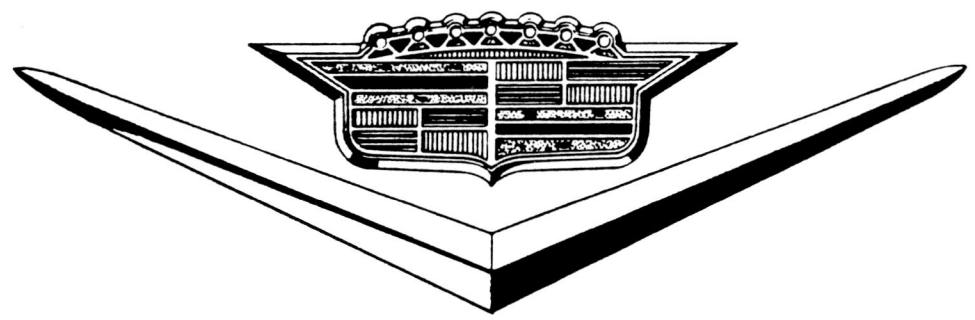

AN ILLUSTRATED GUIDE TO 1950 THRU 1959 MOTOR CARS

Edited by
Roy A. Schneider

Copyright © 1978 by the Automobile Heritage Publishing Company, © 1990 Royco Publishing. This book was manufactured in the United States of America and published simultaneously in Sweden. Copyrighted under International and Pan-American Copyright Conventions. All rights reserved. No part of this work may be reproduced or copied in any form or by any means — graphic, electronic, or mechanical, including photocopying, recording, taping, or information and retrieval systems — without written permission of the publisher, except in the case of brief quotations embodied in critical articles and reviews.

I.S.B.N. 0-917104-02-1

CONTENTS

	Page
PUBLISHER'S FOREWORD	4
MODEL YEAR COMPARISON PHOTOS	5
NINETEEN FIFTY	12
NINETEEN FIFTY-ONE	28
NINETEEN FIFTY-TWO	40
NINETEEN FIFTY-THREE	56
NINETEEN FIFTY-FOUR	82
NINETEEN FIFTY-FIVE	106
NINETEEN FIFTY-SIX	130
NINETEEN FIFTY-SEVEN	156
ELDORADO BROUGHAM	182
NINETEEN FIFTY-EIGHT	190
NINETEEN FIFTY-NINE	212
PRODUCTION STATISTICS	240

Published by
CADILLAC MOTORBOOKS
A Division of Royco
POST OFFICE BOX 7
TEMPLE CITY, CALIFORNIA 91780

PUBLISHER'S FOREWORD

The post-war years of the 1950s produced an unprecedented phenomenon — the Cadillac Renaissance. Cadillac has been America's marque of excellence since the dawn of the motoring age, but during the Fifties Detroit's oldest automaker experienced a resurgence of demand that hadn't been witnessed since the late 1920's. In the 1950s Cadillac had all the glamor, excitement and spectacle of those grand classic years, plus one added dimension, almost universal popular appeal. Its impact on the Country was without parallel. FORTUNE, the nation's most respected business publication, reported that *polls indicated at least one out of two Americans would buy a Cadillac before any other car if they had the money.*

Industry leaders were awed by what became known as the *Cadillac Phenomenon.* The Division consistently set new production records, yet the overwhelming backlog of unfilled new car orders persisted. Expansion programs yielded higher production totals, but an unveiled and unrelenting pent-up demand for Cadillacs continued. General Motors itself wasn't sure exactly what the parameters of the potential Cadillac market were.

For the *Standard of the World* it was a decade of irresistible styling, incomparable performance and, above all, continuing prestige. Each model year introduced magical new engineering advances to chassis and engine; and along came power steering, air conditioning, power brakes, electric windows, six-way power seats, cruise control and much more.

It was the era of the fabulous Motoramas and magnificent Cadillac showcars. *Eldorado, Brougham, Seville, Sedan de Ville,* names that have become synonymous with the ultimate in motoring luxury, were all spawned in the 1950s.

This book is about that amazing period of Cadillac's heritage. We have drawn from institutional literature such as data books, press kits, sales catalogs and technical publications. Thus, the material contained within these pages provides a unique source of primary information for both enthusiast and historian. As you use this book remember that an effort has been made to give editorial and subject balance to the project. This has necessitated considerable rearrangement and editing of original material. Certain information that was duplicated from one year to the next has not been repeated, and in some instances new data has been added. However, this volume constitutes a complete survey of the Cadillacs produced in the 1950s.

We are especially appreciative of the assistance provided by the Cadillac Motor Car Division, G.M. Styling, the G.M. Proving Ground and the National Automotive History Collection of the Detroit Public Library. A personal note of thanks to Bill Knight, Norb Bartos and their staff who, along with Tom Clarke, have given freely of their own time in order to preserve historical data at the factory. To David R. Holls and Pierre Ollier of GM Styling goes our continuing gratitude. Their interest in automotive design goes far beyond their professional involvements. Finally, to James J. Bradley of the Detroit Public Library, the guardian of American automotive lore, our sincere appreciation.

In 1978, when this book was first published, serious collector interest in Cadillacs of the 1950s was still embryonic. A core of preservation-minded enthusiasts, many of them members of the Cadillac-La Salle Club, had already saved many prime examples from the crusher. Now, a dozen years and three printings later, these Cadillacs are among the most sought after and valuable collector cars on earth. Across this great Country and around the globe, to Europe, Australia and Japan, this highly distinctive generation of Cadillacs stand as iconistic symbols of the USA's glorious post-war era. This book is dedicated to those enthusiasts, past, present and future, who restore, preserve and enjoy these legendary Cadillacs of yesteryear.

RAS

PRINTED IN THE
UNITED STATES OF AMERICA

1954

1955

1956

Photos used in this comparison study are originally from the files of the GM Proving Ground in Milford, Michigan. Their extensive testing program is regularly documented with photographic records such as these. The actual testing data remains classified for a number of years. The editors acknowledge this fine contribution and thank the officials at the Proving Ground for their cooperation and interest.

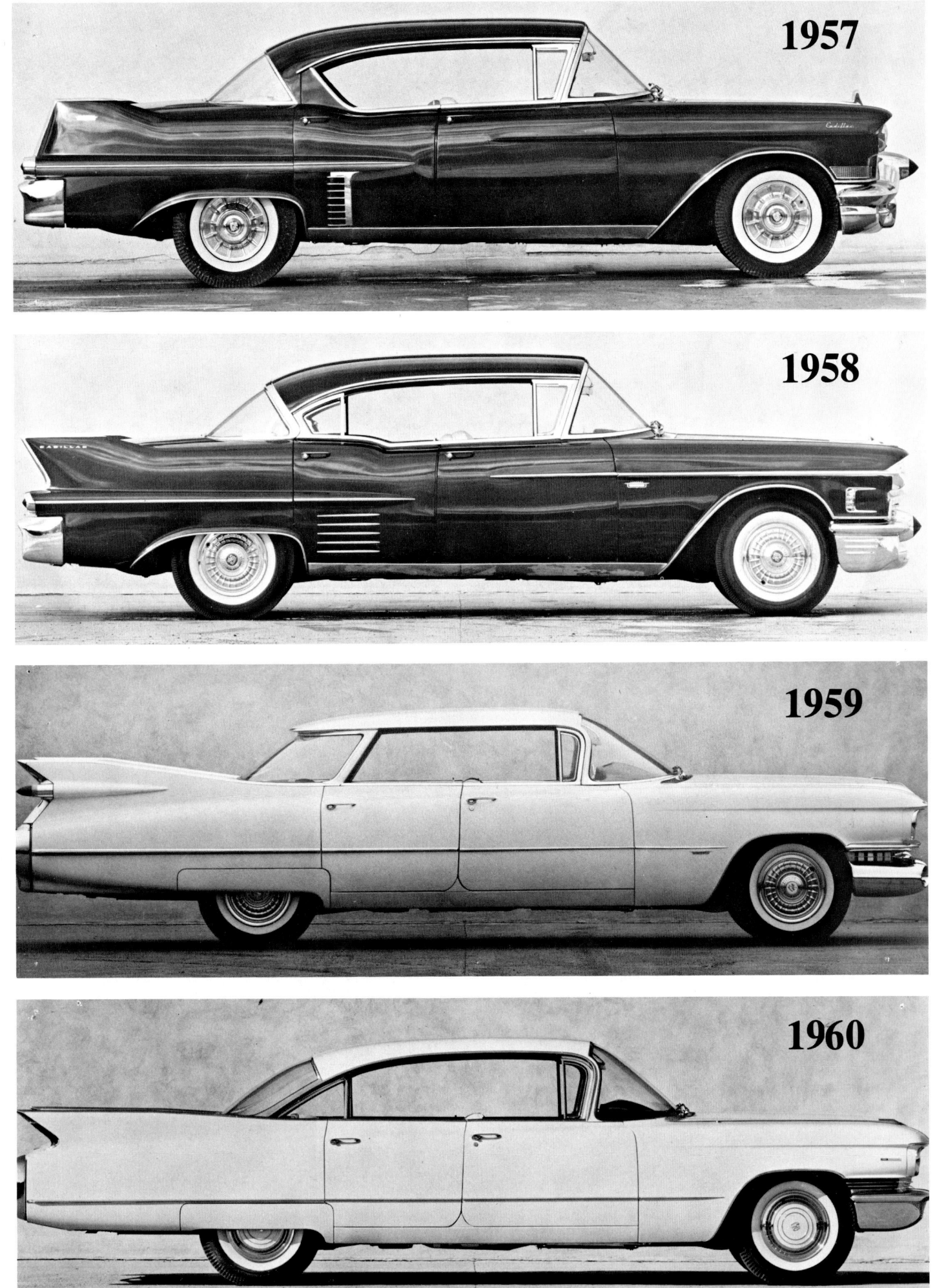

1950

1951

1952

1953

1954

1955

1956

1957

1958

1959

1960

1950 *Features*

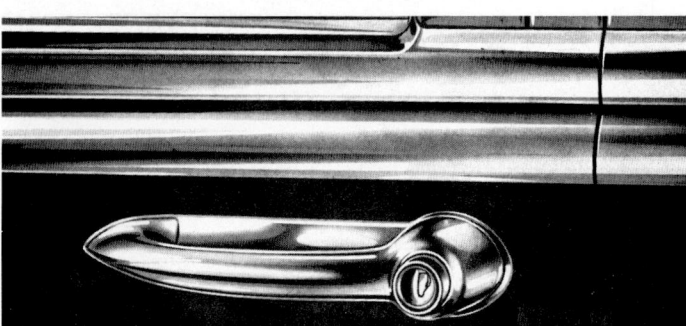

Exterior door handles are of new design. Mounted below the bright chrome door molding, the handle is gracefully curved and is stationary. The door latch control is a button which is inset in the end of the door handle. A protective bright chrome escutcheon plate fits flush against the door and follows the contour of the door handle. Both front doors are fitted with outside locking buttons while rear doors of sedan models, except the Series 75 which has an outside right rear door lock, are locked from the inside.

An important feature of the 1950 design is the new bright chrome ornamental fender insert which is shaped to follow the front fender contour. The insert is mounted between the lower grille bar and the bottom of the fender. Above the insert the upper chrome bar continues back along the edge of the fender wheel opening and joins the decorative chrome fender and door molding spear. One basic advantage of this over-all design is the increased strength added along the edge of the front fender. A painted metal splash guard below the grille covers the bumper mounting brackets attached directly to the frame.

The new rear fender door stone guard is a chrome simulated air scoop which follows the fender and door contour and connects at the bottom with the wheel cover molding. The name, Cadillac, in script appears on all front fenders above the fender molding. There is a lower door sill molding which runs from the front fender opening to the rear stone guard on all models except the Series 61. A rear fender molding in chrome is also used on all models except the Series 61.

Below, 1950 Sixty-Special

1950 *Features*

The radio is installed in the center of the instrument panel above the grille. Controls are mounted in the insert panel directly under the map lights. The winged Cadillac crest finished in chrome is used on all series except the 60 Special which uses the Fleetwood crest in gold. Upper and lower level heat controls are in the left side of the radio grille—ash receiver at right. Right and left air inlet controls are under the grille.

An extra large cloth lined glove box is at the right of the instrument panel. A convenient storage space for maps, gloves or small parcels is automatically illuminated when the door is opened. The new electric clock is mounted above the glove box in the insert panel. The adjustment controls for fast or slow regulation and setting the bands are mounted in the bright chrome molding.

Driver's instruments are grouped in the recessed panel directly above the steering column. A large speedometer dial with a new, narrow, illuminated hand provides high visibility. Odometer and gauges are directly below. The starter button ignition switch and cigar lighter are at the right of the steering column below the insert panel. At the left of the instrument cluster in the insert panel is the headlight switch. The windshield wiper control is mounted directly below in the lower portion of the instrument panel. The hand brake and hood latch controls, not shown, are mounted under the instrument panel to the left of the steering column.

The new curved windshield is one piece, accurately ground to prevent distortion. The curved contour blends gracefully into the flowing body lines. Wider and higher, the windshield is framed in bright chrome. Extra narrow corner pillars and more than 7 square feet of windshield glass area provide exceptional vision. The new full width rear window in sedan models contains approximately 6 square feet of area. Curved to follow the body and roof contour, the rear window is divided into 3 sections. The exceptionally narrow rear corner pillar minimizes the usual blind spot. Side windows are wider and higher. All Cadillacs for 1950 have more than 3300 square inches of glass area.

Many features of the 1950 Cadillac, such as the massive chrome grille, large full-across wrap-around bumpers, integrally designed parking and direction lamp, chrome headlight moldings, new wide "V" with the traditional Cadillac crest, bomb type bumper guards, chrome front fender stone guards and decorative chrome fender moldings and the chrome inserts are common to all series.

Cadillac Series 61 Sedan 1950

The new curved rear window is molded to fit the top contour and extends across the width of the car. Increased visibility is a feature of 1950 Cadillacs.

The smooth flowing lines of the Series 61 Sedan feature an extra wide rear window, graceful rear deck, distinctive rear fenders.

The deck line on the Series 61 Coupe is longer than on the 61 Sedan but features the same graceful fender and new rear bumper.

Characteristic of Cadillac design for 1950 is its rear fender treatment featuring a simulated air inlet at the forward end and terminating in an upward flare at the rear.

Series 61 Sedan interiors are tailored in rich, fine-quality fabrics of gray pattern broadcloth or corded cloth. Seats and seat backs carry light tone cloths and are finished with French seams. Door panels are trimmed in dark tone cloths deeply tufted and fitted with six buttons. A narrow stainless steel molding above imitation leather seat kick pad and door kick panels, together with bright chrome hardware, brightens the appearance. Door trim panels and window molding are morocco brown. Front carpets are gray rubber to match rear pile carpets. Center and side arm rests assure luxurious comfort.

Cadillac Series 61 Coupe *1950*

Cadillac motor cars for 1950 bear all of the traditional hallmarks of Cadillac design and quality. The Series 61, offered in two body styles, is identical in front-end appearance and basic features of design with all other 1950 Cadillac models. The 61 Series offers the distinction of Cadillac ownership at the lowest cost consistent with Cadillac's traditionally high standards of quality.

As on all 1950 Cadillac models front fenders flow gracefully and become an integral part of the body design. Fender molding sweeps from the grille to the door molding.

Coupe interiors are trimmed in two-tone effect. Seats and seat backs are light tone, while door panels and seat cushion edges are dark tone. Ash trays are inset in the wide box-type side arm rests. When door and rear quarter windows are rolled down, the entire area is free from obstructions, since there is no center pillar. The narrow rear quarter pillar and extra large rear window afford unusual vision. Window moldings and trim panels are morocco brown. All hardware is bright chrome. Rubber carpets match in color the dark-tone upholstery. Door handles and window regulators have bright chrome shanks, escutcheon plates and knobs designed and styled in keeping with the new interior motif. Set in a morocco brown panel with a gray insert, they add a touch of style and luxury.

Cadillac Series 62 Coupe 1950

The 62 Standard Coupe is upholstered in two-tone cloth combinations of gray broadcloth with either plain or pattern cloth or bedford cord. Body sides are trimmed with a horizontal pleat motif with narrow chrome moldings. A wide center arm rest and large side arm rests with inset ash receivers enhance the comfort and convenience of this fine car. Floors are covered with fine-pile carpeting which harmonizes with the dark tone upholstery. The convenient metal parcel shelf behind the rear seat is attractively covered with artificial grained leather. Hydraulically operated window controls and front seat adjustment are available in this model at extra cost.

The instrument panel is functionally designed with controls and instruments grouped for quick visibility and convenience. The panel is beautifully finished in morocco brown while the insert is a pattern design in light tone. The panel with the distinctive Cadillac crest and wings in bright chrome curves gracefully to blend with flowing lines of the door molding.

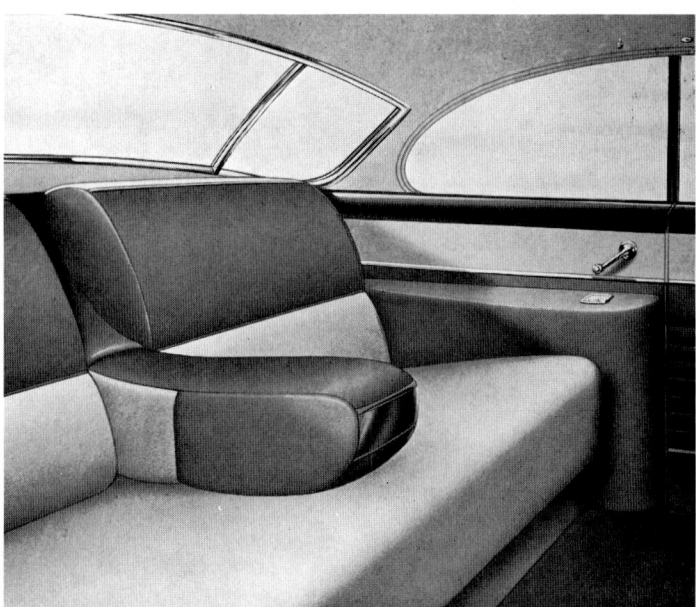

A feature of the Series 62 Coupe is its extra long rear deck which adds to the appearance of the car and provides additional luggage space. The wide rear window and narrow corner pillars give better vision.

Cadillac Series 62 Sedan 1950

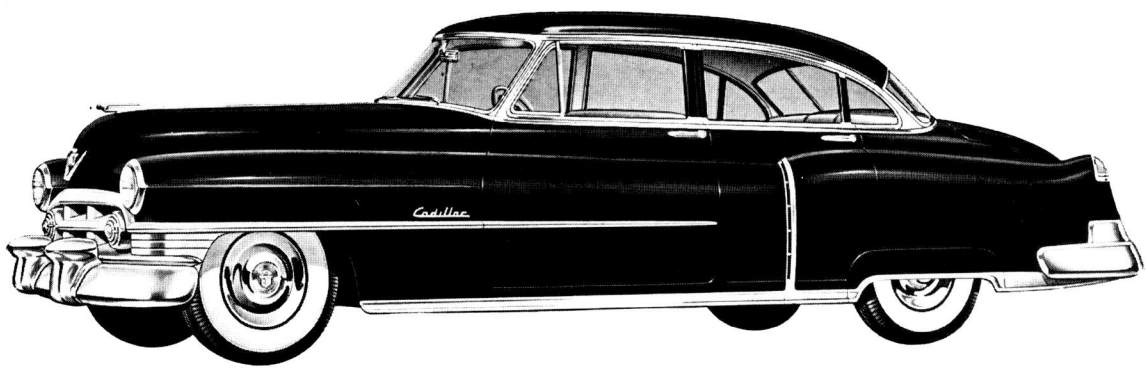

The front compartment of the 62 Sedan is distinctively styled and neatly tailored. Available in two-tone combinations of broadcloth, striped cloth or bedford cord in gray tone, seats and seat backs are light color while bolsters and seat cushion sides are dark. Door panels are two-toned featuring an extra long arm rest, chrome moldings and French-seamed pleats. Window moldings and door trim panels are morocco brown— while quarter ventilator moldings are chrome. Wool pile floor carpet matches dark tone upholstery. Front hardware, except window regulator, is grouped in a panel insert of pearl beige. Imitation leather for door and seat kick panels is in a dark finish to harmonize with the dark tone upholstery.

The 62 Sedan uses the same rear deck and rear fender as used on the Series 61 Sedans. Dual backup lights are standard equipment on all Cadillac models. The wide rear window is framed in bright chrome as is the new narrow corner pillar. Chrome molding along the lower edge of the rear fender, the rocker sill and wheel shield gives added beauty and strength.

The rear compartment of the 62 Sedan is **luxuriously trimmed in rich quality upholstery.** Seats and seat backs are severely tailored in two-tone gray combinations of bedford cord, striped cloth and broadcloth with French seams. The large center arm rest and extra large side arm rests add to the comfort and convenience. A new narrow rear corner pillar combined with a large, full width rear window increases visibility. The large rear quarter venti-pane increases rear vision and improves ventilation. Door panels are in two-tone combinations matching seat upholstery. Dark tone carpets, imitation leather door and seat kick pads, chrome moldings and bright chrome hardware enhance the over-all beauty of the styling and luxury of this popular model. Hydraulic window and front seat control is available at extra cost.

Cadillac Series 62 Convertible 1950

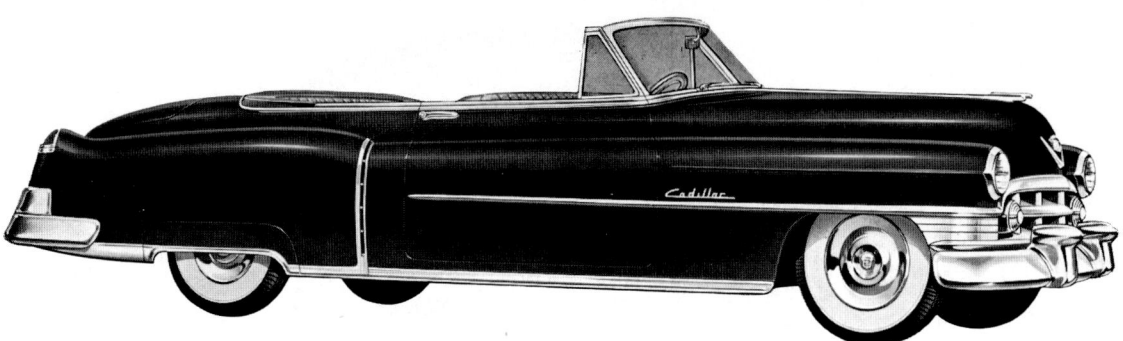

Available only in the Series 62, the convertible is truly the last word in sport models. Long and low, the long type rear deck and rear fenders contribute to its sleek appearance. Rear quarter windows which pivot completely out of sight, as well as side windows and front seat adjustment are hydraulically controlled. The power operated top which is available in either black or tan material, folds neatly into the panel behind the rear seat back. The spare tire and wheel, as in all Cadillac models, is mounted vertically in the right side of the trunk.

Convertible Interiors are trimmed in all leather. Options are available in either three single colors or in two two-tone combinations of green or blue. Seats and seat backs are piped with leather while seat tops and edges are plain. Bright chrome hardware and hydraulic window controls are grouped in the door panel which is framed in molding painted to match body color and contrasted with a light tone insert. Floors are carpeted in fine-pile to match dark tone leather. Each door panel is in leather with a decorative chrome "V".

The new rear deck lid ornamental "V" and traditional crest serve a dual purpose, as a trunk lid handle as well as an identifying characteristic.

The convertible coupe side arm rests contain the rear quarter window hydraulic control button and ash receiver.

Right, a restored 1950 Series 62 Convertible.

Cadillac Series 62 Coupe de Ville 1950

Shown above is the 62 Sedan door featuring hydraulic controls which are optional at extra cost. Moldings are morocco brown with pearl beige insert. Hardware is bright chrome beautifully designed and styled in keeping with interior appointments. Door panels are two-toned with extra long arm rest.

Rear and side vision is greatly improved by the new narrow rear quarter pillar which also increases structural strength. The wide clear-across curved rear window frame and corner pillar are in bright chrome.

Coupe de Ville interiors are rich in styling and luxury. Upholstery combinations in striking two-tone leather and broadcloth options of either gray leather with dark blue cloth or tan leather with tan broadcloth, are available. Leather in 3" pipes is used on bolsters and upper door panels while plain cloth is used on seat cushions and backs as well as lower door panels. Imitation leather headlining with chrome simulated top bows and bright chrome hardware enhances the beauty and distinction of this luxurious sport car. Chrome window and trim moldings with painted door moldings lend a note of distinction. Window and front seat controls are hydraulic. Ash receivers and cigar lighters are inset in the rear compartment side arm rests. Front seat backs have individual robe cords.

A distinctive feature of all Cadillac cars is the neat combination rear tail and directional signal lamps. The left unit also serves to conceal the gasoline tank filler cap.

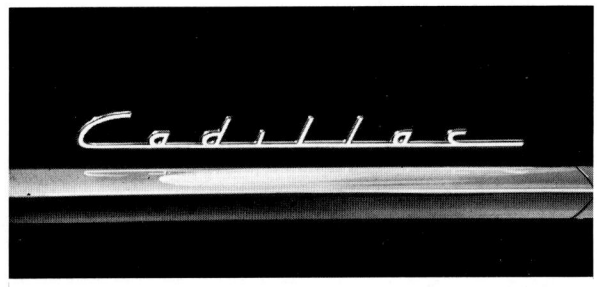

1950 SERIES 75

The Cadillac Fleetwood 75 for 1950 is completely new and similar in basic design to all other Cadillac models. Long and low, its modern exterior appearance strikes a new note in cars of this exclusive type and character. The chassis wheelbase has been increased to 146" to provide the ultimate in interior room and riding comfort. Available either as a 7-passenger limousine with auxiliary seats which fold into the dividing front partition, or as a luxurious 7-passenger sedan, this new Cadillac is luxurious in its appointments and brilliant in its performance. It is constructed with but one thought in mind—to create an automobile for an exacting clientele whose requirements can be satisfied by no other motor car.

The Series 75 has the standard rear sedan deck and the same rear fenders as those on the 62 sedan model. A distinguishing feature is the rear window which is made narrower than other sedan models to accommodate a closed rear-quarter panel for added privacy. Both 75 sedan and limousine exteriors are identical with the same chrome moldings and trim.

The limousine division, shown above, is upholstered in broadcloth. Seat back molding with inserted electric clock is finished in brown burl walnut grain. A cloth covered robe cord fits into the assist handles which are mounted on the seat back. The two auxiliary seats fit flush with the seat back panel and are slotted at the bottom to allow warm air to enter the rear compartment from the underseat heater. The lower portion of the division glass can be hydraulically operated from the rear seat. The upper curved section is stationary. This is a new, original Cadillac design which increases visibility and eliminates the upholstered header normally used. The limousine front seat is stationary.

The front compartment of Series 75 limousine models is trimmed in black leather throughout. The seat and seat backs all have 2½" pipes with French seamed leather. Door panels are black leather with black trim molding, chrome window molding and bright chrome hardware. The left door contains hydraulic controls for all windows. The head lining is black imitation leather. Floor carpeting is mottled black rubber. The division glass is framed in bright chrome. The steering wheel column and instrument panel are black with standard chrome hardware.

Rear compartment interiors of the Series 75 are unusually commodious and trimmed in luxurious fabrics. The rear seat cushion and seat back are in a tufted motif, accentuated by wide plain bolsters. A choice of either bedford cord or broadcloth is optional in pleasing shades of tan or gray. Garnish moldings, door panels and floor carpets are in harmonizing colors with bright chrome hardware and decorative trim. Equipment and appointments include side arm rests with map compartments under the hinged cover as well as ash receivers and cigar lighters, a large center arm rest, robe cord, assist grips, foot rests, an electric clock in the front seat back, hydraulic window and sedan front seat adjustment controls.

SERIES 60 SPECIAL 1950

There is only one Cadillac-Fleetwood 60 Special—a beautiful sedan whose extra length and graceful flowing lines distinguish it from all other cars. Emphasis in the 60 Special is upon luxury. Wheelbase, rear deck, and rear fenders are long and low, giving a sleek, smooth appearance. Easily identified by the eight louvres on the rear fender door cap, the 60 Special is a car designed for those whose choice is unrestricted. Offered in a wide choice of body colors and a variety of upholstery options, this fine car is tastefully tailored, large and roomy. Every detail from the fine fabrics, hydraulic window and seat controls to full curved windshield, features superb taste, roominess and comfort. America's finest owner-driven motor car.

60 Special interiors are beautifully tailored in rich upholstery. They are available in four colors including green, tan, blue or gray. The upholstery is either plain or patterned material and is offered in combinations of pattern or cord seats and seat backs with plain cloth bolsters, or in plain cloth throughout. Seats and seat backs are divided into biscuits with cloth covered buttons for trim. Door panels have a biscuit panel with plain cloth above and below. Door kick pads are bright chrome. The driver's door contains the hydraulic window controls for all windows, set in a panel with a pattern insert framed by molding painted to blend with upholstery colors. Windows are framed in chrome. Hardware is beautifully designed. The front compartment floor has a pile carpet with an artificial leather heel pad under the foot controls.

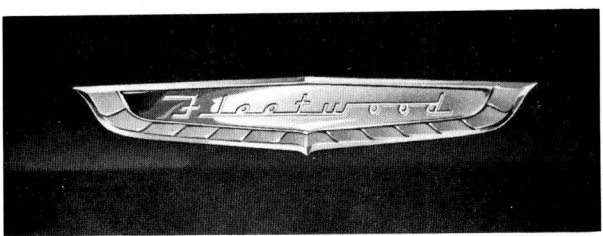

The soft, wide, deep seats with large center arm rests and wide side arm rests accent the comfort and luxury so much a part of the 60 Special. The full-across rear window, the narrow rear corner pillar, the large rear quarter venti-pane and full rear door window give unsurpassed vision to rear seat passengers. Hydraulic window controls in each rear door as well as door latch handle are in bright chrome. A convenient ash receiver and cigar lighter as well as a cloth covered robe cord are mounted in the recessed, heavily padded, front seat back. Liberal use of chrome in window moldings, door trim, kick pads and garnish moldings brightens the interior appearance. The floors are carpeted in wool pile matching in color the upholstery and trim color selected.

From every angle the 60 Special is refreshingly new in design. Viewed from the rear the graceful body lines show practicality as well as beauty. The full-width rear window and narrow body pillars create better rear vision. The long rear deck, with correspondingly long fender line, in addition to providing more luggage space, compliments the long, low lines of the body and accents its appearance of fleetness and grace. A few distinguishing features of the 60 Special include its extra long wheelbase and corresponding body room, luxurious comfort, practically unlimited vision in any direction and increased trunk space. (The spare tire is carried vertically.) The ornamental crest, shown below, is also designed to be used as the deck handle. Unlocking the trunk automatically releases the latch and allows the counterbalanced deck lid to rise. Hydra-Matic Drive, backup lights and glare proof mirror are now standard equipment on the Series Sixty Special Sedan.

THE 1950 ENGINE

FEATURES OF THE NEW ENGINE

★

BETTER PERFORMANCE

★

SMOOTHER, QUIETER OPERATION

★

GREATER DURABILITY

★

LESS WEIGHT

★

GREATER ECONOMY

★

INCREASED HORSEPOWER

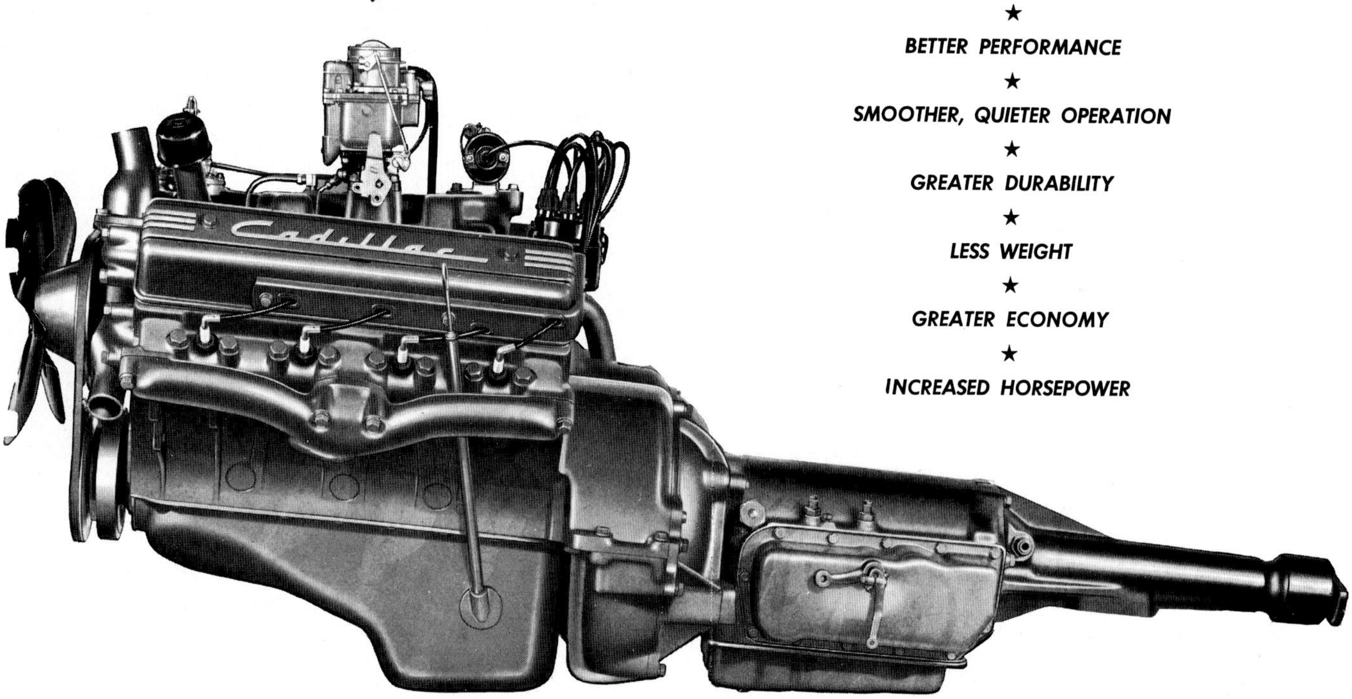

THE NEW CADILLAC V-TYPE OVERHEAD VALVE ENGINE

(Now In Its Second Year of Production)

The new Cadillac engine is a revelation in automotive design and efficiency. Many advanced features literally establish it as a new standard of the world in motor car power. Among these is the new overhead valve combustion chamber design which assures controlled burning of the compressed gas to create a smooth power thrust. This design also permits the use of a higher compression ratio producing gains in power and economy. The combination of a new, larger cylinder bore and shorter piston stroke contributes to efficient operation by exposing about 12% less cylinder wall area to flame. This results in lower heat loss and greater cooling efficiency. The shorter piston stroke reduces frictional power losses by reducing piston travel approximately 20%. At 4000 R.P.M. the pistons travel at the rate of only 2400 feet per minute against 3000 feet per minute in previous models. Thus, high mechanical and thermal efficiency contribute to increased power output.

Main crankshaft bearings have been increased from 3 to 5 and placed in heavy bulkheads which help form a rigid, box-like crankcase structure. This feature is partially responsible for creating the smoothest, quietest running Cadillac engine ever built. Other features contributing to smooth, quiet operation include a newly-designed valve mechanism with high rigidity factors, hydraulic valve lifters and reduction in air cleaner and exhaust system noises.

This new Cadillac engine is the result of years of research both in laboratory and on the road. It will take only a few moments of your time—with your own foot on the accelerator—to prove to you that Cadillac has given the world a new standard for automotive engines.

Dual down-draft carburetor with newly-designed manifold is centered between the cylinder heads for effective distribution of fuel.

IMPROVEMENTS have been made in the design of the fuel intake system to allow freer breathing of gas into the combustion chambers. To accomplish this, a new oil-bath air cleaner has been designed which increases intake capacity of the filtered air to the dual down-draft carburetor. In the 1950 engine a completely new design of both carburetor and manifold eliminates any possibility of icing. Heat passages from the intake manifold run through the carburetor warming the air around the idle posts, thus preventing moisture in the air from freezing.

THE HYDRA-MATIC STORY

Cadillac reaches its highest approach to perfection when Hydra-Matic Drive is used with the new Cadillac overhead valve engine. In this combination, Cadillac engineers have effectively brought together two great engineering achievements which assure maximum efficiency and performance. From the moment the Cadillac is put in motion until it is brought to a complete stop, all operations of driving, except steering, are completely and smoothly automatic, bringing new driving ease and safety to motoring. There are three separate developments in this great Cadillac power train: Cadillac's 160 horsepower engine—a fluid coupling—a 4-speed automatic transmission. The fluid coupling, between engine and transmission, transmits power by means of a pair of steel rotors housed in a sealed casing filled with fluid. The automatic transmission contains three planetary gear units, each having a different gear ratio. Two are 2-speed units used for forward operation. All three are used in reverse.

As power flows from the engine, the driving member of the fluid coupling is set in motion through a forward planetary set of gears. As this member is revolved, it sets the fluid in motion and causes it to flow against the vanes of the driven member which transmits power through the main transmission shaft and rear planetary gear unit to the rear wheels.

Gone is the familiar task of clutching and gear changing, for all that is needed is pressure on the accelerator and the Cadillac automatically goes through four gear ratio changes—changes that occur at the precise instant for best performance. More than a dozen operations of clutch pedal, gearshift lever and accel-

The planetary gears and main transmission shaft which have been removed from housing.

erator have been eliminated every time the Hydra-Matic Cadillac is accelerated from a standing start.

The advantages of Hydra-Matic operation are clearly apparent to the driver whether in slow, heavy traffic or cruising along the open highway. With Hydra-Matic, the driver can relax and smoothly and effortlessly maintain perfect car control, using only accelerator and brake pedal, for Hydra-Matic eliminates guesswork. Proper gear ratio is automatically selected to meet the power required of the engine and the car speed.

Driving and driven members of fluid coupling removed from casing and opened to show vane structure

Hydra-Matic Drive which is standard equipment on the Series 62 and 60 Special and optional on the Series 61 and 75 is vastly improved for 1950. An important new feature is modulated line pressure which regulates the line pressure according to the throttle opening. This eliminates any noticeable downshift in gear ratio from second to first.

Ratio changes in Hydra-Matic are made as follows:

"DR" RANGE "UP-SHIFTS"

Ratio	M.P.H. Minimum Throttle	M.P.H. Full Throttle
1st to 2nd	5-7	11-15
2nd to 3rd	11-14	29-37
3rd to 4th	17-19	61-69

"LO" RANGE "UP-SHIFTS"

1st to 2nd	11-15	23-28

"DR" RANGE "DOWN-SHIFTS" (test made on up-grade)

4th to 3rd	12-15	55-63
3rd to 2nd	....	11-13
3rd to 1st	3-7	....
2nd to 1st	....	6-9

"LO" RANGE "DOWN-SHIFTS" (test made on up-grade)

4th to 2nd	42-50	....
2nd to 1st	5-9	12-15

Note: Miles per hour at which shift is made is dependent on throttle opening. Actually no gears shift. Term used for clarity of meaning only.

REGULAR CADILLAC
3.77 Standard Axle—Series 61
4.27 Standard Axle—Series 75

HYDRA-MATIC CADILLAC
3.36 Axle—Series 61, 62, 60S
3.77 Axle—Series 75

TRANSMISSION AND CAR RATIOS

	Transmission Ratios	Over-all Reduction With 3.77 Axle	Over-all Reduction With 4.27 Axle	Transmission Ratios	Over-all Reduction With 3.36 Axle	Over-all Reduction With 3.77 Axle
Low	2.39	9.00	10.20	3.819	12.83	14.40
Second	1.53	5.76	6.63	2.634	8.85	9.93
Third	1.00	3.77	4.27	1.450	4.87	5.47
Fourth	....	....	....	1.000	3.36	3.77
Reverse	2.39	9.00	10.20	4.304	14.46	16.23

1950/1951

Accessories

Spotlight is mounted through the door. The spotlight has been designed with a built-in rear view mirror enabling the driver to adjust the mirror from inside the car.

License Plate Frames enhance the appearance and protect the license plates. Chrome plated, these frames are supplied in pairs.

Fleetwood Robe is custom tailored of finest broadcloth and lined with either alpaca or crushed silk plush or broadcloth.

Windshield Washer sprays water on the windshield so that mud or slush may be removed by the windshield wipers. In summer, the tank is filled with water—in winter, a special anti-freeze solution is available.

Seat Cover. Again Cadillac offers a wide selection of fine seat covers. Paratwill, illustrated, and sea breeze all mat covers will be available in a variety of patterns and colors.

Outside Rear View Mirror is available for installation on either side. It is heavily chrome-plated and designed to harmonize with exterior trim.

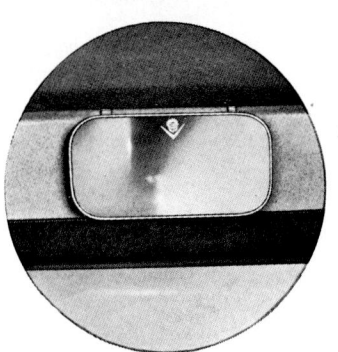

Vanity Mirror—A new vanity mirror is now available for installation on either sun visor. The mirror may be used by lowering the visor—when the visor is raised the mirror is out of sight.

Foglamp Combinations incorporate a parking light, directional signal, and foglamp. It is designed to replace the standard parking and direction lights which are recessed in the front grille.

Cadillac Outside Sun Visor—Chrome-trimmed and painted to match the car color, the new Outside Sun Visor reduces sun and sky glare while keeping hot sun from striking front-seat occupants' laps. This beautifully styled visor provides full forward visibility, yet reduces accumulation of freezing rain and snow on windshield.

Telescopic antenna is vacuum operated by pushing in or pulling out volume control knob while engine is running.

The Automatic Push Button Radio
—With elliptical speaker, offers fine reception under all conditions. Station selectors are set by using the push-pull lock-up tuner. Control knobs and illuminated dial are designed to match the clock and instrument dials.

Wheel Discs completely cover the wheels. The discs which are chrome plated, rust and rattle-proof, add a note of smartness to the exterior appearance.

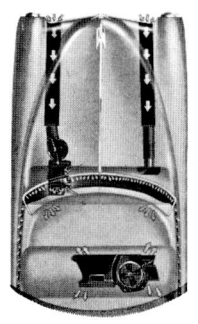

Syncro-Matic Radio and Rear Speaker—The new Syncro-Matic Radio with Bar tuning and individual signal seeking adjustment is the most modern car radio available. By turning signal seeking control to any of five positions radio will automatically receive stations from 2500 watts to 50,000 watts. As many as 50 stations may be received by simply touching the tuning bar. An auxiliary rear compartment speaker is standard equipment with this radio.

Trim Rings are available for those owners who prefer to contrast bright chrome with wheel colors. The trim rings are stainless steel, heavily chromed.

NEW ALL-WEATHER VENTILATING SYSTEM

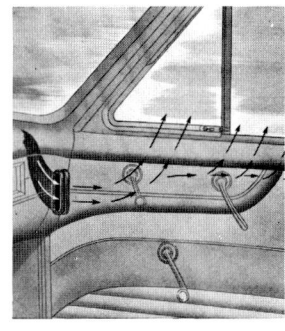

For 1950, Cadillac has designed and engineered a completely new all-weather ventilating system. It consists of an underseat recirculating hot water heater for lower area heating and a heater-defroster for upper area heating. Outside air enters through two ducts which run along the sides of the car under the hood. The left side duct feeds the outside air into the inlet of the heater-defroster unit. This outside air is warmed and then forced by blower and impact through the upper area heating ducts. The heated air is blown across the full width of the windshield. Heated air is blown through ducts extending into the front doors. This air defrosts the windshield, quarter ventilators, and door glass and also circulates heated air into the upper area of the car. The underseat heater and fan heat the lower car area by circulating warm air through ducts into both the front and rear compartments. Upper and lower area heating is thermostatically maintained by individually operated manual controls. In summer, air enters the front compartment through both the right and left side ventilating ducts, which may be controlled separately.

Automatic Heating System—completely new, provides separate control of upper and lower level temperatures. This thermostatically controlled automatic heating system combines an underseat recirculating hot water heater with a heater-defroster unit. Windshield, quarter vents and front door glass areas are defrosted.

Automatic controls located on radio grille maintain the desired temperature.

Standard Heater and Defroster. Front compartment passengers will enjoy the new heater designed for use in mild climates. The heater and defroster unit is controlled thermostatically. The defroster outlet is so designed that warm air is blown across the complete windshield width.

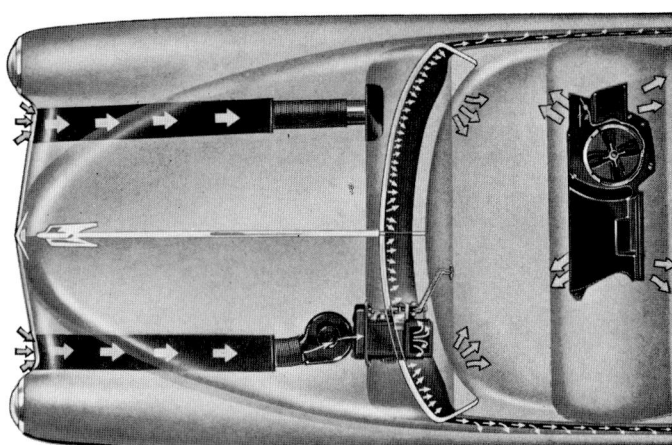

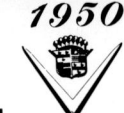

DETAILED SPECIFICATIONS

Engine, Electrical

Generator:	
Make	Delco-Remy
Number	#1102700
Type	Current and voltage regulated
Voltage at cut-out closing	5.9-6.8 (adjust to 6.4)
Amperes to open cut-out	0 to 3
Generator normal charging rate	40 amps. peak. Due to voltage regulation actual charging rate is controlled by state of charge of battery
Peak charging speed	27 M.P.H. up
Generator ventilation	Forced air
Generator:	
Commutator end bearing	
Type	Bronze bushing
Size	9/16" x 3/4" x 3/4"
Drive end bearing:	
Make and type	N. D. Ball
Number	#954378
Starter motor:	
Make	Delco-Remy
Number	#1107969—4 pole
Drive	Solenoid shifted gear
Automatic starting device	Delco-Remy push button
Starter motor:	
Commutator end bearing:	
Type	Durex bushing
Size	3/4" x 5/8" x 9/16"
Outboard bearing:	
Type	Durex bushing
Size	9/16" x 5/8" x 3/4"
Starting motor pinion meshes with flywheel	Front
Flywheel teeth, integral or steel ring	Steel ring
Gear ratio between starter armature and flywheel	16.1 to 1
Spark advance	Centrifugal and vacuum
Ignition unit:	
Make	Delco-Remy
Number	#1110819
Manual advance	None
Maximum centrifugal advance	32° crankshaft
Vacuum advance	22° crankshaft
Distributor breaker gap	.013"-.018"
Initial spark advance	0°-5° B.T.C.
Firing order	1-8-4-3-6-5-7-2
Ignition coil:	
Make	Delco-Remy
Number	#1115380
Amperage draw of coil:	
With engine stopped	4.5 to 5.5
With engine idling	2 to 3
Spark plug:	
Make	A.C.
Model	46.5
Thread	14 mm.
Gap	.033—.038

Transmission—(Standard)

	Series 61	75
No. of forward speeds	3	
Control on steering column	Manual	
Transmission, make	Own	
Gear ratio in high	Direct drive	
Gear ratio in second	1.53 to 1	
Gear ratio in low and reverse	2.39 to 1	
Type of gears:		
First and reverse	Sliding—helical	
Second	Constant mesh—helical	
Synchronous meshing second and third gears?	Yes	
Transmission oil capacity	3.75 pints	
Transmission oil grade recommended, S.A.E. viscosity	S.A.E. 90 E.P.	
Transmission main shaft front pilot bearing, make and type	Hyatt roller	
Number	#1294780	
Transmission main shaft intermediate bearing, make and type	N. D. Ball	
Transmission main shaft rear bearing, type	Steel-backed babbitt	
Transmission countershaft front bearing, type	Needle bearing	
Transmission countershaft rear bearing, type	Needle bearing	
Transmission reverse idler bearing, type	Steel-backed babbitt	

Fuel Tank and Exhaust System

Gasoline tank, capacity	20 gals.
Muffler, type	3 pass

Engine-Clutch

Clutch: (With Standard transmission, available in Series 61 and 75 only)		
Make	Long Mfg.	
Operated, dry or in oil	Dry	
No. of clutch driven discs	1	
Vibration insulator or neutralizer	Coil spring type	
Clutch facing material	Woven	
Area	96.16 sq. in.	103.4 sq. in.
Inside dia.	7"	
Outside dia.	10½"	11"
Thickness	.137"	
No. of facings required	2	
Clutch throwout bearing:		
Make	Bearings Co. of America	
Type	Ball	
Number	CTDS—56	

Steering Mechanism

	Series 61, 62, 60S	75
Steering gear:		
Type	Recirculating ball	
Make	Saginaw	
Over-all steering ratio	25.47—1	
Car turning radius (outside) bumper to bumper sweep	(61) 22′ (60) 23′	(62) 22.5′ (75) 25.5′
Camber angle	−3/8° to +3/8°	
Toe-in inches	1/32" to 3/32"	

Wheels & Tires

Tire:		
Make	U.S. Royal—Firestone and Goodrich	
Size	8.00 x 15	8.20 x 15
No. of plys	4	6
Inflation pressure:		
Front	24 lbs.	28 lbs.
Rear	24 lbs.	28 lbs.
Wheels:		
Type	Slotted disc	
Make	Kelsey Hayes	
Rim, diameter	15"	15"
Rim, width	6.00"	6.00"
Tread:		
Front	59"	59"
Rear	63"	63"
Wheelbase	(61) 122", (62) 126", 60S—130"	146¾"

Chassis Electrical System, Instruments & Instrument Panel

Battery:	
Make	Delco K4W
Number of plates	17
Capacity (amp. hrs.)	115

Chassis Electrical System, Instruments & Instrument Panel—Continued

	Series 61, 62, 60S	75
Battery bench charging rate:		
Start	10	
Finish	8	
Which battery terminal is grounded?	Negative	
Location of battery	Under hood on tray attached to R.H. dash to frame brace front of dash	
Headlight, make	Guide sealed beam	
Headlight cover glass, dia.	6 11/16"	
Parking light, make	Guide	
Tail light, make	Guide	
Lighting switch, make	Delco-Remy	
How are headlights dimmed?	Depressed beam—foot switch	
Horn:		
Make	Delco-Remy	
Type	Airtone	
Amperage draw of horns	Low note 21 High note 19	

Radiator

Radiator core:	
Make	Harrison
Type	Tube and fin
Cooling capacity	18 qts.

Miscellaneous Final Assembly Items

	All Series
Car lifting device, jack	Bumper type
Engine lubrication, type	Pressure
Chassis lubrication, type	High pressure
Axle lubrication, type	Splash
Transmission lubrication, type	Splash

Capacities and Grades

	All Series
Engine oil	5 qts.
Recommended viscosity	Min. anticipated temperature +32°F. 20W or S.A.E. 20; +10°F. 20W; −10°F. 10W; Below −10°F. 5W
Drain	2000 miles (after initial 500 mile change)
Rear axle oil	5 pints
Recommended viscosity	90 hypoid
Transmission oil	3.75 pints
Recommended viscosity	S.A.E. 90 E.P.
Cooling system—water	18 qts.
Gasoline	20 gals.

FEATURES OF DESIGN AND CONSTRUCTION OF CHASSIS

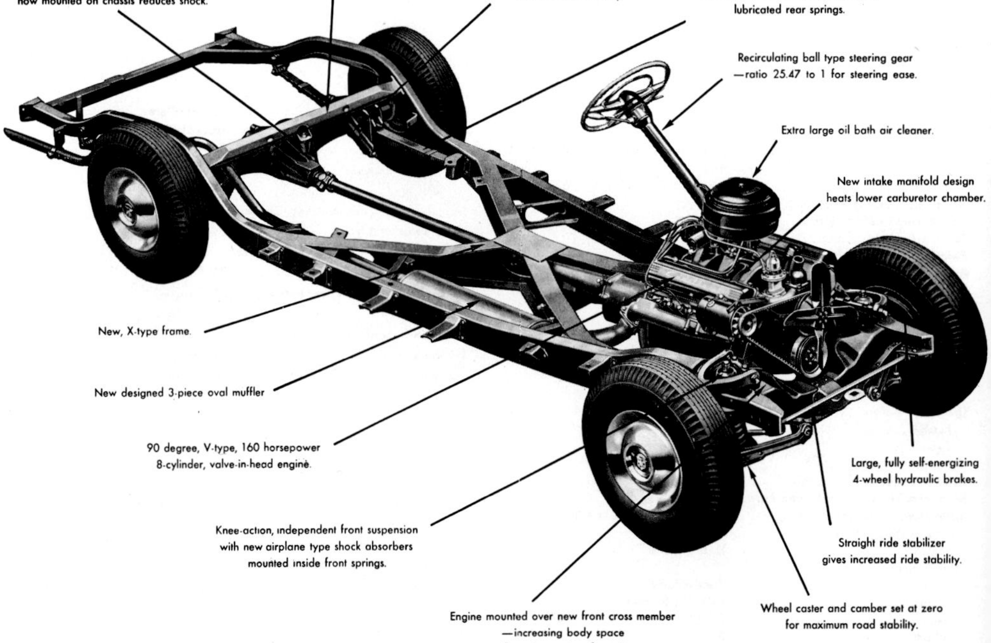
New, more rigid boxed cross-member
Axle compression bumper now mounted on chassis reduces shock.
Airplane type, angle-mounted rear shock absorbers improve ride and increase stability
Hotchkiss drive through permanently lubricated rear springs.
Recirculating ball type steering gear—ratio 25.47 to 1 for steering ease.
Extra large oil bath air cleaner.
New intake manifold design heats lower carburetor chamber.
New, X-type frame.
New designed 3-piece oval muffler
90 degree, V-type, 160 horsepower 8-cylinder, valve-in-head engine.
Large, fully self-energizing 4-wheel hydraulic brakes.
Knee-action, independent front suspension with new airplane type shock absorbers mounted inside front springs.
Straight ride stabilizer gives increased ride stability.
Wheel caster and camber set at zero for maximum road stability.
Engine mounted over new front cross member —increasing body space —lowering center of gravity

Body	Series 61	62	60S	75
Types	2	4	1	2 pleasure
Construction	Fisher Unisteel	Fisher Unisteel	Fleetwood Unisteel	Fleetwood Unisteel
Running boards	Concealed scuff plate	Concealed scuff plate	Concealed scuff plate	Concealed scuff plate
Total glass area (sq. in.)	3377	3539	3539	3609
SEDAN DIMENSIONS: (Based on New Approved GM Dimensioning System)				
Headroom—Front	35⅛″	35½″	35½″	37″
Rear	35¼″	36¼″	36¼″	35″
Legroom—Front	43 7/16″	44″	44″	43 5/16″
Rear	40⅝″	40⅝″	40⅝″	
Seat width—Front:				
Hip	63½″	63½″	63½″	64″
Shoulder	58¼″	58⅛″	58⅛″	58⅛″
Seat width—Rear:				
Hip	64½″	64½″	64½″	56⅞″
Shoulder	56⅞″	56½″	56½″	56⅛″
Ground to Door Sill (rear door)	13¾″	13¾″	13¾″	12″
Over-all length bumper		6237-D & 6267 220⅞″		
to bumper	211⅞″	215⅞″	224⅞″	236⅝″
Over-all width—				
Front	80″	80″	80″	80″
Rear	80⅛″	80⅛″	80⅛″	80⅛″

Frame	Series 61, 62, 60S			75
Frame make	A. O. Smith	A. O. Smith	A. O. Smith	A. O. Smith
Frame depth, maximum	7⅛″	7 5/32″	7 3/16″	7 3/16″
Frame thickness, maximum	⅛″	9/64″	5/32″	5/32″
Flange width, maximum	2 9/16″	2 37/64″	2 19/32″	2 19/32″
Frame—Type	Girder	Girder	Girder	Girder

Front End Suspension

Front suspension, make	Own
Front suspension, type	Forked arms
Forked arm bearings, type	Threaded
Kingpin upper bearing, type	Bronze bushing
Kingpin lower bearing, type	Bronze bushing
Front wheel inner bearing, make and type	N. D. Ball
Front wheel outer bearing, make and type	N. D. Ball
Front spring, type	Helical coil
Front spring, material	GM #9260 steel
Knee-Action coils	Enclosed by frame sidebars
Caster angle	Neg. ½° to Pos. ½°
Camber angle	−⅜° to +⅜°
Toe-in, inches	1/32—3/32
Crosswide inclination of kingpin, degrees	5° 51′ at 0° Camber
Shock absorber, type	Hydraulic direct-acting type
Front stabilizer	Torsion rod

Rear Axle & Rear End Suspension

	Series 61, 62, 60S	75
Rear axle, make	Own	
Rear axle, type	Semi-floating	
Minimum road clearance under center of rear axle, tires inflated	8.34	8.44
Differential gear, make	Own	
Rear axle		
Oil capacity	5 pints	
Grade recommended:		
S.A.E. viscosity	90 hypoid	
Type of final gearing	Hypoid	
Gear ratio:		
Standard	3.77 (available on 61 only)	4.27
Hyd. Trans.	3.36	3.77
No. of teeth in ring gear (Std.)	49	47
No. of teeth in pinion (Std.)	13	11
Pinion adjustment	None	
Pinion bearing adjustment	None (Preloaded)	
Are pinion bearings in sleeve?	No	
Backlash between pinion and ring gear	.003-.010″	
Rear axle pinion shaft		
Front bearing, type	Tapered roller	
Rear bearing, type	Tapered roller	
Differential bearing,		
Right, type	Tapered roller	
Left, type	Tapered roller	
Universal, make	Mechanics	
Model	#3-RCR	
Type	Needle bearing	
Universal joints, lubricated	Permanently	
Drive & torque taken through	Rear springs	
Rear wheel bearing, make and type	N. D. Ball	
Spring leaves lubricated with	Wax impregnated liners	
Spring bushings, type	Rubber	
Stabilizers	Rear—None	
Rear Springs:		
Type	Semi-elliptic	
Material	GM #9260 steel	
Length	54½″	56½″
Width	2″	
No. of leaves	8 60S—9	10
Shackles, type	Compression link	

Rear Axle & Rear End Suspension—Continued	Series 61, 62, 60S	75
Rear spring shackle bolt,		
Upper	Rubber mounted	
Lower	Rubber mounted	
Shock absorbers, type	Hydraulic direct-acting type	

Brakes

	Series 61, 62, 60S	75
No. of complete brakes	4	
Foot brakes:		
Make and type	Bendix-Hydraulic	
Total area	224.5 sq. in.	258.5 sq. in.
Braking ratio:		
Front	55.8%	
Rear	44.2%	
Vacuum booster	None	
Brake lining, molded or woven	Molded	
Brake drum material	Composite	
Front brake drum diameter	11	12
Front brake drum, internal or external	Internal	
Front brake lining, length per wheel:		
Forward shoe	10.55	12.92
Reverse shoe	11.90	12.92
Total	22.45	25.84
Front brake lining width	2½″	
Front brake lining thickness	3/16″	
Front brake clearance	.007-.010″	
Rear brake drum diam.	11	12
Rear brake drum, internal or external	Internal	
Rear brake lining, length per wheel:		
Forward shoe	Same as front	
Reverse shoe	Same as front	
Total	Same as front	
Rear brake lining width	2½″	2½″
Rear brake lining thickness	3/16″	
Rear brake clearance	.007-.010″	
Hand brake location	Left side of dash	
Hand brake lever operates on	Rear service brakes	

Engine

	Series 61, 62, 60S	75
No. of cylinders	8	
Engine make	Own	
Engine model	50-61, 50-62, 50-60S	75
Cylinder arrangement	90° V-type	
Numbering arrangement:		
Left cylinder	1-3-5-7	
Right cylinder	2-4-6-8	
Piston displacement	331 cu. in.	
Taxable horsepower	46.5	
Maximum brake horsepower at R.P.M.	160—3800	
Standard compression ratio	7.5 to 1	
Standard compression pressure lbs/sq. in.	194 at 1000 R.P.M.	
Bore and stroke	3 13/16″ x 3⅝″	
First serial number	61 —506100000 62 —506200000 60S—506000000	507500000
Serial number location	Upper right corner on front face of right hand block—numbered at right angles to crankshaft	
Main bearing:		
Make and type	Moraine Durex	
Poured, spun or separate	Separate (precision inserts)	
Clearance	.0015″-.0025″	
No. 1 main bearing journal, diameter and length	2½″ x 1′	
No. 2, 3, 4 main bearing journal, diameter and length	2½″ x 1 1/16″	
No. 5 main bearing journal, diameter and length	2½″ x 1⅞″	
Crankpin journal, diameter and length	2¼″ x 2″	
Main bearings	5	
Which main bearing takes thrust?	Rear (No. 5)	
Vibration dampener	Torsional	
Torsional vibration, dampener type	Rubber absorption type	
Crankshaft counterweights	6	
Crankshaft end play	.001″-.005″	
Clutch pilot bearing:		
Make and type	Moraine Durex	
Piston material	Aluminum alloy	
Piston features	T-T-slot Stannate-treated finish	
Piston weight, lbs.:		
Without rings, pin	1.206	
With rings, pin	1.726	
Piston length	3 15/16″	
Piston clearance	.0013″-.0017″	
No. of rings per piston:		
Compression	2	
Oil	1	

Engine—Continued	Series 61, 62, 60S	75
Wrist pin length	3 3/32″	
Wrist pin diameter	1″	
Wrist pin	Pressed into rod	
Wrist pin clearance	.00005″-.0001″ at 70°F.	
Wrist pin hole finish	Diamond bore in rod, bearingized stannate-plate in piston	
Connecting rod:		
Length, center to center	6⅝″	
Material	#1041 steel	
Weight, including bearings	1.649 lbs.	
Connecting rod bearing:		
Make and type	Moraine Durex	
Poured, spun or separate	Separate (precision insert)	
Clearance	.001″-.0035″	
Connecting rod end play	.008″-.014″ (total for two rods)	
Rods and pistons removed from	Above	
Oil reservoir capacity	5 qts.	
Oil pump, type	Helical gear	
Normal oil pressure lbs. at M.P.H.	35 lbs. at 30 M.P.H.	
Pressure at which relief valve opens	40 lbs.	
Type of oil drain	Threaded plug	
Oil reservoir gauge, type	Dip stick	
Engine lubrication:		
Lubricating system, type	Pressure	
Valve lifter lubrication	Pressure	
Main bearing, lubrication	Pressure	
Connecting rod bearing lubrication	Pressure	
Wrist pin, lubrication	Splash	
Camshaft bearing, lubrication	Pressure	
Timing gear, lubrication	Positive	
Crankcase ventilation	Road draft type	
Cooling system capacity	18 quarts	
Accessory drive belt (fan, pump and generator):		
Type	Wedge type Vee	
Width, maximum	.380″	
Length (outside circumference)	57″	
Fan blades	4	5
Coolant circulation, type	Pump	
Water pump, type	Centrifugal—dual outlet	
Blocking thermostat, make, control and type	Fulton Sylphon or Dole Vernatherm	
Carburetor, make	Carter—742S	
Size	1¼″	
Type	Plain tube	
Up or down draft	Down draft	
Single or dual	Dual	
Heat adjustment	None	
Automatic choke:		
Make	Carter	
Type	Thermostatic	
Air cleaner and intake silencer:		
Make	A.C.	
Type	Concentric	
Fuel feed type	Camshaft pump	
Engine mounted on	Vulcanized synthetic rubber	
No. of points of suspension:		
Front	2	
Rear	1	
Timing chain:		
Type	Side guide	
Make	Link belt	
Model	57 TCE—11	
Length	23″	
Number of links	46	
Width	11/16″	
Pitch	.500″	
Adjustment	None	
Valve arrangement	Over-head	
Valve timing at .001 tappet lift:		
Intake opens	24° B.T.D.C. at .001 cam-lift	
Intake closes	98° A.B.C. at .001 cam-lift	
Exhaust opens	63° B.B.C. at .001 cam-lift	
Exhaust closes	49° A.T.C. at .001 cam-lift	
Cylinder head material	Cast iron, GM 13M	
Intake valve:		
Actual over-all diameter of head	1.750″	
Angle of seat	44°	
Seat insert	None	
Cooled by	Directed water circulation	
Stem clearance	.0005″-.0025″	
Lift	.330″	
Spring pressure and length:		
Valve closed	60 lbs.—1.696″	
Valve open	135 lbs.—1.366″	
Exhaust valve:		
Actual over-all diameter of head	1.4375″	
Angle of seat	44°	
Seat insert	None	
Cooled by	Directed water circulation	
Stem clearance	.0015″-.0035″	
Lift	.330″	
Spring pressure and length:		
Valve closed	60 lbs.—1.696″	
Valve open	135 lbs.—1.366″	
Tappet clearance, adjustment	Automatic	
Camshaft	Cast iron alloy	

1951

During the half-century of its existence, the Cadillac motor car has stood uniquely alone in the way it looks, in the way it performs, and in the prestige it bestows upon its owners. So well has it been designed and so soundly built during these many years, in fact, that Cadillac now enjoys a reputation for quality and goodness that is probably without parallel in all our industrial history. But it is, nevertheless, always an extremely happy occasion with us when we find ourselves embarking on a year that promises to increase still more the measure of Cadillac's leadership in the world of motor cars. As the ensuing pages will reveal—1951 is destined to be still another such year.

A feature of all 1951 Cadillacs is the new ornamental grille extension beneath the headlights, which adds to massive appearance. The headlight rims are of new distinctive design. A simulated air scoop, which follows the fender and door contour, is mounted at the body edge of the rear fender. Cadillac appears in script above the front fender molding.

All Cadillacs for 1951 feature the same exclusive design and front end appearance. The massive chrome grille conceals an outside hood latch behind the top horizontal bar. A new grille extension continues the smooth flow of chrome across the front of the fenders. New combination grille and bumper guards add to lower appearance of the front. The traditional crest with a wider, more massive V is lower on the hood. Newly designed and exclusively styled chrome headlight rims add a new note of distinction. Such features as the sturdy wrap-around bumpers, integrally designed parking and directional signal, add to the smart appearance of all Cadillacs for 1951.

Trunks on all 1951 Cadillacs are unusually large and roomy. The standard trunk on every sedan series, except the 60 Special, contains approximately 13.5 cu. ft.—accommodating up to eleven standard pieces of luggage including a golf bag. The 60 Special trunk is even larger, containing over sixteen cubic feet. Convertible trunks contain approximately 17.7 cubic feet. All trunk interiors are carpeted to prevent scuffing of luggage.

The Instrument Panel for 1951 features a recessed light-tone insert. The speedometer is inset above the steering column, which is enclosed in a new, streamlined housing. Radio and electric clock are in the middle and right. The speedometer is inset over the odometer and the telltale gauges, which light whenever oil or generator should be attended. When the integral starter switch is turned, a special light in the instrument panel cluster indicates the emergency brake is on by lighting the word "Brake" in red. The steering wheel provides a handsome dual grip for driving convenience. The Hydra-Matic dial is contained in the top half of a circular panel enclosing the horn.

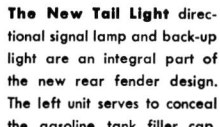

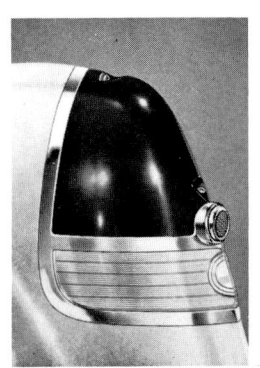

The New Tail Light directional signal lamp and back-up light are an integral part of the new rear fender design. The left unit serves to conceal the gasoline tank filler cap.

In Models containing hydraulic window lifts, all of the window regulators are placed within the door insert panel. The left front door contains master controls for raising and lowering all windows except on the 75 limousine. The door molding and color pattern insert harmonize with the interior color motif.

The Traditional Crest and "V" on the rear deck are not only decorative, but functional as well, the "V" serving as the trunk lid handle.

Interiors are completely re-styled with new trim motif and fine rich fabrics and designs. Increased interior size adds to passenger comfort and convenience.

Cadillac Series 61 Sedan   1951

The new Cadillac Series 61, available in two body styles, offers the distinction of Cadillac ownership at the lowest possible cost consistent with Cadillac standards. It is identical in front-end appearance and in basic features to other 1951 Cadillacs. Because of its moderate price this series is particularly popular with motorists first moving up to the "Standard of the World."

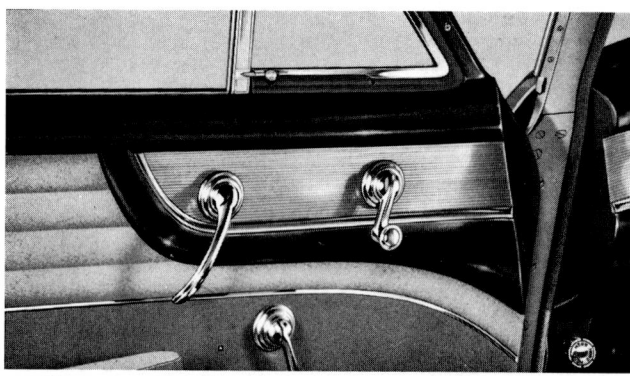

The Series 61 has a decorative insert panel which sweeps across the instrument panel to the front doors. This insert is carried into each front door and houses door handles and front ventilator window regulators. The light color tone of this panel contrasts with the darker tones of the trim panels.

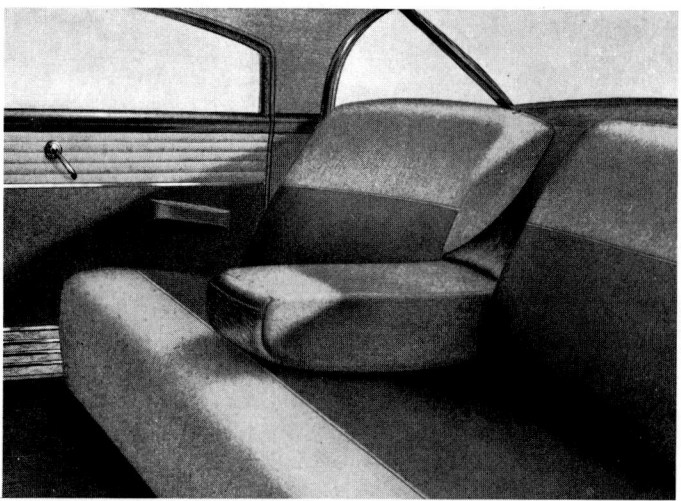

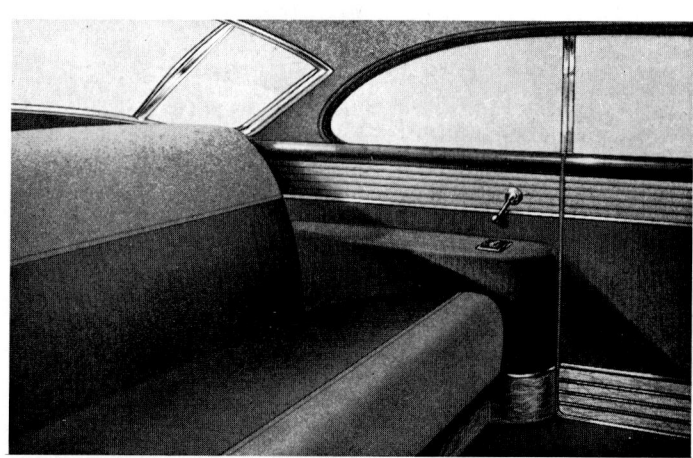

Series 61 Sedans and Coupes strike a fresh note in interior beauty. Bolstered two-tone seats and seat backs are available in pattern or plain cloth with a choice of either gray or tan, combined with light-tone broadcloth. Doors feature light-tone cloth risers above plain or patterned cloth panels. Stainless steel moldings with leather risers serve as a kick panel, while headlining is light in tone. Window moldings and trim panels are painted to match the trim motif. Wool pile carpeting in front and rear compartments complements interior color. Features of the coupe include large rear side windows, a full-width rear window with narrow quarter panel . . . extra large side arm rests, ash receiver and robe cord in back of front seat. Rear seat leg room has been increased through the use of newly designed recessed front seat back on the sedan model and new rear seat-back cushions on both sedan and coupe.

Cadillac Series 61 Coupe   1951

Cadillac Series 62 Sedan

The Series 62 Sedan rear compartment offers the same general interior motif as the Coupe. Deep, soft, wide seat cushions and backs are tailored in either pattern, cord or plain material, in a choice of tan or gray. The large center arm rest and side arm rests enhance the comfort and luxury of this model. A robe cord and ash receiver are inset in the recessed front seat back. Harmonizing carpets, chrome moldings and bright chrome hardware enhance the over-all beauty of styling. All garnish moldings and trim panels are painted to harmonize with the upholstery color. The narrow rear corner pillar, which increases structural strength, and the large full width rear window increase visibility. The wool pile carpeting matches the trim.

The interior of the Series 62 Coupe is distinctively styled and beautifully tailored in two-tone combinations of either tan or gray, in either pattern, cord or plain cloth. Seats and seat backs are upholstered in 6" pleats, while light and dark tones give sparkling new appearance to side and door panels. Doors feature a flowing line of cloth risers with brilliant chrome trim moldings and painted window molding. Extra large side arm rests with insert ash receivers and a large center arm rest add to comfort and convenience. Narrow rear quarter panels and large rear windows which pivot at the front increase visibility.

Cadillac Series 62 Coupe

Cadillac Series 62 Convertible — 1951

Convertible Interiors are trimmed entirely in leather and are available in either three single colors or in two-tone combinations of green or blue. Seat cushions and seat backs are pleated with dark-toned leather as are the top and bottom of the door and side panels. In two-tone trim, plain leather of a light tone is used in the door and side panel and across the top of the seat backs. Bright chrome hardware highlights the all-over color scheme. Instrument and trim panels are painted to match the exterior color while the floor carpeting matches the dark-toned leather. Windows, top and front seat adjustment are hydraulically operated. Quietness and extra rigidity are assured in convertibles due to the extra heavy frame and the addition of more body bolts and extra rigid body supports.

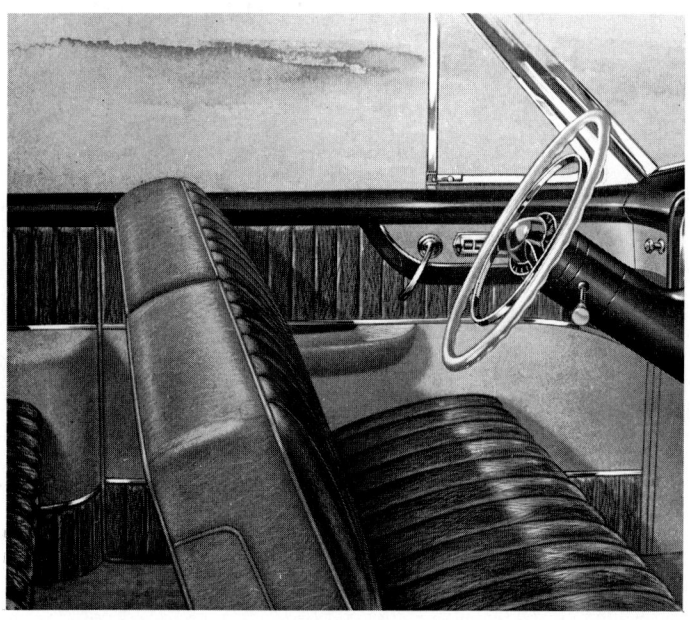

Here is an interior so beautiful that it is destined to endear itself to all whom it surrounds. The Coupe de Ville this year is striking beyond description—carrying the sports motif to its fullest expression. Dark, rich broadcloth of either blue, green or tan is used on seats, side and door panels. Light tone leather in gray, green or buff is used on both the upper half of the seat backs and the top and bottom of both the side and door panels. The headlining matches the leather color, while chrome simulated top bows and bright chrome hardware highlight the whole gorgeous picture. The instrument and trim panels match interior trim. Wool pile carpeting is of either blue, green or tan to match the trim. Window and front seat controls are hydraulically operated.

Cadillac Series 62 Coupe deVille — 1951

Above, the 1951 Series 62 Coupe. Below, the 1951 Series 62 Convertible. Veteran Cadillac watchers generally look at the lower grill extensions for a quick reference in identifying the various model years in the early 1950s — horizontal grooves for 1950, cross-hatched grills for 1951 and the gold-finished winged crests for 1952.

Cadillac Fleetwood 60 Special

1951

Easily identified by the extra long rear deck and the long rear fenders with eight louvers on the rear fender door cap, the 60 Special is a car designed for those who desire America's finest owner-driven motor car. Every detail places the emphasis on luxury. A wide choice of fine upholstery fabrics in a variety of colors meets the desire of the most discriminating. This magnificent sedan, whose extra length and graceful flowing lines distinguish it from all other cars, is beautiful and fleet in appearance. Every luxurious detail—from the hydraulic window and seat controls, large one-piece windshield, narrow rear quarter panel, affording exceptional vision —has been included in this most exclusive of all Cadillacs.

The interior of the magnificent 60 Special is a perfect example of the coachmaker's art at its finest. Richly upholstered in a choice of fabric colors—green, tan, blue or gray—it features harmonizingly blended color variations, highlighted by bright chrome appointments. The seats and seat backs are pleated in flowing, graceful lines, in rich broadcloth. Contrasting light and dark tones with chrome moldings highlight the door panels. Instrument and trim panels are painted to match the general color scheme. Headlining is in lighter tones while the wool pile carpeting matches the trim. All front compartment hardware, including a hydraulically operated master window control in the driver's door, is set in an individual panel in the front doors. A large center arm rest in the rear seat adds to comfort. A robe cord, ash tray and lighter combination, and large assist grips are inset in the recessed front seat back.

The narrow rear quarter pillars of the Series 62 and 60 Special provide the maximum rear and side vision while greatly increasing structural strength. The window frames and narrow pillars are finished in bright chrome.

The Rear Quarter Panel, seen here from the interior, affords excellent vision for both driver and passengers. Large rear venti-panes provide air circulation without allowing disturbing drafts to enter the car.

The magnificent Cadillac Fleetwood 60 Special — a car so distinguished and lovely that it knows no rival for the affections of the motoring public. Significantly, there is but one model in this series — a model which has, perhaps, played the major role in building Cadillac's reputation as the "Standard of the World." A natural and logical choice of fine car owners who want the most distinguished owner-driven car the industry affords.

Cadillac Fleetwood Series 75 — 1951

The Cadillac-Fleetwood Series 75 is constructed with but one thought in mind—to create an automobile for an exacting clientele whose requirements can be satisfied by no other motor car. Available either as a 7-passenger limousine with a stationary dividing front partition, or as a luxurious 7-passenger sedan, this distinguished motor car is luxurious in all of its appointments, distinctive in its appearance, and brilliant in its performance. Although similar in basic design to all other Cadillac models, its long, low lines emphasize the sleek appearance of this exclusive model. The ultimate is achieved in interior room and riding comfort by providing this model with a chassis whose wheel base is 146″.

The front compartment of the Series 75 limousine is trimmed in black leather. Seat cushions are pleated in flowing lines while the door panels are plain black leather with black trim molding. The window molding, hardware and division glass frame are all bright chrome. The headlining is in black imitation leather and the floor carpeting in black wool pile. The steering wheel column and instrument panel are black with standard chrome hardware. The left door panel contains a master hydraulic control for operating rear windows only. The stationary limousine division adds greatly to motoring convenience. The back is upholstered in broadcloth while the top molding which houses the electric clock is finished in Carpathian burl walnut grain. The cloth-covered robe cord fits into the assist handles. The two auxiliary seats fit flush with the seat back panel and are slotted at the bottom to allow heat to enter from underneath. The lower portion of the division glass can be hydraulically operated from the rear seat while the upper curved section is stationary.

The distinguished beauty of the magnificent Series 75 is carried with luxurious taste into its beautiful interior. The tufted rear seat and back cushions accentuated by wide plain bolsters, afford maximum beauty and comfort. Luxurious upholstery fabrics are offered in a choice of either Bedford cord or broadcloth in either gray or tan. Garnish moldings,

THE 75 BUSINESS SEDAN

Cadillac-Fleetwood styling and quality are offered in the Business Sedan, designed expressly for rental or livery service. The interior of the Business Sedan is especially trimmed in tan broadcloth on seats, seat backs and door panels. The full across rear seat and extra wide auxiliary seats accommodate 6 passengers in the rear compartment.

THE 1951 Cadillac

ENGINE

So basically sound and mechanically perfect was the original design of this great engine, in fact, that while this will mark its third year beneath the Cadillac hood, only minor refinements have been possible. These, however, have resulted in even quieter operation and lower oil consumption.

One of the prime objectives in the original development of this engine, for example, was to increase horsepower and fuel economy by taking advantage of the higher octane fuels that appeared on the post-war market. The Grand Canyon Economy Run, in which each of Cadillac's passenger series averaged over 22 miles per gallon, is eloquent testimony of the success of this effort. Recent experimentation and testing, however, have demonstrated that the fuels now on the market, as well as those expected in the near future, do not warrant any change in its initial $7\frac{1}{2}$ to 1 compression ratio—and that to do so would mean a sacrifice in Cadillac's all-around performance. While its basic design could accommodate a ratio as high as 12 to 1, the original estimate of Cadillac engineers has proved accurate beyond reproach.

This does not mean, however, that the 1951 Cadillac engine has not been improved. Indeed, delighted Cadillac owners will find it still quieter, still smoother, still generally more efficient. And while anyone who experienced its performance during the past few years will find this a challenging thought, it is undeniably true. For this, there can be no doubt, is the finest engine Cadillac ever built—the perfect power plant for so splendid a motor car.

Among the advanced features of this modern, new engine is the new overhead valve combustion chamber design which assures controlled burning of the compressed gas to create a smooth power thrust. This design, which permits the use of a high compression ratio, produces maximum power and economy. The combination of the large cylinder bore and short piston stroke contributes to efficient operation by exposing less cylinder wall area to flame. The short piston stroke reduces frictional power losses by reducing piston travel. At 4,000 R.P.M. the piston travels at the rate of only 2,400 feet per minute. Thus, high mechanical and thermal efficiency contribute to increased power output.

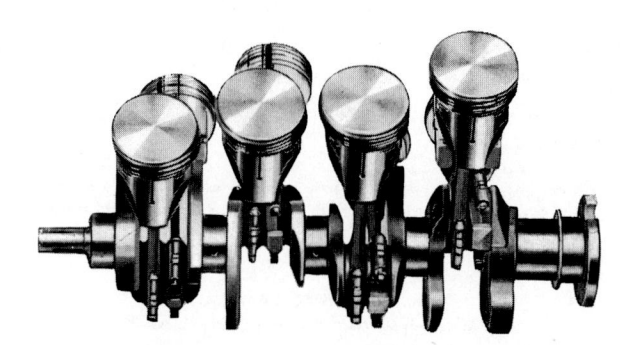

Main crankshaft bearings have been placed in heavy bulkheads which help form a rigid, box-like crankcase structure. This feature is partially responsible for creating the smoothest, quietest running Cadillac engine ever built. Other features contributing to smooth, quiet operation include a scientifically designed valve mechanism with high rigidity factors, hydraulic valve lifters, and a minimum of air cleaner and exhaust system noises.

Vital to good engine performance is a well-designed piston and crankshaft assembly. The use of small, light, scientifically designed engine parts has been an effective method of reducing friction and weight while increasing power in the new Cadillac engine. A short engine design with five bearing supports reduces both size and weight of crankshaft and camshaft. The 5 main-bearing crankshaft has great rigidity and offers great torsional resistance, which increases engine smoothness and quietness in operation.

The fuel intake system allows free breathing of gas into the combustion chambers. The oil-bath cleaner has been designed with large intake capacity of the filtered air to the dual downdraft carburetor. The 1951 design of both carburetor and manifold eliminates any possibility of icing. Heat passages from the intake manifold run through the carburetor warming the air around the idle ports, thus preventing moisture in the air from freezing.

An integral casting, comprising water-pump housing and inlet and outlet water manifolds, eliminates all hose connections except those running to lower and upper radiator tanks. The coolant is circulated by the pump from the bottom of the radiator to the lower manifold, through cylinder block and cylinder head water jackets into the upper manifold to the upper radiator tank. A by-pass in the casting between upper and lower manifolds allows the coolant to recirculate through cylinder block and heads until it reaches the proper temperature to open the thermostat valve, which is mounted in the housing above the water pump, thus allowing the water to circulate into the radiator.

36

THE 1951 HYDRA-MATIC DRIVE

The General Motors Hydra-Matic Drive, as designed and built for Cadillac, has proved so successful over the years that it has been made standard equipment on all series of Cadillac passenger cars. Hydra-Matic Drive consists of an automatic, 4 speed transmission operating in conjunction with a fluid coupling placed between the transmission proper and the smoothly-operating 160 horsepower V-type, overhead valve engine. There is no clutch pedal—no gearshift lever.

Scientific Design and precision workmanship feature the Cadillac-built Hydra-Matic Drive Transmission. Shown above is the main transmission shaft removed from housing, with planetary gears and other parts separated for the purpose of illustration.

A New and Important Feature of the 1951 Cadillac Hydra-Matic Transmission is a cone-type friction reverse control, shown in insert. It is very smooth in operation as it does not require the meshing of gears but picks up its load merely by inserting the conical shape disk, shown at right, under pressure, into the corresponding coupling, shown at left. The rapidity and smoothness with which this manual operation can be accomplished permits rocking the car in sand or snow.

Members of the fluid coupling are here shown separated to illustrate vane structure. The coupling is precision-balanced with fluid to insure smoothest possible operation.

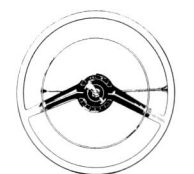

From the moment the car is put in motion until it is brought to a complete stop, all driving operations, except steering, accelerating and braking are completely and smoothly automatic.

As power flows from the engine, the driving member of the fluid coupling is revolved through a set of forward planetary gears. This causes the fluid to flow against the vanes of the driven member and transmit engine power through the main transmission shaft and rear planetary gearset to the rear wheels. All gear ratio changes occur automatically at the precise instant for best car performance.

The advantages and desirability of Hydra-Matic Drive have been proved in the hands of hundreds of thousands of Cadillac owners over nearly a 10-year period. In the opinion of Cadillac engineers, nothing else has yet been developed that will provide the all-around efficiency, the driving comfort, and the operating economy of Hydra-Matic Drive. Adopting it this year as standard equipment on all passenger car models is a great tribute to the basic soundness of the General Motors Hydra-Matic Drive principle as designed and built for Cadillac.

A new feature of the 1951 Cadillac Hydra-Matic transmission is a new "finger-tip" cone-type friction reverse control. It permits shifting into reverse without clash or delay and facilitates "rocking" the car forth and back when in heavy sand or snow. The advantages of Hydra-Matic operation are clearly apparent to the driver whether in slow, heavy traffic or cruising along the open highway. With it he can relax, yet smoothly and effortlessly maintain perfect car control. Once under way, his manual operations have been reduced to merely steering, accelerating and braking, regardless of traffic conditions.

FACTS AND FIGURES

Ratio changes in Hydra-Matic are made as follows:

"DR" RANGE "UP-SHIFTS"

Ratio	M.P.H. Minimum Throttle	M.P.H. Full Throttle
1st to 2nd	5-7	11-15
2nd to 3rd	11-14	29-37
3rd to 4th	17-19	61-69

"LO" RANGE "UP-SHIFTS"

1st to 2nd	11-15	23-28

"DR" RANGE "DOWN-SHIFTS" (test made on up-grade)

4th to 3rd	12-15	55-63
3rd to 2nd	....	11-13
3rd to 1st	3-7	....
2nd to 1st	....	6-9

"LO" RANGE "DOWN-SHIFTS" (test made on up-grade)

4th to 2nd	42-50	....
2nd to 1st	5-9	12-15

Note: Miles per hour at which shift is made is dependent on throttle opening. Actually no gears shift. Term used for clarity of meaning only.

HYDRA-MATIC CADILLAC
3.36 Axle—Series 61, 62, 60S • 3.77 Axle—Series 75

TRANSMISSION AND CAR RATIOS

	Transmission Ratios	Over-all Reduction With 3.36 Axle	Over-all Reduction With 3.77 Axle
Low	3.819	12.83	14.40
Second	2.634	8.85	9.93
Third	1.450	4.87	5.47
Fourth	1.000	3.36	3.77
Reverse	4.304	14.46	16.23

Body

	Series 61	62	60S	75
Types	2	4	1	3
Construction	Fisher Unisteel	Fisher Unisteel	Fleetwood Unisteel	Fleetwood Unisteel
Running boards	Concealed scuff plate	Concealed scuff plate	Concealed scuff plate	Concealed scuff plate
Total glass area (sq. in.)	3377	3539	3539	3609

Frame

	Series 61, 62, 60S			75
Frame make	A. O. Smith	A. O. Smith	A. O. Smith	A. O. Smith
Frame depth, maximum	7 1/8"	7 5/32"	7 3/16"	7 3/16"
Frame thickness, maximum	1/8"	9/64"	5/32"	5/32"
Flange width, maximum	2 9/16"	2 37/64"	2 19/32"	2 19/32"
Frame—Type	Girder	Girder	Girder	Girder

Front End Suspension

Front suspension, make	Own
Front suspension, type	Forked arms
Forked arm bearings, type	Threaded
Kingpin upper bearing, type	Bronze bushing
Kingpin lower bearing, type	Bronze bushing
Front wheel inner bearing, make and type	N. D. Ball
Front wheel outer bearing, make and type	N. D. Ball
Front spring, type	Helical coil
Front spring, material	GM #9260 steel
Knee-Action coils	Enclosed by frame sidebars
Caster angle	Neg. 1/2° to Pos. 1/2°
Camber angle	−3/8° to +3/8°
Toe-in, inches	1/32—3/32
Crosswide inclination of kingpin, degrees	5° 51' at 0° Camber
Shock absorber, type	Hydraulic direct-acting type
Front stabilizer	Torsion rod

Rear Axle & Rear End Suspension

Rear axle, make	Own	
Rear axle, type	Semi-floating	
Minimum road clearance under center of rear axle, tires inflated	8.34	8.44
Differential gear, make	Own	
Rear axle		
Oil capacity	5 pints	
Grade recommended:		
S.A.E. viscosity	90 hypoid	
Type of final gearing	Hypoid	
Gear ratio:		
Hyd. Trans. Std. Equip.	3.36	3.77
No. of teeth in ring gear (Std.)	47	49
No. of teeth in pinion (Std.)	14	13
Pinion adjustment	None	
Pinion bearing adjustment	None (Preloaded)	
Are pinion bearings in sleeve?	No	
Backlash between pinion and ring gear	.003-.010"	
Rear axle pinion shaft		
Front bearing, type	Tapered roller	
Rear bearing, type	Tapered roller	
Differential bearing,		
Right, type	Tapered roller	
Left, type	Tapered roller	
Universal, make	Mechanics	
Model	#3-RCR	
Type	Needle bearing	
Universal joints, lubricated	Permanently	
Drive & torque taken through	Rear springs	
Rear wheel bearing, make and type	N. D. Ball	
Spring leaves lubricated with	Wax impregnated liners	
Spring bushings, type	Rubber	
Stabilizers	Rear—None	
Rear Springs:		
Type	Semi-elliptic	
Material	GM #9260 steel	
Length	54 1/2"	56 1/2"
Width	2"	
No. of leaves	8 60S—8	10
Shackles, type	Compression link	
Rear spring shackle bolt,		
Upper	Rubber mounted	
Lower	Rubber mounted	
Shock absorbers, type	Hydraulic direct-acting type	

Brakes

No. of complete brakes	4	
Foot brakes:		
Make and type	Bendix-Moraine Hydraulic	
Total area	224.5 sq. in.	258.5 sq. in.
Braking ratio:		
Front	55.8%	
Rear	44.2%	
Vacuum booster	None	
Brake lining, molded or woven	Molded	
Brake drum material	Composite	

Brakes—Continued

	Series 61, 62, 60S	75
Anchor-Type	Self Adjusting	Adjustable Eccentric
Front brake drum diameter	11	12
Front brake drum, internal or external	Internal	
Front brake lining, length per wheel:		
Forward shoe	10.55	12.92
Reverse shoe	11.90	12.92
Total	22.45	25.84
Front brake lining width	2 1/2"	
Front brake lining thickness	3/16"	
Front brake clearance	.007-.010"	
Rear brake drum diam.	11	12
Rear brake drum, internal or external	Internal	
Rear brake lining, length per wheel:		
Forward shoe	Same as front	
Reverse shoe	Same as front	
Total	Same as front	
Rear brake lining width	2 1/2"	
Rear brake lining thickness	3/16"	
Rear brake clearance	.007-.010"	
Hand brake location	Left side of dash	
Hand brake lever operates on	Rear service brakes	

Engine

No. of cylinders	8	
Engine make	Own	
Engine model	50-61, 50-62, 50-60S	50-75
Cylinder arrangement	90° V-type O. H. Valve	
Numbering arrangement:		
Left cylinder	1-3-5-7	
Right cylinder	2-4-6-8	
Piston displacement	331 cu. in.	
Taxable horsepower	46.5	
Maximum brake horsepower at R.P.M.	160—3800	
Standard compression ratio	7.5 to 1	
Standard compression pressure lbs/sq. in.	194 at 1000 R.P.M.	
Bore and stroke	3 13/16" x 3 5/8"	
First serial number	61 —516100000 62 —516200000 60S—516000000	517500000
Serial number location	Upper right corner on front face of right hand block—numbered at right angles to crankshaft	
Main bearing:		
Make and type	Moraine Durex	
Poured, spun or separate	Separate (precision inserts)	
Clearance	.0008"-.0025"	
No. 1 main bearing journal, diameter and length	2 1/2" x 1'	
No. 2, 3, 4 main bearing journal, diameter and length	2 1/2" x 1 1/16"	
No. 5 main bearing journal, diameter and length	2 1/2" x 1 7/8"	
Crankpin journal, diameter and length	2 1/4" x 2"	
Main bearings	5	
Which main bearing takes thrust?	Rear (No. 5)	
Vibration dampener	Torsional	
Torsional vibration, dampener type	Rubber absorption type	
Crankshaft counterweights	6	
Crankshaft end play	.001"-.005"	
Piston material	Aluminum alloy	
Piston features	T-T-slot Stannate-treated finish	
Piston length	3 15/16"	
Piston clearance	.0013"-.0017"	
No. of rings per piston:		
Compression	2	
Oil	1	
Wrist pin length	3 3/32"	
Wrist pin diameter	1"	
Wrist pin	Pressed into rod	
Wrist pin clearance	.00005"-.0001" at 70°F.	
Wrist pin hole finish	Diamond bore in rod, bearingized stannate-plate in piston	
Connecting rod:		
Length, center to center	6 5/8"	
Material	#1041 steel	
Connecting rod bearing:		
Make and type	Moraine Durex	
Poured, spun or separate	Separate (precision insert)	
Clearance	.001"-.0035"	
Connecting rod end play	.008"-.014" (total for two rods)	
Rods and pistons removed from	Above	
Oil reservoir capacity	5 qts.	
Oil pump, type	Helical gear	
Normal oil pressure lbs. at M.P.H.	28 lbs. at 30 M.P.H.	
Pressure at which relief valve opens	26 lbs.	
Type of oil drain	Threaded plug	
Oil reservoir gauge, type	Dip stick	
Engine lubrication:		
Lubricating system, type	Pressure	
Valve lifter lubrication	Pressure	
Main bearing, lubrication	Pressure	
Connecting rod bearing lubrication	Pressure	

Engine—Continued

	Series 61, 62, 60S	75
Wrist pin, lubrication	Splash	
Camshaft bearing, lubrication	Pressure	
Timing gear, lubrication	Positive	
Crankcase ventilation	Road draft type	
Cooling system capacity	18 quarts	
Accessory drive belt (fan, pump and generator):		
Type	Wedge type Vee	
Width, maximum	.380"	
Length (outside circumference)	57"	
Fan blades	4	5
Coolant circulation, type	Pump	
Water pump, type	Centrifugal—dual outlet	
Blocking thermostat, make, control and type	Dole Vernatherm	
Carburetor, make	Carter—845S-Roch.	
Size	1 1/4"	
Type	Plain tube	
Up or down draft	Down draft	
Single or dual	Dual	
Automatic choke:		
Make	Carter—Roch.	
Type	Thermostatic	
Air cleaner and intake silencer:		
Make	A.C.	
Type	Concentric	
Fuel feed type	Camshaft pump	
Engine mounted on	Vulcanized synthetic rubber	
No. of points of suspension:		
Front	2	
Rear	1	
Timing chain:		
Type	Side guide	
Make	Link belt	
Model	57 TCE—11	
Length	23"	
Number of links	46	
Width	11/16"	
Pitch	.500"	
Adjustment	None	
Valve arrangement	Over-head	
Valve timing at .001 tappet lift:		
Intake opens	24° B.T.D.C. at .001 cam-lift	
Intake closes	98° A.B.C. at .001 cam-lift	
Exhaust opens	63° B.B.C. at .001 cam-lift	
Exhaust closes	49° A.T.C. at .001 cam-lift	
Cylinder head material	Cast iron, GM 13M	
Intake valve:		
Actual over-all diameter of head	1.750"	
Angle of seat	44°	
Seat insert	None	
Cooled by	Directed water circulation	
Stem clearance	.0005"-.0025"	
Lift	.327"	
Spring pressure and length:		
Valve closed	60 lbs.—1.696"	
Valve open	135 lbs.—1.366"	
Exhaust valve:		
Actual over-all diameter of head	1.4375"	
Angle of seat	44°	
Seat insert	None	
Cooled by	Directed water circulation	
Stem clearance	.0015"-.0035"	
Lift	.327"	
Spring pressure and length:		
Valve closed	60 lbs.—1.696"	
Valve open	135 lbs.—1.366"	
Tappet clearance, adjustment	Automatic	
Camshaft	Cast iron alloy	

Engine, Electrical

Generator:	
Make	Delco-Remy
Number	#1102700
Type	Current and voltage regulated
Voltage at cut-out closing	5.9-6.8 (adjust to 6.4)
Amperes to open cut-out	0 to 3
Generator normal charging rate	40 amps. peak. Due to voltage regulation actual charging rate is controlled by state of charge of battery
Peak charging speed	27 M.P.H. up
Generator ventilation	Forced air
Generator:	
Commutator end bearing	
Type	Bronze bushing
Size	9/16" x 3/4" x 3/4"
Drive end bearing:	
Make and type	N. D. Ball
Number	#954378
Starter motor:	
Make	Delco-Remy
Number	#1107969—4 pole
Drive	Solenoid shifted gear
Automatic starting device	Comb. Ign. & Starter Switch

Engine, Electrical—Continued	Series 61, 62, 60S	75
Starter motor:		
Commutator end bearing:		
Type	Durex bushing	
Size	¾" x ⅝" x 9/16"	
Outboard bearing:		
Type	Durex bushing	
Size	9/16" x ⅝" x ¾"	
Starting motor pinion meshes with flywheel	Front	
Flywheel teeth, integral or steel ring	Steel ring	
Gear ratio between starter armature and flywheel	16.1 to 1	
Spark advance	Centrifugal and vacuum	
Ignition unit:		
Make	Delco-Remy	
Number	#1110820	
Manual advance	None	
Maximum centrifugal advance	32° crankshaft	
Vacuum advance	22° crankshaft	
Distributor breaker gap	.013"-.018"	
Initial spark advance	0°-5° B.T.C.	
Firing order	1-8-4-3-6-5-7-2	
Ignition coil:		
Make	Delco-Remy	
Number	#1115380	
Amperage draw of coil:		
With engine stopped	4.5 to 5.5	
With engine idling	2 to 3	
Spark plug:		
Make	A.C.	
Model	46.5	
Thread	14 mm.	
Gap	.033—.038	

Transmission	Series 61, 62, 60S	75
Hydra-Matic	Standard	

Fuel Tank and Exhaust System	
Gasoline tank, capacity	20 gals.
Muffler, type	3 pass

Steering Mechanism	Series 61, 62, 60S	75
Steering gear:		
Type	Recirculating ball	
Make	Saginaw	
Over-all steering ratio	25.47—1	
Car turning radius (outside) bumper to bumper sweep	(61) 22′ (62) 22.5′ (60) 23′ (75) 25.5′	
Camber angle	−⅜° to +⅜°	
Toe-in inches	1/32" to 3/32"	

Wheels & Tires		
Tire:		
Make	U.S. Royal—Firestone and Goodrich	
Size	8.00 x 15	8.20 x 15
—61 Series—Blackwall 7.60 x 15	Whitewall 8.00 x 15	
Ply Rating	4	6
Inflation pressure:		
Front	24 lbs.	28 lbs.
Rear	24 lbs.	28 lbs.
Wheels:		
Type	Slotted disc	
Make	Kelsey Hayes	
Rim, diameter	15"	15"
Rim, width	6.00"	6.00"
Tread:		
Front	59"	59"
Rear	63"	63"
Wheelbase	(61) 122", (62) 126", 60S—130"	146¾"

Chassis Electrical System, Instruments & Instrument Panel	
Battery:	
Make	Delco K4W
Number of plates	17
Capacity (amp. hrs.)	115
Battery bench charging rate:	
Start	10
Finish	8
Which battery terminal is grounded?	Negative

Chassis Electrical System, Instruments & Instrument Panel—Continued	Series 61, 62, 60S	75
Location of battery	Under hood on tray attached to R.H. dash to frame brace front of dash	
Headlight, make	Guide sealed beam	
Headlight cover glass, dia.	6 11/16"	
Parking light, make	Guide	
Tail light, make	Guide	
Lighting switch, make	Delco-Remy	
How are headlights dimmed?	Depressed beam—foot switch	
Horn:		
Make	Delco-Remy	
Type	Airtone	
Amperage draw of horns	Low note 21 High note 19	

Radiator	
Radiator core:	
Make	Harrison
Type	Tube and fin
Cooling capacity	18 qts.
Core & Tank	5½ qts.

Capacities and Grades	All Series
Engine oil	5 qts.
Recommended viscosity	Min. anticipated temperature +32°F. 20W or S.A.E. 20 +10°F. 20W −10°F. 10W Below 10°F. 5W
Drain	2000 miles (after initial 500 mile change)
Rear axle oil	5 pints
Recommended viscosity	90 hypoid
Auto Trans. Fluid Type 'A'	12 qts. dry
Cooling system—water	18 qts.
Gasoline	20 gals.

COUPE DIMENSIONS

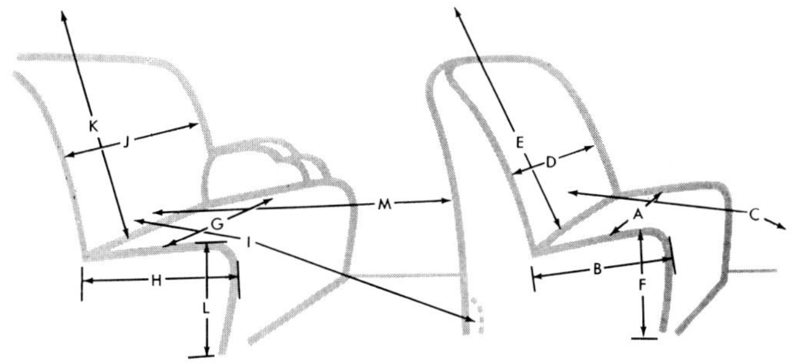

SEDAN DIMENSIONS

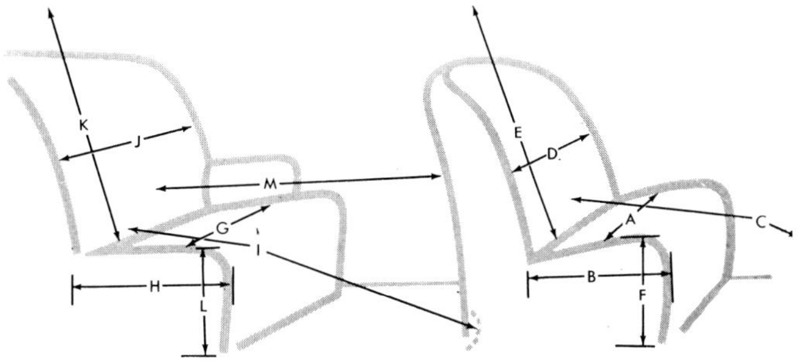

N—63⅛
O—15 5/16
P—34⅞
Q—12 15/16

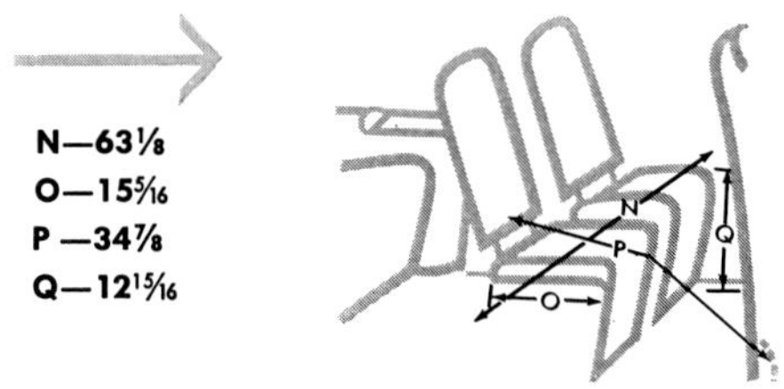

Dim.*	61 Coupe	61 Sedan	62 Coupe & Coupe Déville	62 Sedan	62 Conv.	60 Special	75 Sedan	75 Business Sedan
A	63⅜	63⅞	63⅜	63½	63⅜	63½	64	64
B	18⅜	18 5/16	18⅜ 18¼	18⅜	18⅜	18⅜	18 9/16	18 9/16
C	42 15/16	43½	43 13/16 43 11/16	43⅝	42 11/16	43⅝	43⅛	43⅛
D	56⅛	58¼	56⅛	58⅛	56⅛	58⅛	58⅛	58⅛
E	35⅜	35 13/16	35⅜ 35 11/16	35½	36⅛	35½	37	37
F	13 5/16	13⅜	13 5/16	14 3/16	13 5/16	14 3/16	13 11/16	13 11/16
G	54 9/16	64⅝	54 9/16	64½	51	64½	56⅞	56⅞
H	18 11/16	19	18 11/16	19	18 11/16	19	19 13/16	19 11/16
I	38 9/16	40 13/16	37⅞	40 3/16	37⅞	40 3/16	—	—
J	56¼	56⅞	56¼	56½	47½	56½	56⅛	56⅛
K	34⅞	35¼	34⅞	36	35 3/16	36	35	34 13/16
L	12	12⅛	11¾	12⅛	11¾	12⅛	14 5/16	13⅛
M	30 1/16	33	30 1/16	35 9/16	30 1/16	35 9/16	52 5/16	54⅞

*FRONT SEAT IN FULL REAR POSITION

1952 *Cadillac*

The appearance of the Golden Anniversary Cadillac should be a source of tremendous pride to all of us—to those who build it, to those who sell it, and to those who own it. For not only does it once again raise the world's conception of what constitutes a truly fine motor car—but it represents, in all that it is, looks and does, a full half-century of continuous automotive development. Since the appearance of the first Cadillac car in 1902, each passing year has seen Cadillac's position as the "Standard of the World" more firmly fixed in the minds of the motoring public. So consistently and unfailingly, in fact, have the good things come from Cadillac that motorists look to it, almost as a matter of routine, for their standards of automotive quality. The Golden Anniversary Cadillac will, we feel certain, strengthen this attitude to a conviction. For never before has so fine an automobile been presented for their consideration. In beauty, in performance, in riding comfort, in everything that contributes to motoring goodness, this is the finest motor car Cadillac has ever built.

IN ITS 50TH YEAR AS STANDARD OF THE WORLD!

A NEW CONCEPT IN LUXURY

The 1952 Cadillac cars present an utterly new concept in luxurious interiors. At every hand . . . on every side . . . are features that add a sparkling difference in beauty and convenience. Rich colors, fabrics of superb textures and jewel-like appointments are blended to create settings of unusual charm. Here in the 1952 Cadillac cars, is offered a new "Standard of the World" in automotive fashions—presented to perfection in flawless workmanship and an unequalled, extravagant beauty of line.

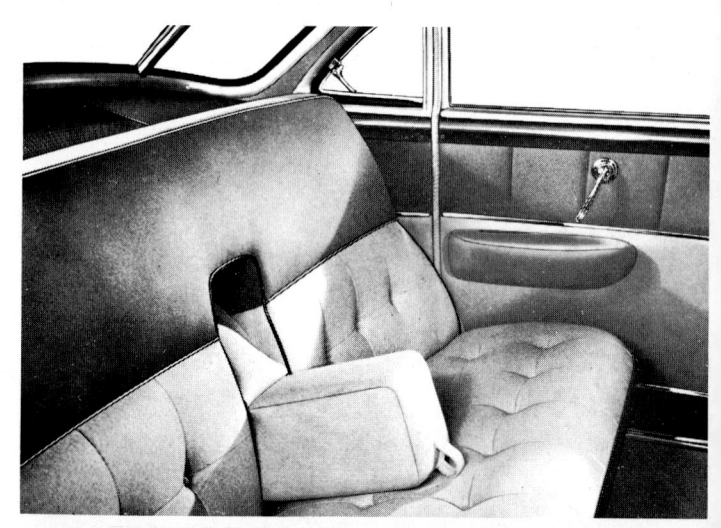

NEW 1952 FRONT-END ENSEMBLE

In all 1952 Cadillac cars, improvements have been made in the front-end ensemble. The lower grille extensions have been redesigned to add a massive yet graceful note. Beautiful "Cadet Visor" headlamp bezels in sparkling chrome are again part of the over-all effect that accentuates the flowing lines to blend pleasingly with the over-all design. The horizontal grille bars focus attention on the beautiful, wider Cadillac V and crest. Fog lights, optional at additional cost, are integral with the center grille member and also carry the new beautifully styled Cadillac "Cadet Visor" bezels in sparkling chrome.

The Golden Anniversary models had the highest passenger car hoursepower rating in the industry and still delivered outstanding fuel economy. Above, a 1952 Series 62 Sedan. Center, a Series 75 Limousine. Below, a Series 62 Coupe with accessory sun visor. During this era pre-owned 1950 and 1951 Cadillacs often brought more on the used car lot than comparable brand new competitve '52s.

IN ITS 50TH YEAR AS

STANDARD OF THE WORLD!

NEW 62 SEDAN REAR DECK CONTOUR

For the ultimate result in sleekness of line and long, low silhouette, the rear deck contour of the Cadillac 62 Sedan and the rear deck contour of the Series 75 cars has been raised. This new slipstream styling distinguishes these cars in appearance of grace and provides roomy luggage compartments of more spacious proportions.

NEW DUAL EXHAUST THROUGH BUMPER

The wrap-around protection of the Cadillac rear bumper has taken on a glamorous new continental custom styling where "split" exhaust systems terminate in beautifully designed dual exhaust ports through gleaming chrome bumper bars. This new customized dual-exhaust-through-bumper is attractive in appearance and functional in design. The value of this new feature has been proven in terms of better engine performance because it reduces back-pressure. It is standard on all 1952 Cadillac cars.

NEW CADILLAC POWER STEERING

Cadillac's power steering, a grand new 1952 alliance of the proven Cadillac steering system and a hydraulic booster system, is the latest, safest and most modern engineering innovation in sheer effortless driving.

Cadillac introduces with its Golden Anniversary models a new Hydra-Matic Drive. This new unit retains all of the advantages of the Hydra-Matic transmission developed over the past decade, plus new flexibility, better performance, and a higher degree of economy than before.

Simply stated, this new transmission has two driving ranges instead of one—a range for the open road and a range for congested city traffic and mountainous driving.

The quadrant selector dial, located just above the horn button, provides for five positions of the lever—"Neutral," two "Drive" positions, "Low" and "Reverse."

SETTING FOR GRACIOUS DRIVING

There is a sturdy tradition behind the studied simplicity of the Cadillac front compartment. This setting for gracious driving comes into its distinctive best in 1952. The instrument panel, distinguished by a new gold and brushed silver crest, is finished in subtle, sophisticated colors. Highlight of the panel is the convenient group of instruments. Instruments and other appointments are richly chromed. Other features are the extra large steering wheel with sparkling colored plastic rim, the easy-to-reach radio controls, smart clock and deep glove box. Finishing touches of the front compartment are the heavy wool pile carpet and the massive steering column-jacket which pick up the basic interior colors once more.

1952 SPECIFICATIONS

EXTERIOR BODY DIMENSIONS

All 1952 Cadillac Models

	Wheelbase	Over-all Length	Over-all Height	Minimum Road Clearance
Series 62 Convertible Coupe	126"	220 1/2"	61 1/8"	7 1/4"
Series 62 Sedan	126"	215 1/2"	62 11/16"	7 1/4"
Series 62 Coupe	126"	220 1/2"	60 15/16"	7 1/4"
Series 62 Coupe de Ville	126"	220 1/2"	60 15/16"	7 1/4"
Series 60 Fleetwood Special	130"	224 1/2"	62 11/16"	7 1/4"
Series 75 8-Passenger Sedan	146 3/4"	236 1/4"	64 1/16"	6 3/4"
Series 75 Imperial Sedan	146 3/4"	236 1/4"	64 1/16"	6 3/4"

INTERIOR BODY DIMENSIONS

All 1952 Cadillac Models

	Front Seat Hip Room	Front Seat Shoulder Room	Front Seat Leg Room	Rear Seat Hip Room	Rear Seat Shoulder Room	Rear Seat Leg Room	Front Head-room	Rear Head-room	Front Seat Height to Floor	Rear Seat Height to Floor	Steering Wheel Clear-ance to Seat
Series 62 Convertible Coupe	62 13/16"	56 1/8"	43 15/16"	51"	47 1/2"	38 5/8"	34 15/16"	34 5/8"	14 7/16"	12 1/2"	5 1/16"
Series 62 Sedan	63 9/16"	58 1/8"	43 15/16"	64 1/4"	56 1/2"	42 1/8"	35 13/16"	35 9/16"	14 7/16"	12 13/16"	5 1/16"
Series 62 Coupe	62 13/16"	56 1/8"	43 15/16"	54 9/16"	56 1/4"	38 5/8"	34 3/16"	34 5/16"	14 7/16"	12 1/2"	5 1/16"
Series 62 Coupe de Ville	62 13/16"	56 1/8"	43 15/16"	54 9/16"	56 1/4"	38 5/8"	34 3/16"	34 5/16"	14 7/16"	12 1/2"	5 1/16"
Series 60 Fleetwood Special	63 3/4"	58 1/8"	43 15/16"	64 1/2"	56 1/2"	42 1/8"	35 13/16"	35 9/16"	14 7/16"	12 13/16"	5 1/16"
Series 75 8-Passenger Sedan	64"	58 1/8"	44 1/8"	56 7/8"	56 1/8"		37"	35"	13 11/16"	12 13/16"	5 7/8"
Series 75 Imperial Sedan	64"	58 1/8"	43 15/16"	56 7/8"	56 1/8"		36 7/8"	35"	13 11/16"	12 13/16"	5 7/8"

1952 CADILLAC SERIES 62

Wonderful to the eye and colorfully accented, the Cadillac Series 62 offers a variety of coupe and sedan models, including two of the most strikingly beautiful cars in the entire Cadillac series—the 62 Convertible Coupe and the Coupe de Ville. In addition this series presents the lovely Cadillac 62 Coupe and the smoothly streamlined Cadillac 62 Sedan. All the interiors of this series have been brightened and enriched. Exteriors, too, have been brightened—Series 62 cars are available in a choice of 12 beautiful new solid colors, and 5 new two-tone color combinations. The Coupe de Ville is available in one additional solid color, and one extra two-tone combination. The Convertible is available in one added color. Many other fashionable design features characterize the graceful flowing lines, wonderful riding comfort and beauty of motion unequalled in any other motor car.

1952 CADILLAC SERIES 62 COUPE

SERIES 62 COUPE
PAGEANT OF INTERIOR FASHIONS

The cushions and seat back inserts in the Series 62 Coupe are distinguished by deep tufting, styled in light tone fabrics of pattern broadcloth or cord. Wide seat backs and cushion bolsters are tailored in harmonizing dark broadcloth. Four color schemes are available to choose from. Dark green is combined with beautiful light-tone green. Brown is coupled with tan. Dark blue and a lighter blue form another fashionable combination. Delicate gray tailored with gray of a much darker hue offers flattering beauty. Extreme lower seat-facings are protected by simulated leather. Door panels are trimmed in six-inch pipes of dark broadcloth and sidewall cloth of light tone. Hydraulic controls for windows and front seat are available as an option. The same striking motif is carried into the rear compartment of the Series 62 Coupe with the traditional skill of Cadillac craftsmen. Another luxury and convenience feature is the soft, lounge-type center arm rest that folds into the rear seat back. It adds to the comfort of the rear seat passengers. The front doors and rear compartment sides are equipped with arm rests positioned for ease and comfort. The wool pile carpeting of fashionable hue, combined with other sound-deadening material, minimizes road noise.

Cadillac rear seats are restful because of the large number of individually wrapped and tied coil springs. They are topped by thick fabric padding, deep foam rubber and heavy upholstery cloth. Front seats in all Cadillac cars, except Series 75, are built up as illustrated below with the new type zig-zag springs topped by thick padding.

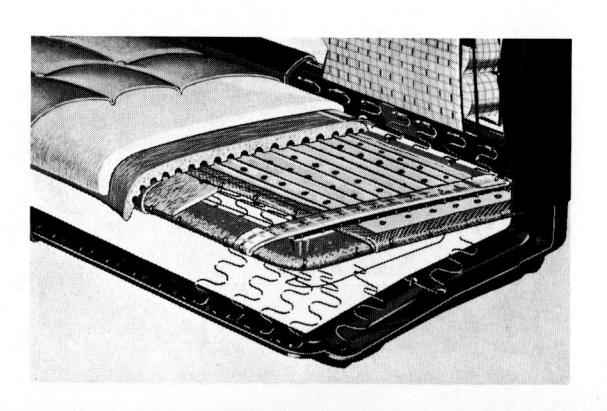

44

1952 CADILLAC SERIES 62 SEDAN

SERIES 62 SEDAN
PAGEANT OF INTERIOR FASHIONS

The interior of the 62 Sedan is softly mannered and deftly tailored. Upholstery material is in two-tone combinations of dark broadcloth with either cord or patterned cloth of light color. Seat back inserts and cushions are deeply tufted for exquisite design and the traditional Cadillac custom-made look. Doors are trimmed in dark broadcloth in six-inch pipes above door panel trim cloth of light color. Four height-of-the-season color combinations are available. They are dark gray tailored with light gray for an incredibly beautiful combination—rich brown broadcloth blended with tan cord or patterned cloth—darkly brilliant green that accents a green of delicate shade—or lovely pale blue combined with a crisp blue of darker hue. A center arm rest and large door arm rests enhance the comfort and convenience of this fine car. Floors are covered with wool pile carpets which harmonize with the upholstery. The go-everywhere charm of the Cadillac 62 Sedan continues throughout the front compartment. Heavy vinyl welts accent dark and light-colored upholstery cloth for a tailored appearance.

The interior of the 62 Sedan is both functional and attractive. Every item is harmoniously related to the whole—to create an atmosphere of luxury. Lower side panels of the front seat are of scuff resistant simulated leather. The robe cords and chrome roll-cover ash receiver accent the fact that fabrics, trim, carpets and appointments all blend with the general styling of these wonderful cars.

Cadillac's advanced-type door check-links are designed for double service to hold doors positively in open position . . . and to help counterbalance the doors for easier opening.

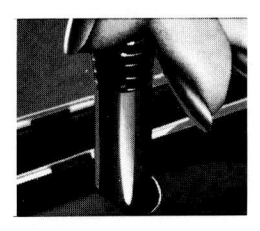

Sedan rear doors are fitted with door locks adjusted to disengage from the inside door handle. This safety feature safeguards children. When the doors are shut and the inside locking-knobs are pressed down (see photos), they cannot be opened from the inside.

45

1952 CADILLAC SERIES 62 CONVERTIBLE COUPE

SERIES 62 CONVERTIBLE COUPE
PAGEANT OF INTERIOR FASHIONS

The Cadillac 62 Convertible is radiantly tailored all around in genuine leather which protects it with sheer enchantment against harsh winds and sun. Five beautiful choices of two-tone and solid color leathers are available in 1952. Of the five different trim selections, three are two-tone combinations of light metallic and darkly brilliant leathers of the same color, two are tailored in shimmering leather of solid hue. Cadillac interprets one interior trim in the flattery of brown combined with light tan leather combination, a second in dark and light metallic blue, and a third in softly lighted metallic green leather coupled with leather of a rich dark green shade. Choice number four includes a fashion-future interior of solid red leather throughout. For a suave midnight effect the Convertible interior may also be trimmed all around in fine leathers of solid black. Top material is available in four matching colors—black, tan, blue and green.

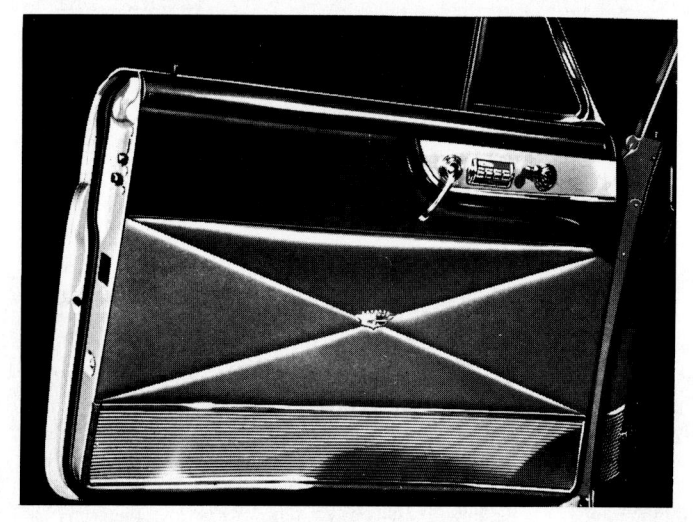

The two-tone or solid leather tailoring in the Convertible Coupe is dramatically carried even to the front seat back. In two-tone trim selections, the dark-tone leather bolster back contrasts with a recessed center panel of light leather. The robe cord is covered in dark leather. Seat backs and cushion inserts are trimmed in the leather of fine metallic light-tones with diagonal tufting. Wide back bolsters and lower seat fronts are fashioned in rich dark leathers. The doors are also paneled in diagonally-tufted leather of two shades. Where solid red leather or solid black leather is selected, seats and door panels are tufted in a single color. The Cadillac crest in chrome is mounted in the center of each interior door panel. Door and cowl kick pads are in beautiful patterned chrome metal.

1952 CADILLAC SERIES 62 COUPE de VILLE

COUPE DE VILLE
PAGEANT OF INTERIOR FASHIONS

Here cited for outstanding beauty, the Coupe de Ville interior glories in distinguished styling and the fine hand of Cadillac tailoring. Highly metallic leather of light matching tone graces the diagonally tufted upper seat back. Leather bolsters and door panels are regally contrasted with a choice of classic dark cord body cloth. Four exclusive color combinations are available to choose from. A shadow-blue fabric combines with light blue metallic leather for a real beauty bonus. Dark gray cord body cloth is available with light tone leather. A provocatively lovely green cloth with a lighter green leather of exciting hue is another choice. An exquisite brown nylon fabric with a fashionable tan leather is also available. Each of these is the inspired answer to 1952 Coupe de Ville interior styling. The rear compartment of the Cadillac 62 Coupe de Ville is trimmed in smooth and exotic harmony with the rest of the car. A large center arm rest and side arm rests add to beauty, comfort and convenience.

Perfect styling and the custom-tailored look are further enhanced in this model by chrome roof bows, chrome garnish moldings and bright hardware. Hydraulic window controls are a convenient feature. Dark tone carpets harmonize with the trim. Door and kick pads are in patterned chrome metal. A chrome Cadillac crest is centrally mounted in each diagonally tufted door panel. Distinctive leather of light tone, combined with dark cord, is carried clear around the front seat. The robe cords are also of light leather brightened by chrome escutcheons to add further grace to this great car.

Below a restored 1952 Convertible. Wire wheels didn't appear until a year later but many were purchased for use on earlier models, as seen here.

SERIES 60 SPECIAL

Here, beyond all doubt, is the most magnificently luxurious owner-driven automobile on the highways—a long and low-silhouetted beauty designed for those whose choice is unrestricted. This lovely Cadillac 60 Special knows no rival for the affections of the motoring public. It offers such outstanding and exclusive features, brilliant style and dazzling performance that it has helped play a major role in building Cadillac's reputation as the "Standard of the World." Every feature of design, construction and performance places the emphasis on luxury.

CADILLAC-FLEETWOOD 60 SPECIAL
PAGEANT OF INTERIOR FASHIONS

There is only one Cadillac-Fleetwood 60 Special—a car designed for those whose choice is unrestricted. Distinguished appearance and the elusive magic of Cadillac interior styling, combine in a finished masterpiece for discriminating clientele. Seats and seat back inserts are tastefully trimmed in light cord or an alternate choice of light tone plain broadcloth. Both are fashioned in 2" pipes with tailored welts of contrasting color. Richly padded and cushioned bolsters are styled in luxurious dark-tone broadcloth. Four beautiful two-tone color combinations are available to choose from. They are a shadowy dark green upholstery contrasted with a pastel green combination, a tawny brown coupled with golden tan interior, a trim of dark gray tailored with light gray for an incredibly beautiful effect, and a crisp dark blue blended with a blue of lighter matching shade. Light-tone matching leather is tailored into heavily padded door pipes to contrast with door sidewall broadcloth of similar color. All trim combinations in the Cadillac-Fleetwood 60 Special are wonderful in conception and exquisite in workmanship for regal beauty and comfort.

Lasting echoes of magnificent Cadillac styling are reflected by the tailored appearance of the front seat back. Dark leather robe cords, roll ash receiver of chrome, and endlessly useful chrome assist-handles accent the careful detail inherent in Cadillac cars. Examples of the light tone and darkly brilliant motif are the 2" light-tone leather seat back pipes harmonizing with light-tone broadcloth. Lower seat bottoms and seat sides are faced in dark leather for lasting beauty. The exquisite styling of the Cadillac-Fleetwood 60 Special also carries into the front compartment. Jewel-like front hardware is grouped in an attractive panel insert. Window moldings are of sparkling chrome. Arm rests are integral with the door panels. This is a new feature for '52. The metal door and cowl kick pads are attractively styled. Hydraulic window controls are another convenience feature.

For 1952, the accent is also on color. This grand sedan is available in 17 color choices—12 solid colors and 5 two-tone combinations. The Cadillac 60 Special is also distinguished by its graceful flowing lines, its extra length and fleet appearance. Symbolic of the distinctive marking of the 60 Special, is the new broad decklid V and gleaming "Fleetwood" script. Here, too, is value and quality beyond all other cars—so distinctively different, so refined and elegant—that it has won enthusiastic acclaim throughout the world as a motor car unequaled.

SERIES 75

The Cadillac Series 75 is the plus ultimate in the automotive fashion world. Long and low—extravagant in grace—its exterior appearance presents to perfection an exquisite flawless beauty of line. Never before have luxurious interior appointments presented such enchantment of sophisticated tailoring—every luxury fabric inside harmonizes with the gleaming dark elegance of exterior design. Never before has such smooth performance, quiet comfort and wonderful convenience been available in cars of this exclusive type and character. Built on a chassis wheelbase of 146" to provide the maximum interior room, Series 75 cars are powered by the Cadillac 190-horsepower engine. Available either as an 8-passenger limousine with a stationary dividing partition, or as a luxurious 8-passenger sedan, this motor car is constructed with but one thought in mind—to create an automobile for an exacting clientele whose requirements can be satisfied by no other motor car now being manufactured.

CADILLAC-FLEETWOOD SERIES 75
PAGEANT OF INTERIOR FASHIONS

Unmistakably Cadillac, the interior styling of the Series 75 lends a warm vibrant accent interpreted by master-tailors for an exacting clientele whose requirements can be satisfied by no other motor car. The rear compartment interiors are unusually commodious and trimmed in luxurious fabrics. The rear seat cushion and seat back are in a fashion-future tufted motif, accentuated by wide plain bolsters and harmonizing leather welts. A choice of either bedford cord or broadcloth is optional in pleasing shades of light tan or light gray. Garnish moldings are in Australian Lacewood grain pattern with bright chrome hardware and decorative trim. Door panels and floor carpets are in harmony. Equipment and appointments include cushioned side arm rests with package compartments, ash receivers and lighters, a newly designed center arm rest, robe cord, assist grips, foot rests, an electric clock in the front seat back, hydraulic window lifts, front seat adjustment controls and two new under-rear-seat heaters. An additional Cadillac heater is under the front seat.

LIMOUSINE FRONT COMPARTMENT

The front compartment of the Series 75 limousine is trimmed in black leather. Seat cushions are pleated in flowing lines while the door panels are plain black leather with black trim molding. The window molding, hardware and division glass frame are all bright chrome. The headlining is in black imitation leather and the floor carpeting in black wool pile. The steering wheel column and instrument panel are black with standard chrome hardware. The left door panel contains a master hydraulic control for operating rear windows only. The limousine division adds greatly to Cadillac motoring convenience.

THE NEWEST STANDARD OF THE WORLD IN MOTOR CAR ENGINES

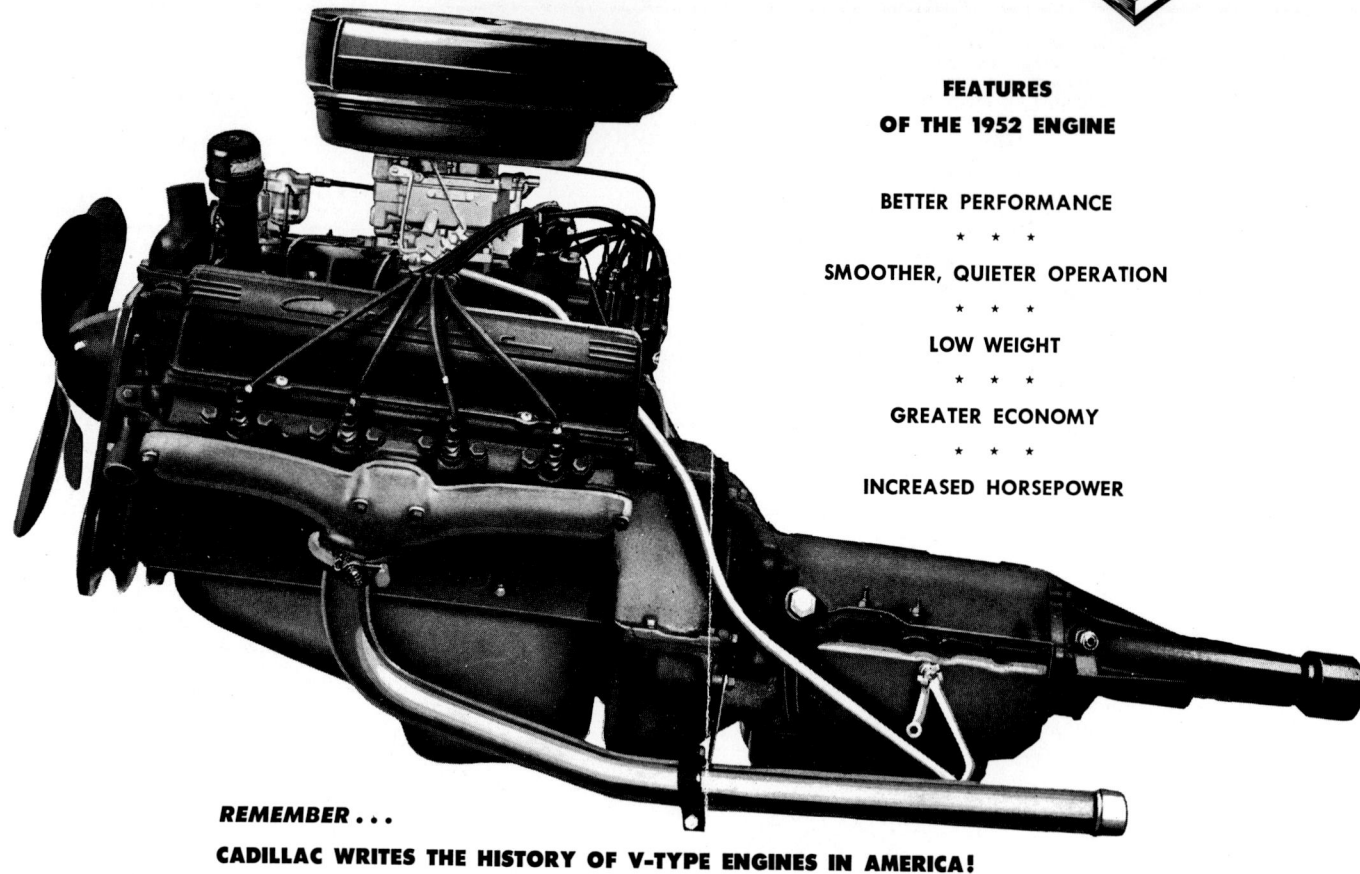

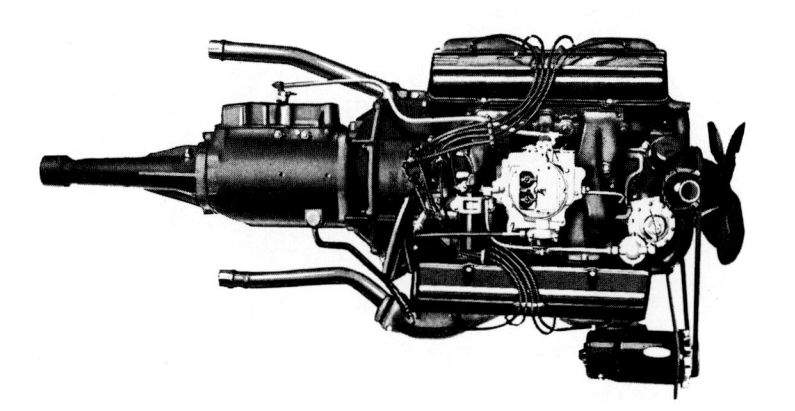

FEATURES OF THE 1952 ENGINE

BETTER PERFORMANCE

★ ★ ★

SMOOTHER, QUIETER OPERATION

★ ★ ★

LOW WEIGHT

★ ★ ★

GREATER ECONOMY

★ ★ ★

INCREASED HORSEPOWER

REMEMBER...
CADILLAC WRITES THE HISTORY OF V-TYPE ENGINES IN AMERICA!

MILES AND YEARS OF TESTING

It is an undeniable fact that no motor car engine ever built has back of it a history of development, testing and achievement, that is comparable to that of this new 190-horsepower Cadillac power plant. Its basic design, in addition to laboratory tests, has been proved over a period of 37 years in the hands of the world's most exacting motorists. In the course of testing, the 1952 Cadillac engine, like all of the models that have preceded it, has been exposed to every conceivable strain and hazard—sustained high speeds on the road; pulling tests up grades as steep as 27%; mud roads designed to draw everything out of an engine; water baths that search out any weak spots. Those who know best—test drivers and experimental engine specialists—say without reservation that the new 190-horsepower Cadillac engine is more powerful, more durable, more efficient than any stock car engine ever built—including the great previous Cadillac engines.

The spotlight of Cadillac engineering progress moves rapidly forward, and following in its path is the shadow of obsolescence, creeping over and obscuring yesterday's best. A head-on view of the powerful 1952 Cadillac engine reveals its low silhouette. As brilliant as the past performance of Cadillac engines has been, the 1952 engine surpasses its history-making V-type predecessors.

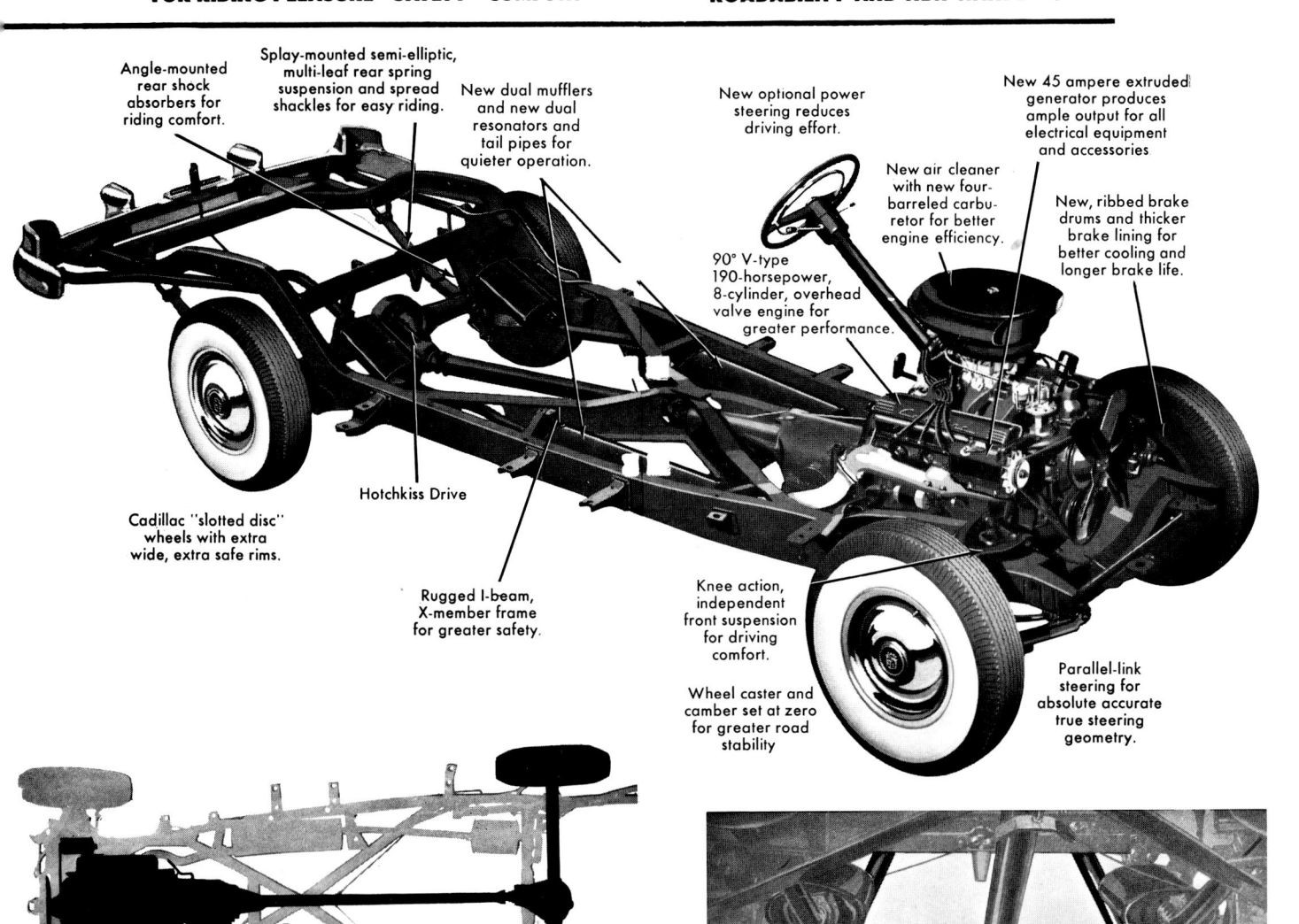

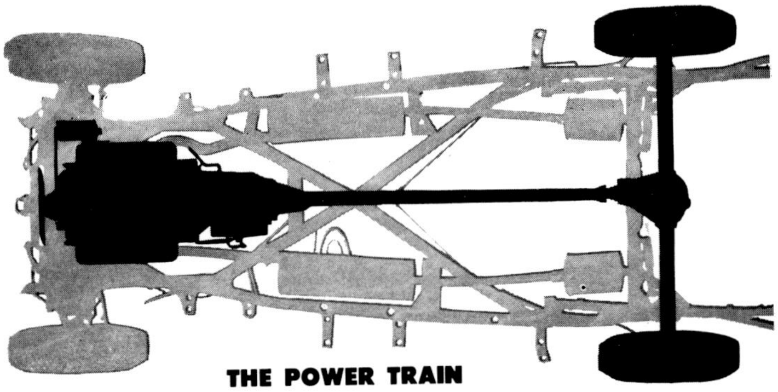

FOR RIDING PLEASURE—SAFETY—COMFORT   ROADABILITY AND NEW HANDLING EASE

Angle-mounted rear shock absorbers for riding comfort.

Splay-mounted semi-elliptic, multi-leaf rear spring suspension and spread shackles for easy riding.

New dual mufflers and new dual resonators and tail pipes for quieter operation.

New optional power steering reduces driving effort.

New air cleaner with new four-barreled carburetor for better engine efficiency.

New 45 ampere extruded generator produces ample output for all electrical equipment and accessories.

New, ribbed brake drums and thicker brake lining for better cooling and longer brake life.

90° V-type 190-horsepower, 8-cylinder, overhead valve engine for greater performance.

Cadillac "slotted disc" wheels with extra wide, extra safe rims.

Hotchkiss Drive

Rugged I-beam, X-member frame for greater safety.

Knee action, independent front suspension for driving comfort.

Wheel caster and camber set at zero for greater road stability

Parallel-link steering for absolute accurate true steering geometry.

THE POWER TRAIN

Component parts of the power train include the new Hydra-Matic transmission. A second and alternate component is the famous Cadillac Synchro-Mesh transmission standard on Series 75 cars as well as Cadillac commercial cars.

Other important components of the Cadillac power train are the precision-built, tubular propeller shaft, and full needle-bearing universal joints. These are designed to give much longer life and smooth, vibrationless operation.

Also part of the power train is Cadillac's semi-floating rear axles, with Hypoid gears. These gears are cut so that the driving pinion meshes with the ring gear, well below the center line of the differential. This accounts for the lower drive-shaft, lower floors and almost unnoticeable tunnel in the floor of the car. A new ribbed carrier for the hypoid gears is a 1952 feature. It provides a more rigid mounting and improved oiling. It reduces rear axle noise.

ALTERNATE REAR AXLE RATIO AVAILABLE

Cadillac Series 62 and Series 60 Special cars are built at the factory with a rear axle ratio of 3.36:1 which provides excellent "get away" and wonderful performance. However many Cadillac owners may prefer an alternate rear axle ratio of 3.07:1 and, upon request *only*, cars will be built with this alternate ratio. The 3.07:1 alternate rear axle ratio offers economy of as much as ⅝ of a mile more per gallon in city driving, as much as from 1 to 2 miles more per gallon for country driving—depending upon the driver. At higher cruising, the 3.07:1 rear axle also offers lower and quieter engine speeds.

REAR "SEA LEG" SHOCK ABSORBERS

For a combination that further adds to riding comfort—Cadillac's angle-mounted, rear shock absorbers control side-to-side movement at the rear of the car and cushion road shocks. Engineered to control spring action, the result is boulevard riding comfort over the roughest roads.

HOTCHKISS DRIVE

Hotchkiss Drive, a Cadillac chassis feature, provides an easier ride, protects the mechanism, and isolates road shocks from the car body. Passenger comfort is increased by Hotchkiss Drive because the driving force is transmitted and cushioned through the splay-mounted rear springs, which are equipped with "spread shackles" to reduce lateral movement. Less tire noise is transmitted to the sturdy body with this Cadillac chassis feature.

51

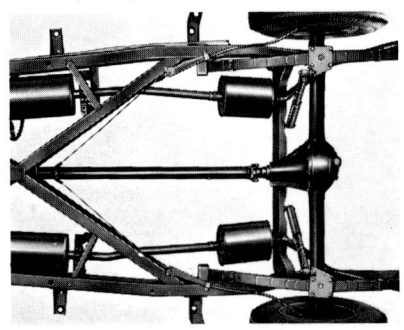

1952 ACCESSORIES

CADILLAC ACCESSORIES GROUPS

GROUP G1

Windshield Washer	Fog Lights
Wheel Discs	License Frames
Oil Filter Vanity Mirror	Outside Mirror

GROUP G2

Windshield Washer	Fog Lights
Wheel Discs	License Frames
Oil Filter	Vanity Mirror

GROUP G3

Windshield Washer	Fog Lights
Wheel Discs	Outside Mirror
Oil Filter	Vanity Mirror

GROUP G4

Windshield Washer	License Frames
Wheel Discs	Outside Mirror
Oil Filter	Vanity Mirror

GROUP G5

Windshield Washer	Oil Filter
Wheel Discs	Fog Lights

GROUP G6

Windshield Washer	Oil Filter	Wheel Discs

WINDSHIELD WASHER—The Cadillac windshield washer is not only a convenience but also a safety accessory. It sprays two jets of clean water or solvent on the windshield so that mud, slush or insects may be removed by the windshield wipers. The tank is filled with Cadillac Solvent and water in winter or summer. Finger-tip pressure on button in the center of the windshield wiper control starts a pump which gives immediate action.

LICENSE PLATE FRAMES—These Cadillac license plate frames enhance the appearance of the license plates, cover their sharp edges and protect them from weathering. Chrome-flashed, these attractive frames sell in pairs.

SIGNAL SEEKING RADIO WITH REAR SPEAKER—The signal seeking radio with rear speaker and automatic station selector is available. Foot tuning control can be added. It is one of the most modern car radios available.

THE AUTOMATIC PUSH BUTTON RADIO—With elliptical speaker, offers fine reception under all conditions. Station selector buttons are easily set on the "push-pull" lock-up tuner which is the smoothest and most accurate mechanical tuner ever developed for any car radio.

SPOTLIGHTS—Right-hand or left-hand mounted spotlights are designed with a built-in rear view mirror—enabling the driver to adjust the mirror from inside the car. Both left and right spotlights add distinctive beauty to the 1952 Cadillac car.

AUTOMATIC HEATING SYSTEM—The Cadillac Automatic Heating System consists of one underseat heater, a defroster with an outside air inlet on the left side of the front compartment. In addition the Deluxe Model for Series 60 Special, and Series 62 cars (except Convertible), includes a rear window blower for defogging the rear window. The Deluxe Model for Series 75 cars has three underseat heaters and also includes a rear window blower for defogging this vital rear-window area.

FOG LAMPS—The new 1952 Cadillac fog lamps improve visibility under adverse weather conditions. These fog lamps also incorporate the turn-signal lights. The location of the front compartment control switch for the fog lamps depends upon whether Signal Seeking or Automatic Push Button radio is used.

PARATWILL SEAT COVERS—Cadillac seat covers for 1952 have been restyled. The Rayon-Cotton Paratwill line is available in three patterns. The first, a two-tone stripe pattern is available in green, blue or maroon with bolster in solid matching color. Solid colors of green, blue or maroon with self-woven stripes are also available. The new Neoline Paratwill pattern comes in two-tone colors of blue, maroon or green with bolster of solid color.

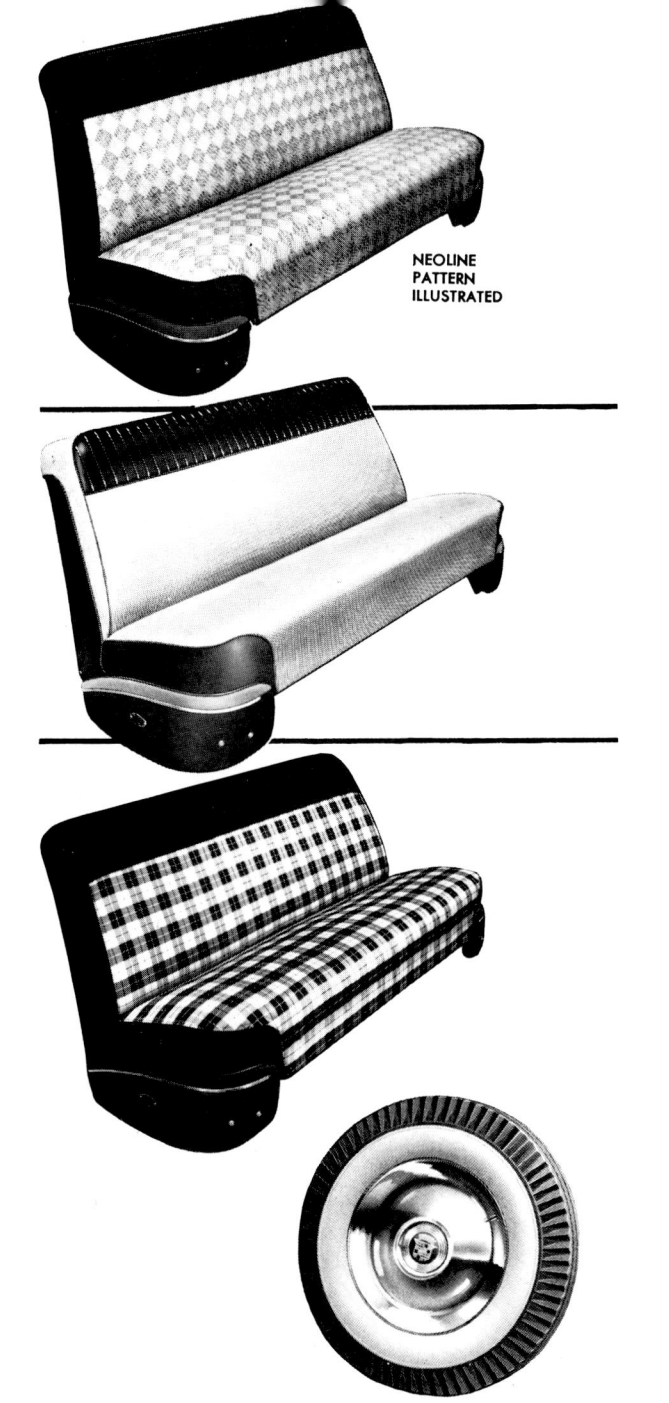

PLASTIC COVERS—Are available in two distinct patterns and a range of three color combinations. An over-all diamond-cross pattern is available in either blue, green or maroon with a solid colored bolster of Paratwill. A houndstooth pattern is also available in a choice of green, blue or maroon. This pattern has a black simulated leather bolster with channel design.

TARTAN PLAID SEAT COVERS—Are fabricated from 100% durable double-twist rayon. A green and gray plaid with green Paratwill bolster is an attractive choice. Other color combinations available include blue and gray plaid with blue Paratwill bolster and a maroon and gray plaid combination with maroon Paratwill bolster.

MIRRORS—Among the beautiful Cadillac accessories are listed two pairs of endlessly useful mirrors. The first set, the visor vanity mirrors, are convenient 4″ x 8″ mirrors distinctively decorated with the Cadillac name in script. They clamp on the back of either sun visor. The second set of mirrors, for better rear view, are the outside mirrors. They are plate glass, 4½ inches in diameter and can be adjusted for the best driving angle.

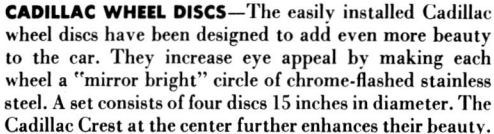

CADILLAC WHEEL DISCS—The easily installed Cadillac wheel discs have been designed to add even more beauty to the car. They increase eye appeal by making each wheel a "mirror bright" circle of chrome-flashed stainless steel. A set consists of four discs 15 inches in diameter. The Cadillac Crest at the center further enhances their beauty.

CADILLAC WHEEL TRIM RINGS Enable the owner to build up the eye appeal of the wheels. Whether the car is in motion or standing still, the trim rings add to the over-all impression of Cadillac smartness. The trim rings are fabricated from durable and heavy stainless steel.

CADILLAC BLUE CORAL—During the past 20 years, the Cadillac Blue Coral Treatment goes far beyond ordinary wash and polish or waxing. It cleans away dirt, grime and traffic film. It restores the original beauty of the finish and then seals it with a lustrous, glass-hard enduring protective coating. It may be applied in the Service Department or is available for individual application.

SUN VISOR—Cadillac's attractive, Plexiglas sun visor is easy on the eyes the year around. It is installed on the inside top portion of the windshield in the matter of only a few minutes. In all seasons of the year, it filters out strong sun rays ... cuts sky and snow glare and offers better daytime driving visibility.

VENTSHADES—These beautiful, stainless steel window shields not only dress up the car but cut down sun glare, reduce draft when the windows are open, and when it's raining, permit opening the windows two or three inches without letting in rain. Handsomely styled to harmonize with the car's appearance, they fit smoothly.

53

1952 CADILLAC GENERAL SPECIFICATIONS

	Series 62 Sedan	Series 62 Convertible Coupe	Series 62 Coupe	Series 62 Coupe de Ville	Series 60 Fleetwood Special	Series 75 8-Passenger Sedan	Series 75 Imperial Sedan
Wheelbase	126″	126″	126″	126″	130″	146¾″	146¾″
Over-all Length	215½″	220½″	220½″	220½″	224½″	236¼″	236¼″
Over-all Width	80⅛″	80⅛″	80⅛″	80⅛″	80⅝″	80⅛″	80⅛″
Over-all Height	62¹¹⁄₁₆″	61⅛″	60¹⁵⁄₁₆″	60¹⁵⁄₁₆″	62¹¹⁄₁₆″	64¹⁄₁₆″	64¹⁄₁₆″
Steering Ratio—Over-all	25.47	25.47	25.47	25.47	25.47	25.47	25.47
Turning Radius	22½′	22½′	22½′	22½′	23′	25½′	25½′
Tread—Front	59″	59″	59″	59″	59″	59″	59″
Tread—Rear	63″	63″	63″	63″	63″	63″	63″
Tires—Size	8:00 x 15	8:00 x 15	8:00 x 15	8:00 x 15	8:00 x 15	8:20 x 15	8:20 x 15
Tires—Ply Rating	4-ply	4-ply	4-ply	4-ply	4-ply	6-ply	6-ply
Engine	190-horsepower Cadillac V-8	190-horsepower Cadillac V-8	190-horsepower Cadillac V-8	190-horsepower Cadillac V-8	190-horsepower Cadillac V-8	190-horsepower Cadillac V-8	190-horsepower Cadillac V-8
Compression Ratio	7.5:1	7.5:1	7.5:1	7.5:1	7.5:1	7.5:1	7.5:1
Piston Displacement	331 cu. in.	331 cu. in.	331 cu. in.	331 cu. in.	331 cu. in.	331 cu. in.	331 cu. in.
Valve Arrangement	Overhead	Overhead	Overhead	Overhead	Overhead	Overhead	Overhead
Carburetor	4-Barrel	4-Barrel	4-Barrel	4-Barrel	4-Barrel	4-Barrel	4-Barrel
Exhaust System	Dual	Dual	Dual	Dual	Dual	Dual	Dual
Transmission	New Hydra-Matic	New Hydra-Matic	New Hydra-Matic	New Hydra-Matic	New Hydra-Matic	*Synchro-Mesh	*Synchro-Mesh
Steering Gear	Ball Nut with optional power steering	Ball Nut with optional power steering	Ball Nut with optional power steering	Ball Nut with optional power steering	Ball Nut with optional power steering	Ball Nut with optional power steering	Ball Nut with optional power steering
Frame	I-Beam, X-Member	I-Beam, X-Member	I-Beam, X-Member	I-Beam, X-Member	I-Beam, X-Member	I-Beam, X-Member	I-Beam, X-Member
Springs	Coil front, semi-elliptic-leaf rear	Coil front, semi-elliptic-leaf rear	Coil front, semi-elliptic-leaf rear	Coil front, semi-elliptic-leaf rear	Coil front, semi-elliptic-leaf rear	Coil front, semi-elliptic-leaf rear	Coil front, semi-elliptic-leaf rear
Drive	Hotchkiss	Hotchkiss	Hotchkiss	Hotchkiss	Hotchkiss	Hotchkiss	Hotchkiss
Axle Ratio with Hydra-Matic	3.36:1	3.36:1	3.36:1	3.36:1	3.36:1	3.77:1*	3.77:1*
Axle Ratio—Series 75 (Std. Manual Trans.)	.....	.....	.....	.....	.....	3.77:1	3.77:1
Alternate Axle Ratio Series 60 Special and 62s	3.07:1	3.07:1	3.07:1	3.07:1	3.07:1	.....	.....

*New Hydra-Matic transmission is optional on Series 75 cars.

DETAILED SPECIFICATIONS

ENGINE
- Number of cylinders: 8
- Cylinder arrangement: 90° bank-type
- Valve arrangement: Overhead
- Bore and stroke: 3¹³⁄₁₆″ x 3⅝″
- Block and cylinder head material: Cast iron
- Piston displacement: 331 cu. in.
- Taxable horsepower: 46.5
- Max. brake horsepower: 190 @ 4000 r.p.m.
- Max. engine torque—lbs.-ft.: 322 @ 2400 r.p.m.
- Compression ratio: 7.5:1
- Engine mounts: Vulcanized rubber
- Number of points of suspension: 3

PISTONS AND RINGS
- Make: Alcoa—Bohn—Stearling
- Material: Aluminum alloy
- Type: T-slot, cam ground
- Weight: 18.752 oz.
- Clearance: .0015″
- Number of oil rings per piston: 1
- Number of comp. rings per piston: 2

RODS AND PINS
- Wristpin length: 3.093″
- Wristpin material: Steel alloy
- Type: Locked in rod
- Connecting rod length: 6.625″
- Material—connecting rod: Forged steel alloy
- Weight—connecting rod: 23.95 oz.
- Crankpin journal diameter: 2¼″
- Lower bearing material: Steel back Durex
- Connecting rod bearing clearance: .001″–.0035″
- Connecting rod bearing end play: .008″–.014″ (total two rods)

CRANKSHAFT
- Material: Forged alloy steel
- Weight: 61.5 pounds
- Main bearing thrust: Rear main
- Crankshaft end play: .001″ to .005″
- Main bearing type: Slip-on
- Main bearing removable: Yes
- Main bearing material: Steel back Durex
- Main bearing clearance—rear: .0015″ to .0025″
- Main bearing journal Diameter x Length:
  - Number 1: 2.5″ x 1″
  - Number 2: 2.5″ x 1.0625″
  - Number 3: 2.5″ x 1.0625″
  - Number 4: 2.5″ x 1.0625″
  - Number 5: 2.5″ x 1.875″

CAMSHAFT
- Drive: Chain
- Camshaft sprocket material: Cast iron
- Timing chain—make: Link Belt
- Timing chain—no. of links: 46
- Timing chain—width: .6875″
- Timing chain—pitch: .500″

VALVES
- Valve arrangement: Overhead
  - Intake opens: 14° B.T.C. without ramp
  - Intake closes: 58° A.B.C. without ramp
  - Exhaust opens: 48° B.B.C. without ramp
  - Exhaust closes: 24° A.T.C. without ramp

INTAKE
- Material: Alloy steel
- Over-all length: 4.539″ to 4.559″
- Diameter of head: 1.750″
- Angle of seat: 44°
- Lift: .327″

EXHAUST
- Material: Alloy steel
- Over-all length: 4.529″ to 4.559″
- Diameter of head: 1.562″
- Angle of seat: 44°
- Lift: .327″
- Hydraulic valve lifters: Yes
- Valve inserts: None
- Valve seats cooled by: Direct water circulation

LUBRICATION
- Type: Full pressure
- Oil Under Pressure to:
  - Main bearings: Yes
  - Connecting rods: Yes
  - Wristpins: Splash
  - Camshaft bearings: Yes
  - Tappets: Yes
- Oil pump type: Gear
- Normal oil pressure: 30 to 35 lbs. @ 30 m.p.h.
- Capacity of oil reservoir: Dry, 5 Qts.; Refill, 5 Qts.
- Type of oil level gauge: Dip stick
- Make of pressure gauge: AC

FUEL

Gasoline tank capacity	20 gallons
Type of fuel feed	Camshaft pump
Carburetor—make	Rochester & Carter
Carburetor—type	Four barrel down draft
Manifold heat control	Automatic
Type of air cleaner	Oil bath
Dual tail pipe diameters	2.094" to 2.099"

COOLING

Water pump type	Centrifugal—dual outlet
Pressure relief valve	Yes
Choke for re-circulation	Yes
Radiator core	Tube and fin
Full-length cylinder water jacket	Yes
Water all around cylinders	Yes
Fan belt length	57"
Fan belt width	3/8"
Fan—No. of blades, Series 62 & 60	4
Fan—No. of blades, Series 75	5

GENERATOR

Make	Delco-Remy
Voltage at cut-out closing	5.9 to 6.8 (adjust to 6.4)
Amperes to open cut-out	0 to 4
Generator maximum charging rate	45 to 51 amp. (adjust to 47)
Minimum charging speed	28 m.p.h. and up
Generator ventilation	Forced air

STARTING MOTOR

Make	Delco-Remy
Flywheel teeth, integral or ring	Steel ring

IGNITION

Spark advance	Centrifugal and vacuum
Ignition Unit:	
Make	Delco-Remy
Manual advance	None
Maximum centrifugal advance	Crankshaft (31° to 35°)
Vacuum advance	Crankshaft (19° to 22°)
Distributor breaker gap	.010" to .015"
Initial spark advance	5° B.T.C.
Firing order	1-8-4-3-6-5-7-2
Ignition Coil:	
Make	Delco-Remy
Amperage Draw of Coil:	
With engine stopped	4.5 to 5.5
With engine idling	2 to 3
Spark Plugs:	
Make	AC
Model	48
Thread	14 mm.
Gap	.035"

BATTERY

Make	Delco K4W
Number of plates	17
Capacity (amp. hrs.)	115
Battery Bench Charging Rate:	
Start	10
Finish	8
Terminal grounded	Negative
Location of battery	Under hood on tray attached to right-hand dash to frame brace front of dash

LAMPS AND HORN

Headlight—make	Guide sealed-beam
Headlight cover glass, dia.	6 11/16"
Parking light—make	Guide
Tail light—make	Guide
Lighting switch—make	Delco-Remy
How are headlights dimmed?	Depressed beam—foot switch
Horn:	
Make	Delco-Remy
Type	Vibrator, seashell electric

CLUTCH (75 Series only)

Make	Long semi-centrifugal
Drive type	Direct to flywheel
Vibration neutralizer	Spring friction type
Number of driving discs	1
Number of driven discs	1
Clutch facing	Woven asbestos
Clutch facing inside diameter	7"
Clutch facing outside diameter	11"
Clutch facing thickness	.137"
Clutch facing number required	2

SYNCHRO-MESH TRANSMISSION (Standard on 75 Series)

Number of forward speeds	3
Type of shift	Manual
Gear ratio, high	1:1
Gear ratio, second	1.53:1
Gear ratio, low	2.39:1
Gear ratio, reverse	2.39:1
Type of gears	Helical, constant mesh in 1st, 2nd and reverse
Oil capacity	3 3/4 pints
Grade recommended, summer	S.A.E. 90
Grade recommended, winter	S.A.E. 90 Extreme cold 80

HYDRA-MATIC DRIVE

Type	High Efficiency fluid coupling and fully automatic transmission
Gearing	Planetary
No. of forward speeds	4
No. of forward speeds in "City" dr. range	3
No. of forward speeds in "Country" dr. range	4
No. of forward speeds in Lo range	2
Transmission ratio, first	3.8195:1
Transmission ratio, second	2.6341:1
Transmission ratio, third	1.45:1
Transmission ratio, fourth	1:1
Transmission ratio, reverse	4.3045:1
Oil capacity	10.5 qts.
Type of fluid	Hydra-Matic fluid

FRAME

	Series 62	Series 60S	Series 75
Frame make	A. O. Smith	A. O. Smith	A. O. Smith
Frame depth, maximum	7 5/32"	7 3/16"	7 3/16"
Frame thickness, maximum	9/64"	1/2"	1/2"
Flange width, maximum	2 37/64"	2 11/32"	2 11/32"
Frame—Type	Box girder	Box girder	Box girder

FRONT END SUSPENSION

Front suspension, make	Own
Front suspension, type	Forked arms
Forked arm bearings, type	Threaded
Kingpin upper bearing, type	Bronze bushing
Kingpin lower bearing, type	Bronze bushing
Front wheel inner bearing, make and type	N. D. ball
Front wheel outer bearing, make and type	N. D. ball
Front spring, type	Helical coil
Front spring, material	Spring steel
Shock absorber, type	Hydraulic direct-acting type
Front stabilizer	Torsion rod

PROPELLER SHAFT

	Series 62-60	Series 75
Number used	1	2
Type	Exposed	Exposed

UNIVERSAL JOINTS

Make	Mechanics and Saginaw
Number used	2 3
Type	Cross and Trunnion
Bearing	Needle
Universal joints, lubricated	Permanently
Drive and torque taken through	Rear springs

REAR AXLE

	Series 62-60	Series 75
Rear axle, make	Own	
Rear axle, type	Semi-floating	
Differential gear, make	Own	
Rear axle:		
Oil capacity	5 pints	
Grade recommended:		
S.A.E. viscosity	90 hypoid	
Type of final gearing	Hypoid	
Gear ratio:		
Hyd. Trans. Std. Equip.	3.36:1	3.77:1
Pinion adjustment (Except 75)	None	
Pinion bearing adjustment	None (Preloaded)	
Are pinion bearings in sleeve?	No	
Backlash between pinion and ring gear	.003-.010"	
Rear axle pinion shaft:		
Front bearing, type	Tapered roller	
Rear bearing, type	Tapered roller	

TIRES AND WHEELS

Tires:		
Make	U.S. Royal—Firestone and Goodrich	
Size	8.00 x 15	8.20 x 15
Ply rating	4	6
Inflation pressure:		
Front	24 lbs.	28 lbs.
Rear	24 lbs.	28 lbs.
Wheels:		
Type	Slotted disc	
Make	Kelsey-Hayes	
Rim, diameter	15"	15"
Rim, width	6.00"	6.00"
Tread:		
Front	59"	59"
Rear	63"	63"

SPRINGS (Rear)

	Series 62-60	Series 75
Rear springs:		
Type	Semi-elliptic	
Material	Spring steel	
Length	54 1/2"	56 1/2"
Width	2"	
No. of leaves	8	10
Spring leaves lubricated with	Wax impregnated liners	
Spring bushings, type	Rubber	
Stabilizers	Rear—None	

SHOCK ABSORBERS (Rear)

Type	Direct Acting

STEERING

Steering gear:	
Type	Recirculating ball
Make	Saginaw
Over-all steering ratio	25.47-1
Car turning radius (outside) bumper to bumper sweep	(62) 22.5' (75) 25.5' (60) 23'

BRAKES

	Series 62-60	Series 75
Front brake drum diameter	12"	12"
Front brake drum, internal or external	Internal	Internal
Front brake lining, length per wheel:		
Forward shoe	12.92	12.92
Reverse shoe	12.92	12.92
Total	25.84	25.84
Front brake lining width	2 1/2"	2 1/2"
Front brake lining thickness	1/4"	1/4"
Front brake clearance	.007-.010"	.007-.010"
Rear brake drum diam.	11"	12"
Rear brake drum, internal or external	Internal	Internal
Rear brake lining, length per wheel:		
Forward shoe	10.55	Same as front
Reverse shoe	11.90	Same as front
Total	22.45	Same as front
Rear brake lining width	2 1/2"	2 1/2"
Rear brake lining thickness	1/4"	1/4"
Rear brake clearance	.007-.010"	
Hand brake location	Left side of dash	
Hand brake lever operates on	Rear service brakes	

MISCELLANEOUS SPECIFICATIONS

Car lifting device, jack	Bumper type
Engine lubrication, type	Pressure
Chassis lubrication, type	High pressure
Axle lubrication, type	Splash

LUBRICANTS

Engine oil	5 qts.
Recommended viscosity	Min. anticipated temperature: +32°F. 20W or S.A.E. 20 +10°F. 20W -10°F. 10W Below -10°F. 5W
Drain	2000 miles (after initial 500-mile change)
Rear axle oil	5 pints
Recommended viscosity	90 hypoid
Auto trans. fluid type "A"	12 qts. dry
Cooling system—water	19 qts. (20 with heater)
Gasoline	20 gals.

Cadillac for 1953

The year 1953 is, in a sense, a turning point for Cadillac. For it not only brings to a close one of the most brilliant chapters in automotive history—the first half-century of Cadillac leadership—but it also begins a *second* half-century of Cadillac progress and development. The 1953 Cadillac brings to fruition all the good and wonderful things that Cadillac has pioneered and achieved during these past fifty years—and, at the same time, heralds a new era of automotive advancement. It is both the climax of Cadillac's historic past—and a brilliant promise and pledge for the future. In building this motor car, we of Cadillac have spared nothing by way of styling, of engineering or of craftsmanship. It is a Cadillac designed without compromise in any way—and built to the most exacting standards that can be enforced in the production of a motor car. Anyone who has the pleasure of driving it or the privilege of owning it, will recognize instantly that it has brought the automotive science to a higher degree of perfection than has ever before been attained. In its beauty, in its performance and in its distinction—it is the greatest Cadillac car of all time!

AS ALWAYS—THE STANDARD OF THE WORLD!

NEW PARKING LIGHTS... AND NEW GRILLE GUARDS

Look closely at the refined and elegant styling of this sparkling new Cadillac grille. The style accent is on full-width horizontal lines to give a low, wide look. The parking lamps have been set in and integrated with the entire front-end design and they are protected by heavy, yet gleamingly attractive metal work. Too, there is an appearance of authority in the clean lines of the newly designed and more massive "bullet-like" front bumper guards... which provide rugged protection when it is needed. The blended effect of these two features is one of beauty and low road-hugging security.

NEW 1953 FRONT-END ENSEMBLE

The magic of Cadillac styling transforms the 1953 front-end ensemble in all Cadillac cars into more massive and even more graceful lines. Cars were restyled *to retain* many of Cadillac's most popular and captivating appearance characteristics. The 1953 hood, topped by a chromed goddess of newly streamlined proportions, is wider and lower. This appearance feature for 1953 is accentuated by the addition of a *wider Cadillac V and crest* in familiar gold motif. Chromed *horizontal* grille bars are heavy. The center grille bar is built integral with new and larger bumper guards. This combination of features adds a solid, lower-and-wider appearance to the ensemble. Chrome-plated *vertical* grille bars retain the characteristic Cadillac appearance. The lower grille extensions have been redesigned for 1953. They are tailored to retain newly designed parking lights which have moved to the outside of the ensemble as shown in the photo on the right. Cadillac "Cadet Visor" headlamp bezels, in sparkling chrome, add to the flowing lines and blend pleasingly with the over-all design. Fog lights, optional at extra cost, are designed to nest into the lower grille extensions to replace the parking lights.

NEW "CADET VISOR" BEZELS

Cadillac's beautiful new "Cadet Visor" headlamp bezels have been redesigned in sparkling chrome. This lovely design is distinctive and extremely practical . . . it directs the headlamp-beam downward to reduce glare and guards the lens against damage, dirt and bugs. While retaining the characteristics of Cadillac appearance, these newly designed bezels add greatly to the wonderfully symmetrical appearance of the 1953 front-end ensemble.

NEW, WIDER AND LOWER HOOD

Here is massiveness, strength and beauty all coordinated into a balanced and pleasing new hood design of streamlined proportions. Topped by a lovely redesigned chrome ornament, the hood tapers deeply downward and at a greater forward angle to dramatize the neatly paralleled grill members, and to emphasize the width of this new Cadillac.

This designer's magic has been made possible by an over-all, basic harmony of design . . . by discreet use of chromium trim . . . by keeping the center of eye interest low.

BEAUTIFUL NEW FOG LIGHTS

Look closely at the functional design of this sparkling new 1953 Cadillac Fog Light (optional at extra cost). It has been set in and integrated with the entire front-end ensemble. The gentle and graceful design of these new Fog Lights is destined to become one of the major recognition marks that people everywhere identify as belonging strictly to Cadillac.

NEW, WIDER V AND CREST

On the 1953 Cadillacs, the horizontal grille bars focus attention on the beautiful, wider Cadillac V and crest. This distinguished Cadillac emblem is a heritage—a heritage that has left its imprint on every Cadillac product ever built. Topping the grille in the center of the newly designed hood . . . this Cadillac V and shield in gleaming gold and colorful plastic tells all the world that for 1953 there is no sacrifice in traditional Cadillac *quality*.

57

NEW REAR-END APPEARANCE

This ensemble of massive rear bumper and new "bullet-like" rear bumper guards combines with the big, husky rear deck contour, decorative Cadillac V and crest, and giant chrome and red plastic twin tail lamps. The result is a new sleekness of line and long, low silhouette. Shown above is the rear deck contour of the Cadillac 62 Sedan.

This slipstream styling distinguishes the 62 Sedan in appearance of grace and makes available a roomy luggage compartment. Series 75 Cadillac cars for 1953 also use this impressive rear deck contour to provide a luggage compartment of "cross country" proportions. The smooth continuity of design shown in this "going away" view is typical of the entire car.

NEW AIRSCOOP STONE GUARD

Viewed from any angle, the 1953 Cadillac cars are beautiful to look at. The symmetrical front fenders flow gently into the body . . . to meet a *newly-designed* simulated airscoop stone guard. This new guard retains the familiar characteristics that have made it a sparkling hallmark of Cadillac recognition and appearance since 1949. And yet, it adds a new distinctive note to Cadillac styling for 1953 by giving the rear fender bulge the modern, tailored, trim look.

NEW WHEEL DISC

Shown above is the new Cadillac wheel disc. These newly-designed, concentric-ring wheel discs offer a large concave area in sparkling chrome within which the famous and colorful Cadillac crest is attractively mounted on a convex chrome-plated dome. In addition to style advantages, these new Cadillac wheel discs reduce wind noise and wind drag to a new low point in streamlined automotive design.

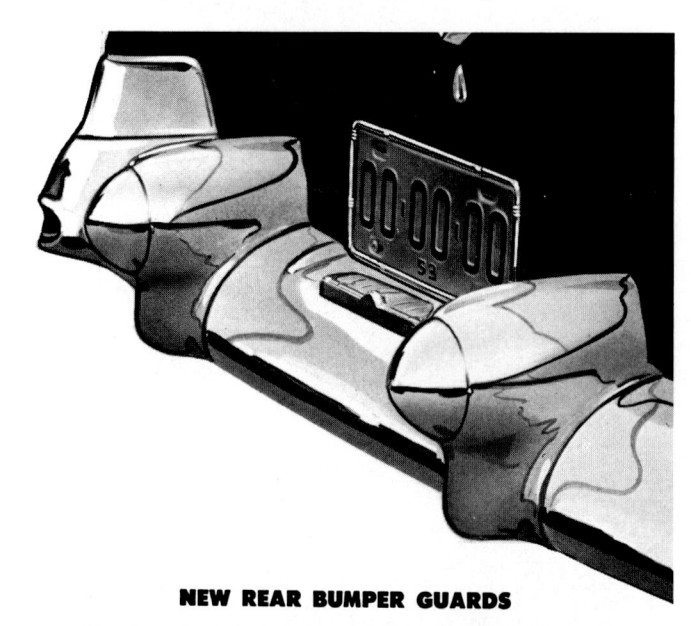

NEW REAR BUMPER GUARDS

Here is a close-up photograph of the two new massive and streamlined rear bumper guards. This rugged protective feature blends with the rear ensemble to give the 1953 car a trim appearance that is completely refreshing.

DUAL EXHAUST THROUGH BUMPER

The wrap-around protection of the Cadillac rear bumper retains a glamorous continental custom styling where "split" exhaust systems terminate in beautifully designed dual exhaust ports through each end of the gleaming chrome bumper bars. This customized dual exhaust-through-bumper system is attractive in appearance and functional in design. The value of this feature has been proven in terms of better engine performance because it reduces engine back-pressure.

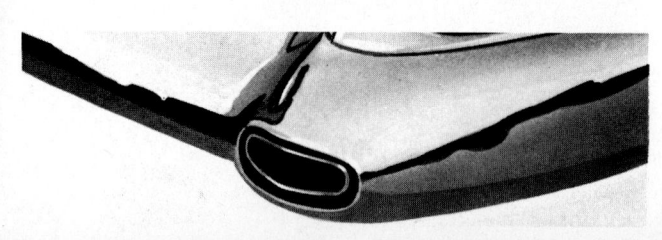

Above, the 1953 Series 62 Sedan. Center, the 1953 Sixty-Special Sedan. Below, the 1953 Series 62 Convertible, with optionally available wire wheels. Approximately 95% of all '53s were factory-equipped with power steering — a fact that prompted the Division to make it standard equipment in 1954. Roughly 10% of the total production had factory air conditioning.

1953 CADILLAC SERIES 62 SEDAN

The fashion future interiors of the Series 62 Sedan are magnificent in their superb styling and two-tone combinations. Luxurious fabrics and deep cushioning are sumptuously combined for armchair comfort. Appointments feature wide arm rests, new door hardware, ash receivers, deep pile rugs and new accents of scintillating chrome throughout. Upholstery material for seat and seat backs is available in *EIGHT* choices of pattern BROADCLOTH or durable CORD fabrics of light color. Following are the available color choices.

EIGHT BEAUTIFUL INTERIORS TO CHOOSE FROM

1. *Light blue* NYLON CORD fabric upholstery ... with rich *dark blue* BROADCLOTH on seat bolsters and trim.
2. *Deep gray color* BROADCLOTH combined with *mist gray* PATTERN BROADCLOTH.
3. *Light blue* PATTERN BROADCLOTH material coupled with *dark blue* BROADCLOTH.
4. *Gray* NYLON CORD fabric matched with *dark gray* BROADCLOTH.
5. *Light tan* NYLON CORD upholstery on seats and seat-back inserts, with a darker *brown* BROADCLOTH for bolsters and trim.
6. *Dark brown* BROADCLOTH combined with *light tan* PATTERN BROADCLOTH on seats, seat-back inserts and trim.
7. *Light green* woven NYLON CORD cloth for seats, seat backs and trim, with *dark green* BROADCLOTH for seat bolsters and trim.
8. *Dark green* BROADCLOTH combined with PATTERN BROADCLOTH in *light green* for seats, seat backs and inserts.

The front compartment permits the driver and front seat passengers to ride relaxed with space to spare, and everything is within easy reach. Generous size doors are outstanding examples of Cadillac engineering genius ... and new door details for 1953 are distinctively styled to good taste and accent the soft manners and deft tailoring in this gorgeous car.

Once inside, the driver and front seat passengers enjoy leg room galore ... picture-window visibility ... overhead room even for milady's hat ... plenty of hip room and shoulder room.

The Series 62 Sedan rear compartment, with its rich upholstery over supple foam rubber padding and individually covered and tied coil springs, offers the utmost in comfort and "room to spare." This car offers all the comfort of an overstuffed easy chair. The luxurious "two person" arm rest is 12 inches across. Heavy vinyl welts accent dark and light colored upholstery.

For ease and comfort, the rear compartment is equipped with built-in arm rests, with inset hand grips on doors. The convenient parcel shelf behind the seat is attractively finished in simulated grained leather.

Door panels in the Series 62 Sedan are trimmed with side wall cloth of light color. A new dark-toned metal finish upper door panel with light tone metallic insert is mounted with new bright and satin-finish door hardware. Hydro-electric controls for windows and the front seat are available as optional equipment at extra cost. Wide built-in door arm rests are "topped" with simulated leather of light tone and contain a new cup grip of matching color. Chrome finish moldings, appointments and door kick-pad of polished tinted stainless steel add to the appearance. Simulated leather hand grips on the steering wheel add that extra luxury touch for which Cadillac is famous, as the Standard of the World.

1953 CADILLAC SERIES 62 COUPE

The front seat in the Cadillac Series 62 Coupe is 62⅝ inches wide. There is head room and leg room to spare in this beautiful automobile. The seat-back bolster is tailored with tufted buttons. Heavy vinyl welts accent dark and light colored upholstery. Lower side panels of the front seat are of scuff-resistant simulated leather. Floors are covered with luxurious wool pile carpets which harmonize with the interior trim. The steering wheel column and instrument panel are painted to match the interior motif chosen from any one of *eight* selections.

The same striking motif is carried into the rear compartment. The rear seat has wide side arm rests and a lounge-type center arm rest. The back of the front seat bolster is upholstered in dark toned cloth to contrast with the light toned seat back.

The interior of the 1953 Cadillac Series 62 Coupe is both functional and lovely to the eye. It is softly and deftly tailored. Every item of the Coupe interiors is harmoniously related to the appearance as a whole—to create an atmosphere of luxury. There is "living room" space in both the front and rear compartments of this car. The rear seat features a center arm rest a full foot wide, for complete arm chair relaxation.

Upholstery material for seats and seat backs is available in eight choices of patterned body cloth or durable cords of light color. Seat back inserts are styled in lovely biscuits with buttons. Seat cushions are given the Cadillac mark of distinction, with a styling of biscuits gathered with buttons.

EIGHT COLOR FASHIONS TO CHOOSE FROM

1. *Mist gray* woven NYLON CORD for seats and seat-back inserts . . . combined with rich *deep gray* plain BROADCLOTH on seat bolsters and trim.
2. Plain BROADCLOTH of *deep gray* color, combined with *mist gray* PATTERN CLOTH for seats, seat-back inserts and trim.
3. *Sky-blue* NYLON CORD material for seats and seat-back inserts, coupled with a *dark blue* plain BROADCLOTH for bolsters and trim.
4. *Light blue* BROADCLOTH combined with a *dark blue* PLAIN cloth upholstering for seats, seat-back inserts and trim.
5. *Light tan* woven NYLON CORD upholstery on seats and seat-back inserts, with a *darker brown* BODY CLOTH for bolsters and trim.
6. *Dark brown* BODY CLOTH combined with *light tan* PATTERN CLOTH on seats, seat-back inserts and trim.
7. *Light green* woven NYLON CORD cloth for seats, seat-backs and trim, combined with a *dark green* plain BROADCLOTH.
8. *Dark green* BROADCLOTH combined with PATTERN BROADCLOTH in *light green*.

Doors in the Series 62 Coupe are trimmed in a light colored cloth. A continuous round-the-car valance of metal, attractively lacquered in light metallic colors, sets off the beautiful new satin finish which is contrasted with bright, jewelry-like chrome metal door hardware.

Hydro-electric controls for windows and the front seat are available in the Coupe as optional equipment at extra cost. Ample door arm rests are "topped" with simulated leather of light tone and feature new finishing cups of matching color. Chrome finish moldings, appointments, and a wide door kick-pad in tinted, polished, stainless steel prove that nothing has been left out of this car.

1953 CADILLAC SERIES 62 COUPE DE VILLE

Here is the 1953 Cadillac Series 62 Coupe de Ville with interiors that are vibrant, airy, gay—and as enchanting as a breath of spring! And here, too, are *hardy* interiors, fashioned in rugged leathers and long-wearing Nylon fabrics that defy travel and wear. For 1953, Cadillac presents a choice of EIGHT interior combinations and color styles in the Coupe de Ville. *Four* of these interior combinations include *leather* trim, featuring classic dark leathers matched with Tapestry Pattern Nylon of lighter tone. Optional *four* interior selections in this car offer Vee and Crest patterned Nylon fabrics for seats and seat-back inserts, coupled with dark leathers.

The rear compartment of the Cadillac Series 62 Coupe de Ville is trimmed in smooth and exotic harmony with the rest of the car. A new 12" wide center arm rest and side arm rests add to beauty, comfort and convenience. There's ample leg room—and foot room, too. Proper seat height gives adequate support for leg comfort. Chrome finish moldings and roof bows add a note of luxury to the interior of the De Ville.

In the front, there is 62⅝ inches of seat space. The seat is generously padded with soft, resilient foam rubber that outwears ordinary cushions. The *custom-tailored* look of the front compartment is enhanced by a steering wheel of new design, new bright and satin-finish hardware.

There is exceptional room for leg movement in the rear compartment of the Coupe de Ville. Proper seat height assures adequate support for leg comfort. Generous sized recesses in the front seat backs add to the roominess by permitting extra leg and foot room. Front seat backs tip forward and inward and the entire seat pivots toward the car center to provide extra entrance room to the back seat.

Deep wool pile carpeting of fashionable hue, combined with new sound-deadening material, minimizes road noise in the rear compartment. Chrome finish moldings and roof bows add a note of luxury . . . robe cords increase convenience . . . side and center arm rests provide complete comfort.

EIGHT COLOR FASHIONS TO CHOOSE FROM

1. *Gray* Tapestry Nylon on lower door panels, seats, seat-back inserts, the back of the front seats and other trim. *Dark gray* leather bolsters, seat fronts, panels and headlining.
2. The same combinations using *light toned blue* Tapestry Nylon, with *Royal blue* leather for matching ensembles.
3. *Light tan* Tapestry Nylon, coupled with the darker beauty of genuine leathers in *saddle tan* color.
4. *Light green* Tapestry Nylon with a *darker green* genuine leather.
5. Seats, seat backs and trim in Nylon Vee and Crest cloth of light *mist gray*, with the bolsters and matching trim styled in genuine leathers of *dark gray*.
6. Nylon Vee and Crest fabric in *light blue* color, with bolsters and trim in *dark blue* genuine leathers.
7. *Dark brown* leathers with pattern Vee and Crest Nylon fabrics of *light tan*.
8. *Dark green* leathers with matching trim tailored in *light green* Vee and Crest patterned Nylon.

1953 CADILLAC SERIES 62 CONVERTIBLE COUPE

The eye is quick to appreciate the radiantly tailored interiors offered in the 1953 Cadillac Series 62 Convertible Coupe. Beautiful, wide and handsome seats and panels are fashioned in genuine leathers to protect this car against harsh winds and sun! This newest and most exciting Cadillac Convertible Coupe offers interior styling in *SEVEN* beautiful choices of two-tone or solid colors. *Three* of the choices include two-tone combinations of light metallic and dark leathers of the same color: *two* choices include white leather with light metallic bolsters, *two* are tailored in genuine leather of solid hue.

The two-tone luxury and convenience features of the 1953 Cadillac Convertible Coupe extend into the ample rear compartment. Rear compartment sides are equipped with arm rests positioned for ease and comfort. Cadillac's window controls are self-contained hydro-electric units in the Convertible. A control button is conveniently located for each rear window on each side of the rear compartment. A master control for all windows is located on the driver's door.

The two-tone or solid leather tailoring in the Convertible Coupe is carried to the front seat back. The robe cord is covered in dark leather. Thick, dark tone wool pile carpets are color matched to the interior trim and upholsteries.

SEVEN COLOR FASHIONS TO CHOOSE FROM

1. A combination of genuine leather of *light blue* shade of metallic finish, combined with the *dark blue* leathers of solid hue.
2. *Light tan* genuine leathers of metallic finish with genuine leathers of *dark brown* hue.
3. *Pastel green* leathers of metallic finish, coupled with genuine *dark green* leathers.
4. Genuine *solid red* leathers throughout.
5. Fine leathers of *solid black*.
6. White leather with light blue metallic bolsters.
7. White leather with light green metallic bolsters.

In two-tone trim selections, the seat backs and cushion inserts are tastefully upholstered in pipes . . . in genuine leathers of fine *light* metallic tones. Tailored leather welts of contrasting color finish the ensemble. Wide back bolsters are smoothly sculptured in rich dark leathers enhanced by Cadillac's new "flowing-vee" Convertible seat styling. Bright chrome hardware highlights the over-all styling scheme. Convertible windows, top, and front seat adjustment are hydraulically operated, for greater driver convenience and comfort.

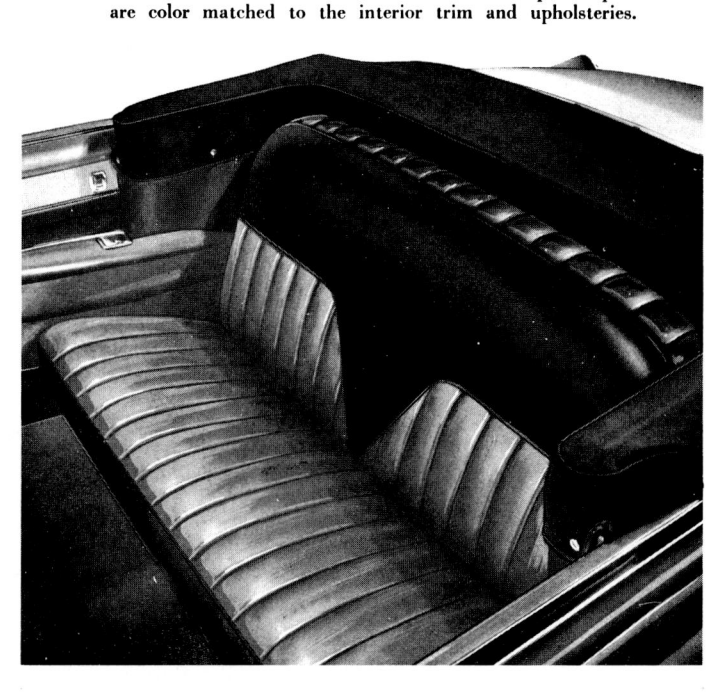

FOUR "TOP" COLORS TO CHOOSE FROM

Cadillac Convertible tops for 1953 are carefully tailored in durable, high-count rayon dragnol cotton fabric. They are cushioned with an inner layer of rubber for waterproofing. When the top has been folded down, Cadillac top material will not crease. It stays fresh and clean much longer, and is shrinkage controlled. Top material is available in four matching colors—black, tan, blue and green.

Cadillac's new Convertible interior door design features finish moldings of sparkling chrome. Bright new door hardware blends into the white and silver-stripe pattern on which these controls are mounted. Convertible doors are panelled in fine leathers of two shades, contrasted by a wide stainless steel door kick-molding.

THE Cadillac ELDORADO

DRAMATICALLY STYLED BY FLEETWOOD   TO CAPTURE THE HEART OF ALL AMERICA...

NOW IN LIMITED PRODUCTION...

FOR THE ENJOYMENT

OF AMERICA'S MOST DEMANDING

MOTOR CAR ENTHUSIASTS!

For 1953, Cadillac proudly presents the classic new Cadillac *El Dorado*. Its rugged chassis offers superb riding characteristics, better roadability, greater comfort, easier handling and more safety features than ever before offered in one American open type car. What's more, it is powered by the great new Cadillac 210-horsepower engine. Add to this combination the fact that Cadillac stylists have created a special convertible body that sets a new pace in seating room, style and beauty ... and the result is the exciting new *El Dorado*.

Into this new *El Dorado*, Cadillac engineers and stylists have combined the features most desirable in a sports car. It has a wide over-all width (80⅛ inches), a low, road-hugging silhouette (58⅛ inches), comfortable seating for *six* passengers, and ample room for luggage. The *El Dorado* meets the full needs of an American sports car. Body surfaces in the Cadillac *El Dorado* are accentuated in subtly rounded shapes and curves. The long hood, low doors, the top and the rear decklid are carefully proportioned to emphasize the sports car flavor. The durable, disappearing top is inner-lined with a layer of rubber to assure a waterproof interior, and is available in *WHITE* or *BLACK*. When the top is folded down, it is concealed by a metal cover in the rear deck to give a smooth, flush appearance. The cover for the disappearing top matches the car color.

Interior trims are available in three solid tones of leather— RED, BLUE and BLACK, and in three two-tone leather combinations—BLUE and WHITE, RED and WHITE, and BLACK and WHITE. Any one of the interior choices may be had with any one of the twelve standard 1953 exterior colors or with four new colors exclusive to the *El Dorado*.

The following equipment is furnished as Standard on the *El Dorado*: Heater, Radio, Windshield Washer, Oil Filter, Power Steering, Wire Wheels, White Wall Tires, and License Frame.

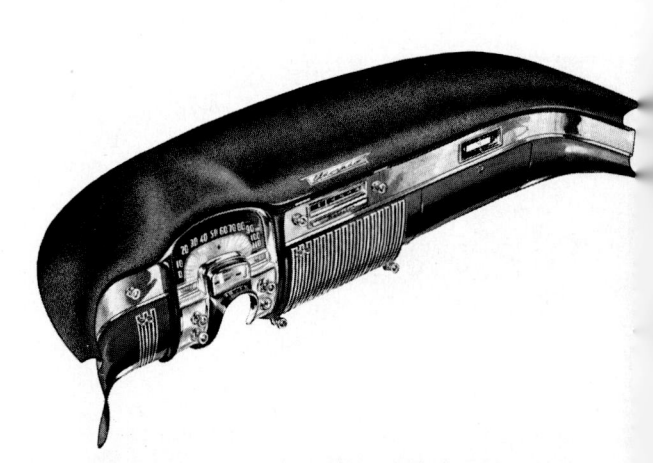

The *El Dorado* instrument panel features a plastic royalite, anti-glare cover that keeps annoying instrument reflections off the windshield. It is color-matched to interior trim. The instrument cluster and control knobs are of chrome finish. Other features are a new *El Dorado* steering wheel with plastic leather hand grips ... smart new clock ... deep glove box.

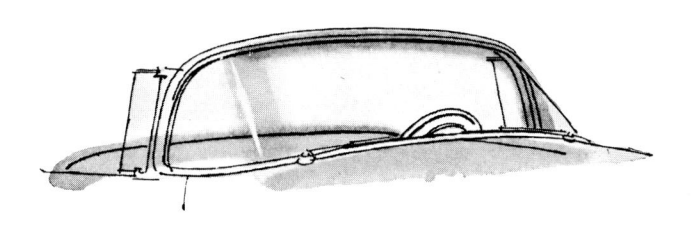

PANORAMIC WINDSHIELD

The Eldorado has been designed to give both driver and passengers a feeling of freedom and openness on the highway. The extraordinary "panoramic" windshield is an excellent example of this design. By eliminating corner pillars, it provides an uninterrupted view of the road and completely eliminates "blind spots."

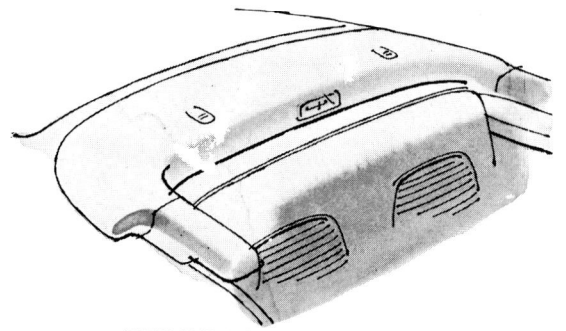

DISAPPEARING TOP

One particularly distinctive feature of the Eldorado's styling is this special metal covering which conceals the top and gives the entire rear deck a smooth, flowing appearance. The top itself is made of a special Orlon fabric and is available in either white or black.

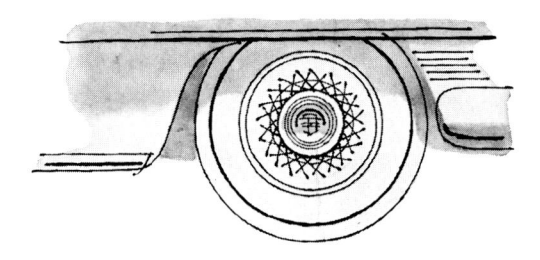

WIRE WHEELS

Purely aside from their eye-catching beauty, the Eldorado's wire wheels assure better brake cooling. White sidewall tires are also standard equipment—as are the fog lights, side view and vanity mirrors, spotlight, and Cadillac Signal-Seeking, Pre-Selector Radio.

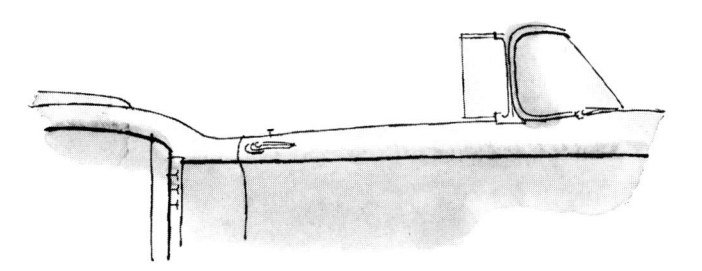

UNIQUE DROPPED-DOOR LINE

The unusual lowness of the Eldorado is accentuated by this unique and distinctive dropped-door design. At the rear of the door, the Eldorado is only 37 inches in height—and is from 3 to 4 inches lower than the standard Cadillac convertible in its all-over silhouette.

El Dorado interiors are smartly tailored in genuine leathers. The front compartment seat, seat-back inserts and a portion of the leather door panels are finished in ¾-inch saddle-stitched pipes. Hip room in front is over 63 inches. The rear compartment is similarly fashioned in leather. It features wide side armrests . . . generous-sized recesses in the front-seat backs for exceptional leg room . . . and 51 inches of hip room. Genuine leather seat bolsters . . . chrome garnish moldings and door hardware add a final touch of elegance and quality.

CADILLAC-FLEETWOOD SERIES 60 SPECIAL

Cadillac is proud to present the magnificently luxurious Cadillac-Fleetwood Series 60 Special . . . *the* fine car designed and built for the discriminating buyer. Examined from any angle, this car gives a true impression of regal size. It is 224 inches in length—with a wheelbase of 130 inches. And yet, ladies among Cadillac drivers will discover that this magnificent possession is *so easy to maneuver* that they will thrill at the chance to command it. It is only 62 inches high and it is considerably wider than it is high—wider by more than 18 inches. And here in this car is new massiveness, new strength and new beauty for 1953 . . . all coordinated into a new balanced and pleasing design. For descriptions of upholstery color choices see the Interior Section.

1953 CADILLAC-FLEETWOOD SERIES 60 SPECIAL

The 1953 Cadillac-Fleetwood Series 60 Special is the most luxurious 5-passenger automobile on the highways—a long, low-silhouetted beauty. This lovely Cadillac 60 Special knows no rival for the affections of the motoring public. It offers many new, outstanding and exclusive features inside and out PLUS such brilliant style and dazzling new performance that it will play a major part in maintaining Cadillac's reputation as "Standard of the World." Every feature of 1953 design, construction and performance places the emphasis on luxury. The engine is more powerful than ever before and the appearance of the Series 60 has been streamlined in a refreshingly different manner. The interior of this wonderful car has been redesigned in a fashion as beautiful as it is convenient and comfortable. The accent for 1953 is also on color. This sedan is available in twelve lovely solid colors and five two-tone color combinations. The Cadillac 60 Special is distinguished by its graceful flowing lines, its extra length and fleet appearance. Symbolic of the distinctive marking of the 60 Special is a broad decklid V and gleaming "Fleetwood" script of gold. Here, too, is value and quality beyond all other cars—so distinctively different, so refined and elegant—that it has won enthusiastic acclaim throughout the world.

There is *only* ONE Cadillac-Fleetwood Special. Distinguished appearance and the elusive magic of Cadillac interior styling combine in a finished masterpiece for discriminating clientele. Seats and seat-back inserts are tastefully trimmed in light-tone BEDFORD CORD fabrics or alternate choices of plain BROADCLOTH or Vee and Crest Pattern cloth. All are fashioned in 1" pipes, with tailored welts of harmonizing and contrasting colors. Richly padded and cushioned bolsters are styled in luxurious dark-tone BROADCLOTH of long-wearing quality.

Here is Cadillac's new Series 60 Special interior-door design for 1953. From top to bottom . . . here again are some of the most brilliantly wonderful automotive styling features of all time. Finish moldings are of bright chrome. A simulated "ostrich-skin" insert between darker metal-finish panels mount the latest in "rear pull" door handles elaborately styled in bright chrome. Arm rests are integral. Genuine leather welts lend accents to this setting of beauty.

Entering these extra-wide doors is an effortless movement. Once inside, deep, wide seats invite passengers to stretch out and relax. There are wide, luxury arm rests to provide comfort . . . sponge-backed frieze pile carpets . . . bright chrome ash trays with snap covers in each rear door arm rest . . . in every contour and appointment the emphasis is on luxury.

CADILLAC-FLEETWOOD SERIES 60 SPECIAL

Lasting echoes of magnificent Cadillac styling are also reflected by the tailored appearance of the front seat back. A flat, richly-dark leather robe cord, Cadillac V and coronet . . . all help accent the careful detail inherent in Cadillac cars. Examples of the light-tone and darkly brilliant motif are the 1" light-tone pipes styled in BROADCLOTH. Padded seat top is tailored in gleaming leather. Lower seat fronts and seat sides are faced in dark leather for lasting beauty.

All trim combinations in the Cadillac-Fleetwood 60 Special are wonderful in conception and exquisitely executed. All door hardware is new for 1953 . . . the jewel-like front door appointments are grouped in a new deep finish panel insert.

TWELVE BEAUTIFUL TRIM STYLES

1. Light green BEDFORD CORD combined with dark green BROADCLOTH.
2. Light green BROADCLOTH combined with dark green BROADCLOTH.
3. Light green VEE and CREST PATTERN CLOTH with dark green BROADCLOTH.
4. Light tan BROADCLOTH combined with brown BROADCLOTH.
5. Light tan BEDFORD CORD combined with brown BROADCLOTH.
6. Light tan VEE and CREST PATTERN CLOTH with brown BROADCLOTH.
7. Light gray BEDFORD CORD combined with dark gray BROADCLOTH.
8. Light gray BROADCLOTH combined with dark gray BROADCLOTH.
9. Light gray VEE and CREST PATTERN CLOTH with dark gray BROADCLOTH.
10. Light blue BEDFORD CORD combined with dark blue BROADCLOTH.
11. Light blue BROADCLOTH combined with dark blue BROADCLOTH.
12. Light blue VEE and CREST PATTERN CLOTH with dark blue BROADCLOTH.

SETTING FOR GRACIOUS DRIVING

There is a sturdy tradition behind the studied simplicity of the Cadillac front compartment. The instrument panel, distinguished by a new gold and brushed silver crest on Series 62 cars, or by the word "Fleetwood" on the Series 60 or 75, is finished in subtle, sophisticated colors. Highlight of the panel is the new style convenient group of instruments. Instruments and other appointments are richly chromed. Other features are the new steering wheel with light-tone simulated leather hand grips, the new easy-to-reach controls, smart clock and deep glove box.

1953 CADILLAC-FLEETWOOD SERIES 75

Here is the 1953 Cadillac-Fleetwood Series 75—*a car that is proudly built to be proudly owned!* For 1953, it is powered by the newest and mightiest Cadillac engine of all time—a great, new 210-horsepower power plant. There is no single attribute of a motor car in which this new Series 75 does not brilliantly excel. This luxurious car is 236 inches in length—with a wheelbase of 146¾ inches. The Series 75 Cadillac is a *big* car with interior room to spare, yet it is unbelievably quick and nimble. Although similar in basic design to all other Cadillac models, long, low lines emphasize it's sleek appearance. Also for 1953, Cadillac makes available to Series 75 owners the proven Hydra-Matic transmission and Cadillac Power Steering. Both are optional at extra cost.

Cadillac
FLEETWOOD SERIES 75

The Cadillac-Fleetwood Series 75 is the plus-ultimate in the automotive fashion world. It is the outstanding car in the Cadillac line whether owner- or chauffeur-driven. For 1953, the appearance of this car becomes even more distinctive and its comfort even more luxurious. It is long, low and extravagant in its new exterior appearance for 1953—a picture of perfection and flawless beauty of line. And never before in the automotive fashion world have luxurious interior appointments and lovely new hardware presented such "high fashion" enchantment and sophistication—every tailoring detail of the luxurious fabric inside this car harmonizes with the colorful elegance of exterior design. Never before has such smooth performance, quiet comfort and wonderful convenience been available in cars of this *exclusive* type and character. For 1953, there are many new engineering achievements built into the Series 75 Cadillac to make it more wonderful to ride in and more wonderful *to drive* than ever before. *With its great new 210-horsepower engine, this car is unbelievably nimble, quick and powerful.* Cadillac's marvelous Hydra-Matic Drive, improved for 1953 and featuring a special "performance" range for city driving... IS AVAILABLE AT EXTRA COST IN THIS CAR FOR 1953. Proven Cadillac Power Steering, an option available at extra cost, eliminates as much as 75% of normal steering effort, and is the answer to complete perfection in automotive driving and riding luxury. The Series 75 8-Passenger Sedan is available in twelve lovely solid colors and five two-tone color combinations.

Unmistakably Cadillac, the interior styling of the Cadillac-Fleetwood Series 75 lends a warm vibrant accent interpreted by master-tailors for an exacting clientele whose requirements can be satisfied by no other motor car. This car has become inevitably the choice of those who want only the finest. And because more and more Cadillac connoisseurs are ordering the exteriors of these Series 75 cars painted in vibrant, airy and gay pastel colors... Cadillac has styled the interiors of these wonderful cars in light custom colors for 1953! Highly appropriate for the most formal function, the interior of this great car provides unusual comfort for "cross continent" travel.

Custom details of the rear compartment view shown below reflect Cadillac craftsmanship. Note how neatly the two auxiliary seats fit into the front seat back when not in use. Footrests provide additional passenger comfort. The rear compartment is upholstered in BROADCLOTH or BEDFORD CORD of either *two-tone* or *single-tone* color interior styling. The seat-back finish molding, with inserted electric clock, is painted in dark tones. A simulated "ostrich-skin" insert panel is decorated with a characteristic Cadillac V in chrome finish. A dark-toned robe cord fits into the assist grip handles. On the limousine, the lower portion of the division glass may be raised and lowered hydraulically from the rear seat.

Shown here are a few of the custom details of the Limousine division which reflect the time-honored Cadillac craftsmanship. Exceptionally broad floors, front and rear seats of davenport dimensions, and center-joined seats of armchair size allow eight people to ride for miles and hours in uncramped ease and comfort.

CADILLAC-FLEETWOOD SERIES 75

The front compartment of the Series 75 Limousine is available upholstered in *black* or *blue* genuine leathers. *Black* leather is supplied with *gray* or *tan* trims. *Dark blue* leather is available in the front compartment where rear compartments are trimmed in *blue* BROADCLOTH or CORD fabrics. The Limousine seat is stationary. Garnish molding, hardware, and the division-glass frame are all bright chrome. Headlining in the front compartment is tailored in simulated leather. The carpet is wool pile. The Series 75 Imperial Limousine is the most luxurious chauffeur-driven automobile in America.

SIX TWO-TONE INTERIORS FOR 1953

1. A two-tone combination of *light gray* BROADCLOTH tailored with seat bolsters and trim in shadowy *dark gray* BROADCLOTH.

2. *Light gray* BEDFORD CORD to be combined with *dark gray* BROADCLOTH.

3. *Light blue* BEDFORD CORD for seats and seat backs and other trim, coupled with *dark blue* BROADCLOTH for seat bolsters and trim.

4. *Light blue* BROADCLOTH in combination with *dark blue* BROADCLOTH.

5. Seat backs tufted in *tan* BROADCLOTH matched with seat bolsters, door trim panels and other trim in *brown* BROADCLOTH.

6. *Brown* BROADCLOTH combined with BEDFORD CORD of a *tan* color and matching ensemble.

Above colors are in limited production.

SIX SOLID COLOR INTERIORS FOR 1953

1. *Tan* BEDFORD CORD.
2. *Tan* BROADCLOTH.
3. *Mist-gray* BROADCLOTH.
4. *Mist-gray* BEDFORD CORD.
5. *Pale-blue* BROADCLOTH.
6. *Pale-blue* BEDFORD CORD.

NOTE: These interiors' upholstery choices apply to both front and rear compartments of the 75 Series Sedan but only to the rear compartment of the 75 Series Limousine. The front compartment is available in a choice of dark leathers. *Black* leather is supplied with *gray* and *tan* trims. *Dark blue* leather is available for the front compartment when rear compartments are trimmed in *blue* fabrics.

The auxiliary seat shown above not only looks comfortable—it is! It is one of the two auxiliary seats in the rear compartment of the Series 75 . . . when not in use, it fits flush with the seat-back panel and pulls are covered with cloth to match the trim. The new, wide, rear-seat arm rest, shown in the "down" position in the photograph above, offers unusual passenger comfort. Door panels and heavy wool carpets are in harmony with this gracious interior. Two under-rear-seat heaters PLUS the Cadillac Air Conditioner, which is available as an option at extra cost, assure comfortable traveling "weather" within the car in any climate . . . at any time of the year!

Note, too, the wide, plain seat-back bolsters and harmonizing leather welts . . . new "pull-to" door hardware . . . brushed chrome ash trays, cigarette lighters. Courtesy lights and side arm rests with package compartments add to this brilliant ensemble.

Other appointments include an electric clock in back of the front seat and hydro-electric operated windows.

Here is the spacious Cadillac Series 75 Sedan front seat where in every contour and appointment the emphasis is on luxury. The *convenience* dimensions in this softly upholstered front compartment offer the maximum in leg room, shoulder room and head room. This gorgeous front seat is 64 inches wide and seats three in restful comfort. Included among the many luxurious features of the Series 75 Sedan are hydro-electric operated window controls for all windows with a master control panel on the left door, hydro-electric front seat adjustment, generous size doors, and maximum driver visibility. Ash trays, arm rests and newly styled hardware lend sparkling accents to this setting of beauty.

The doors feature simulated "ostrich-skin" inserts and "pull-to" door handles.

1953 CADILLAC ENGINE OWES MUCH TO CADILLAC ENGINES OF THE PAST

Advances in the 1953 Cadillac engine have been brought about by a process of evolution—by the cumulative effect of innumerable small improvements. But, having arrived by such process at a given state of Cadillac excellence, occasionally developments are introduced that accelerate progress by a greater than ordinary increment. Many such new developments have been incorporated in the 1953 Cadillac engine. These new developments will be discussed in the following pages of this section. First, however, see how much the 1953 Cadillac engine owes to the famous V-type Cadillac engines which have borne the Cadillac name during 38 of the past 50 years of Cadillac progress:

1914
America's first V-type automotive engine was introduced by Cadillac in 1914. This—the first in a distinguished series of Cadillac V-type engines — immediately created a whole new idea of automotive performance.

1948
In the following 34 years, a whole series of Cadillac superlative motor car power plants was built. Each year brought improvements and engineering developments that pioneered the way for today's modern power plants.

1949
In 1949, Cadillac introduced a totally new engine improved in every way. This, then new, 160-horsepower, high-compression valve-in-head engine was destined to set new standards for the automotive world.

1952
In 1952, Cadillac offered 190-horsepower. The Cadillac four-barrel carburetor, exclusive dual exhaust, high-capacity air cleaner, larger exhaust valves and wider "free-flow" exhaust ports were among the many features.

1953 A NEW ERA IN "HIGH-COMPRESSION" EFFICIENCY!

A NEW ERA IN "HIGH-COMPRESSION" EFFICIENCY!

For 1953, Cadillac again brings to the American motoring public an engine that is destined to go down in automotive history as the *power sensation of the highways* . . . 210-horsepower, eager and ready to provide flashing response, surging power and smooth, swift acceleration. This *greatest* in a long line of Cadillac V-type engines brings a *new* "high-compression" ratio of 8.25:1 . . . with smoother, quieter, more economical performance than ever before! It features a brand new combustion chamber for greater fuel efficiency! It offers the latest automotive development in a "high-lift" valve mechanism which raises the valves higher to charge the cylinders with a greater volume of fuel-air mixture. The result is MORE POWER from every drop of gasoline.

There are many Cadillac *"features of the future"* available in the 1953 Cadillac engine *today!* The 1953 Cadillac engine incorporates the big Cadillac four-barrel carburetor that means added mileage, better performance and the safety and convenience of rapid acceleration . . . a new 12-volt electrical system for better performance and easier starting . . . new pistons that allow closer fits and give whisper-quiet operation. Cadillac's dual exhaust system and dual pipes with dual mufflers and resonators *double* the capacity of the engine exhaust system and provide a substantial reduction in engine back pressure and correspondingly better engine performance. These features and many more covered in this section of the 1953 *Data Book* are proof that CADILLAC WRITES THE HISTORY OF V-TYPE ENGINES IN AMERICA.

FEATURES OF THE 1953 ENGINE

New Smoother Performance
New Quieter Operation
New "High Lift" Valve Mechanism
New 8.25:1 "High Compression"
New 210-Horsepower
New Swifter Acceleration
New 12-Volt Ignition System
New Greater Economy
Cadillac Four-Barrel Carburetor
Cadillac Dual Exhaust
And Many Other Features

BIG "FREE-FLOW" INTAKE MANIFOLD

The breathing efficiency of the 1953 Cadillac engine has also been greatly improved by the development of an improved intake manifold. The 1953 manifold has large and smooth passages. It is designed to deliver uniform charges of fuel-air mixture to cylinders.

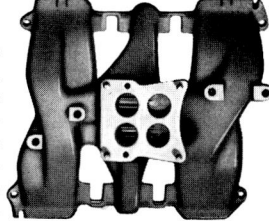

BIG AIR CLEANER AND INTAKE SILENCER

For 1953, the high-capacity carburetor air cleaner directs a flow of air into the carburetor for better engine breathing. As in past years, the air cleaner is of the heavy duty oil-type to provide efficient air filtering, and this year it is mounted with a center stud to improve sealing at the carburetor gasket.

BIG FOUR-BARREL CARBURETOR

For added mileage, better performance and the safety and convenience of smooth and rapid acceleration—Cadillac offers a four-barrel carburetor of advanced design. This unit, in combination with Cadillac's unrestricted engine intake and dual-exhaust manifolding, plays an important role in the high output of the 1953 Cadillac 210-horsepower engine.

This four-barrel "carburetor of tomorrow"—made available today for Cadillac owners—works in two sets of dual-barrel carburetors mounted on the engine in tandem. The forward dual-barrel unit is the basic operating or "primary" carburetor. The aft dual-barrel unit is the "booster" or "secondary" carburetor, and comes into play as needed. At low speeds, the engine works from the primary carburetor. In driving emergencies on the highway, or when sparkling acceleration is required in city driving, the secondary carburetor comes into action by additional pressure on the accelerator pedal. The result is smooth, powerful and satisfying acceleration. No noticeable "bump" is felt by the driver at the entrance of the secondary carburetor into engine use.

Better, smoother performance in the top half of speedometer range requires a larger quantity of fuel-air mixture rather than a richer mixture. One of the major advantages of the Cadillac four-barrel downdraft carburetor is that the "secondary" carburetor permits the engine cylinders to be packed more effectively due to the higher pressure in the intake manifold at the beginning of the compression stroke before the intake valve is closed.

ADVANTAGES

- Quick starts in cold weather.
- Freedom from stalling.
- Greater fuel economy.
- More power and speed.
- More rigid construction.
- Smooth and ultra-fast acceleration.

MORE HORSEPOWER WITH DUAL-EXHAUST

Each bank of four cylinders in the 1953 Cadillac engine exhausts directly into separate manifolds—one on each side of the engine. The dual pipes double the capacity of an exhaust system, provide a substantial reduction in exhaust back pressure and better engine performance.

Road horsepower is increased by this Cadillac feature and fuel mileage boosts of up to two miles per gallon of gasoline are not uncommon. Other advantages are higher all-around engine efficiency and added driver satisfaction.

NEW "HIGH LIFT" CAMSHAFT

All Cadillac camshafts are machined from high alloy castings. The cam and bearing surfaces are specially treated to give them permanent friction-resisting qualities. Five bearing supports make the short Cadillac camshaft even more rigid, thereby maintaining split-second timing of the valves.

NEW LONGER PISTONS

New Cadillac pistons for 1953 feature the slipper-type skirt in which part of the skirt is cut away to reduce both weight and friction in the engine. This design allows the use of a short connecting rod of great strength. Cadillac pistons nest into the crankshaft counterweights. The light weight of these aluminum alloy pistons reduces inertia when the engine is operating at high speeds and permits faster acceleration. A special heavy-duty oil ring adds to oil mileage.

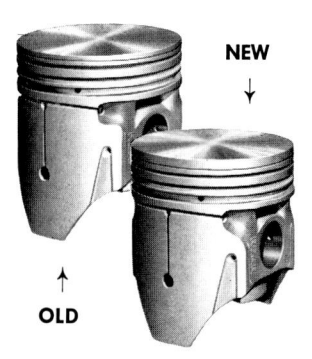

NEW "HIGH LIFT" VALVE MECHANISM

Cadillac offers an amazingly efficient new "high lift" valve mechanism in the 1953 engine. It is closely related to the type used in high-speed racing car engines in popular use on American tracks. This new mechanism provides a larger opening through which more fuel-air mixture can enter the cylinder. Cadillac's *newly designed pistons* for 1953 then compress the gasoline vapor and air into less space than ever before. This adds greatly to making the 1953 Cadillac engine the most powerful and the most efficient engine of all time!

NEW COMBUSTION SMOOTHNESS

The illustration indicates the compact shape of the 1953 combustion chamber. The flame front progresses evenly across the combustion chamber. This means uniform pressure on the piston head and a smooth delivery of power. Detonation is limited by the "quenching effect" of the small clearance area between the piston and the combustion chamber at a point opposite the spark plug. Complete burning of the fuel-air mixture is thus accomplished.

NEW "HIGH VOLTAGE" DISTRIBUTOR

Under all weather conditions, Cadillac's new 1953 Distributor can safely handle up to 5,000 more volts than previous models. A strong spark is assured for smooth operation and full power. The cap, rotor, breaker lever arm, breaker plate and vacuum advance unit of the 1953 Cadillac Distributor are of advanced design. Also, the vacuum advance mechanism has been redesigned to provide a greater spark advance.

NEW 12-VOLT STARTING MOTOR

The new 12-volt starting motor used in connection with Cadillac's 1953 electrical and ignition system is designed for extremely heavy-duty operation. It assures *quick-starting* in all kinds of weather and offers the Cadillac owner the most dependable starting motor ever built since 1911, when the invention of the starter helped make the automobile a necessity. Cadillac's new 12-volt starter provides over 50% greater engine cranking speed at zero temperature.

NEW 12-VOLT BATTERY

Cadillac engineers have also set the pace for the automotive industry in helping to develop a new 12-volt battery for 1953. This new battery has a 46 per cent gain in rated capacity. It is longer and narrower to conserve space and mounts in a new battery box on the dash under the hood.

HIGHWAY FUEL ECONOMY

| 1952 | (3.36 AXLE RATIO) | 16.2 |
| 1953 | (3.07 AXLE RATIO) | 18.2 |

MILES PER GALLON 0 5 10 15 20 25

ACCELERATION FOR FIRST 20 SECS.

| 1952 | (3.36 AXLE RATIO) | 100 FT. BEHIND |
| 1953 | (3.07 AXLE RATIO) | |

DISTANCE IN FEET 0 100 200 300 400 500 600 700 800 900 1000 1100 1200 1300 1400 1500

WONDERFUL NEW ECONOMY

Cadillac engineers have built real economy into the 1953 Cadillac engine and chassis by combining the advantages of 8.25:1 "high-compression" engine efficiency with Dual-Range Hydra-Matic and a *numerically lower* rear axle ratio for 1953. A standard 3.07:1 rear axle ratio for 1953 means that the Cadillac engine is required to make only 3.07 revolutions for one complete revolution of the rear wheels. In other words, the Cadillac 210-horsepower engine in company with Hydra-Matic and the 3.07:1 rear axle is required to make only 2,198 revolutions per mile. Even with the terrific performance of the Cadillac engine in 1952 . . . the engine was required to make 2,404 revolutions per mile when coupled with Hydra-Matic and a numerically higher rear axle ratio of 3.36:1. For 1953, Cadillac's extra 20-horsepower makes possible the use of the lower rear axle ratio *with ECONOMY of operation and even IMPROVED ACCELERATION.* The bar chart above demonstrates how these extra miles obtained by the 1953 Cadillac add up to savings on gasoline! This combination also offers savings on oil, reduced engine maintenance costs . . . *and longer engine life.*

NEW 12-VOLT ELECTRICAL SYSTEM

For better engine performance, quicker and easier starting in all kinds of weather, and to provide available reserves of electrical energy for ignition, lighting and accessories . . . Cadillac has again taken the initiative in the automobile industry by designing and incorporating a new and advanced 12-volt electrical system for 1953 Cadillac cars.

This new system which replaces the 6-volt electrical system, standard on American passenger cars for many years, solves two problems of unusual importance to 1953 Cadillac owners. The compression ratio of the Cadillac engine increases the 1952 ratio of 7.5:1 to the 1953 high-compression ratio of 8.25:1. In addition, more and more electrical owner-convenience accessories have been built into the 1953 Cadillac.

These two factors add up to a greatly expanded demand on the 1953 Cadillac electrical system. Previous 6-volt electrical systems, still in use on some makes of cars, were inadequate for the new higher Cadillac compression ratio where engine performance depends on the delivery of consistent high-voltage to the spark plugs.

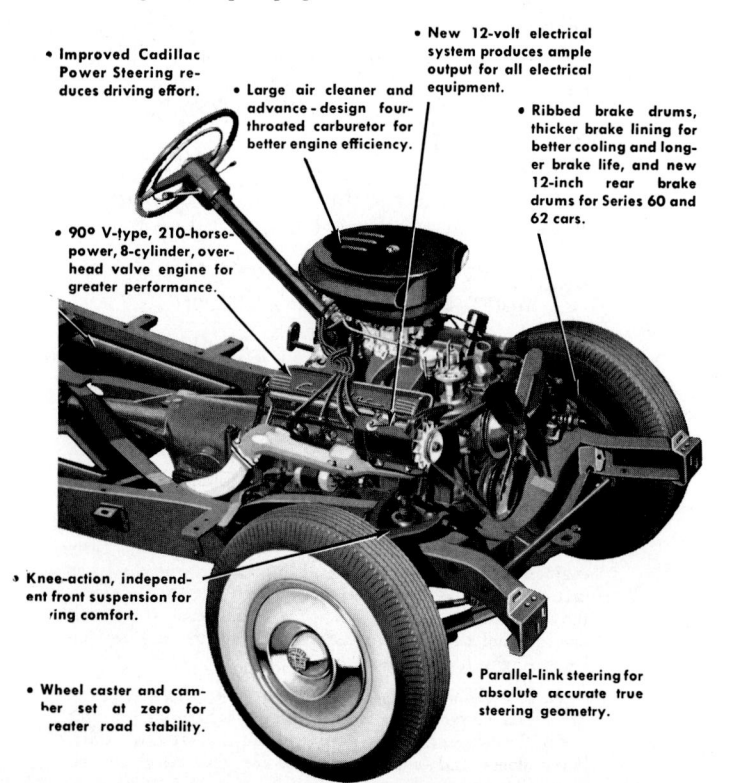

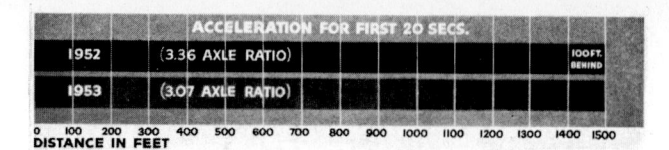

- Improved Cadillac Power Steering reduces driving effort.
- Large air cleaner and advance-design four-throated carburetor for better engine efficiency.
- New 12-volt electrical system produces ample output for all electrical equipment.
- Ribbed brake drums, thicker brake lining for better cooling and longer brake life, and new 12-inch rear brake drums for Series 60 and 62 cars.
- 90° V-type, 210-horsepower, 8-cylinder, overhead valve engine for greater performance.
- Knee-action, independent front suspension for riding comfort.
- Parallel-link steering for absolute accurate true steering geometry.
- Wheel caster and camber set at zero for greater road stability.

FLASHING NEW ACCELERATION

Since its introduction, the Cadillac V-8 "high-compression" overhead valve engine for 1953 has exceeded all expectations. In addition to added horsepower, new efficiency and improved performance . . . this great new 210-horsepower Cadillac engine, coupled with Hydra-Matic and a 3.07:1 rear axle ratio, is destined to become even more famous for its flashing response at traffic lights or on the open highway. Eager, willing power responds to the slightest pressure on the accelerator. Response is in one smooth surge of action through all forward speeds. The bar chart above is graphic proof that again Cadillac offers the engine sensation of the nation. It surpasses its history-making 1952 predecessor. The 1952 Cadillac, equipped with 190-horsepower engine and a 3.36:1 rear axle, *is left 100 feet behind the 1953 Cadillac in 20 seconds.* And tests made at General Motors Proving Grounds reveal many other dramatic advantages in favor of the 1953 Cadillac engine and chassis.

NEW HIGHER COMPRESSION RATIO

The compression ratio of the 1953 Cadillac engine has been increased from 7.50:1 in 1952 to 8.25:1 in order to gain two desirable results. The first of these is *more power and a higher standard of Cadillac performance.* This fact is probably more important to Cadillac owners than the second reason— *economical operation.* In the new Cadillac combustion chamber a larger amount of fuel-air mixture is compressed.

210-HORSEPOWER PLUS ECONOMY . . . PLUS BETTER ROAD PERFORMANCE

The 1953 Cadillac engine offers dramatic road performance . . . sparkling acceleration and get-away. As brilliant as the past performance of Cadillac engines has been, the 1953 engine surpasses its history-making V-type predecessors. In the chart below, you can compare the maximum power output of the 1953 engine with its 1952 Cadillac counterpart. Note the amazing increase in efficiency and power output of the 1953 engine.

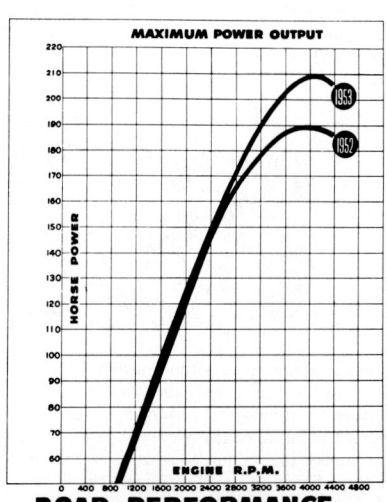

MAXIMUM POWER OUTPUT

ROAD PERFORMANCE

1953 CADILLAC WITH TWIN-TURBINE DYNAFLOW PROVIDES DRIVING EASE, SMOOTHNESS, SAFETY

Cadillac's brilliant 210-horsepower engine combined with the Dynaflow automatic transmission provides the Cadillac owner with a new experience in flexibility, driving ease and convenience.

All power transmission is oil-cushioned through the torque converter. There is no shifting of gears. Thus, acceleration or deceleration is accomplished with exceptional smoothness.

Here, briefly, is what each position of the quadrant selector lever accomplishes for the driver—

P—Park. This position provides a second, positive parking brake. Setting the indicator on "P" drops a steel pawl into its ratchet, locking the rear wheels. Naturally, it can be used only when the car is at a complete standstill. Engine may be started in this position.

N—Neutral. The same as on conventional transmissions. Engine may also be started in this position. The drive shaft is disconnected from the engine, and the car will roll freely down a grade or when pushed. A disabled car should be pushed in Neutral.

D—Drive. For all normal forward driving.

L—Low. This extra powerful range should be used only for starting trailers or when towing or pushing heavy cars; for starting extra heavy loads up steep grades; for extra "engine breaking" going down long, steep grades; or for "rocking" the car out of mudholes or snow. It can also be used when extremely fast getaway is desired.

R—Reverse. For backing—also an extra powerful range.

The engine cannot be started when the car is in gear. A safety switch keeps the starter from engaging unless the shift lever is either in "Park" or "Neutral" position.

The engine can instantly be used as a brake. At any speed below 40 miles an hour, Dynaflow can be shifted into "Low" position with a flick of the hand, giving quick yet gentle deceleration. This feature helps reduce brake wear on long, winding downhill stretches.

The car can't roll, even when parked on the steepest grade, when the indicator is in "Park" position.

Dynaflow's easy feeding of power enables the car to get under way without wheel spinning. This is especially valuable in slippery weather.

Other than having its oil level checked regularly, and changing the oil every 25,000 miles, Dynaflow needs no servicing at all. In fact, Twin-Turbine Dynaflow is easily the most foolproof and trouble-free of any torque converter in use today. It has four torque converter elements. These elements serve to provide automatically the power called for by the driver's foot on the accelerator or required to overcome the resistance of any type of road surface or degree of grade. Here, simply, is how the Dynaflow transmission works:

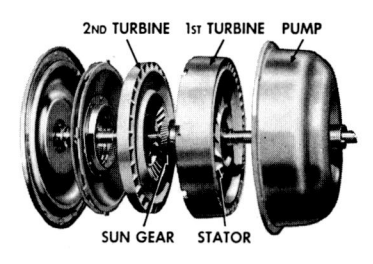

The pump, which is also the housing for all the elements, is fastened to the engine and turns as fast as the engine turns. The entire Dynaflow unit is filled with oil. As the pump turns, vanes on the inside of the pump force oil against the vanes of the turbines which also begin to turn, but more slowly than the pump. Since the turbines are geared to the drive shaft which leads to the rear axle, the car also begins to move.

Dynaflow, however, is a torque converter. It multiplies the torque or twisting action exerted on the drive shaft. This is accomplished by an additional vaned unit called a stator. The vanes on the stator are arranged so as to direct the oil back to the pump at high velocity. The force of the returning oil serves to increase the power output of the pump. In other words, the oil returning to the pump actually multiplies the torque or turning power of the pump itself.

The turning force on the drive shaft is increased still further by a set of gears which multiply the turning force of the first turbine by 1.6 or a little over one and a half times. Thus, when the added torque supplied by the oil being redirected to the pump by the stator is combined with the torque added to the drive shaft by the step-down gearing, it amounts to increasing the turning power or torque of the engine by 2.45 or almost two and a half times. The result is a tremendous thrust of power to the rear wheels during acceleration or as needed in heavy going in soft terrain, on hills or when pulling heavy loads.

As the car attains cruising speed, less and less torque or twisting force on the drive shaft is required to keep the car moving. Dynaflow transmission automatically adjusts itself to meet these diminishing torque requirements. The first turbine gradually picks up speed until it is turning at about the same speed as the pump and the second turbine begins to take over and drive the car. During this transition the returning oil gradually begins to strike the back of the stator vanes instead of the front. This change results in a shifting of pressure permitting the stator and the sun gear to which it is coupled to free-wheel. The second turbine now takes over completely and the entire transmission of power from engine through the drive shaft is at a 1 to 1 ratio as it is in high gear in other transmissions.

At any change in the driving situation, however, where a sudden spurt of acceleration is required or a steep hill is encountered, simply depressing the accelerator brings the torque multiplication feature of Dynaflow into play. As the engine speeds up and the attached pump revolves faster than the turbines, the stator and gear-reduction unit again come into use to provide the additional thrust of power required. In effect, Dynaflow provides an infinite number of gear ratios to exactly meet any driving requirements.

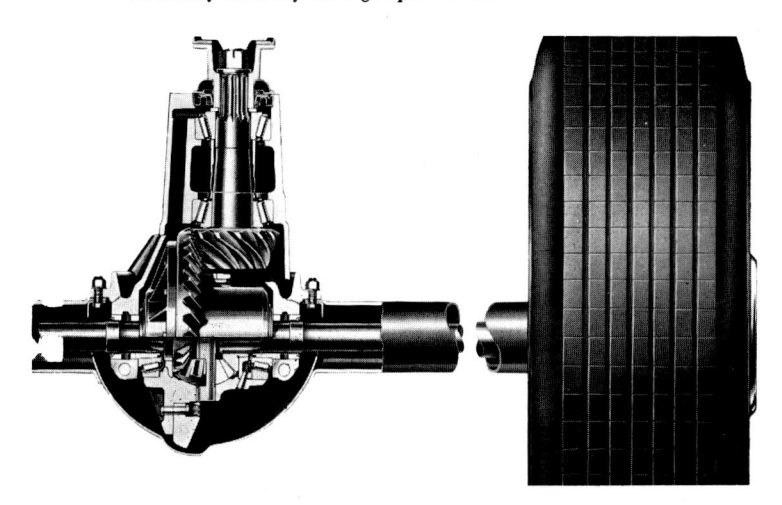

1953 REAR AXLE RATIO MEANS QUIETNESS, ECONOMY, DURABILITY

1953 Cadillac cars equipped with Twin-Turbine Dynaflow are provided with a 3.36 to 1 rear axle ratio for maximum performance combined with quietness, durability and excellent economy. With this rear axle ratio, the 1953 Cadillac engine is required to make only 3.36 revolutions for one complete revolution of the rear wheels at cruising speeds. In other words, the new 1953 210-horsepower Cadillac engine in company with the Dynaflow automatic transmission and the 3.36:1 rear axle ratio is required to make only 2,405 revolutions per mile. Cars with higher rear axle ratios require their engines to work much harder, turn more revolutions per mile and wear faster than the Cadillac engine. On this basis, the extra Cadillac miles obtained not only mean savings on gasoline and oil, but also reduce maintenance and provide longer engine life.

Gears in Cadillac's semi-floating rear axles are cut so that the driving pinion meshes with the ring gear, well below the center line of the differential. This accounts for the lower drive-shaft, lower floors and almost unnoticeable rear floor tunnel.

1953 CADILLAC ACCESSORIES

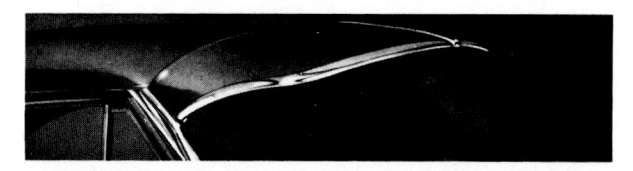

OUTSIDE SUN VISOR—Cadillac Outside Sun Visor is a wise investment in beauty, protection and safety. It protects against sun glare . . . gives full forward visibility . . . provides comfort from summer heat . . . reduces freezing rain and snow on windshield. Construction is unusually sturdy. It is free of rattles and wind noise.

VENTSHADES—Functional stainless steel window shields not only dress up the car but, in addition, perform many useful duties. They cut annoying sun glare . . . reduce drafts from open windows . . . permit lowering windows two or three inches during a rain storm without letting rain in.

LICENSE PLATE FRAMES—Cadillac license plate frames enhance the appearance of the car by making the license plates an integral part of the design. Unsightly sharp edges are eliminated. These attractive, chrome-flashed frames sell in pairs.

CADILLAC WIRE WHEELS—The fleet, low, graceful lines of the car are further enhanced by wire wheels because the center of eye interest is kept low. A note of practical value is improved brake cooling. These wire wheels hit a new high in good taste and functional value. They are available in sets of five.

WINDSHIELD WASHER—Once considered a convenience item, the Cadillac windshield washer has rapidly come to be accepted by owners as a safety must. It sprays two jets of water and solvent mixture on the windshield so that mud, slush, road spray or insects can be easily swept away by the windshield wipers. A touch of the button in the center of the wiper switch gives immediate action.

FOG LAMPS—The new 1953 Cadillac fog lamps improve visibility under adverse weather conditions. They are designed to nest in the lower grille extensions directly below the headlights. These fog lamps also incorporate the parking and turn-signal lights.

AUTRONIC-EYE—Gives Cadillac owners added safety and convenience for night driving. The headlights of oncoming cars automatically control the switch from bright headlight beams to dims. The Autronic-Eye includes an over-riding foot switch to signal oncoming drivers who neglect to reduce their lights.

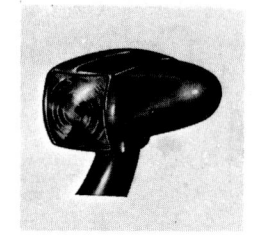

MIRRORS—Among the beautiful Cadillac accessories are listed two pairs of endlessly useful mirrors. The first set, the visor vanity mirrors, are convenient 4" x 8" mirrors distinctively decorated with the Cadillac name in script. The second set of mirrors, for better rear view, are outside mirrors. They are plate glass, 4½ inches in diameter and can be adjusted to the best angle.

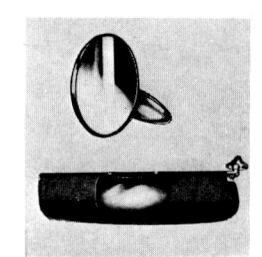

CADILLAC ACCESSORIES

GROUP 62
Windshield Washer • Fog Lights
License Frame • Outside Mirror
Oil Filter • Vanity Mirror • Autronic-Eye

GROUP 63
Windshield Washer • Fog Lights
Autronic-Eye • Outside Mirror
Oil Filter • Vanity Mirror

GROUP 64
Windshield Washer • Outside Mirror
Fog Lights • Oil Filter • Vanity Mirror
License Frame

GROUP 65
Windshield Washer • Oil Filter
Vanity Mirror • Outside Mirror

GROUP 66*
Windshield Washer • Oil Filter • Fog Lights
Autronic-Eye • Vanity Mirror • License Frame

GROUP 67*
Oil Filter • Vanity Mirror • Fog Lights
Windshield Washer • Autronic-Eye

GROUP 68*
Oil Filter • Windshield Washer • Vanity Mirror
Fog Lights • License Frame

GROUP 69*
Oil Filter • Windshield Washer • Vanity Mirror

*This group may be ordered for any model, but must be specified for Convertible models because Outside Mirror in other groups is standard on Convertible models.

SIGNAL SEEKING—PRE-SELECTOR RADIO—This new radio simplifies tuning for the Cadillac driver. In addition to the tuning bar which automatically selects the strongest signal in the area, each of five push buttons can be pre-set to select any one of five favorite stations. Rear speaker included except on Convertibles.

CADILLAC WHEEL DISCS—The increased eye-appeal of the new Cadillac wheel discs is apparent at a glance. They enhance the beauty of the car by making each wheel a circle of chrome. The strikingly attractive Cadillac crest on a raised cone at the center of each disc accentuates their smartness. A set consists of four.

REAR COMPARTMENT REMOTE CONTROL RADIO—For complete enjoyment of motoring in the rear compartment of a Cadillac Series 75, a rear compartment radio with remote control tuning is available. High fidelity tones, a wide range of reception and convenient controls permit passengers to enjoy radio at its finest.

CADILLAC WHEEL TRIM RINGS—Whether the car is in motion or at a standstill, the trim rings add to the over-all impression of Cadillac smartness. They are fabricated from heavy gauge, durable stainless steel and attached to the wheels with patented locking clips that keep them snug and rattle-free. A set consists of five rings.

INSTRUMENT PANEL ANTI-GLARE COVER—Designed to prevent annoying instrument reflections on the windshield. The anti-glare cover is contour-molded to fit the instrument panel. It is available in wolf-grain black with the same Cadillac wings and crest as the instrument panel.

CADILLAC SPOKE WHEEL DISCS—Available in sets of four, spoke wheel discs give a sleek, sports-car look to any Cadillac body style. They are constructed of rugged stainless steel flashed with bright chrome. This durable finish resists corrosion, makes cleaning a quick, simple operation.

NYLON SEAT COVERS—

All Cadillac seat covers for 1953 have been restyled. This year a new, satin-smooth, self-woven striped nylon—richly styled and superbly tailored for solid beauty and long life—is available in blue, green or maroon.

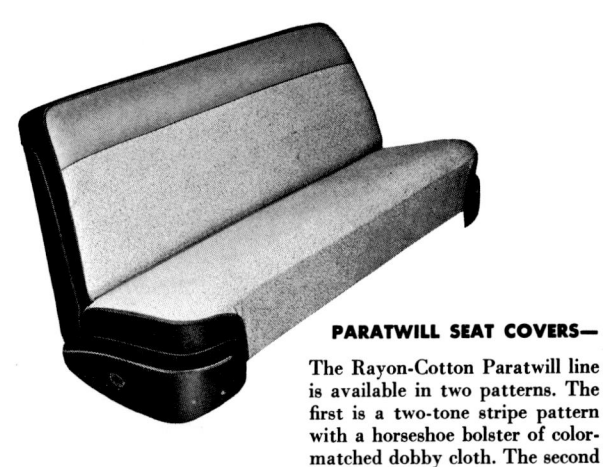

TARTAN PLAID SEAT COVERS—

These covers are fabricated from 100% durable double-twist rayon. They have matching horseshoe bolsters and facing material with a small rectangular pattern. Color combinations are: green and gray plaid with matching bolster, blue and gray, maroon and gray, also with matching bolsters.

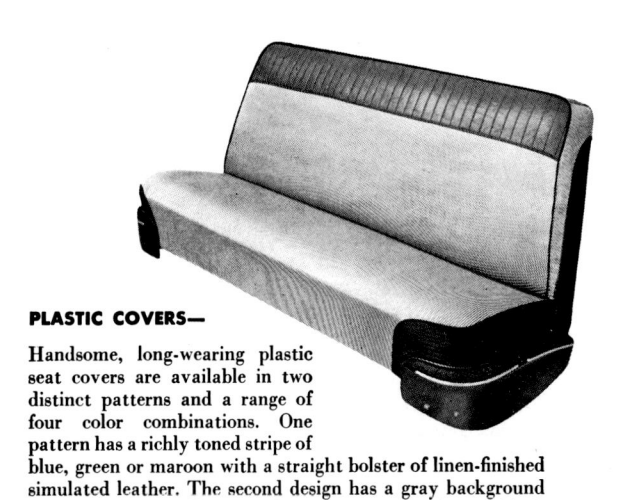

PARATWILL SEAT COVERS—

The Rayon-Cotton Paratwill line is available in two patterns. The first is a two-tone stripe pattern with a horseshoe bolster of color-matched dobby cloth. The second is a crescent pattern with matching straight bolster of naugahyde. Both patterns are in shades of green, blue and maroon.

PLASTIC COVERS—

Handsome, long-wearing plastic seat covers are available in two distinct patterns and a range of four color combinations. One pattern has a richly toned stripe of blue, green or maroon with a straight bolster of linen-finished simulated leather. The second design has a gray background with a gold metallic thread interwoven to give a block effect. The bolster is of linen-finished simulated leather.

CADILLAC POWER STEERING MAKES DRIVING EASIER... MORE ENJOYABLE

...POWER STEERING DOES THE WORK!

During ordinary driving, Cadillac Power Steering becomes effective when a manual effort of about three pounds is required at the rim of the steering wheel. The maximum effort required of the driver under any condition does not exceed about eight pounds—as opposed to the approximately fifty pounds that are often required with conventional steering.

It should be remembered that this hydraulic system is only a booster and takes away none of the driver's steering initiative. On a curve, for instance, the car follows the path directed by the driver and will not go beyond the arc he has set. It will recover from the turn in the normal way.

Thus, Cadillac Power Steering not only increases the joy of motoring, but greatly reduces physical effort. It provides greater safety than before by giving the driver complete control.

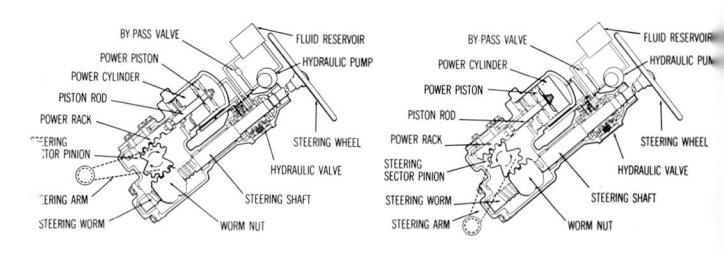

The above two simplified drawings show what happens when the Cadillac driver turns the steering wheel of his car. When he turns the wheel to the left, the hydraulic valve mechanism is actuated to permit the hydraulic power pump to force oil under pressure to the lower end of the power cylinder as indicated by the solid color in the drawing at the left. The resultant upward movement of the piston transmits motion through the power rack to rotate the steering sector pinion as indicated. The slight manual effort applied at the steering wheel raises the worm nut at the base of the steering shaft which simultaneously transmits some motion to the sector pinion. The driver retains the feel of the wheel while all except the slightest effort is assumed by the power cylinder. Turning the wheel to the right reverses the action.

CADILLAC AUTOMATIC HEATING SYSTEM

An automobile heating system must meet many requirements if the car's occupants are to enjoy utmost comfort and motoring pleasure. The system must supply fresh air... provide ample heat... seal out dust... hold to a steady temperature ... rapidly defrost and de-fog windows... and have a low noise level. Cadillac heating systems meet all of these demands.

For all models except the 75 Series, the heating system for 1953 consists of one dash heater and defroster, and one underseat heater located under the *front* seat. The dash heater supplies warm air to the front compartment, while the underseat heater blankets the rear compartment with warm air.

The Cadillac Series 75 heating system consists of one dash heater and defroster, and *two* underseat heaters located under the *rear* seat.

Convenient controls in easy reach of the driver make temperature adjustment a simple operation. *Temperature Control Knob* controls the amount of heat—moving this lever down raises the temperature; *Heater Control Knob* regulates direction of heated air to the driver's feet and to windshield and also operates the underseat heater. *Upper Vent Lever* directs cool air to the windshield; *Blower Lever* regulates the amount of air through the dash heater and defroster and is used for summer ventilation. Detailed operation of heating system is explained fully in Cadillac Owner's Manual.

NEW CADILLAC AIR CONDITIONER

Summer heat was the incentive for this wonderful new system ... and with its advent, Cadillac again sets the pace for the entire automotive industry by offering 1953 Cadillac owners a cool, comfortable car interior while driving in the most torrid of semi-tropical climates or even in the northern part of the United States during the hot summer months.

A flick of a switch will permit owners to cool off a Cadillac car that has been parked in the sun for hours. The manner in which cool weather is manufactured within Cadillac cars is best explained by using the drawing shown at left. The system consists of a condenser, compressor, refrigerant, evaporator, and two blowers. The compressor operates off the crankshaft.

1. Outlet Air Ducts
2. Evaporator Case
3. Return Air Grill
4. Compressor
5. Condenser
6. Receiver Tank

HERE'S HOW IT WORKS IN THE CADILLAC CAR

In the Cadillac Air Conditioner system the belt-driven compressor draws refrigerant from the evaporator (cooling unit located in back of rear seat), compresses and discharges the refrigerant in gaseous form into the condenser coils, where it is changed back to liquid.

In this new air conditioning system there are two optional methods of cool air delivery to the car interior. The first—best suited to climates that don't reach excessively high temperatures—will be to discharge cool air from grilles on each side of the rear package shelf. Warm air is then returned through a center grille on the shelf panel.

The second method—for extremely hot areas of the country—discharges cool air via ducts mounted below the headlining and running from the package shelf up to the front compartment. At the rear these ducts are of clear plastic. The remainder of the ducts are flocked and color-matched to the headlining material. Individual airliner-type vents allow separate adjustments of cool air for both front and rear compartments. Warm air is returned through a center grille on the rear compartment package shelf.

In both systems, fresh air is introduced into the car with fresh air scoops on the sides of the car body.

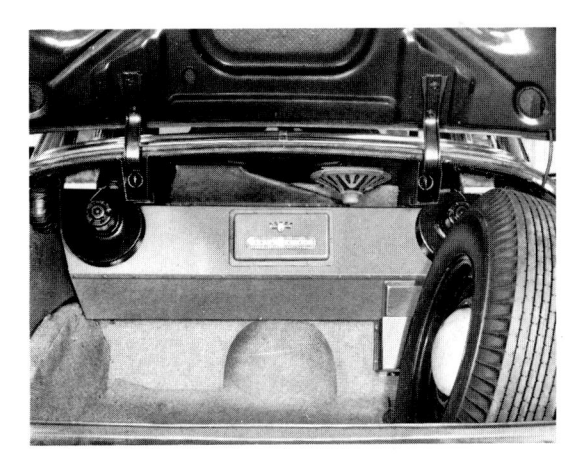

OUTSIDE IT MAY BE 120 DEGREES ... INSIDE IT'S A COMFORTABLE 78 DEGREES

Tests of the new Cadillac Air Conditioner prove that these units perform excellently in dry desert heat and in humid areas. Cadillac owners who buy this system will arrive at their destination clean, well pressed and rested. They will not have to contend with bugs or wind noises as the windows will be closed while driving.

In this new Cadillac air conditioning system the evaporator and blower housing unit is mounted behind the rear seat. It subtracts very little trunk space from the ample cubic content of the big 1953 trunk. Only the switch panel on the dashboard and the visible air ducts indicate that this comfort and convenience system is present in the car.

1953 CADILLAC

SMOOTH STARTS AND CUSHIONED STOPS . . . PROVIDED BY CADILLAC'S HOTCHKISS DRIVE

Passenger comfort in Cadillac cars is greatly increased through the use of Hotchkiss Drive. In this Cadillac system, the driving force of the rear axle is transmitted and cushioned through Cadillac's splay-mounted rear springs . . . *this means smoother starts and cushioned stops.* Passengers ride easier, and the chassis mechanism of the car is more fully protected.

CADILLAC STEERING TAKES THE "FIGHT" . . . OUT OF THE TOUGHEST ROADS

Parallel Link steering in all 1953 Cadillac cars provides steering stability at all speeds, and takes the "fight" out of the toughest roads. The Cadillac Steering system is perfectly balanced to take the sharpest turn . . . easily and sweetly. A short-turning radius and absolute accurate steering geometry are among the features of this system. It is simpler and more accurate than many other systems and a ratio of 25 to 1 and a newly designed 18-inch steering wheel provide maximum steering ease with minimum wheel rotation.

CADILLAC SHOCK ABSORBERS . . . PROVIDE A SMOOTH RIDE

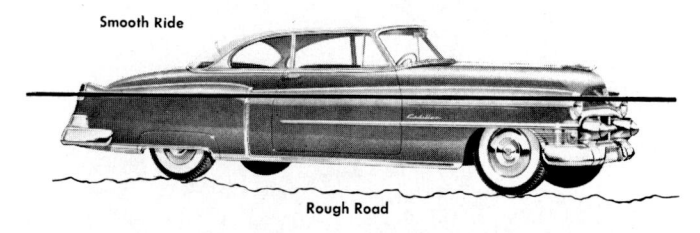

A direct-acting, high-volume, variable control shock absorber is mounted within each front coil spring. Each shock absorber has a small metering orifice for smooth city streets, a pressure blow-off spring for moderately rough roads, and a restriction for cross country or very rough roads. For a combination that further adds to riding comfort—Cadillac's angle-mounted, rear shock absorbers control side-to-side movement at the rear of the car and cushion road shocks. Engineered to control spring action, the result is boulevard riding comfort.

RUGGED I-BEAM, X-TYPE FRAME

The rugged Cadillac frame provides support and holds in their proper position virtually all other major parts of the car. This hardy Cadillac frame is built up of extra-strong channel-section side rails, joined together with a rugged I-Beam, X-Member to provide the most sturdy kind of backbone for the power, transmission and suspension units. Husky cross-members and diagonal braces of steel reinforce the frame, and provide additional support for the engine and wheels. All Cadillac frame joints are either welded or riveted together for the greatest possible strength. The center section of the "double drop" Cadillac frame makes possible the beautiful low body silhouette, low center of gravity, excellent road stability and easier handling. The frame narrows at the front to give front wheels "short-turning-circle" steering

ROUGH ROADS LEVEL OUT

Cadillac's individual front wheel spring suspension is of the angularly set type. Independent heavy steel coil springs are assembled between the frame and the front wheels in such a way that the front springs support the front weight of the Cadillac frame evenly. This weight puts each spring under initial compression. Each spring will further compress as the wheel passes over an obstruction in the road, or expands if the wheel encounters a hole in the road. Thus Cadillac independent Knee-Action coil springs are relieved of all braking and driving duties and function to "level out" bumps in the road *without* transmitting road shocks to the steering system or the car body. In all 1953 Cadillac cars, the front wheel suspension and steering systems are coordinated to furnish Cadillac drivers and passengers with excellent riding quality; safe steering; unusual stability; a continuous contact of wheels with the road surface and less tire wear.

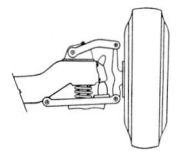

Cadillac front coil spring compresses as front wheel encounters a bump in the road. Wheel is in contact with road surface at all times for smooth ride!

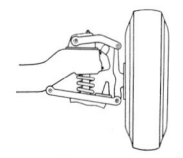

Cadillac front coil spring expands as wheel encounters a hole in the road—wheel is in contact with road surface at all times for smooth ride!

EXTRA-LONG REAR SPRINGS ADD SAFETY . . . CUSHIONED RIDE

The Cadillac system of rear springing is one of the most costly in the industry and is engineered to coordinate perfectly with the coil springs used in Cadillac's independent front suspension. This combination of coil front suspension and the two extra-long, semi-elliptic Cadillac rear springs offers unusual road-holding advantages PLUS greater driving comfort. Cadillac rear springs are mounted in splayed position at a scientifically selected angle . . . *they smooth out up-and-down motion and reduce side-sway and rolling on curves.*

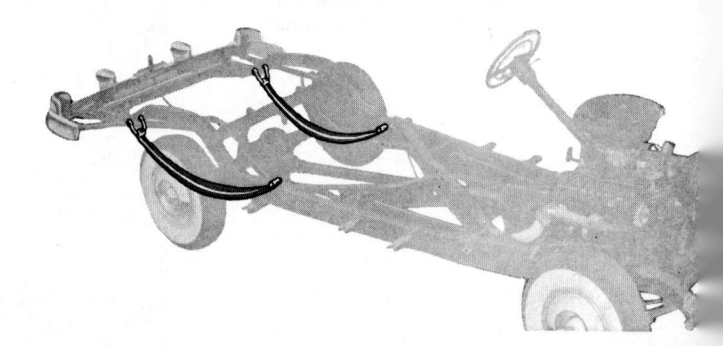

1953 CADILLAC GENERAL SPECIFICATIONS

	Series 62 Sedan	Series 62 Convertible Coupe	Series 62 Coupe	Series 62 Coupe de Ville	Series 60 Fleetwood Special	Series 75 8-Passenger Sedan	Series 75 Imperial Sedan
Wheelbase..........	126"	126"	126"	126"	130"	146 3/4"	146 3/4"
Over-all Length......	215 13/16"	220 13/16"	220 13/16"	220 13/16"	224 13/16"	236 9/16"	236 9/16"
Over-all Width......	80 1/8"	80 1/8"	80 1/8"	80 1/8"	80 5/8"	80 1/8"	80 1/8"
Over-all Height......	62 11/16"	61 1/8"*	60 15/16"	60 15/16"	62 11/16"	64 1/16"	64 1/16"
Steering Ratio—Over-all	25.47	25.47	25.47	25.47	25.47	25.47	25.47
Turning Radius.......	22 1/2'	22 1/2'	22 1/2'	22 1/2'	23'	25 1/2'	25 1/2'
Tread—Front........	59.12"	59.12"	59.12"	59.12"	59.12"	59.12"	59.12"
Tread—Rear........	63.10"	63.10"	63.10"	63.10"	63.10"	63.16"	63.16"
Tires—Size..........	8:00 x 15**	8:00 x 15**	8:00 x 15**	8:00 x 15**	8:00 x 15**	8:20 x 15	8:20 x 15
Tires—Ply Rating.....	4-ply	4-ply	4-ply	4-ply	4-ply	6-ply	6-ply
Engine..............	210-horsepower Cadillac V-8	210-horsepower Cadillac V-8	210-horsepower Cadillac V-8	210-horsepower Cadillac V-8	210-horsepower Cadillac V-8	210-horsepower Cadillac V-8	210-horsepower Cadillac V-8

*58 1/8" on Special El Dorado Sports Coupe. **8:20 x 15 supplied in white wall tires.

Compression Ratio....	8.25:1	8.25:1	8.25:1	8.25:1	8.25:1	8.25:1	8.25:1
Piston Displacement...	331 cu. in.	331 cu. in.	331 cu. in.	331 cu. in.	331 cu. in.	331 cu. in.	331 cu. in.
Valve Arrangement...	Overhead	Overhead	Overhead	Overhead	Overhead	Overhead	Overhead
Carburetor..........	4-Barrel	4-Barrel	4-Barrel	4-Barrel	4-Barrel	4-Barrel	4-Barrel
Exhaust System.......	Dual	Dual	Dual	Dual	Dual	Dual	Dual
Transmission.........	Automatic	Automatic	Automatic	Automatic	Automatic	Automatic	Automatic
Steering Gear.......	Ball Nut with optional power steering	Ball Nut with optional power steering	Ball Nut with optional power steering	Ball Nut with optional power steering	Ball Nut with optional power steering	Ball Nut with optional power steering	Ball Nut with optional power steering
Frame.............	I-Beam, X-Member	I-Beam, X-Member	I-Beam, X-Member	I-Beam, X-Member	I-Beam, X-Member	I-Beam, X-Member	I-Beam, X-Member
Springs............	Coil front, semi-elliptic-leaf rear	Coil front, semi-elliptic-leaf rear	Coil front, semi-elliptic-leaf rear	Coil front, semi-elliptic-leaf rear	Coil front, semi-elliptic-leaf rear	Coil front, semi-elliptic-leaf rear	Coil front, semi-elliptic-leaf rear
Drive..............	Hotchkiss	Hotchkiss	Hotchkiss	Hotchkiss	Hotchkiss	Hotchkiss	Hotchkiss
Axle Ratio..........	3.36:1	3.36:1	3.36:1*	3.36:1	3.36:1	3.77:1**	3.77:1**

*3.07:1 on El Dorado with Hydra-Matic. **4.27:1 on Series 75 with Dynaflow.

Right, a 1953 Series 62 Coupe. Because of the transmission plant fire in August of 1953, approximately 28,600 '53 Cadillacs were equipped with *Dynaflow* transmissions.

DETAILED SPECIFICATIONS

1953

ENGINE

Number of cylinders	8
Cylinder arrangement	90° bank-type
Valve arrangement	Overhead
Bore and stroke	3 13/16" x 3 5/8"
Block and cylinder head material	Cast iron
Piston displacement	331 cu. in.
Taxable horsepower	46.5
Max. brake horsepower	210 @ 4150 r.p.m.
Max. engine torque—lbs.-ft.	330 @ 2700 r.p.m.
Compression ratio	8.25:1
Engine mounts	Vulcanized rubber
Number of points of suspension	3

PISTONS AND RINGS

Make	Alcoa—Bohn—Stearling
Material	Aluminum alloy
Type	T-slot, cam ground
Weight	19.680 oz.
Clearance	.0015"
Number of oil rings per piston	1
Number of comp. rings per piston	2

RODS AND PINS

Wristpin length	3.093"
Wristpin material	Steel alloy
Type	Locked in rod
Connecting rod length	6.625"
Material—connecting rod	Forged steel alloy
Weight—connecting rod	23.49 oz.
Crankpin journal diameter	2 1/4"
Lower bearing material	Steel back Durex
Connecting rod bearing clearance	.001"-.0035"
Connecting rod bearing end play	.008"-.014" (total two rods)

CRANKSHAFT

Material	Forged alloy steel
Weight	61.5 pounds
Main bearing thrust	Rear main
Crankshaft end play	.001" to .005"
Main bearing type	Slip-on
Main bearing removable	Yes
Main bearing material	Steel back Durex
Main bearing clearance—rear	.0015" to .0025"
Main bearing journal Diameter x Length:	
Number 1	2.5" x 1"
Number 2	2.5" x 1.0625"
Number 3	2.5" x 1.0625"
Number 4	2.5" x 1.0625"
Number 5	2.5" x 1.875"

CAMSHAFT

Drive	Chain
Camshaft sprocket material	Cast iron
Timing chain—make	Link Belt
Timing chain—no. of links	46
Timing chain—width	.6875"
Timing chain—pitch	.500"

VALVES

Valve arrangement	Overhead
Intake opens	22° B.T.C. without ramp
Intake closes	67° A.B.C. without ramp
Exhaust opens	63° B.B.C. without ramp
Exhaust closes	27° A.T.C. without ramp

INTAKE

Material	Alloy steel
Over-all length	4.586" to 4.566"
Diameter of head	1.750"
Angle of seat	44°
Lift	.365"

EXHAUST

Material	Alloy steel
Over-all length	4.574" to 4.594"
Diameter of head	1.562"
Angle of seat	44°
Lift	.365"
Hydraulic valve lifters	Yes
Valve inserts	None
Valve seats cooled by	Direct water circulation

LUBRICATION

Type	Full pressure
Oil Under Pressure to:	
Main bearings	Yes
Connecting rods	Yes
Wristpins	Splash
Camshaft bearings	Yes
Tappets	Yes
Oil pump type	Gear
Normal oil pressure	30 to 35 lbs. @ 30 m.p.h.
Capacity of oil reservoir	Dry, 5 Qts.; Refill, 5 Qts.
Type of oil level gauge	Dip stick
Make of pressure gauge	AC—Tell Tale Lite

FUEL

Gasoline tank capacity	20 gallons
Type of fuel feed	Camshaft pump
Carburetor—make	Rochester & Carter
Carburetor—type	Four barrel down draft
Manifold heat control	Automatic
Type of air cleaner	Oil bath
Dual tail pipe diameters	2.094" to 2.099"

COOLING

Water pump type	Centrifugal—dual outlet
Pressure relief valve	Yes
Choke for re-circulation	Yes
Radiator core	Tube and fin
Full-length cylinder water jacket	Yes
Water all around cylinders	Yes
Fan belt length	57"
Fan belt width	3/8"
Fan—No. of blades, Series 62 & 60	4
Fan—No. of blades, Series 75	5

GENERATOR

Make	Delco-Remy
Voltage at cut-out closing	12–13.2 (adjust to 12.5)
Voltage regulator setting	13.4–14.6 (adjust to 14.2 at 90°)
Generator maximum charging rate	34 to 40 amp. (adjust to 37)
Minimum charging speed	28 m.p.h. and up
Generator ventilation	Forced air

STARTING MOTOR

Make	Delco-Remy
Flywheel teeth, integral or ring	Steel integral

IGNITION

Spark advance	Centrifugal and vacuum
Ignition Unit:	
Make	Delco-Remy
Manual advance	None
Maximum centrifugal advance	Crankshaft (22.5°-26.5°)
Vacuum advance	Crankshaft (26°-29°)
Distributor breaker gap	.010" to .015"
Initial spark advance	2 1/2° B.T.C.
Firing order	1-8-4-3-6-5-7-2
Ignition Coil:	
Make	Delco-Remy
Spark Plugs:	
Make	AC
Model	46.5
Thread	14 mm.
Gap	.035"

LAMPS AND HORN

Headlight—make	Guide sealed-beam
Headlight cover glass, dia.	6 11/16"
Parking light—make	Guide
Tail light—make	Guide
Lighting switch—make	Delco-Remy
How are headlights dimmed?	Depressed beam—foot switch
Horn:	
Make	Delco-Remy
Type	Vibrator, seashell electric

BATTERY

Make	Delco 3EE70
Number of plates	11
Capacity (amp. hrs.)	70
Terminal grounded	Negative
Location of battery	Under hood on tray attached to right-hand dash to frame brace front of dash

CLUTCH (75 Series only)

Make	Long semi-centrifugal
Drive type	Direct to flywheel
Vibration neutralizer	Spring friction type
Number of driving discs	1
Number of driven discs	1
Clutch facing	Woven asbestos
Clutch facing inside diameter	7"
Clutch facing outside diameter	11"
Clutch facing thickness	.137"
Clutch facing number required	2

SYNCHRO-MESH TRANSMISSION

Number of forward speeds	3
Type of shift	Manual
Gear ratio, high	1:1
Gear ratio, second	1.53:1
Gear ratio, low	2.39:1
Gear ratio, reverse	2.39:1
Type of gears	Helical, constant mesh in 1st, 2nd and reverse
Oil capacity	3 3/4 pints
Grade recommended, summer	S.A.E. 90
Grade recommended, winter	S.A.E. 90 Extreme cold 80

AUTOMATIC TRANSMISSION

Type	Torque Converter with Gears
Gearing	Planetary
No. of forward speeds	2
Transmission ratio, Low	1.82 x Converter Ratio
Transmission ratio, Drive	1. x Converter Ratio
Transmission ratio, Reverse	1.82 x Converter Ratio
Oil capacity	10 qts.
Type of automatic transmission fluid	Type "A"

FRAME

	Series 62	Series 60S	Series 75
Frame make	A. O. Smith	A. O. Smith	A. O. Smith
Frame depth, maximum	7 1/2"	7 1/2"	7 1/2"
Frame thickness, maximum	3/64"	1/2"	1/2"
Flange width, maximum	2 3/64"	2 1/2"	2 1/2"
Frame—Type	Box girder	Box girder	Box girder

FRONT END SUSPENSION

Front suspension, make	Own
Front suspension, type	Forked arms
Forked arm bearings, type	Threaded
Kingpin upper bearing, type	Bronze bushing
Kingpin lower bearing, type	Bronze bushing
Front wheel inner bearing, make and type	N. D. ball
Front wheel outer bearing, make and type	N. D. ball
Front spring, type	Helical coil
Front spring, material	Spring steel
Shock absorber, type	Hydraulic direct-acting type
Front stabilizer	Torsion rod

PROPELLER SHAFT

	Series 62-60	Series 75
Number used	1	2
Type	Exposed	Exposed

UNIVERSAL JOINTS

Make	Mechanics and Saginaw
Number used	2 3
Type	Cross and Trunnion
Bearing	Needle
Universal joints, lubricated	Permanently
Drive and torque taken through	Rear springs

REAR AXLE

	Series 62-60	Series 75
Rear axle, make	Own	
Rear axle, type	Semi-floating	
Differential gear, make	Own	
Rear axle:		
Oil capacity	5 pints	
Grade recommended:		
S.A.E. viscosity	90 hypoid	
Type of final gearing	Hypoid	
Gear ratio:		
Dynaflow Trans.	3.36:1	4.27:1
Hyd. Trans.	3.07:1	3.77:1
Pinion adjustment (Except 75)	None	
Pinion bearing adjustment	None (Preloaded)	
Are pinion bearings in sleeve?	No	
Backlash between pinion and ring gear	.003-.010"	
Rear axle pinion shaft:		
Front bearing, type	Tapered roller	
Rear bearing, type	Tapered roller	

TIRES AND WHEELS

Tires:		
Make	U.S. Royal—Firestone and Goodrich	
Size	8.00 x 15*	8.20 x 15
Ply rating	4	6
Inflation pressure:		
Front	24 lbs.	28 lbs.
Rear	24 lbs.	28 lbs.

*8.20 x 15 when White Walls are ordered.

TIRES AND WHEELS—Continued

Wheels:		
Type	Slotted disc	
Make	Kelsey-Hayes	
Rim, diameter	15"	15"
Rim, width	6.00"	6.00"
Tread:		
Front	59.12"	59.12"
Rear	63.10"	63.16"

SPRINGS (Rear)

	Series 62-60	Series 75
Rear springs:		
Type	Semi-elliptic	
Material	Spring steel	
Length	54½"	56½"
Width	2"	
No. of leaves	8	10
Spring leaves lubricated with	Wax impregnated liners	
Spring bushings, type	Rubber	
Stabilizers	Rear—None	

SHOCK ABSORBERS (Rear)

Type	Direct Acting

STEERING

Steering gear:		
Type	Recirculating ball	
Make	Saginaw	
Over-all steering ratio	25.47-1	
Car turning radius (outside) bumper to bumper sweep	(62) 22.85' (60) 23.35'	(75) 25.85'

BRAKES

	Series 62-60	Series 75
Front and Rear		
Brake drum diameter	12"	12"
Brake drum, internal or external	Internal	Internal
Brake lining, length per wheel:		
Forward shoe	12.92	12.92
Reverse shoe	12.92	12.92
Total	25.84	25.84
Brake lining width	2½"	2½"
Brake lining thickness	¼"	¼"
Brake clearance	.007-.010"	.007-.010"
Hand brake location	Left side of dash	
Hand brake lever operates on	Rear service brakes	

MISCELLANEOUS SPECIFICATIONS

Car lifting device, jack	Bumper type
Engine lubrication, type	Pressure
Chassis lubrication, type	High pressure
Axle lubrication, type	Splash

LUBRICANTS

Engine oil	5 qts.	
Recommended viscosity	Min. anticipated temperature: +32°F. 20W or S.A.E. 20 +10°F. 20W −10°F. 10W Below −10°F. 5W	
Drain	2000 miles (after initial 500-mile change)	
Rear axle oil	5 pints	
Recommended viscosity	90 hypoid	
Auto trans. fluid type "A"	10 qts.	
Cooling system—water	20 qts.	(21 with heater)
Gasoline	20 gals.	

INTERIOR BODY DIMENSIONS

All 1953 Cadillac Models

	Front Seat Hip Room	Front Seat Shoulder Room	Front Seat Leg Room	Rear Seat Hip Room	Rear Seat Shoulder Room	Rear Seat Leg Room	Front Head-room	Rear Head-room	Front Seat Height to Floor	Rear Seat Height to Floor	Steering Wheel Clear-ance to Seat
Series 62 Convertible Coupe	62⅝"	55⅞"	43¾"	51"	47½"	37 15/16"	34 15/16"	34⅝"	14 7/16"	12 5/16"	5⅛"
Series 62 Sedan	63¾"	57 7/16"	43¾"	64¼"	55⅝"	43⅝"	35 13/16"	35 9/16"	14 9/16"	12½"	5⅛"
Series 62 Coupe	62⅝"	55⅞"	43¾"	54 7/16"	55¾"	37 13/16"	34 3/16"	34 3/16"	14 9/16"	12 5/16"	5⅛"
Series 62 Coupe de Ville	62⅝"	55⅞"	43¾"	54 7/16"	55¾"	37 13/16"	34⅜"	34 3/16"	14 9/16"	12 5/16"	5⅛"
Series 62 El Dorado Sports Coupe	63¼"	57⅛"	43 9/16"	51"	47⅝"	37 5/16"	34 15/16"	34⅝"	13 9/16"	11 5/16"	5⅛"
Series 60 Fleetwood Special	61 13/16"	57 7/16"	43¾"	63⅛"	55⅝"	43⅝"	35 13/16"	35 9/16"	14 9/16"	12½"	5⅛"
Series 75 8-Passenger Sedan	64⅛"	57 5/16"	43 13/16"	56⅝"	56⅛"		36 9/16"	35"	13¾"	14"	5 15/16"
Series 75 Imperial Sedan	64"	57 3/16"	43 11/16"	56⅝"	56⅛"		36⅜"	35"	13 13/16"	14"	5⅞"

EXTERIOR BODY DIMENSIONS

All 1953 Cadillac Models

	Wheelbase	Over-all Length	Over-all Height	Minimum Road Clearance
Series 62 Convertible Coupe	126"	220 13/16"	61⅛"	6⅝"
Series 62 Sedan	126"	215 13/16"	62 11/16"	7¼"
Series 62 Coupe	126"	220 13/16"	60 15/16"	7¼"
Series 62 Coupe de Ville	126"	220 13/16"	60 15/16"	7¼"
Series 62 El Dorado Sport Coupe	126"	220 13/16"	58⅛"	5⅝"
Series 60 Fleetwood Special	130"	224 13/16"	62 11/16"	7¼"
Series 75 8-Passenger Sedan	146¾"	236 9/16"	64 1/16"	6¾"
Series 75 Imperial Sedan	146¾"	236 9/16"	64 1/16"	6¾"

It is an undeniable fact that no motor car engine ever built has back of it a history of development, testing and achievement that is comparable to that of this new 210-horsepower Cadillac power plant. Its basic design, in addition to laboratory tests, has been proved over a period of 38 years in the hands of the world's most exacting motorists. In the course of testing, the 1953 Cadillac engine, like all of the models that have preceded it, has been exposed to every conceivable strain and hazard—sustained high speeds on the road; pulling tests up grades as steep as 27%; mud roads designed to draw everything out of an engine; water baths that search out any weak spots. Those who know best—test drivers and experimental engine specialists—say without reservation that the 1953 210-horsepower Cadillac engine is more powerful, more durable, more efficient than any stock car engine ever built—including the great previous Cadillac engines.

1954 CADILLAC Styling

In the new 1954 Cadillac motor cars, every styling detail, from the new, gracefully contoured front bumper, bumper guards and new grille to the new circular exhaust ports in the rear bumper, has been designed to make them the most beautiful motoring creations ever to bear the distinguished Cadillac name. The 1954 Cadillac cars are longer and lower. They have a longer wheelbase and a wider front tread. The new panoramic windshield with vertical corner pillars and vertical front vent wings lends a striking continental air, and at the same time, vastly increases visibility. New, and almost certain to be copied, are the two-inch windshield visors on Sedans and the new overhanging reveal moldings across the top of each door on all models. The new lower hood features a newly designed hood ornament, a new "V" and crest. Fenders, front and rear, are styled with new, straighter, swifter lines. The rear fender tail-light fins break upward more sharply, accentuating this famous Cadillac style note. Smart in appearance, and functional as well, is the new cowl air intake extending across the top of the hood at the base of the windshield. These are but a few of the many styling features illustrated in this section of your Data Book. They are features that lend new distinction to the magnificent new Cadillac for 1954 . . . a car that is destined to set the pace in automotive styling for many years to come.

NEW CONTINENTAL-TYPE VENTI-PANES

One of the leading new style changes in the 1954 Cadillac, and one that is almost certain to be copied in the years ahead, is the new rectangular design of the chrome-framed vent wings. In conjunction with the vertical pillar posts, this type of construction provides exceptionally strong roof support. The newly designed vent wings, not only provide exactly the amount of draft-free ventilation desired, but contribute to the eye-catching beauty of the car as well.

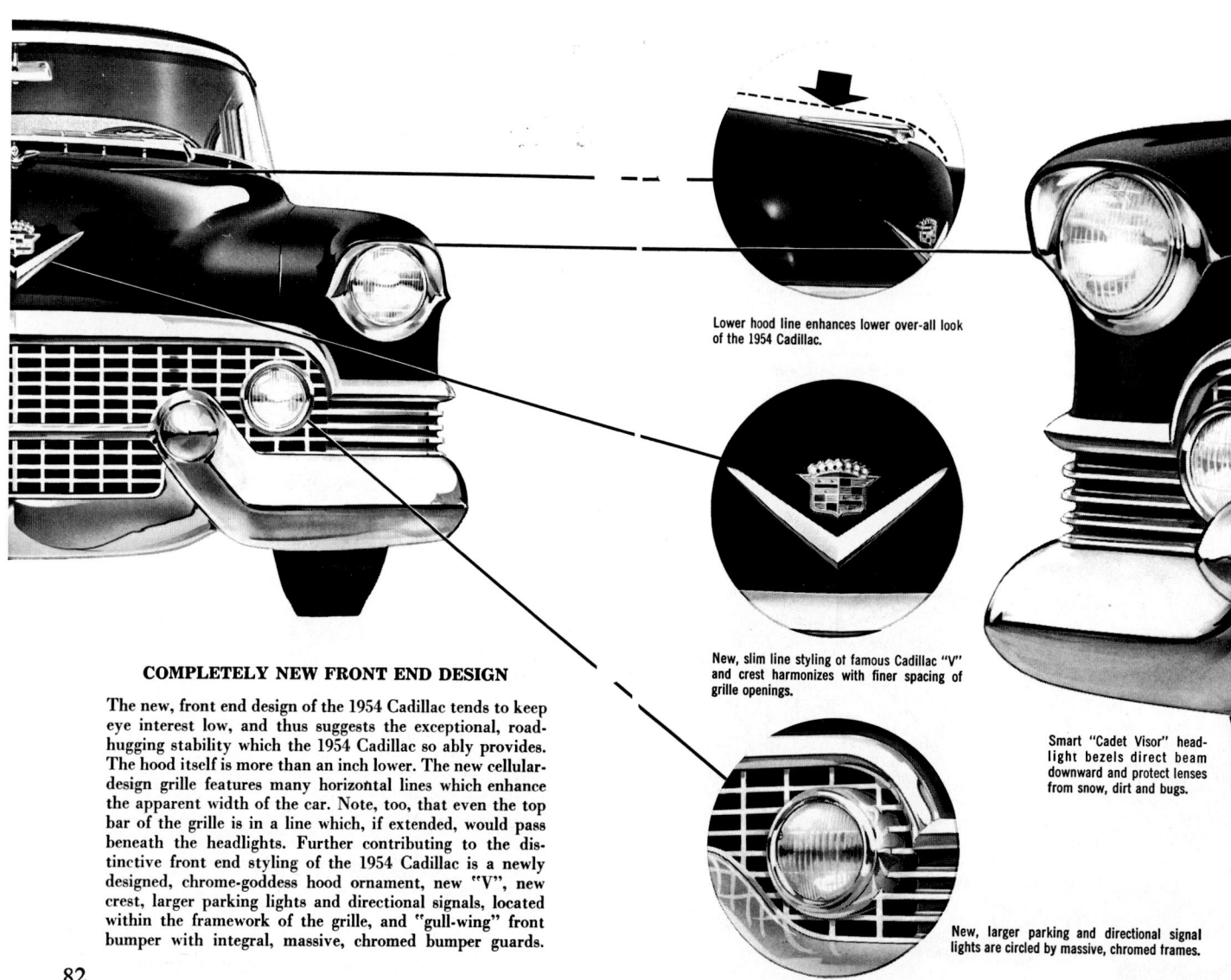

COMPLETELY NEW FRONT END DESIGN

The new, front end design of the 1954 Cadillac tends to keep eye interest low, and thus suggests the exceptional, road-hugging stability which the 1954 Cadillac so ably provides. The hood itself is more than an inch lower. The new cellular-design grille features many horizontal lines which enhance the apparent width of the car. Note, too, that even the top bar of the grille is in a line which, if extended, would pass beneath the headlights. Further contributing to the distinctive front end styling of the 1954 Cadillac is a newly designed, chrome-goddess hood ornament, new "V", new crest, larger parking lights and directional signals, located within the framework of the grille, and "gull-wing" front bumper with integral, massive, chromed bumper guards.

Lower hood line enhances lower over-all look of the 1954 Cadillac.

New, slim line styling of famous Cadillac "V" and crest harmonizes with finer spacing of grille openings.

Smart "Cadet Visor" headlight bezels direct beam downward and protect lenses from snow, dirt and bugs.

New, larger parking and directional signal lights are circled by massive, chromed frames.

NEW WINDSHIELD VISOR

The new 1954 Cadillac sedan models have a visor-like, two-inch roof overhang extending across the entire windshield. It accentuates the low roof line of the car and the sweeping width of the new panoramic windshield. It prevents the accumulation of snow or ice across that part of the windshield farthest from the defrosters, and protects against excessive glare from sun and sky.

NEW COWL AIR INTAKE

One of the most distinctive, as well as most functional, features of the beautiful Cadillac for 1954 is the new hood-width cowl air intake. In conjunction with the new panoramic windshield, the wide design of the cowl air intake adds to the apparent width of the car. At the same time, it is an ideally located source of fresh, clean air for ventilation, or for heating and defrosting in cars equipped with the Cadillac Heater. The entrance of road dust or exhaust fumes into the ventilation system, an annoyance sometimes associated with underhood air inlets, is virtually eliminated with the new cowl air intake. A series of baffles prevents the entrance of rain water by trapping the water and permitting it to drain through a tube to the ground.

NEW DOOR REVEAL MOLDINGS

Another Cadillac style "first" is the new upper door reveal moldings which extend outward above the windows. This permits door windows to be opened slightly during rainy weather to give ventilation and to prevent window fogging.

NEW REAR STYLING DETAILS

Viewed from the rear, the 1954 Cadillac presents many pleasing new style details. The famous rear fender tail-light fins are smarter than ever with a new, more abrupt upsweep from the fenders and a new, modish, squared-off design. The equally famous Cadillac twin tailpipe outlets in the rear bumper continue to remind of the Dual Exhaust system and its contribution to the tremendous power of the great Cadillac engine. However, they, too, have been given the fresh beauty of a new circular design. New bumper guards present pleasing style harmony with the vertical bumper extensions at the lower edge of each rear fender. New license plate lights, now located on the inside of each bumper guard, are better protected from dust, snow and ice.

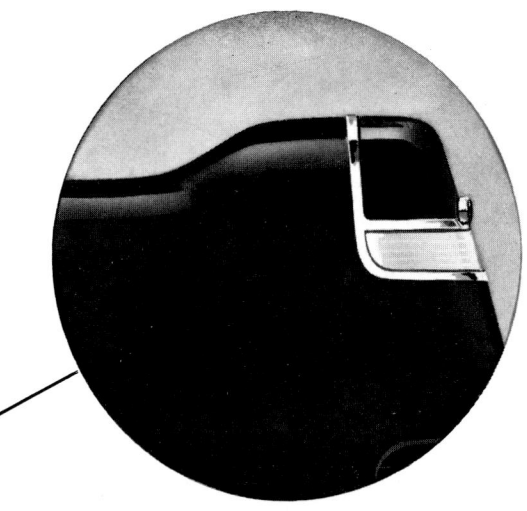

NEW SQUARED-OFF FENDER CONTOUR

NEW ROUND DUAL EXHAUST OUTLETS

1954 CADILLAC SERIES 62 SEDAN

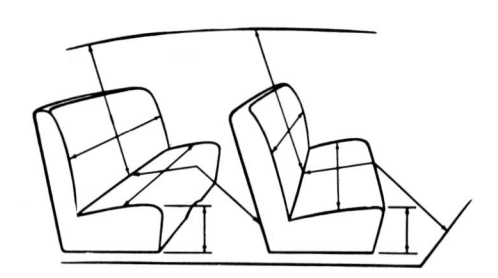

INTERIOR DIMENSIONS

	REAR	FRONT
Head room	35.6"	35.8"
Shoulder room	58.9"	59.4"
Hip room	65.2"	64.3"
Leg room	45.8"	43.3"
Seat height	12.3"	14.8"

STANDARD EQUIPMENT

Air Cleaner, oil-bath type
Armrest, center-rear
Cadillac Power Steering
Cigarette Lighters, front and rear
Clock, Electric
Hydra-Matic Transmission
Lights, Back-up (dual)
Light, Courtesy or Map (automatic)
Lights, Directional Signal
Light, Glove Box (automatic)
Light, Luggage Compartment (automatic)
Mirror, Glare-proof, rear-view, flip-type
Oil Filter
Outside Mirror, left side
Paint, two-tone
Parking Brake Warning Signal
Robe Cord on back of front seat
Vanity Mirror
Visors, dual sun
Wheel Discs (set of four)
Windshield Washers

OPTIONAL EQUIPMENT (Extra Cost)

Cadillac Air Conditioner
Cadillac Power Brakes
E-Z-Eye Tinted Glass
Fog Lamps (pair)
Front Seat Adjustment (2-way), Electrically-operated
Front Seat Adjustment (4-way), Electrically-operated
Headlight Dimmer, automatic
Heater
License Frames
Radio
Window Lifts, Electrically-operated
Wire Wheels (set of five)
Whitewall Tires, 8.20 x 15 (set of five)

Again, in 1954, the Cadillac body presents the proven features of construction that have contributed so much to its reputation as the Standard of the World. In addition, there are many new features that assure the owner of a 1954 Cadillac even more comfort and quietness . . . even greater safety . . . than ever before.

The new, one-piece, panoramic windshield and the new vertical corner pillars, for example, provide greatly increased visibility. As a result, the driver can be more relaxed and at ease. Greater safety is provided, too, by new side-welded body construction and by the welding of rear quarter panels and rear fenders into a single, extra-strong and rigid unit.

Sedan rear doors are fitted with push-down door locks designed to safeguard children by disengaging the inside door handle when button is in down position. When doors are shut and button pushed down, doors cannot be opened from the outside without a key, nor can they be opened with the inside door handle. If preferred by owner, locks can be adjusted so that inside handles will open doors when push button is in down position.

Just as the Cadillac body is designed to provide lasting style and beauty . . . so is it engineered and built to provide comfort, quiet and safety throughout the life of the car. These benefits provided by Cadillac's advanced body construction methods mean a great deal to the peace of mind and motoring enjoyment of the Cadillac owner. At the same time, the enduring quality of Cadillac body construction is a contributing factor to the continued strong demand for used Cadillac cars . . . a demand that assures not only the original owner but each subsequent owner maximum protection for his investment.

THE CADILLAC SERIES 62 SEDAN

The magnificent interiors of the Cadillac Series 62 Sedan are distinctively styled and finely tailored. New luxury of upholstery and trim fabrics is provided by two-tone combinations of all-wool gabardine or all-wool gabardine combined with beautifully patterned nylon. All combinations are available in a choice of gray, blue or green. Completely redesigned door panels, as shown on the opposite page, are typical of the all-new interior styling of the Series 62 Sedan for 1954. Eye-pleasing color contrast is provided by the light-tone upper and lower sections and the dark-tone center section of the door panel. Gleaming, stainless steel moldings extend across the lower width of the doors to form beautiful and protective panels. The grille openings in bottom molding of front doors form the heater outlets for the rear compartment. Tufted biscuits and buttons across the lower door panels match the seat cushion and seat back inserts in color and styling. The center section of the door panels continues this color harmony with dark-toned fabric to match the seat bolsters. A new door control panel insert with chromed, raised edges and satin-black grooves continues into the instrument panel thus unifying and beautifying the entire front compartment. Built-in armrests and door pulls are covered with smart and serviceable dark-tone vinyl.

The front compartment of the Series 62 Sedan is designed to provide maximum riding comfort and driving convenience combined with beauty and luxury matched by no other fine car. Seat cushion and seat back inserts of light-tone all-wool gabardine or patterned nylon are styled with heavily padded biscuits and deeply recessed buttons. Bolsters and seat cushion sides are of smooth surfaced, dark-toned all-wool gabardine for pleasing contrast of color and style. Foam rubber in the seat cushions gives luxurious, easy-chair comfort, while the front seat height of almost 15 inches enables the driver to enjoy the full visibility provided by the new panoramic windshield. Brushed and bright chrome hardware and gleaming, stainless steel moldings add their highlights to the incomparable elegance of decor that distinguishes the front compartment of the Cadillac Series 62 Sedan.

Traditional Cadillac luxury and comfort are emphasized in every detail of the Cadillac Series 62 Sedan rear compartment. Divan-height rear seats, luxuriously tailored of all-wool gabardine or all-wool gabardine and patterned nylon, provide even greater hip room and shoulder room in 1954. Leg room, too, has been increased. Thick, wool pile floor carpeting, two side armrests and a wide, deeply cushioned center armrest add further to the living-room comfort enjoyed by rear-seat passengers. New beauty is provided by carrying the two-tone colors and tufted upholstery styling of the seat cushion and seat backs into the rear door panels. Leather-grained vinyl lends smartness and durability to door armrests and seat scuff pad. The convenient robe cord which extends across the rear of front seat back is covered in simulated leather. Framed in gleaming chrome, just above the robe cord, is a raised Cadillac "V" in gold against a background of brushed chrome.

SIX COLOR AND FABRIC CHOICES

50. LIGHT GRAY WOOL GABARDINE cushions and seat backs ... DARK GRAY WOOL GABARDINE seat bolsters and trim.
51. LIGHT GRAY PATTERN NYLON cushions and seat backs combined with DARK GRAY WOOL GABARDINE bolsters.
52. LIGHT BLUE WOOL GABARDINE cushions and backs with DARK BLUE WOOL GABARDINE bolsters and trim.
53. LIGHT BLUE PATTERN NYLON cloth on seats and seat backs with DARK BLUE WOOL GABARDINE bolsters and trim.
56. LIGHT GREEN WOOL GABARDINE cushions and backs with DARK GREEN WOOL GABARDINE trim and bolsters.
57. LIGHT GREEN PATTERN NYLON cushions and seat backs with DARK GREEN WOOL GABARDINE bolsters and trim.

1954 CADILLAC SERIES **62** COUPE

INTERIOR DIMENSIONS

	REAR	FRONT
Head room	34.4"	34"
Shoulder room	58.9"	59"
Hip room	56.4"	63.9"
Leg room	41.4"	43"
Seat height	12"	14.9"

STANDARD EQUIPMENT

Air Cleaner, oil-bath type
Armrest, center-rear
Cadillac Power Steering
Cigarette Lighters, front and rear
Clock, Electric
Hydra-Matic Transmission
Lights, Back-up (dual)
Light, Courtesy or Map (automatic)
Lights, Directional Signal
Light, Glove Box (automatic)
Light, Luggage Compartment (automatic)
Mirror, Glare-proof, rear-view, flip-type
Oil Filter
Outside Mirror, left side
Paint, two-tone
Parking Brake Warning Signal
Robe Cords on front seat backs
Vanity Mirror
Visors, dual sun
Wheel Discs (set of four)
Windshield Washers

OPTIONAL EQUIPMENT (Extra Cost)

Cadillac Air Conditioner
Cadillac Power Brakes
E-Z-Eye Tinted Glass
Fog Lamps (pair)
Front Seat Adjustment (2-way), Electrically-operated
Front Seat Adjustment (4-way), Electrically-operated
Headlight Dimmer, automatic
Heater
License Frames
Radio
Window Lifts, Electrically-operated
Wire Wheels (set of five)
Whitewall Tires, 8.20 x 15 (set of five)

86

THE CADILLAC SERIES 62 COUPE

The interior of the Cadillac Series 62 Coupe for 1954 is superbly tailored and beautifully appointed. Seats and seat backs, offering even greater hip room and shoulder room, are fashioned with inserts of deeply tufted biscuits and recessed buttons. This styling is continued across the lower door panels and on the rear of the front seat backs. Pleasing color harmony is provided by the smooth, dark-toned seat bolsters and sides and the center door panel. Six different color and fabric combinations, described on the opposite page, give the owner wide latitude in selecting exactly the interior to meet his preference. Ease of entrance to the rear compartment is provided by the split front seat back and by the pivot mounting of the front seat itself. Ample seat height, nearly 15 inches, combined with the new panoramic windshield assures exceptional visibility for maximum safety and greater motoring enjoyment. Careful attention to every styling detail is evident in the functional beauty of the instrument panel. Control knobs and levers of bright and brushed chrome are placed for maximum convenience. An insert panel of gleaming chromed horizontal lines relieved by satin-black grooves forms a jewel-like setting for radio dial and electric clock. The top and extended edge of the instrument panel are covered with glare-resistant Elascofab, a beautiful leather-like vinyl material.

New, more beautiful door panel styling offers a fitting introduction and a warm invitation to the elegant interiors of the Series 62 Coupe. Light-toned upper and lower sections of the door panel provide pleasing contrast with the dark-toned center section with its vinyl-topped, built-in armrest and door pull. A narrow, stainless steel molding extends nearly across the door panel before gracefully curving down to meet the wide stainless steel kick-pad molding. Grille openings in this lower molding provide heater outlets for the rear compartment. Highlighting the new door panel styling is a new door and window control panel insert of alternating chromed and satin-black horizontal lines.

The Cadillac Series 62 Coupe provides greater comfort and luxury than ever before. In every important interior dimension, shoulder room, hip room, head room and leg room, rear-compartment passengers will find new spaciousness. A wide, center armrest folds forward from the seat back for added comfort and convenience. Seat cushion, seat back inserts and lower sidewalls are fashioned in light-toned fabrics with heavily padded biscuits and deeply recessed buttons. Seat cushion bolsters and the upper section of the sidewalls are in color-harmonizing dark tones. Carpeting of thick wool pile; vinyl seat welts and side armrests and simulated leather on robe cords and seat kick-pad combine smart, textured beauty with durability. Moldings of gleaming stainless steel and brushed and bright chromed hardware complete the elegance of decor that distinguishes the Series 62 Coupe.

SIX DISTINCTIVE CHOICES

50. **LIGHT GRAY WOOL GABARDINE** cushions and seat backs ... **DARK GRAY WOOL GABARDINE** seat bolsters and trim.
51. **LIGHT GRAY PATTERN NYLON** cushions and seat backs combined with **DARK GRAY WOOL GABARDINE** bolsters.
52. **LIGHT BLUE WOOL GABARDINE** cushions and backs with **DARK BLUE WOOL GABARDINE** bolsters and trim.
53. **LIGHT BLUE PATTERN NYLON** cloth on seats and seat backs with **DARK GREEN WOOL GABARDINE** bolsters and trim.
56. **LIGHT GREEN WOOL GABARDINE** cushions and backs with **DARK GREEN WOOL GABARDINE** trim and bolsters.
57. **LIGHT GREEN PATTERN NYLON** cushions and seat backs with **DARK GREEN WOOL GABARDINE** bolsters and trim.

1954 CADILLAC SERIES 62 CONVERTIBLE COUPE

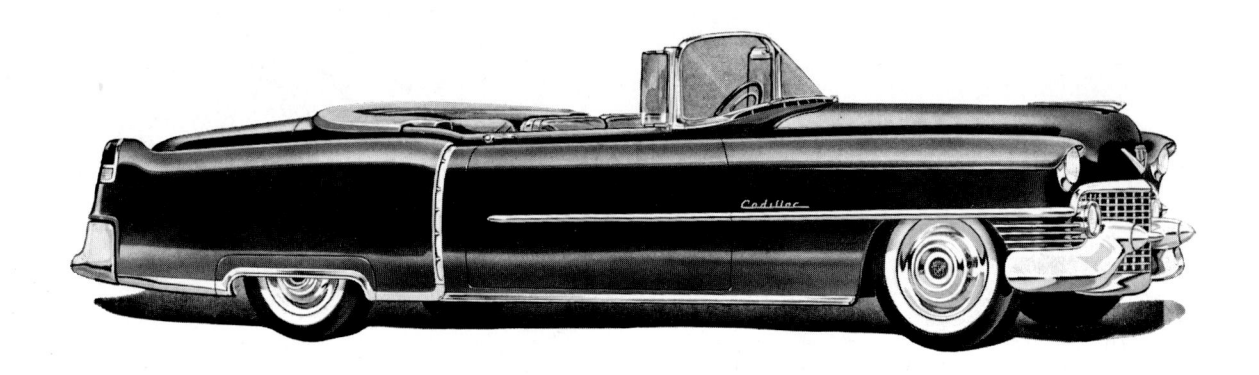

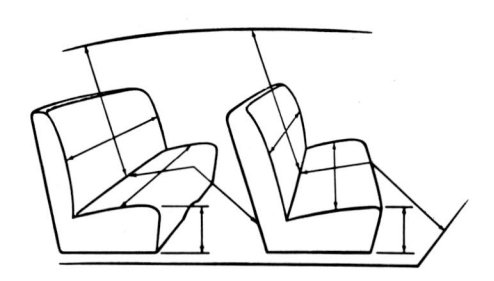

INTERIOR DIMENSIONS

	REAR	FRONT
Head room	34.2"	34.9"
Shoulder room	49.8"	59"
Hip room	53.3"	63.9"
Leg room	40.7"	43"
Seat height	12"	14.9"

STANDARD EQUIPMENT

Air Cleaner, oil-bath type
Cadillac Power Steering
Cigarette Lighters, front and rear
Clock, Electric
Front Seat Adjustment (2-way), Electrically-operated
Hydra-Matic Transmission
Lights, Back-up (dual)
Light, Courtesy or Map (automatic)
Lights, Directional Signal
Light, Glove Box (automatic)
Light, Luggage Compartment (automatic)
Mirror, Glare-proof, rear-view, flip-type
Outside Mirror, left side
Oil Filter
Parking Brake Warning Signal
Robe Cords on front seat backs
Vanity Mirror
Visors, dual sun
Wheel Discs (set of four)
Window Lifts, Electrically-operated
Windshield Washers

OPTIONAL EQUIPMENT (Extra Cost)

Cadillac Power Brakes
E-Z-Eye Tinted Glass
Fog Lamps (pair)
Front Seat Adjustment (4-way), Electrically-operated
Headlight Dimmer, automatic
Heater
License Frames
Radio
Wire Wheels (set of five)
Whitewall Tires, 8.20 x 15 (set of five)

THE CADILLAC SERIES 62

CONVERTIBLE

The buoyant, zestful way of life that is so much a part of those who prefer the thrill of open-air motoring is truly reflected in the gay, colorful, durable interiors of the beautiful Cadillac Series 62 Convertible. Here are interiors richly upholstered in genuine leathers whose beauty seems to increase with the years. And here are color choices from solid Red, Black or Natural to ultra-smart two-tones of Light Blue or Green Metallic Leathers for seat cushion and seat back inserts with White Leather bolsters and trim, or Dark Blue and Green Metallic Leathers with Light Blue and Green Metallic Leathers for bolsters and trim. Door panels and side walls, too, are finished in durable and beautiful leathers in dark-toned color below the distinctive V-shaped door panel molding and in light-toned colors above. Bright and brushed chrome hardware and gleaming stainless steel door moldings add sparkling highlights of enduring beauty. A new door panel insert with satin-black grooves between raised chromed lines frames the door handle and the automatic window controls which enable the driver to raise or lower any or all windows at a touch of his finger. Built-in leather-covered armrests afford convenience and comfort, yet blend smoothly into the door panels.

From any angle the interiors of the Cadillac Series 62 Convertible Coupe present an exceptionally trim, tailored beauty. Leather-upholstered seat cushion and seat back inserts, lower door panels and side walls are fashioned in full two-inch pipes in smart contrast to the smooth leathers of bolsters, seat cushion sides, upper side walls and door panels. Genuine leather welts and French seams are typical of the attention to styling details that is found in the Convertible interior.

The front seat provides even greater roominess in 1954 with more hip room and over three inches more shoulder room. The instrument panel offers new beauty and convenience and the safety of a new glare-proof, padded Elascofab covering across the top and over the extended edge. Instruments and control knobs and levers are all grouped directly ahead of the driver. Radio and electric clock are framed in the new satin-black and chromed insert at the right.

Rear-compartment passengers enjoy the increased comfort of more shoulder room, hip room and leg room in the 1954 Cadillac Series 62 Convertible. Here, too, is the luxury of completely leather-upholstered seats, seat backs and side walls in solid colors or in elegant two-tones. Dark-toned carpeting of luxurious, deep wool pile covers the entire floor and heel pad and protects the lower portion of the front seat back. Chromed ash trays located in the rear seat armrests and two leather-covered robe cords on the rear of the front seat back add to convenience. The ash receivers incorporate the chromed control buttons which permit raising or lowering rear windows at the touch of a finger. When the Convertible top is folded down, it is concealed behind the rear seat back beneath a beautifully tailored snap-on cover in colors of blue, black, tan or green to match the top color.

SEVEN SMART INTERIOR SELECTIONS

41. A complete interior fashioned of BLACK LEATHER.
42. WHITE LEATHER with LIGHT BLUE METALLIC LEATHER.
43. DARK BLUE METALLIC LEATHER seats with LIGHT BLUE METALLIC LEATHER bolsters and trim.
45. Genuine NATURAL LEATHERS throughout.
46. LIGHT GREEN METALLIC LEATHER seats and seat backs; WHITE LEATHER bolsters and trim.
47. DARK GREEN METALLIC LEATHER combined with LIGHT GREEN METALLIC LEATHER.
49. Complete interior of RED LEATHER.

1954 CADILLAC SERIES 62 COUPE DE VILLE

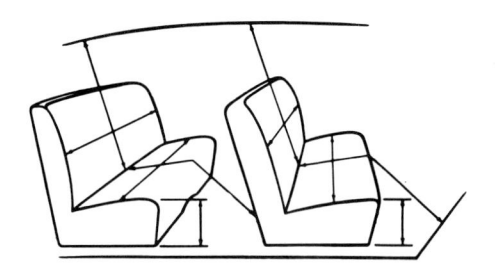

INTERIOR DIMENSIONS

	REAR	FRONT
Head room	34.4"	34"
Shoulder room	58.9"	59"
Hip room	56.4"	63.9"
Leg room	41.4"	43"
Seat height	12"	14.9"

STANDARD EQUIPMENT

Air Cleaner, oil-bath type
Armrest, center-rear
Cadillac Power Steering
Cigarette Lighters, front and rear
Clock, Electric
Front Seat Adjustment (2-way), Electrically-operated
Hydra-Matic Transmission
Lights, Back-up (dual)
Light, Courtesy or Map (automatic)
Lights, Directional Signal
Light, Glove Box (automatic)
Light, Luggage Compartment (automatic)
Mirror, Glare-proof, rear-view, flip-type
Oil Filter
Outside Mirror, left side
Paint, two-tone
Parking Brake Warning Signal
Robe Cords on front seat backs
Vanity Mirror
Visors, dual sun
Wheel Discs (set of four)
Window Lifts, Electrically-operated
Windshield Washers

OPTIONAL EQUIPMENT (Extra Cost)

Cadillac Air Conditioner
Cadillac Power Brakes
E-Z-Eye Tinted Glass
Fog Lamps (pair)
Front Seat Adjustment (4-way), Electrically-operated
Headlight Dimmer, automatic
Heater
License Frames
Radio
Wire Wheels (set of five)
Whitewall Tires, 8.20 x 15 (set of five)

THE CADILLAC SERIES 62 COUPE DE VILLE

Always one of the most lavishly appointed models in the entire Cadillac line, the Coupe de Ville in 1954 offers an enchanting interior decor that is as enduring as it is beautiful. The elegantly upholstered interiors offer a choice of V-Crest patterned nylon seat cushion and seat back inserts in light tones of gray, green or blue combined with dark-toned bolsters of genuine metallic leathers. Another exquisitely beautiful choice combines seat and seat back inserts of gray and silver metallic floral pattern tapestry with white leather bolsters. Enhancing the smart color contrast of the Coupe de Ville interior is the dark-tone, thick wool pile carpet on the floor and on the heel board across the bottom of the rear seat. Full comfort for rear-seat passengers is assured by even greater hip room, shoulder room and leg room, plus the armchair comfort provided by the wide, heavily cushioned center armrest and two convenient side armrests. Lower side walls are fashioned in the same smart piping as the seat cushion and seat back inserts. Genuine leather on side armrests and on the two convenient robe cords lends rich, durable beauty, while stainless steel moldings and bright and brushed chrome hardware add their highlights to the luxurious interior of the Coupe de Ville.

Door panel styling of the Coupe de Ville is distinctively new and different in 1954. Heavily padded, two-inch risers extend vertically from the gleaming stainless steel bottom molding to the rich, genuine leather V-shaped center molding. Just above the V-molding is a leather covered built-in armrest and door pull. The upper portion of the door panels above the armrests is painted in light tones to contrast with dark-toned leather trim or in black where white leather trim has been selected. A further distinguishing note for 1954 is the satin-black and chromed lines of the door panel insert which frames the bright and brushed chromed window and door controls. The door panel insert and the door risers continue into the instrument panel and cowl adding to the pleasing unity of style that is evident throughout the 1954 Coupe de Ville.

AS ALWAYS—THE STANDARD OF THE WORLD

The front compartment of the Cadillac Series 62 Coupe de Ville provides every comfort and convenience to make driving safe, effortless, enjoyable. Here, for example, are electric window lifts that permit the driver to raise or lower any or all windows in the car with the touch of a finger to the convenient controls on the door panel. Seat adjustment, too, forward or back, is automatic at the touch of a control button on the front of the seat. Comfort and safety are provided by foam-rubber-cushioned seats. The front seat, nearly 15 inches high, enables the driver to take full advantage of the tremendous visibility of the panoramic windshield. Additional safety and new beauty are provided by the glare-proof, padded Elascofab cover across the top and around the extended edge of the instrument panel. The instrument panel itself combines new convenience of all control knobs and levers with new, smarter styling. A new panel insert of chromed horizontal lines with satin-black grooves provides a jewel-like background for radio controls and electric clock.

FOUR COLOR FASHIONS TO SELECT FROM

- **60. GRAY AND SILVER METALLIC FLORAL PATTERN TAPESTRY** contrasted with genuine WHITE LEATHER bolsters.
- **61. LIGHT GRAY V-CREST PATTERN NYLON** combined with DARK GRAY METALLIC LEATHER bolsters.
- **63. LIGHT BLUE V-CREST PATTERN NYLON** together with bolsters of DARK BLUE METALLIC LEATHER.
- **67. LIGHT GREEN V-CREST PATTERN NYLON** seats and seat backs; DARK GREEN METALLIC LEATHER bolsters.

1954 CADILLAC

ELDORADO

SPECIAL CONVERTIBLE

In the Eldorado Special Convertible, Cadillac stylists have created a convertible body style that leaves nothing to be desired in beauty of trim and appointments, magnificent performance and handling ease, and the convenience that comes with power-assisted steering, braking, seat adjustments and window lifts. The rubber-lined Orlon top is also raised or lowered without manual effort. Clean lines of the Eldorado are maintained by a three-piece plastic cover which completely conceals the top when it is in the "down" position. Cover is stowed out of sight behind the rear seat when not in use.

INTERIOR DIMENSIONS

	REAR	FRONT
Head room	34.2"	34.9"
Shoulder room	49.8"	59"
Hip room	53.3"	63.9"
Leg room	40.7"	43.2"
Seat height	12"	14.9"

STANDARD EQUIPMENT

Air Cleaner, oil-bath type	Light, Luggage Compartment (automatic)
Cadillac Power Brakes	Mirror, Glare-proof, rear-view, flip-type
Cadillac Power Steering	
Cigarette Lighters, front and rear	Outside Mirror, left side
Clock, Electric	Oil Filter
Fog Lamps (pair)	Parking Brake Warning Signal
Front Seat Adjustment (2-way), Electrically-operated	Radio
Heater	Robe Cords on front seat backs
Hydra-Matic Transmission	Visors, dual sun, translucent plastic, chrome frames
License Frames	
Lights, Back-up (dual)	Window Lifts, Electrically-operated
Light, Courtesy or Map (automatic)	Windshield Washers
Lights, Directional Signal	Wire Wheels
Light, Glove Box (automatic)	Whitewall Tires 8.20 x 15 (6-ply)

OPTIONAL EQUIPMENT (Extra Cost)

E-Z-Eye Glass	Front Seat Adjustment (4-way), Electrically-operated
Headlight Dimmer (automatic)	

THE CADILLAC ELDORADO
SPECIAL CONVERTIBLE

The interiors of the Cadillac Eldorado are as distinctive as might be expected of a car whose ultra-smart exterior beauty and completeness of equipment are unmatched by any other fine car. Precisely tailored of genuine leathers, the seat cushions and seat backs feature such details of the leather-worker's art as French seams, raised leather welts, saddle-stitched piping and embossed "V" and crown insignia. The front compartment provides breath-taking beauty combined with every convenience to make driving the Eldorado an effortless pleasure. Of course, steering, braking, seat adjustment, raising or lowering the windows or the sleek Orlon top are all power assisted. The instrument panel, across the top and around the extended edge, is covered with fine-grained Elascofab. It is padded, glare-proof and finished along the edge with a smart French seam. All instrument panel control knobs and, in fact, all hardware are finished in bright or brushed chrome. In the center of the panel an emblem bears the proud name Eldorado in 18-carat gold against a brushed chrome background. The lower portion of the instrument panel is finished in blue and silver diamond patterned Dinoc. New dual sun visors offer the beauty of translucent, smoke-gray color plastic panels in bright chromed frames.

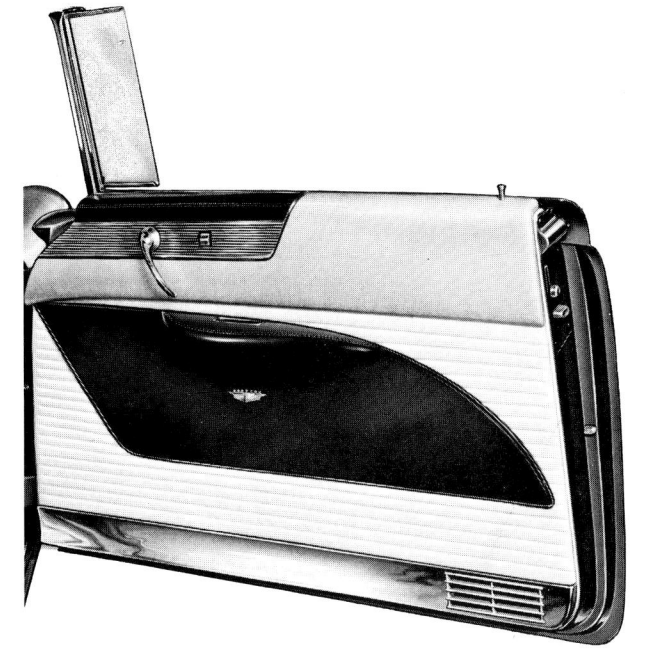

Door panel styling in the Eldorado is distinctively new and decidedly beautiful. Above the wide stainless steel bottom molding is a panel of ¾-inch horizontal risers of light-toned leather inset with a gracefully tapered panel of smooth finish dark-tone leather. The upper portion of the door panel is finished in diamond patterned Dinoc in blue and silver with a door and window control insert panel of satin-black grooves between raised chromed lines. Convenient armrests, extending smoothly out from the door panels, are finished with a smart French seam along their outer edge. The entire door panel treatment is continued into the cowl sides and into and across the instrument panel giving unity and beauty throughout the front compartment. Bright chromed frames around the windows and windshield add their glittering highlights to the fabulous beauty of the 1954 Cadillac Eldorado.

With all of their richly tailored beauty and gorgeous coloring, (see previous page) the foam-rubber-cushioned seats in the Eldorado offer even greater comfort and roominess. In fact, there is up to two inches more hip room, shoulder room and leg room in the rear compartment alone. Smartly modern are the contrasting color tones and plain and patterned finishes used throughout the 1954 Eldorado. Seat cushion and seat back inserts, for example, are fashioned with ¾-inch pipes in light tones in contrast to the smooth finish of dark-toned bolsters and seat cushion sides. Rear compartment side walls, too, combine a lower panel of ¾-inch risers with an upper panel of smooth finish leather around the top operating mechanism and a panel of diamond patterned Dinoc just above the armrests. The floor, heel pad and lower portion of the rear of the front seat back are covered in luxurious Rox Point carpeting in dark tones.

EIGHT COLOR FASHIONS IN LEATHER

30. WHITE LEATHER seat and seat back inserts; BLACK LEATHER bolsters and trim.
31. Complete interior of solid BLACK LEATHER.
32. WHITE LEATHER inserts for cushion and seat back with BLUE LEATHER bolsters and trim.
33. BLUE LEATHER throughout the interior.
34. YELLOW LEATHER for cushion and seat back inserts with BLACK LEATHER bolsters and trim.
35. Genuine YELLOW LEATHER throughout.
38. WHITE LEATHER seat cushion and seat back inserts with RED LEATHER bolsters and trim.
39. Complete interior of genuine RED LEATHER.

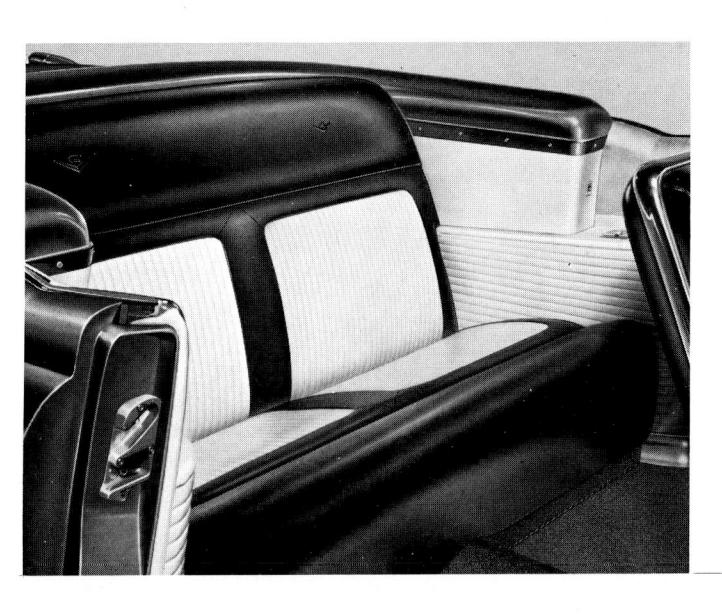

1954 CADILLAC-FLEETWOOD SERIES 60 SPECIAL SEDAN

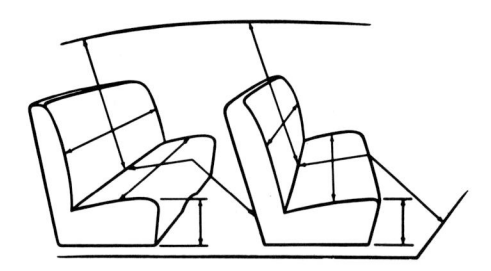

INTERIOR DIMENSIONS

	REAR	FRONT
Head room	35.6″	35.8″
Shoulder room	58.9″	59.4″
Hip room	65.2″	64.2″
Leg room	45.8″	43.3″
Seat height	12.3″	14.8″

STANDARD EQUIPMENT

Air Cleaner, oil-bath type
Armrest, center-rear
Assist Handles (2)
Cadillac Power Steering
Cigarette Lighters, front and rear
Clock, Electric
Front Seat Adjustment (2-way), Electrically-operated
Hydra-Matic Transmission
Lights, Directional Signal
Light, Courtesy or Map (automatic)
Lights, Back-up (dual)
Light, Glove Box (automatic)
Light, Luggage Compartment (automatic)
Mirror, Glare-proof, rear-view, flip-type
Oil Filter
Outside Mirror, left side
Paint, two-tone
Parking Brake Warning Signal
Robe Cord on back of front seat
Vanity Mirror
Visors, dual sun
Wheel Discs (set of four)
Window Lifts, Electrically-operated
Windshield Washers

OPTIONAL EQUIPMENT (Extra Cost)

Cadillac Air Conditioner
Cadillac Power Brakes
E-Z-Eye Tinted Glass
Fog Lamps (pair)
Front Seat Adjustment (4-way), Electrically-operated
Headlight Dimmer, automatic
Heater
License Frames
Radio
Whitewall Tires, 8.20 x 15 (set of five)
Wire Wheels (set of five)

The new panoramic windshield and new vertical corner posts mark another step forward in the design and engineering of the 1954 Cadillac. All forward vision includes a certain amount of side vision without the necessity of turning the head. Previous slanted corner posts cut across the line of side vision creating a blind spot at each corner of the windshield. The new vertical corner posts permit the driver of a Cadillac to enjoy a greater amount of unobstructed side vision. Adding to the driver's comfort and safety is the new 2-inch front overhang of roof panel on sedan models, which cuts off a considerable portion of the glaring rays of the sun. In winter, it prevents that portion of the windshield farthest from the defrosters from getting heavily iced or packed with snow. High and wide window areas on each side of the car and the wide panoramic rear window serve to complete the unsurpassed visibility provided by the 1954 Cadillac.

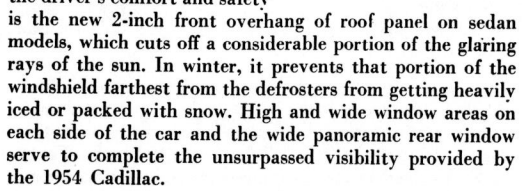

The magnificent luxury of the 1954 Cadillac is nowhere more evident than in the jewel-like appearance of interior hardware and trim. Stainless steel moldings highlight door panels and front seat scuff pads. Bright and brushed chrome adds gleaming beauty and richness to door and window controls, light frames and switches, coat hooks, visor brackets and many other places throughout the interiors. The distinctive chrome and satin-black motif of the instrument panel insert is carried around into the front doors, thus framing the door and window controls with spectacular beauty. Side armrests, front and rear, and a wide center armrest complete the picture of comfort, luxury and beauty that makes the 1954 Cadillac interiors the most elegant in Cadillac history.

The instrument panel in the 1954 Cadillac combines new beauty with unsurpassed convenience. Complete accessibility of all control knobs enables the driver to operate any driving control or accessory without distracting his attention from the wheel. The instrument cluster itself is directly ahead of the driver. A large ash receiver is centered on the instrument panel just below the nameplate. Radio and clock are located to the right in a newly designed insert panel of chromed horizontal lines separated by grooves of satin black. New beauty and additional safety are provided by the padded, glare-resistant Elascofab covering on the instrument panel.

THE CADILLAC SERIES 60 SPECIAL

The interiors of the one and only Cadillac Series 60 Special are designed to please the world's most discriminating clientele. And for their selection Cadillac provides a choice of twelve tasteful trim options utilizing light pattern nylon, plain all-wool broadcloth or V-Crest pattern nylon superbly matched with luxurious, dark-toned plain all-wool broadcloth. Seat cushion and seat back styling of plain bolsters and cushion sides with inserts of heavily padded 1¼-inch pipes is continued into the trimly tailored door panels. Stainless steel door kick-pad moldings provide durable, long-lasting beauty. Another, finer, stainless steel molding frames and accents the elegant, heavily padded vertical risers which form a light-toned panel within a rectangle of dark-toned sidewall cloth. Built-in door armrests which taper smoothly outward from the center of the door panels are covered in genuine leather in dark tones. Above the armrests, door panels are finished in a light-toned painted finish with an insert panel of raised chromed lines with glossy satin-black grooves. In this panel are the automatic window controls, door handle and vent wing control, all in sparkling bright and brushed chrome finish.

TWELVE BEAUTIFUL TRIM STYLES

70. LIGHT GRAY PATTERN NYLON combined with DARK GRAY BROADCLOTH.
71. LIGHT GRAY BROADCLOTH combined with DARK GRAY BROADCLOTH.
81. LIGHT GRAY V-CREST PATTERN NYLON with DARK GRAY BROADCLOTH.
72. LIGHT BLUE PATTERN NYLON combined with DARK BLUE BROADCLOTH.
73. LIGHT BLUE BROADCLOTH combined with DARK BLUE BROADCLOTH.
83. LIGHT BLUE V-CREST PATTERN NYLON with DARK BLUE BROADCLOTH.
74. LIGHT TAN PATTERN NYLON combined with BROWN BROADCLOTH.
75. LIGHT TAN BROADCLOTH combined with BROWN BROADCLOTH.
85. LIGHT TAN V-CREST PATTERN NYLON with BROWN BROADCLOTH.
76. LIGHT GREEN PATTERN NYLON combined with DARK GREEN BROADCLOTH.
77. LIGHT GREEN BROADCLOTH combined with DARK GREEN BROADCLOTH.
87. LIGHT GREEN V-CREST PATTERN NYLON with DARK GREEN BROADCLOTH.

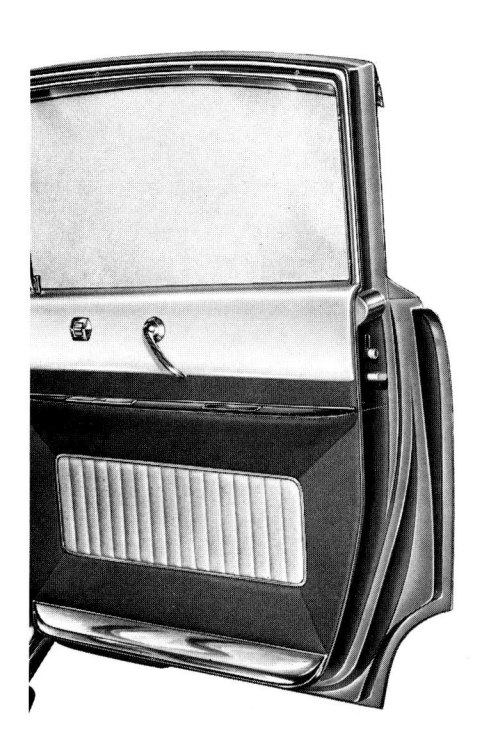

Supreme luxury and comfort have long been a part of the full motoring enjoyment provided by the Cadillac Series 60 Special. In the rear compartment, for example, passengers enjoy the relaxing comfort provided by a divan-height, foam-rubber-padded seat cushion which boasts over sixty-five inches of hip room. Adding to this armchair comfort is a wide, heavily padded center armrest and two wide door armrests. The entire floor is covered with deep carpeting of looped Frieze in rich, dark tones. The elegant tailoring throughout the 60 Special is emphasized by the seam welts of dark-toned genuine leather or fine-grained Elascofab. Final contributions to passenger convenience are the automatic window lift controls on each rear door panel, bright chromed ash receivers in each door armrest and a leather-covered robe cord across the rear of the front seat back.

In the front compartment the driver and passengers will find themselves surrounded with features of beauty, comfort and convenience, new even to those well acquainted with the incomparable luxury of the Cadillac Series 60 Special. First, they will be aware of increased hip room and shoulder room. They will note, too, that the height of the foam-rubber-cushioned front seat, nearly 15 inches, is just right for comfort and to enable them to enjoy the tremendous visibility provided by the new panoramic windshield. And a glance at the instrument panel brings attention to its new glare-proof, padded Elascofab covering which extends not only across the top but around the edge as well. New, too, is the elegant instrument panel insert of glossy satin-black grooves between gleaming chromed horizontal lines. Framed in this panel are the radio controls and electric clock. All instruments and instrument panel control knobs and levers are conveniently located directly ahead of the driver. Centered on the instrument panel against a background of brushed chrome is the name Fleetwood in gold script.

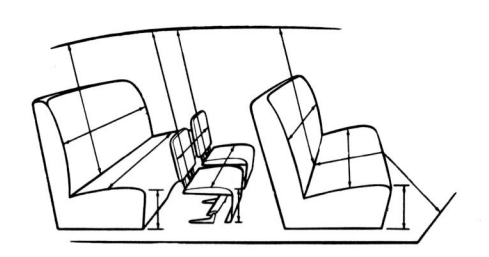

1954 CADILLAC-FLEETWOOD SERIES **75**

INTERIOR DIMENSIONS

	REAR	AUXILIARY	FRONT
Head room	35.5"	37.2"	36.7"
Shoulder room	58.4"	58.9"	58.3"
Hip room	59.4"	65.3"	64.4"
Leg room	—	—	43.3"
Seat height	14.8"	12.8"	14.6"

STANDARD EQUIPMENT

Air Cleaner, oil-bath type
Armrest, center-rear
Assist Handles (2)
Cadillac Power Steering
Cigarette Lighters, front and rear
Clocks, Electric, front and rear compartments
Foot Rests, adjustable (2), rear compartment
Front Seat Adjustment (2-way), Electrically-operated
Hydra-Matic Transmission
Lights, Back-up (dual)
Light, Courtesy or Map (automatic)
Lights, Directional Signal
Light, Glove Box (automatic)
Light, Luggage Compartment (automatic)
Mirror, Glare-proof, rear-view, flip-type
Oil Filter
Outside Mirror, left side
Package Compartments in Side Armrests, rear (2)
Paint, two-tone
Parking Brake Warning Signal
Robe Cord on back of front seat
Vanity Mirror
Visors, dual sun
Wheel Discs (set of four)
Window Lifts, Electrically-operated
Windshield Washers

OPTIONAL EQUIPMENT (Extra Cost)

Cadillac Air Conditioner
Cadillac Power Brakes
E-Z-Eye Tinted Glass
Fog Lamps (pair)
Front Seat Adjustment (4-way), Electrically-operated
Headlight Dimmer, automatic
Heater, with two under-rear-seat units
License Frames
Radio, remote control
Wire Wheels (set of five)
Whitewall Tires, 8.20 x 15 (set of five)

THE CADILLAC SERIES **75** LIMOUSINE

As in the beautiful Series 75 8-passenger Sedan, the Limousine provides every luxury, comfort and convenience for relaxing motor car travel. In fact, the Cadillac Series 75 Imperial Limousine is the most luxurious chauffeur-driven car in America. The rear compartment is identical in upholstery, appointments and trim to the 8-passenger sedan described on the previous pages. The front compartment, however, is separated from the rear by a glass-dividing partition which may be raised or lowered electrically by automatic control buttons located on the rear seat armrests. Front compartment upholstery and trim are of durable and beautiful leathers in black with gray or tan rear compartment upholstery, and in blue with blue rear compartment upholstery. Seat cushions and seat backs are fashioned of 3-inch pipes and finished in dark-toned leather welts. New for 1954 is the electric automatic front seat adjustment operated by a control button located on the front of the seat cushion support just behind the driver's feet. Floor covering in the Limousine is luxurious Kinkomo in the rear compartment and deep, long-wearing wool pile in the front. The instrument panel provides the same features of beauty, safety and convenience as described for the 8-passenger sedan.

NOTE: These interior upholstery choices apply to the rear compartment only in the Series 75 Limousine. The front compartment is upholstered in **black leather** when gray or tan is selected for rear compartment, and in **blue leather** when blue rear compartment upholstery is selected.

SIX COLOR AND TRIM STYLES

90. LIGHT GRAY BEDFORD CORD.
91. LIGHT GRAY PLAIN BROADCLOTH.
92. LIGHT BLUE BEDFORD CORD.
93. LIGHT BLUE PLAIN BROADCLOTH.
94. LIGHT TAN BEDFORD CORD.
95. LIGHT TAN PLAIN BROADCLOTH.

THE CADILLAC SERIES 75

8-PASSENGER SEDAN

The distinguished beauty of the magnificent Series 75 is carried with luxurious taste into its elegant and spacious interiors. The tufted seat cushions and seat backs are fashioned with the style and beauty of heavily padded biscuits and deeply recessed buttons. Six luxurious upholstery choices include Bedford cord or broadcloth in either of three fashionable light-tone colors. The interiors of this great car are appropriate for the most formal occasion, yet provide the comfort that makes cross-continent travel an enjoyable and revealing experience. The front seat of the 8-passenger sedan is truly high, wide and handsome. It enables the driver to ride in fullest comfort, yet in a position to obtain the greatest benefit from the new panoramic windshield with its tremendous wide range visibility. Protection from glare is provided by the beautiful, fine-grained, padded Elascofab covering over and around the extended edge of the instrument panel. The instrument panel itself is a masterpiece of functional beauty. Controls and instrument cluster are all grouped directly ahead of the driver. Radio controls and electric clock are framed in a richly distinctive insert panel of glossy satin-black grooves between lines of gleaming chrome.

The rear of the front seat back is a masterpiece of tailoring excellence with highlights of jewel-like beauty. Auxiliary seats fold flush into the seat back. A panel of ostrich-grained vinyl extends across the top portion and around into the door panels. Midway in the seat back is a beautifully chromed electric clock bearing the exclusive Cadillac crest. Door panels, too, each bear a chromed Cadillac crest symbolic of Cadillac quality craftsmanship. Assist handles and robe cord combine gleaming chrome with the rich beauty of genuine leather in dark tones. Two footrests, adjustable to two positions, are covered with luxurious, light-toned Kinkomo carpeting, as is the entire floor and the rear seat heel pad. Stainless steel moldings and chromed hardware throughout contribute to the elegance of the Series 75 interior decor.

One reason for the tremendous popularity of the Cadillac Series 75 among large families and for company executive use is well illustrated in the rear compartment view above. Here a group of five can ride in uncrowded comfort with room for three more in the front compartment. The finished tailoring and deep cushioning of the two auxiliary seats match the rest of the interior in style and comfort. The conveniences that mean so much to the world's most discriminating clientele are present in the Cadillac Series 75 in full measure. Here are wide, heavily padded side armrests which may be lifted to reveal convenient package compartments. And just forward on the armrests are two automatic window control buttons which permit raising or lowering either rear door window at a finger's touch. Here, too, are chromed ash receivers and cigarette lighters, a large dome light and two additional lights located on the rear quarter panels at each side of the rear seat back.

SIX SOLID-COLOR INTERIORS

90. LIGHT GRAY BEDFORD CORD.
91. LIGHT GRAY PLAIN BROADCLOTH.
92. LIGHT BLUE BEDFORD CORD.
93. LIGHT BLUE PLAIN BROADCLOTH.
94. LIGHT TAN BEDFORD CORD.
95. LIGHT TAN PLAIN BROADCLOTH.

AS ALWAYS—THE STANDARD OF THE WORLD

1954 CADILLAC
Engine

The 1954 Cadillac engine with its tremendous 230-horsepower output is a worthy successor to the famous engine which set new standards of power, performance and economy in 1953.

However, because of many new refinements, plus an almost 10% increase in horsepower, your 1954 Cadillac owners are assured of engine performance and dependability never before attained in an American production automobile.

Naturally, the great majority of your Cadillac owners will be quite content to enjoy the smooth, effortless power that flows quietly and without pause from beneath the broad, low and beautiful Cadillac hood. But a brief reading of the following pages will enable you to reaffirm in fact what is already well known by reputation . . . that Cadillac, year after year, sets the pace in automotive engine development.

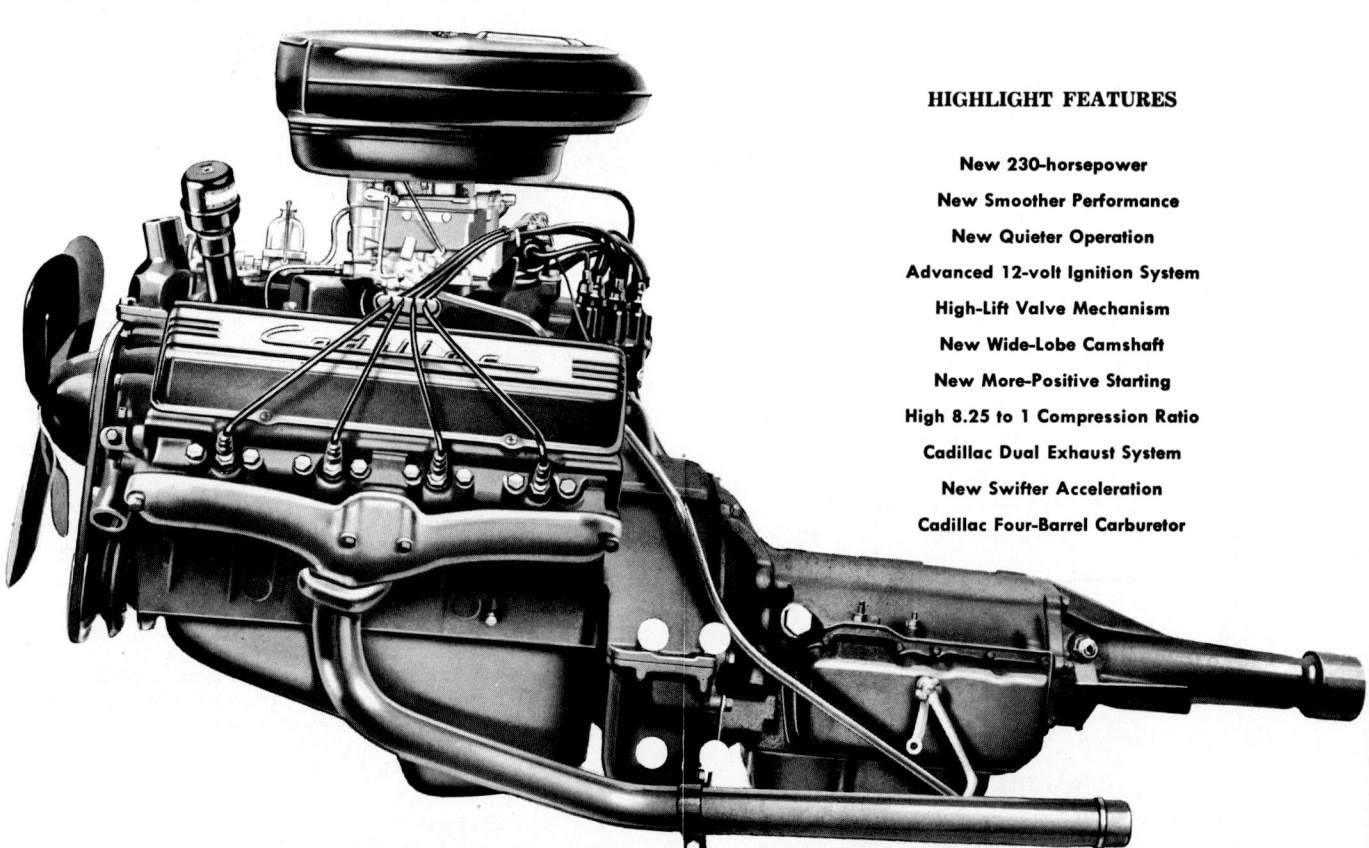

HIGHLIGHT FEATURES

New 230-horsepower
New Smoother Performance
New Quieter Operation
Advanced 12-volt Ignition System
High-Lift Valve Mechanism
New Wide-Lobe Camshaft
New More-Positive Starting
High 8.25 to 1 Compression Ratio
Cadillac Dual Exhaust System
New Swifter Acceleration
Cadillac Four-Barrel Carburetor

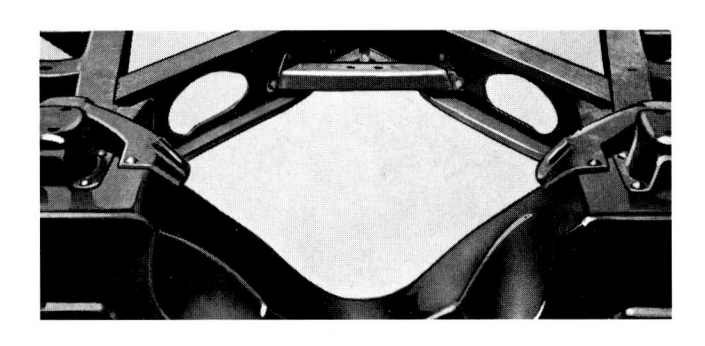

NEW SHOCK ABSORBERS

New double-end-type valving in 1954 Cadillac shock absorbers permits the shock absorbers to quickly counteract spring flexing on small bumps so that they are scarcely perceptible to passengers. On large bumps, the double-end valving permits less abrupt spring control, thus sudden, hard jolts are eliminated. Use of a new high viscosity, aircraft-type shock absorber fluid, less susceptible to temperature changes, assures consistent, full-range shock absorber control in any weather. A baffle tube prevents formation of bubbles in the fluid and consequent loss of shock absorber efficiency.

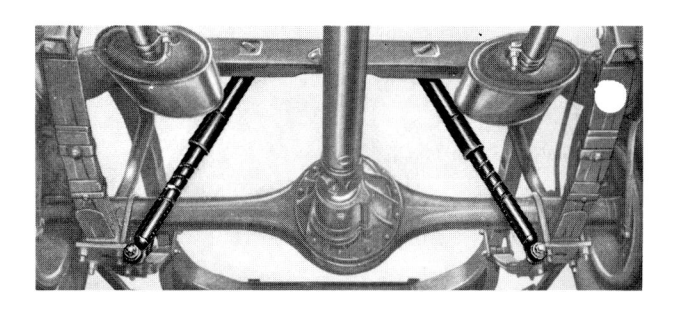

As shown above, the front engine mounting points for the 1954 Cadillac engine are located at an angle, just inside and lower than the top of the frame side rails. These new mounting points are in a natural position to give more stable support to the V-shaped engine, and yet permit the rubber-cushioned engine mountings to absorb the slight remaining torsional vibrations set up by all piston engines. One of the advantages of these new mountings is to provide exceptionally smooth and quiet engine operation at idling speeds.

Lowering the engine position between the frame side rails also serves to straighten the drive line to the rear axle. The result is minimized vibration of the propeller shaft, thus contributing to quieter, trouble-free operation and longer life.

The new lower engine position permits a lower hood line for improved appearance, thus enabling the driver to see more of the road directly ahead of the car.

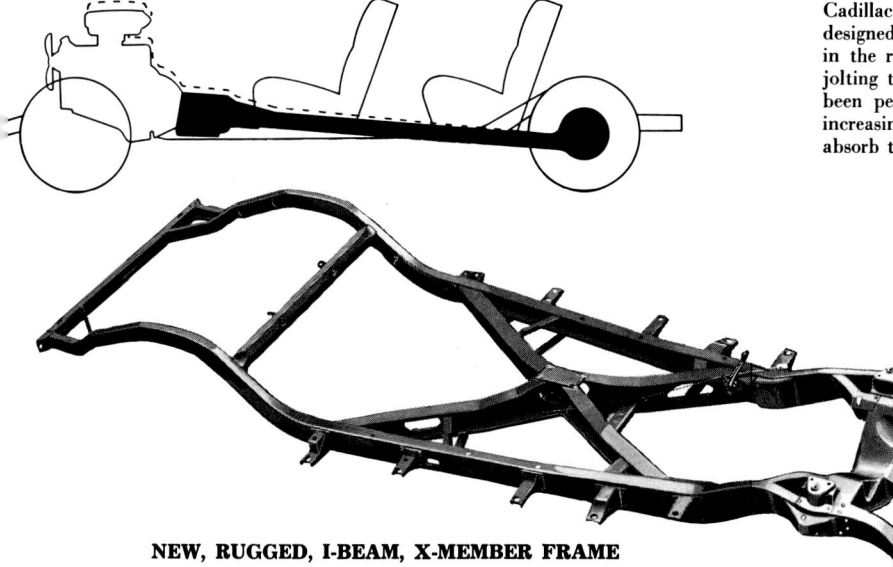

INDIVIDUAL FRONT WHEEL SUSPENSION

Cadillac individual coil spring front wheel suspension is designed to permit either front wheel to pass over bumps in the road without affecting the opposite front wheel or jolting the passengers. In 1954, increased wheel travel has been permitted on both compression and rebound, thus increasing the capacity of the front suspension units to absorb the most severe bumps without "bottoming".

NEW LONGER WHEELBASE

The advantages of a long-wheelbase car are many. For example, when driving over uneven road surfaces there is less tilt to the long-wheelbase car. This can easily be demonstrated to your prospects by laying one end of a long lead pencil and one end of a short lead pencil across a third pencil. Note the greater angle of tilt of the shorter pencil. In addition to a more level ride, the new longer wheelbase permits roomier interiors with 2 inches greater leg room for rear-seat passengers.

NEW, RUGGED, I-BEAM, X-MEMBER FRAME

The new Cadillac frame for 1954, as in the past, provides the safety of sturdy, channel-section side rails with a rugged, I-Beam, X-Member extending beneath the entire passenger compartment. This type of construction, reserved by some car makers for convertible models only, provides an exceptionally strong, rigid backbone for the entire car. The rugged front cross member provides exceptional strength plus sturdy support for engine, steering and front suspension units. The 1954 frame is longer, thus permitting the increased comfort of a 3-inch longer wheelbase and 2 inches more leg room in the rear compartment. It is wider in front, permitting a wider front tread for easier steering and greater stability.

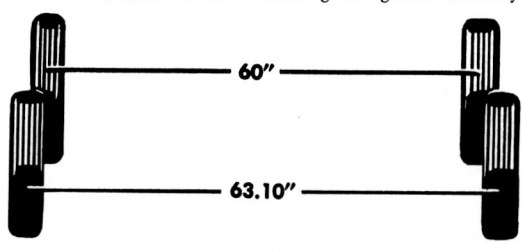

WEIGHT DISTRIBUTION—FRONT: 50% REAR: 50%

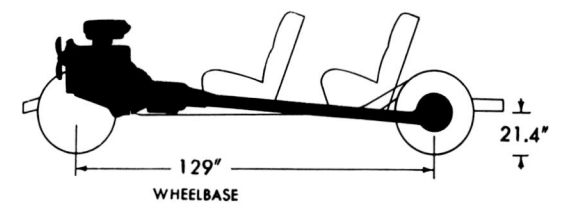

GOOD WEIGHT DISTRIBUTION

Another factor contributing to the ease with which Cadillac cars are kept on a straight course is good weight distribution. For example: Cadillac cars carry approximately 50% of the weight on the front wheels and 50% on the rear wheels. This equitable weight distribution, assuring good traction of all four wheels on the road, is especially important during braking or when rounding curves at highway speeds.

NEW WIDER TREAD

Ample tread width has long been a factor in Cadillac's steadiness on the straightaway; its sure-footedness rounding curves or corners. In 1954, the front tread width has been increased to a full 60 inches for even surer, steadier steering.

LOW CENTER OF GRAVITY

The low, sweeping lines of the 1954 Cadillac are achieved by skillful frame and chassis engineering which permits lowering the entire body without sacrificing interior roominess. This brings Cadillac's center of gravity still closer to the road and results in a truly amazing resistance to roll-over.

AS ALWAYS—THE STANDARD OF THE WORLD

1954 CADILLAC
Special Equipment

All Cadillac optional equipment and accessories are functional and serve a definite purpose for the owner. They increase comfort . . . or convenience . . . or safety and when they are apparent to the eye, they enhance the beauty of the car, for they are engineered and designed to compliment the over-all styling of the Cadillac. What's more, it is these features that enable each owner to individualize *his* car.

CADILLAC AIR CONDITIONER

The Cadillac Power Brake is a vacuum-power unit connected to the hydraulic brake system and to the intake manifold. A piston is enclosed in the unit. With vacuum on either side of the piston, the forces are balanced and the piston does not move. But, when pressure is applied to the brake pedal, air enters one-half of the unit and the difference in pressure actuates the piston. The force produced by the piston assists in the braking. When the brake is released, vacuum again enters both sides of the piston, and a spring returns the piston to released position. Should the power unit be accidentally damaged, the brakes operate as usual, but with no power assistance. Thus, the unit is completely safe.

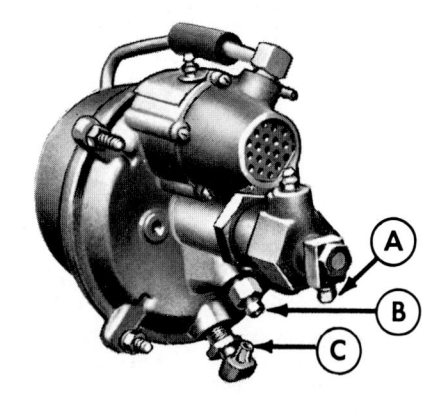

A   Brake line pressure outlet.
B   Brake line pressure inlet.
C   Vacuum line from manifold.

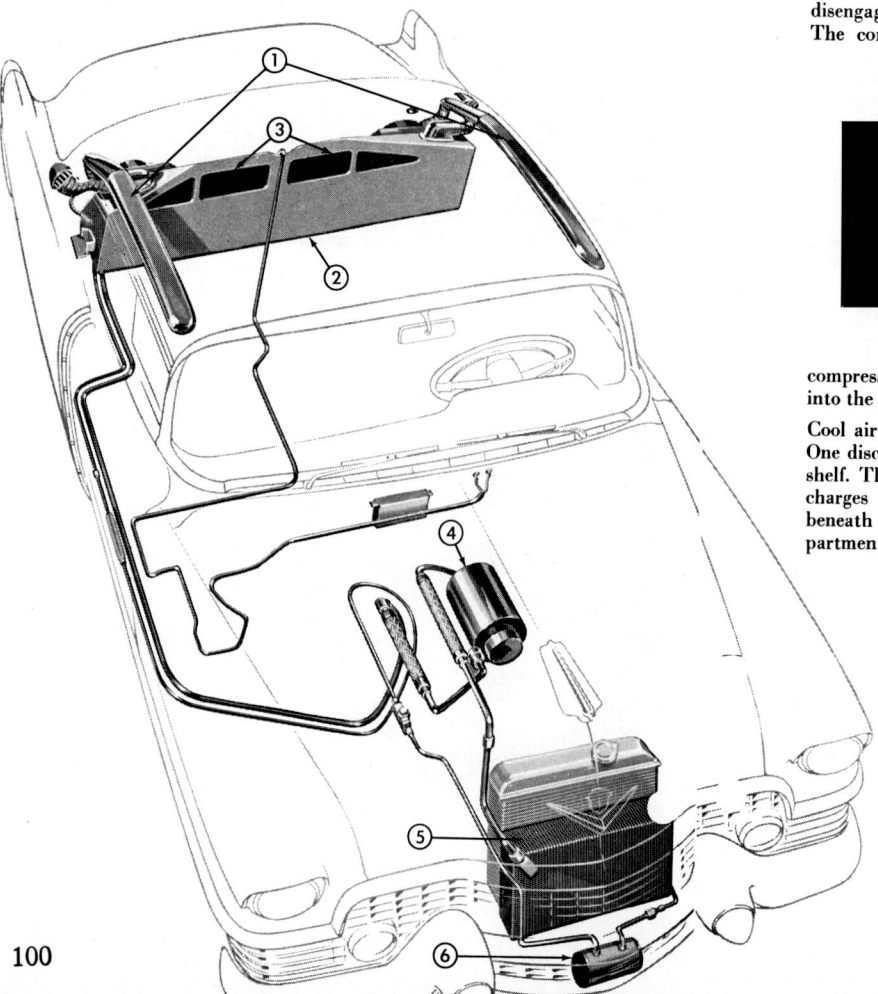

The Cadillac Air Conditioner provides ideal summer temperatures and dust-free interiors for Cadillac owners. Simple to operate, the system consists of a compressor, condenser, refrigerant, evaporator and two blowers. The compressor is belt-driven off the crankshaft through a clutch which disengages the compressor when air conditioner is "Off." The compressor draws refrigerant from the evaporator, compresses and discharges the refrigerant in gaseous form into the condenser coils where it is changed back into liquid.

Cool air enters the car interior by either of two methods. One discharges air from grilles on each side of the package shelf. The second method (available on Sedans only) discharges cooled and freshened air from ducts mounted beneath the headlining, and running up to the front compartment.

1. **Outlet Air Ducts**
2. **Evaporator Case**
3. **Return Air Grille**
4. **Compressor**
5. **Condenser**
6. **Receiver Tank**

FOG LAMPS

The new 1954 Cadillac fog lamps are designed to nest in the grille below, and closer to the center, than the headlights. They improve visibility in adverse weather conditions, and also incorporate the parking and turn-signal lights. A new bar-type filament is used in 1954. It provides more light than V-type filament previously used.

CADILLAC AUTRONIC-EYE

This accessory provides added safety and convenience for Cadillac owners when driving at night. The headlights of oncoming cars automatically dim the lights of your owner's car. Thus, the Cadillac owner's lights avoid blinding other drivers. An overriding switch is provided to signal drivers who neglect to switch from highway beam.

SPOTLIGHTS

Spotlights are available to Cadillac owners for either side of the car. They are handsomely styled and finished in bright chrome. The motorist who travels a good deal at night will find spotlights almost indispensable. They can be used to read road signs on sharp curves and for many other purposes.

SIGNAL SEEKING—PRE-SELECTOR RADIO

This Cadillac Radio is designed to permit hairline tuning with a mere touch of the selector bar just above the dial. In addition to selector bar tuning, which automatically selects the strongest signal in the area, each of five push buttons can be pre-set for immediate selection of favorite stations. This radio is equipped with dual speakers (except in Convertible Coupes). One is located in the usual instrument panel location and the other is at the back of the rear compartment, giving balanced sound to all passengers.

A foot control may also be used for tuning. It makes it unnecessary to take your eyes off the road or your hands off the wheel. And on Series 75 models, remote control tuning for the rear compartment is available.

WINDSHIELD WASHER (STANDARD)

Once considered a convenience item, the Cadillac Windshield Washer has rapidly come to be accepted by owners as a safety "must". A touch of the button in the center of the wiper switch causes two jets of water and solvent mixture to be sprayed on the windshield, and automatically turns on the wipers to full speed long enough to sweep away mud, slush, road spray or insects. Standard on all models.

RIGHT-HAND OUTSIDE MIRROR

A useful Cadillac accessory for better rear view is the outside mirror. It is constructed of plate glass, 4½ inches in diameter, and can be adjusted to the best viewing angle for each individual driver. Left-hand mirror is standard.

E-Z-EYE GLASS

Tinted "E-Z-Eye" Glass is available as an option for all window areas in 1954 Cadillacs. It is a tinted plastic set between layers of polished plate glass. A minimum of eyestrain is assured under all driving conditions. It has also been found to give unusual protection from the sun.

CADILLAC WIRE WHEELS

The fleet, low, graceful lines of the car are further enhanced by wire wheels because the center of eye interest is kept low. A note of practical value is improved brake cooling. These wire wheels hit a new high in good taste and functional value. They are available in sets of five.

1954 CADILLAC

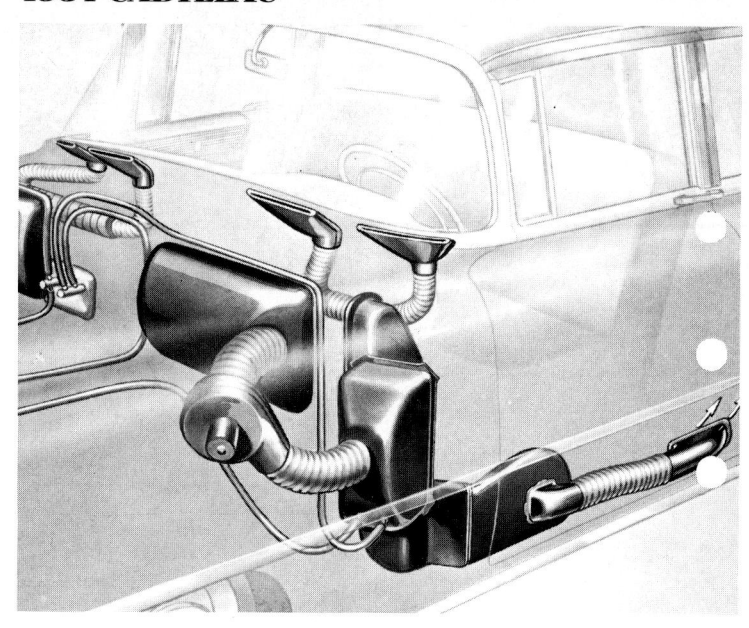

CADILLAC HEATING SYSTEM

The Cadillac Automatic Heating System supplies fresh air . . . provides ample heat . . . seals out dust and moisture . . . holds to a constant temperature . . . rapidly defrosts and de-fogs windows . . . has a low noise level . . . and is simple to operate.

Heated outside air is delivered through two heaters, located on each side of the front compartment. Front-seat passengers receive warm air through grilles in the cowl side panels, and rear passengers receive heated air through ducts and grilles in each front door.

The system is controlled with two levers. There is one on each side of the instrument cluster. The left-hand lever marked "HEATER" turns the heater on and off and also controls the temperature. Under most conditions, the engine is warmed up and this lever is pushed down to the "LOW" position. If more heat is required, the lever is pushed down until a desired temperature is obtained. The right-hand lever is marked "DEFR". It controls ventilating and defrosting air to the windshield. To obtain cool air for ventilation and de-fogging, the lever is moved down to the "FOG" position. For defrosting, the lever is pushed farther down to obtain air heated to the temperature setting of the "HEATER" lever. When a large quantity of hot air is needed for de-icing, the "HEATER" lever should be in the "OFF" position and the "DEFR" lever all the way down to the "ICE" position. This directs all heated air to the windshield.

This heating system is used on all 1954 Cadillac models. However, on Series 75 models, two under-seat heaters located under the rear seat replace the heater outlet grilles on the front doors. This assures a well-heated rear compartment in these larger models.

Additional
CADILLAC ACCESSORIES

Rear Compartment Radio Control	$_____
Radio Foot Control Switch	$_____
Cadillac Cushion Topper	$_____
Cadillac Twill Seat Covers	$_____
Tartan Plaid Seat Covers	$_____
Cadillac Nylon Seat Covers	$_____
Cadillac Plastic Seat Covers	$_____
Visor Vanity Mirrors	$_____
License Plate Frames	$_____
Cadillac Rubber Mats	$_____
Fleetwood Robes	$_____
Windshield Washer Solvent	$_____
Cadillac Body Polish	$_____
Cadillac Fabric Cleaner	$_____
Cadillac Kar-Kleen	$_____
Cadillac Blue Coral	$_____
Cadillac Chrome Cleaner	$_____
Cadillac Chrome Protector	$_____
Cadillac Cooling System Inhibitor	$_____
Cadillac Cooling System Cleaner	$_____

ACCESSORY GROUPS
(Factory-Installed)

GROUP A $_____
White Sidewall Tires • Heater • Radio
License Frame (1)

GROUP B $_____
White Sidewall Tires • Heater • Radio
License Frames (2)

GROUP C $_____
Heater • Radio

GROUP 2 $_____
Power Brakes • E-Z-Eye Glass • Dor-Gards
Fog Lamps • Autronic-Eye • Air Conditioner
(with ducts) • 3.36 to 1 Rear Axle Ratio

GROUP 3 $_____
Power Brakes • E-Z-Eye Glass • Dor-Gards
Fog Lamps • Autronic-Eye • Air Conditioner
(no ducts) • 3.36 to 1 Rear Axle Ratio

GROUP 4 $_____
Power Brakes • E-Z-Eye Glass • Dor-Gards
Fog Lamps • Autronic-Eye • 3.36 to 1 Rear
Axle Ratio

GROUP 5 $_____
Power Brakes • E-Z-Eye Glass • Dor-Gards
Fog Lamps • Autronic-Eye

GROUP 6 $_____
Power Brakes • E-Z-Eye Glass • Dor-Gards
Fog Lamps • 3.36 to 1 Rear Axle Ratio

GROUP 7 $_____
Power Brakes • E-Z-Eye Glass • Dor-Gards
Fog Lamps

GROUP 8 $_____
Power Brakes • E-Z-Eye Glass • 3.36 to 1
Rear Axle Ratio

GROUP 9 $_____
Power Brakes • E-Z-Eye Glass

Do not order any group for Eldorado Convertibles, as most of this equipment is standard.
For Series 75 models order only Groups A, B, C or 9.
On coupe models do not use Group 2, as Air Conditioner with ducts is not available.
The Vertical Seat Adjuster is not available on the Series 75 or the 62 Sedan or Coupe unless it is equipped with Electric Window Controls and Horizontal Seat Adjuster.

1954 CADILLAC GENERAL SPECIFICATIONS

	Series 62 Sedan	Series 62 Convertible Coupe	Series 62 Coupe de Ville	Series 62 Coupe	Eldorado Special Convertible	Series 60 Fleetwood Special	Series 75 8-Passenger Sedan and Limousine
Wheelbase	129"	129"	129"	129"	129"	133"	149¾"
Over-all Length	216 7/16"	223 7/16"	223 7/16"	223 7/16"	223 7/16"	227 7/16"	237 3/16"
Over-all Width	79 5/8"	79 5/8"	79 5/8"	79 5/8"	79 5/8"	79 5/8"	79 5/8"
Over-all Height	62 1/16"	60 1/8"	59 5/8"	59 5/8"	60 1/8"	62 1/16"	63 15/16"
Frame-to-Road Clearance at Center of Wheebase	6½"	6½"	6½"	6½"	6½"	6½"	7½"
Steering Ratio—Over-all	21.5	21.5	21.5	21.5	21.5	21.5	21.5
Turning Radius	22.6'	22.6'	22.6'	22.6'	22.6'	23.1'	27.5'
Tread—Front	60"	60"	60"	60"	60"	60"	60"
Tread—Rear	63.10"	63.10"	63.10"	63.10"	63.10"	63.10"	63.10"
Tires—Size	8:00 x 15*	8:00 x 15*	8:00 x 15*	8:00 x 15*	8:00 x 15*	8:00 x 15*	8:20 x 15
Tires—Ply Rating	4-ply	4-ply	4-ply	4-ply	4-ply	4-ply	6-ply

*8:20 x 15 supplied in whitewall tires (Standard on Special Convertible)

	Series 62 Sedan	Series 62 Convertible Coupe	Series 62 Coupe de Ville	Series 62 Coupe	Eldorado Special Convertible	Series 60 Fleetwood Special	Series 75 8-Passenger Sedan and Limousine
Engine	230-horsepower Cadillac V-8	230-horsepower Cadillac V-8	230-horsepower Cadillac V-8	230-horsepower Cadillac V-8	230-horsepower Cadillac V-8	230-horsepower Cadillac V-8	230-horsepower Cadillac V-8
Compression Ratio	8.25:1	8.25:1	8.25:1	8.25:1	8.25:1	8.25:1	8.25:1
Piston Displacement	331 cu. in.	331 cu. in.	331 cu. in.	331 cu. in.	331 cu. in.	331 cu. in.	331 cu. in.
Valve Arrangement	Overhead	Overhead	Overhead	Overhead	Overhead	Overhead	Overhead
Carburetor	4-Barrel	4-Barrel	4-Barrel	4-Barrel	4-Barrel	4-Barrel	4-Barrel
Exhaust System	Dual	Dual	Dual	Dual	Dual	Dual	Dual
Transmission	Hydra-Matic	Hydra-Matic	Hydra-Matic	Hydra-Matic	Hydra-Matic	Hydra-Matic	Hydra-Matic
Steering	Hydraulic Power	Hydraulic Power	Hydraulic Power	Hydraulic Power	Hydraulic Power	Hydraulic Power	Hydraulic Power
Frame	I-Beam, X-Member	I-Beam, X-Member	I-Beam, X-Member	I-Beam, X-Member	I-Beam, X-Member	I-Beam, X-Member	I-Beam, X-Member
Springs	Coil front, semi-elliptic-leaf rear	Coil front, semi-elliptic-leaf rear	Coil front, semi-elliptic-leaf rear	Coil front, semi-elliptic-leaf rear	Coil front, semi-elliptic-leaf rear	Coil front, semi-elliptic-leaf rear	Coil front, semi-elliptic-leaf rear
Drive	Hotchkiss	Hotchkiss	Hotchkiss	Hotchkiss	Hotchkiss	Hotchkiss	Hotchkiss
Axle Ratio	3.07:1*	3.07:1*	3.07:1*	3.07:1*	3.07:1*	3.07:1*	3.77:1

*3.36:1 Optional (Standard on Air Conditioner equipped models.)

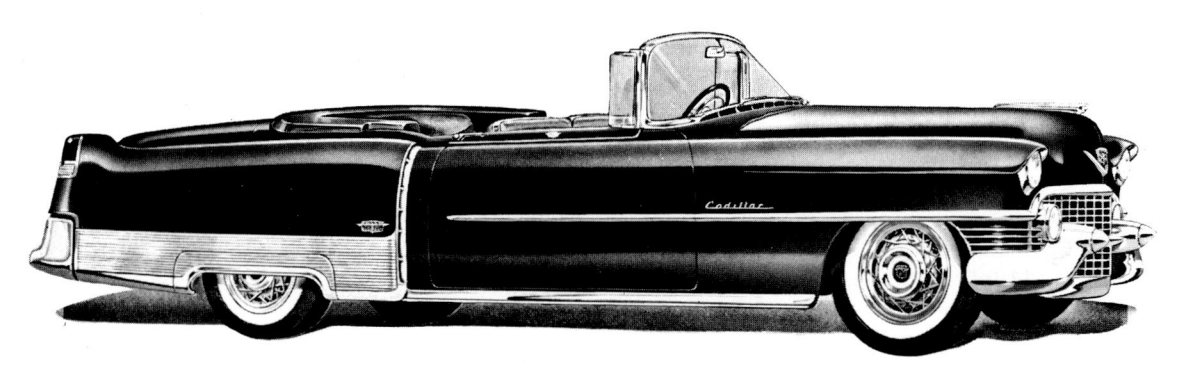

1954 CADILLAC Specifications

ENGINE

Number of cylinders	8
Cylinder arrangement	90° V-type
Valve arrangement	Overhead
Bore and stroke	3 13/16" x 3 5/8"
Block and cylinder head material	Cast iron
Piston displacement	331 cu. in.
Taxable horsepower	46.5
Max. brake horsepower	230 @ 4400 r.p.m.
Max. engine torque—lbs.-ft.	330 @ 2700 r.p.m.
Compression ratio	8.25:1
Engine mounts	Vulcanized rubber
Number of points of suspension	3

PISTONS AND RINGS

Make	Alcoa—Bohn—Stearling
Material	Aluminum alloy
Type	T-slot, cam ground
Weight	19.680 oz.
Clearance	.0015"
Number of oil rings per piston	1
Number of comp. rings per piston	2
Top compression ring	Chrome plated
Wristpin length	3.093"
Wristpin material	Steel alloy
Type	Locked in rod
Connecting rod length	6.625"
Material—connecting rod	Forged steel alloy
Weight—connecting rod	23.49 oz.
Crankpin journal diameter	2 1/4"
Lower bearing material	Steel back aluminum
Connecting rod bearing clearance	.001"-.0035"
Connecting rod bearing end play	.008"-.014" (total two rods)

CRANKSHAFT

Material	Forged alloy steel
Weight	61.5 pounds
Main bearing thrust	Rear main
Crankshaft end play	.001" to .005"
Main bearing type	Slip-on
Main bearing removable	Yes
Main bearing material	Steel back Durex
Main bearing clearance—rear	.0015" to .0025"
Main bearing journal	
Diameter x Length:	
Number 1	2.5" x 1"
Number 2	2.5" x 1.0625"
Number 3	2.5" x 1.0625"
Number 4	2.5" x 1.0625"
Number 5	2.5" x 1.875"

CAMSHAFT

Drive	Chain
Camshaft sprocket material	Steel
Timing chain—make	Link Belt
Timing chain—no. of links	46
Timing chain—width	.6875"
Timing chain—pitch	.500"

VALVES

Valve arrangement	Overhead
Intake opens	22° B.T.C. without ramp
Intake closes	67° A.B.C. without ramp
Exhaust opens	63° B.B.C. without ramp
Exhaust closes	27° A.T.C. without ramp

INTAKE

Material	Alloy steel
Over-all length	4.586" to 4.566"
Diameter of head	1.750"
Angle of seat	44°
Lift	.365"

EXHAUST

Material	Alloy steel
Over-all length	4.574" to 4.594"
Diameter of head	1.562"
Angle of seat	44°
Lift	.365"
Hydraulic valve lifters	Yes
Valve inserts	None
Valve seats cooled by	Direct water circulation

LUBRICATION

Type	Full pressure
Oil Under Pressure to:	
Main bearings	Yes
Connecting rods	Yes
Wristpins	Splash
Camshaft bearings	Yes
Tappets	Yes
Oil pump type	Gear
Normal oil pressure	30 to 35 lbs. @ 30 m.p.h.
Capacity of oil reservoir	Dry, 5 Qts.; Refill, 5 Qts.
Type of oil level gauge	Dip stick
Make of pressure gauge	AC—Tell Tale Lite
Oil Filter	Standard
Type	Partial flow

FUEL

Gasoline tank capacity	20 gallons
Type of fuel feed	Camshaft pump
Carburetor—make	Rochester & Carter
Carburetor—type	Four-barrel down draft
Manifold heat control	Automatic
Type of air cleaner	Oil bath
Dual tail pipe diameters	2.094" to 2.099"

COOLING

Water pump type	Centrifugal—dual outlet
Pressure relief valve	Yes
Choke for recirculation	Yes
Radiator core	Tube and center
Full-length cylinder water jacket	Yes
Water all around cylinders	Yes
Fan belt length	57"
Fan belt width	3/8"
Fan—No. of blades, Series 62 & 60	4
Fan—No. of blades, Series 75	5
Cooling system capacity	19 3/4 qts.
With heater	22 qts. (Series 75 24 1/2 qts.)

GENERATOR

Make	Delco-Remy
Minimum charging speed	22 m.p.h. and up
Generator ventilation	Forced air

GENERATOR REGULATOR

Make	Delco-Remy
Voltage at cut-out closing	11.8—13.6 (adjust to 12.8)
Voltage regulator setting	14—15 (adjust to 14.5 at 90°)
Generator maximum charging rate	27—33 amp. (adjust to 30)

STARTING MOTOR

Make	Delco-Remy
Flywheel teeth, integral or ring	Steel integral

IGNITION

Spark advance	Centrifugal and vacuum
Ignition Unit:	
Make	Delco-Remy
Manual advance	None
Maximum centrifugal advance	Crankshaft (22.25°-26.25°)
Vacuum advance	Crankshaft (26°-29°)
Distributor breaker gap	.016"
Initial spark advance	5° B.T.C.
Firing order	1-8-4-3-6-5-7-2
Ignition Coil:	
Make	Delco-Remy
Spark Plugs:	
Make	AC
Model	46.5
Thread	14mm.
Gap	.035"

BATTERY

Make	Delco 3EM60W
Number of plates	9
Capacity (amp. hrs.)	70
Terminal grounded	Negative
Location of battery	Under hood on tray attached to right-hand body bracket front of dash

LIGHTS AND HORN

Headlight—make	Guide sealed-beam
Headlight cover glass, dia.	6 11/16"
Parking light—make	Guide
Taillight—make	Guide
Lighting switch—make	Delco-Remy
How are headlights dimmed?	Depressed beam—foot switch

HYDRA-MATIC DRIVE

Type	High efficiency fluid coupling and fully automatic transmission
Gearing	Planetary
No. of forward speeds	4
No. of forward speeds in "City" DR range	3
No. of forward speeds in "Country" DR range	4
No. of forward speeds in Lo range	2
Transmission ratio, first	3.8195:1
Transmission ratio, second	2.6341:1
Transmission ratio, third	1.45:1
Transmission ratio, fourth	1:1
Transmission ratio, reverse	4.3045:1
Oil capacity	11 qts.
Type of fluid	Hydra-Matic fluid

SHIFT POINTS:

With Rear Axle Ratio of:

		3.07:1	3.36:1	3.77:1
Upshift	Throttle Opening	M.P.H.	M.P.H.	M.P.H.
DR- 4 Range				
1st to 2nd	Minimum	5.5-8.2	5-7.5	4.5-6.7
	Maximum	20-23	18-21	16.3-18.7
2nd to 3rd	Minimum	11.5-16	10.5-14.6	8.6-13
	Maximum	36-41	33-38	30-34
3rd to 4th	Minimum	21-26	19-24	17-21
	Maximum	73-79	67-72	60-64
Downshift				
DR- 4 Range				
4th to 3rd	Minimum	14.5-17.2	13.2-15.7	12-14
	Maximum	70-75	64-69	57-61
3rd to 2nd	Minimum	8.5-11	8-10.7	7-8.4
	Maximum	21-24	19-22	17-20
2nd to 1st	Minimum	4-6.6	3.6-6	3.3-5.4
	Maximum	8.5-11	7.8-10	7-9
DR- 3 Range				
Same as DR- 4 except				
Upshifts from 3rd to 4th only at		73-79	67-72	60-64
Downshifts from 4th to 3rd only at		70-79	64-72	57-64
LO Range				
1st to 2nd Upshift and Downshift same as DR 4				
Upshifts from 2nd to 4th at		42	39	34
Downshifts from 4th to 2nd at		41	38	33

Note: Miles per hour at which shift is made is dependent on degree of throttle opening. Actually no gears shift. Term used for clarity of meaning.

FRAME

	Series 62	Series 60S	Series 75
Frame make	A. O. Smith	A. O. Smith	A. O. Smith
Frame depth, maximum	7 1/2"	7 3/16"	7 3/4"
Frame thickness, maximum	3/4"	3/4"	3/4"
Flange width, maximum	2 3/4"	2 1/2"	2 1/2"
Frame—Type	Channel side bars with I-beam X-member	Channel side bars with I-beam X-member	Channel side bars with I-beam X-member
Frame-to-road clearance at center of wheelbase	6 1/2"	6 1/2"	7 1/2"

FRONT END SUSPENSION

Front suspension, make	Own
Front suspension, type	Forked arms
Forked arm bearings, type	Threaded
Kingpin upper bearing, type	Bronze bushing
Kingpin lower bearing, type	Bronze bushing
Front wheel inner bearing, make and type	N. D. ball
Front wheel outer bearing, make and type	N. D. ball
Front spring, type	Helical coil
Front spring, material	Spring steel
Shock absorber, type	Hydraulic direct-acting type
Front stabilizer	Torsion rod

PROPELLER SHAFT

	Series 62-60	Series 75
Number used	1	2
Type	Exposed	Exposed

UNIVERSAL JOINTS

Make	Mechanics and Saginaw
Number used	2 3
Type	Cross and Trunnion
Bearing	Needle
Universal joints, lubricated	Permanently
Drive and torque taken through	Rear springs

REAR AXLE

	Series 62-60	Series 75
Rear axle, make	Own	
Rear axle, type	Semi-floating	
Differential gear, make	Own	
Rear axle:		
Oil capacity	5 pints	

104

DETAILED SPECIFICATIONS
Continued

REAR AXLE—Continued	Series 62-60	Series 75
Type of final gearing	Hypoid	
Gear ratio:		
Standard	3.07:1	3.77:1
Optional (standard on Air Conditioner equipped models)	3.36:1	
Pinion adjustment (except 75)	None	
Pinion bearing adjustment	None (Preloaded)	
Are pinion bearings in sleeve?	No	
Backlash between pinion and ring gear	.003″-.010″	
Rear axle pinion shaft:		
Front bearing, type	Tapered roller	
Rear bearing, type	Tapered roller	

TIRES AND WHEELS

Tires:		
Make	U.S. Royal, Firestone and Goodrich	
Size	8.00 x 15*	8.20 x 15
Ply rating	4	6
Inflation pressure:		
Front	24 lbs.	28 lbs.
Rear	24 lbs.	28 lbs.
*8.20 x 15 when Whitewalls are ordered.		
Wheels:		
Type	Slotted disc	
Make	Kelsey-Hayes	
Rim, diameter	15″	15″
Rim, width	6.00″	6.00″
Tread:		
Front	60″	60″
Rear	63.10″	63.10″

SPRINGS (Rear)	Series 62-60	Series 75
Rear springs:		
Type	Semi-elliptic	
Material	Spring steel	
Length	56½″	
Width	2½″	
No. of leaves	5	6
Spring leaves lubricated with	Wax impregnated liners	
Spring bushings, type	Rubber	
Stabilizers	Rear—None	

SHOCK ABSORBERS (Rear)

Type	Direct Acting

STEERING

Steering	Hydraulic power
Type	Bevel gear in rack
Make	Saginaw
Over-all steering ratio	21.5:1
Car turning radius (outside) bumper to bumper sweep	(62) 22.6′ (75) 27.5′ (60) 23.1′

BRAKES	Series 62-60	Series 75
Front and Rear		
Brake drum diameter	12″	12″
Brake drum, internal or external	Internal	Internal
Brake lining, length per wheel:		
Forward shoe	11.15″	11.15″
Reverse shoe	12.23″	12.23″
Total	23.38″	23.38″

BRAKES—Continued	Series 62-60	Series 75
Brake lining width	2½″	2½″
Brake lining thickness	¼″	¼″
Brake lining effective area	211.55 sq. in.	
Brake clearance	.010″ bottom .015″ top	
Hand brake location	Left side of dash	
Hand brake lever operates on	Rear service brakes	
Power brakes	Optional	

MISCELLANEOUS SPECIFICATIONS

Car lifting device, jack	Bumper type
Engine lubrication, type	Pressure
Chassis lubrication, type	High pressure
Axle lubrication, type	Splash

LUBRICANTS

Engine oil	5 qts.
Recommended viscosity	Min. anticipated temperature: +32°F. 20W or S.A.E. 20 +10°F. 20W -10°F. 10W Below -10°F. 5W
Drain	2000 miles (after initial 500-mile change)
Rear axle oil	5 pints
Recommended viscosity	90 hypoid
Auto trans. fluid type "A"	12 qts. dry
Gasoline	20 gals.

The safety and protection of the Cadillac driver and his passengers is evidenced in every detail of construction in the 1954 Cadillac body. Note, in particular, how the many features illustrated and itemized on these pages add up to a rugged ring of steel entirely surrounding the passenger compartments. The Cadillac body is built up from a "rock-solid" foundation. The rigid steel floor, reinforced by sturdy ribbed sections, is welded to box-girder rocker panels and vertical body pillars. The all-steel Turret-Top, reinforced by double-ribbed steel bows and box-girder roof rails, is welded into this assembly. A box-girder reinforced cowl and dash and new, integral, more rigid rear quarter panels and rear fenders assembly complete the sturdy steel framework. The entire Cadillac body is built for the greater protection of Cadillac owners, their families and friends.

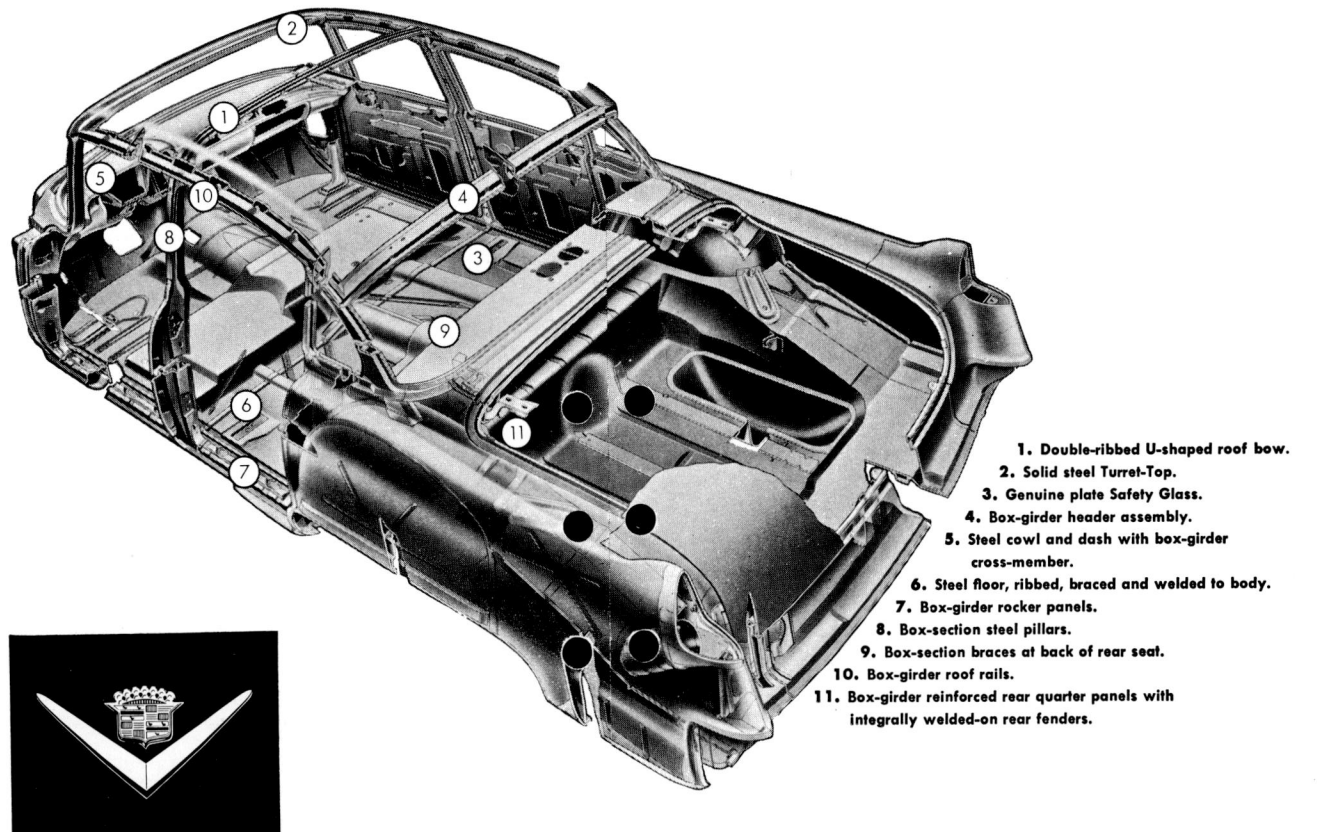

1. Double-ribbed U-shaped roof bow.
2. Solid steel Turret-Top.
3. Genuine plate Safety Glass.
4. Box-girder header assembly.
5. Steel cowl and dash with box-girder cross-member.
6. Steel floor, ribbed, braced and welded to body.
7. Box-girder rocker panels.
8. Box-section steel pillars.
9. Box-section braces at back of rear seat.
10. Box-girder roof rails.
11. Box-girder reinforced rear quarter panels with integrally welded-on rear fenders.

1955 Cadillac Features

However, added to these widely acclaimed features and lending positive new model identification are an entirely new grille and front bumper treatment, new side molding, new simulated air scoop on the leading edge of the rear fender, a new, narrower center door pillar on the 60 Special Sedan, a new wider hood, new parking lights now located in the grille extensions and, on sedan models, new rear windows featuring the smart Florentine curve used only on Cadillac coupes in the past.

In 1955, Cadillac styling continues to improve on the design innovations that, in 1954, set a style standard to be copied for years to come ... the beauty and vision of the panoramic windshield, the hood-width cowl air intake, the overhanging door reveal moldings and the graceful flare of the extended, circular, twin tailpipes in the rear bumper extensions.

The new, front-end design of the 1955 Cadillac tends to keep eye interest low, and thus suggests the exceptional, road-hugging stability which the 1955 Cadillac so ably provides. The new grille features larger openings and narrower dividing bars. The newly designed parking lights have been relocated in the grille extensions directly below the headlights. Here they enhance the lower, wider appearance of the car and add to safety by clearly indicating the car's width to oncoming motorists. Widely spaced and gracefully tapered bumper guards protect radiator and grille. Hood ornament and V and Crest offer new refinements while retaining positive Cadillac identification.

Newly designed parking lights are set into grille extensions.

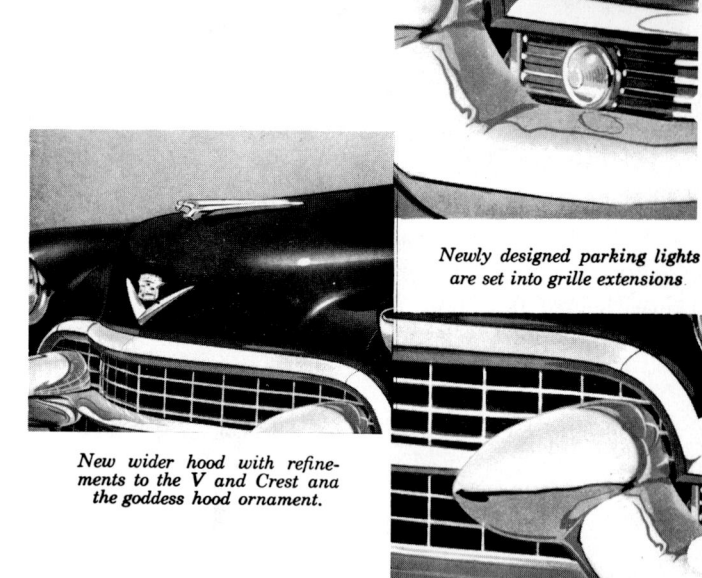

New wider hood with refinements to the V and Crest and the goddess hood ornament.

New, more gracefully tapered gull-wing bumper guards.

Vertical windshield pillar posts eliminate former "blind spots" associated with old-style slanted pillars. The rectangular design of the ventwings lends a smart continental note while permitting exactly the amount of draft-free ventilation desired.

A feature certain to be as popular in 1955 as when introduced last year is the overhanging reveal molding across the top of the door windows. Door windows can be opened slightly for ventilation and to prevent window fogging, yet without permitting the entrance of rain or snow.

106

A style note that contributes greatly to the flowing lines of the 1955 Cadillac is the long, straight, finned rear fenders. They combine with the low, wide rear deck to give an appearance of road-hugging stability. The rear fenders are welded integrally to the rear quarter panels—thus making the entire rear-end structure a single, strong, rigid and rattle-free unit. This blending of beauty of design with greater safety and quietness is typical of the inspired styling and sound engineering which make Cadillac the finest luxury car in America. Note the graceful sweep of the curved pillars at the sides of the rear window. This is now a feature of all of the closed body models in the Cadillac 62 Series and on the 60 Special Sedan.

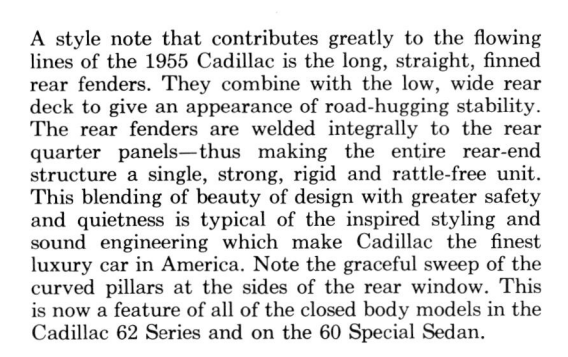

The impressive Cadillac rear-end design again provides the gracefully upswept fender fins and circular exhaust outlets in tapered extensions of the rear bumper. Six chromed vertical moldings on the trunk sill just above the bumper offer a new style note. They tend to make the deck lid appear even lower in 1955. A new deck lid crest is an added styling note on the 62 Series.

Viewed from the side, the 1955 Cadillac presents a number of distinctive design changes. For example, the smart Florentine curve of the rear window pillars, formerly a feature of the closed coupes only, is now a feature of the Series '62 and 60 Special Sedans as well. Additional coupe styling, now on the Series 62 and 60 Special Sedans, is the elimination of the chromed belt molding previously extending beneath the door windows.

Side appearance is further marked by a new chromed vertical molding on the upper half of the leading edge of the rear fender. The lower end of this rear fender molding is met by a chromed horizontal molding mounted on a new contour line pressed into door and fender panels.

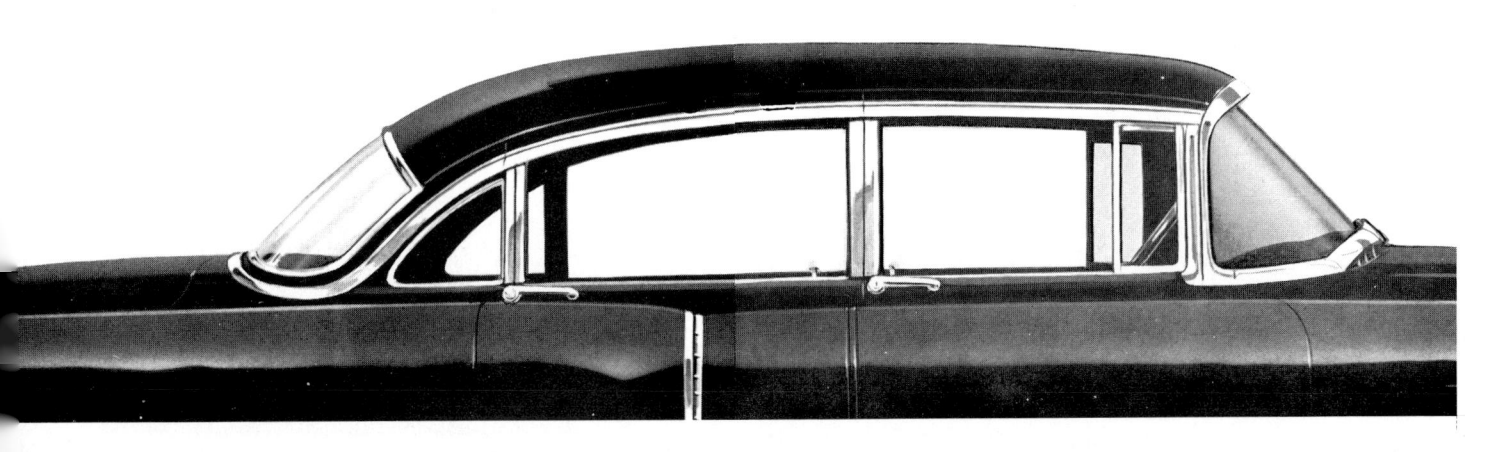

1955 — SERIES 62 SEDAN

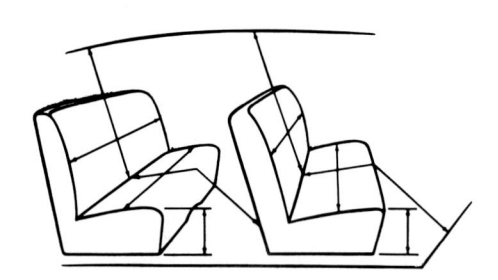

INTERIOR DIMENSIONS

	REAR	FRONT
Head room	35.6"	35.8"
Shoulder room	58.9"	59.4"
Hip room	65.2"	64.3"
Leg room	46.3"	43.3"
Seat height	12.8"	13.8"

STANDARD EQUIPMENT

Air Cleaner, oil-bath type
Armrest, center-rear
Cadillac Power Steering
Cigarette Lighters, front and rear
Clock, electric
Hydra-Matic Transmission
Lights, Back-up (dual)
Light, Courtesy or Map (automatic)
Lights, Directional Signal
Light, Glove Box (automatic)
Light, Luggage Compartment (automatic)
Mirror, glare-proof, rear-view, flip-type
Oil Filter
Outside Mirror, left side
Paint, two-tone
Parking Brake Warning Signal
Robe Cord on back of front seat
Visor Vanity Mirror
Visors, dual sun
Wheel Discs (set of four)
Windshield Washer and Coordinator

OPTIONAL EQUIPMENT (EXTRA COST)

Cadillac Air Conditioner
Cadillac Power Brakes
E-Z-Eye Tinted Glass
Fog Lamps (pair)
Front Seat Adjustment (4-way), electrically operated
Headlight Dimmer, automatic
Heater
License Frames
Radio
Sabre-Spoke Wheels (set of five)
Spotlight(s)
Window Lifts, electrically operated
Whitewall Tires, 8.20 x 15 (set of five)

INSTRUMENT PANEL STYLING

The instrument panel of the 1955 Cadillac combines the utmost in beauty of appearance, convenience of controls and instruments, plus the smartness and safety of a padded, glare-resistant Elascofab covering extending from the front top edge of the instrument panel forward to the windshield.

108

The interior of the 62 Sedan is smartly styled and deftly tailored. Upholstery material is in two-tone combinations of dark gabardine with light gabardine, or dark gabardine with diamond-pattern nylon. Light-toned seat back and seat cushion inserts are fashioned with four large biscuits with a single deeply recessed button. A wide, pleated panel in a harmonizing dark tone divides the right- and left-hand seat and seat back inserts, to provide smartly contrasting style and color. Door panels are newly styled in light-toned colors, with pleasing highlights provided by stainless steel moldings and the bright chrome of the new door panel medallion and door and window controls. Floors are covered with thick, wool pile carpets in dark tones which harmonize with the upholstery. Seat scuff pads are of dark-tone simulated leather. The use of heavy vinyl welts accents the division between light- and dark-tone upholstery cloth and further enhances the well-tailored appearance of 62 Sedan interiors.

Cadillac 62 Sedan interiors are as functional as they are beautiful. Fullest comfort for the driver and passengers is provided by the wide, deeply cushioned front and rear seats. There is, for example, nearly five and one-half feet of hip room across the width of the rear compartment and approximately the same in the front compartment. Both compartments provide ample shoulder room of approximately five feet. Further adding to convenience and comfort are a wide rear seat center armrest, cigarette lighters, front and rear, robe cord across the back of the front seat back, large ash receivers front and rear, a visor vanity mirror and an electric clock. Every item is harmoniously designed to blend into the atmosphere of luxury which marks the 62 Sedan interior.

SERIES 62 SEDAN
COLOR AND FABRIC CHOICES

40. **LIGHT GRAY WOOL GABARDINE** seat cushion and seat back inserts with **DARK GRAY WOOL GABARDINE** seat bolsters and trim.
41. **LIGHT GRAY DIAMOND-PATTERN NYLON** seat and seat back inserts with **DARK GRAY WOOL GABARDINE** seat bolsters and trim.
42. **LIGHT BLUE WOOL GABARDINE** seat cushions and seat back inserts with **DARK BLUE WOOL GABARDINE** seat bolsters and trim.
43. **LIGHT BLUE DIAMOND-PATTERN NYLON** seat and seat back inserts with **DARK BLUE WOOL GABARDINE** seat bolsters and trim.
44. **LIGHT TAN WOOL GABARDINE** seat cushion and seat back inserts with **DARK TAN WOOL GABARDINE** seat bolsters and trim.
46. **LIGHT GREEN WOOL GABARDINE** seat cushion and seat back inserts with **DARK GREEN WOOL GABARDINE** seat bolsters and trim.
47. **LIGHT GREEN DIAMOND-PATTERN NYLON** seat and seat back inserts with **DARK GREEN WOOL GABARDINE** seat bolsters and trim.

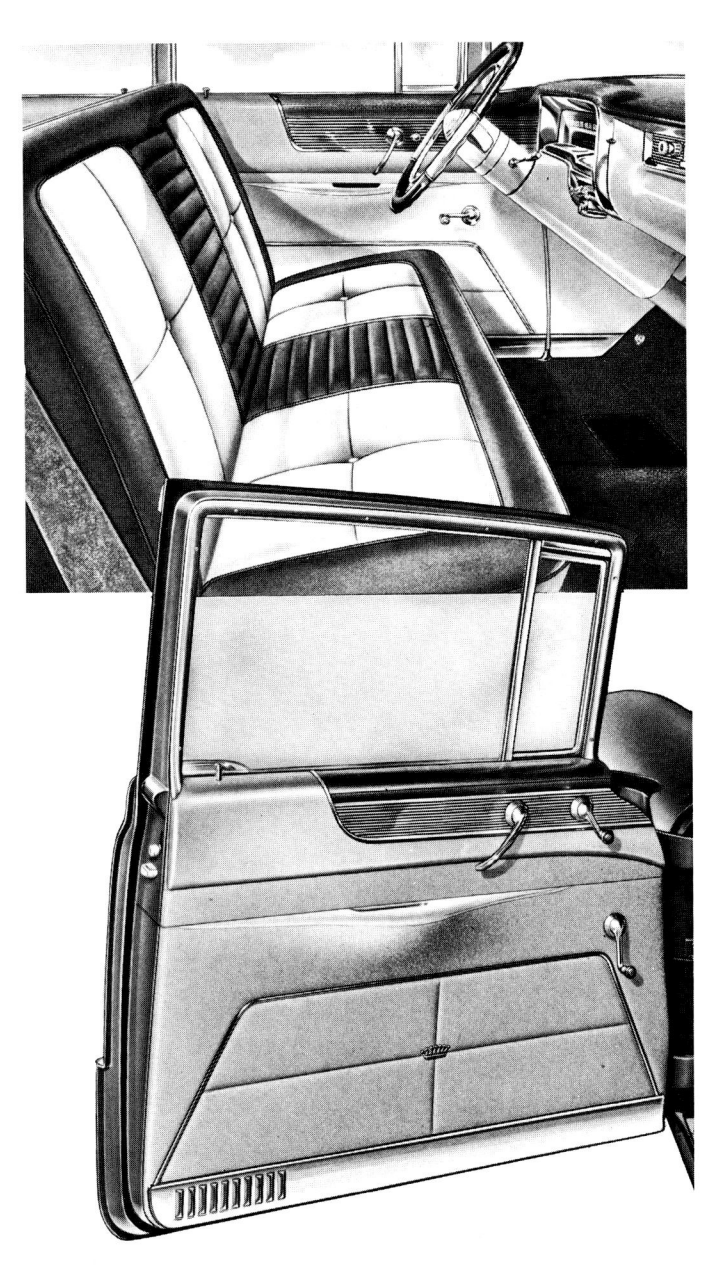

The magnificent luxury of the 1955 Cadillac is nowhere more evident than in its all-new interior styling. Here are new, more glamorous upholstery fabrics and patterns, including all-wool gabardines in solid colors; patterned nylons with gleaming gold or silver Lurex thread; all-wool plain-color broadcloth; smart Bedford cord; and genuine natural and metallic leathers in single and two-tone combinations. Seats and seat backs, too, are entirely re-styled with deep-tufted biscuits and recessed buttons, handsome pleats or in combinations of both. Stainless steel moldings highlight door panels and front seat scuff pads, while bright and brushed chrome adds gleaming beauty and richness to door and window controls, light frames and switches, coat hooks, visor brackets and many other places throughout the interiors. Luxurious carpeting is rich-textured wool pile, nylon loop pile or Kinkomo.

1955 — SERIES 62 COUPE

250 Horsepower   129" Wheelbase   223.3" Over-all Length   Shipping Weight ___ Lbs.

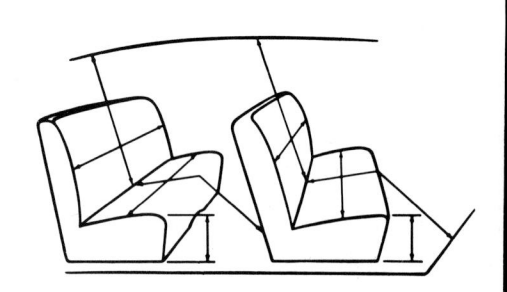

INTERIOR DIMENSIONS

	REAR	FRONT
Head room	34.3"	34.1"
Shoulder room	58.9"	59"
Hip room	56.4"	63.9"
Leg room	41.2"	42.8"
Seat height	12.6"	13.2"

STANDARD EQUIPMENT

Air Cleaner, oil-bath type
Armrest, center-rear
Cadillac Power Steering
Cigarette Lighter, front
Clock, electric
Hydra-Matic Transmission
Lights, Back-up (dual)
Light, Courtesy or Map (automatic)
Lights, Directional Signal
Light, Glove Box (automatic)
Light, Luggage Compartment (automatic)
Mirror, glare-proof, rear-view, flip-type
Oil Filter
Outside Mirror, left side
Paint, two-tone
Parking Brake Warning Signal
Robe Cords on front seat backs
Visor Vanity Mirror
Visors, dual sun
Wheel Discs (set of four)
Windshield Washer and Coordinator

OPTIONAL EQUIPMENT (EXTRA COST)

Cadillac Air Conditioner
Cadillac Power Brakes
E-Z-Eye Tinted Glass
Fog Lamps (pair)
Front Seat Adjustment (4-way), electrically operated
Headlight Dimmer, automatic
Heater
License Frames
Radio
Sabre-Spoke Wheels (set of five)
Spotlight(s)
Window Lifts, electrically operated
Whitewall Tires, 8.20 x 15 (set of five)

The twin four-barrel carburetor set-up introduced in 1955 had a distinctive air cleaner assembly as seen in the photo at the left. This arrangement was typical for the next several years. In 1955, the Eldorado used this dual carburetor intake system and it was optionally available, although rare, on other models.

The all-new interiors of the Series 62 Coupe offer traditional Cadillac quality and beauty. Seats and seat backs are deftly tailored in two-tone combinations of light- and dark-toned gabardine, or diamond-pattern nylon and dark-toned gabardine. The design of seat cushion and seat back inserts provides a new four-biscuit pattern with a single recessed button in the center. Dividing the right- and left-hand seat and seat back inserts is a new, wide, pleated panel in dark tones to contrast with the light-tone color of the inserts. New light-toned door panels display a new chromed Cadillac medallion. Thick wool pile carpeting in dark tones covers the floors in front and rear. Rich, dark-toned simulated leather protects and beautifies seat scuff panels. Further enhancing the smartly tailored appearance of the Series 62 Coupe interior is the use of heavy vinyl welts which serve to accent the division between the light- and dark-tone areas of the upholstery cloth.

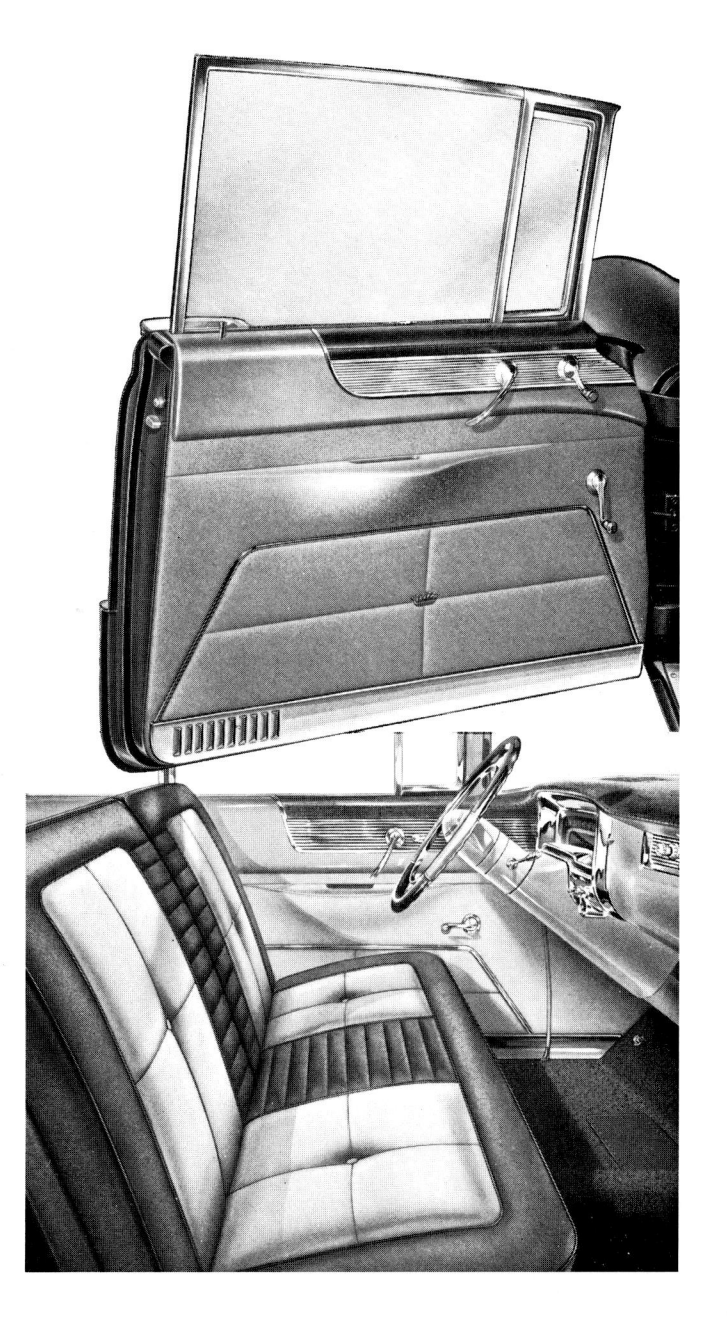

The driver and passengers in a Cadillac Series 62 Coupe enjoy full luxury, comfort and roominess. There is, for example, approximately five feet of hip room and shoulder room in the front compartment and only slightly less in the rear. In convenience, too, the 62 Coupe leaves little to be desired, with its two robe cords, ash receivers front and rear, cigarette lighter, visor vanity mirror, electric clock, convenient side armrests and large rear-seat center armrest. As in the entire Cadillac line, the instrument panel is a harmonious blend of beauty and practicality. Instruments and controls are located for maximum accessibility; while topping the instrument panel is a rich, leather-like Elascofab covering which eliminates glare.

SERIES 62 COUPE
COLOR AND FABRIC CHOICES

40. **LIGHT GRAY WOOL GABARDINE** seat cushion and seat back inserts with **DARK GRAY WOOL GABARDINE** seat bolsters and trim.
41. **LIGHT GRAY DIAMOND-PATTERN NYLON** seat and seat back inserts with **DARK GRAY WOOL GABARDINE** seat bolsters and trim.
42. **LIGHT BLUE WOOL GABARDINE** seat cushion and seat back inserts with **DARK BLUE WOOL GABARDINE** seat bolsters and trim.
43. **LIGHT BLUE DIAMOND-PATTERN NYLON** seat and seat back inserts with **DARK BLUE WOOL GABARDINE** seat bolsters and trim.
44. **LIGHT TAN WOOL GABARDINE** seat cushion and seat back inserts with **DARK TAN WOOL GABARDINE** seat bolsters and trim.
46. **LIGHT GREEN WOOL GABARDINE** seat cushion and seat back inserts with **DARK GREEN WOOL GABARDINE** seat bolsters and trim.
47. **LIGHT GREEN DIAMOND-PATTERN NYLON** seat and seat back inserts with **DARK GREEN WOOL GABARDINE** seat bolsters and trim.

1955 — SERIES 62 CONVERTIBLE COUPE

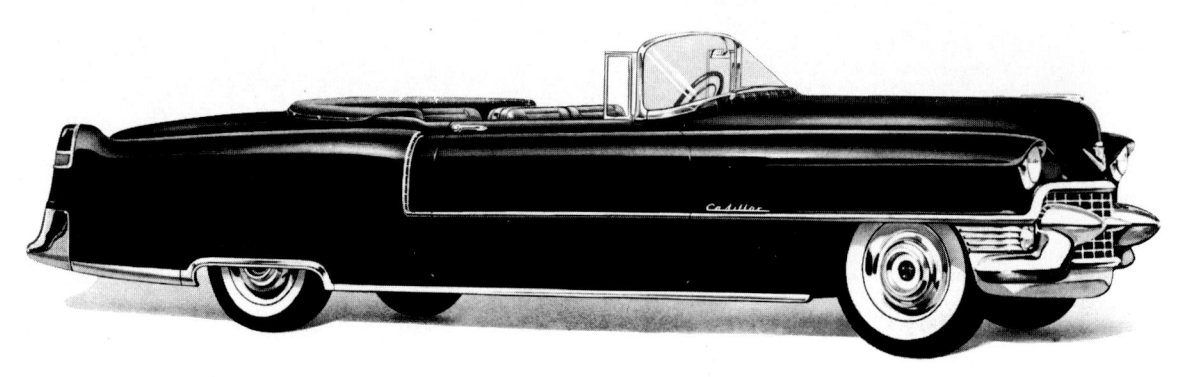

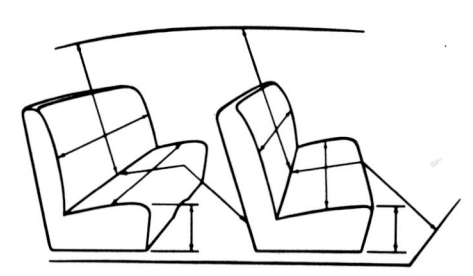

INTERIOR DIMENSIONS

	REAR	FRONT
Head room	34.2"	34.9"
Shoulder room	49.6"	59"
Hip room	52.9"	63.9"
Leg room	40.8"	43.6"
Seat height	12.7"	13.2"

STANDARD EQUIPMENT

Air Cleaner, oil-bath type
Cadillac Power Steering
Cigarette Lighter, front
Clock, electric
Front Seat Adjustment (horizontal), electrically operated
Hydra-Matic Transmission
Lights, Back-up (dual)
Light, Courtesy or Map (automatic)
Lights, Directional Signal
Light, Glove Box (automatic)
Light, Luggage Compartment (automatic)
Mirror, glare-proof, rear-view, flip-type
Oil Filter
Outside Mirror, left side
Parking Brake Warning Signal
Robe Cords on front seat backs
Visor Vanity Mirror
Visors, dual sun
Wheel Discs (set of four)
Window Lifts, electrically operated
Windshield Washer and Coordinator

OPTIONAL EQUIPMENT (EXTRA COST)

Cadillac Power Brakes
E-Z-Eye Tinted Glass
Fog Lamps (pair)
Front Seat Adjustment (vertical), electrically operated
Headlight Dimmer, automatic
Heater
License Frames
Radio
Sabre-Spoke Wheels (set of five)
Spotlight(s)
Whitewall Tires, 8.20 x 15 (set of five)

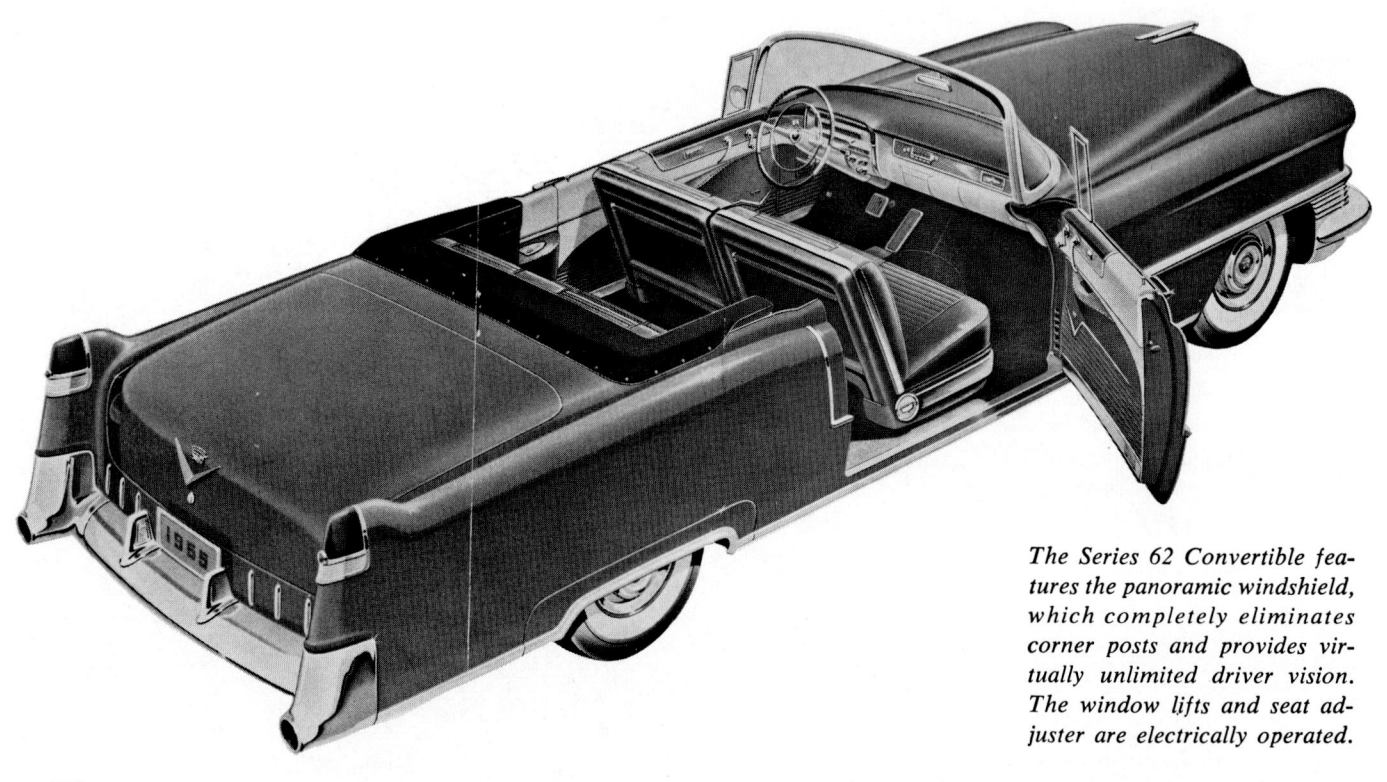

The Series 62 Convertible features the panoramic windshield, which completely eliminates corner posts and provides virtually unlimited driver vision. The window lifts and seat adjuster are electrically operated.

The gay, colorful and durable interiors of the Cadillac Series 62 Convertible hold bright promise of the buoyant, zestful way of motoring that awaits the proud owner. Here are rich-looking leather upholstered interiors whose beauty finds new lustre through the years. Completely restyled seat cushions and seat backs have smartly tailored inserts of horizontal pleats. Door panels and side walls continue this theme with horizontal pleats across the lower portion and smooth leathers above. Upholstery selections, all in durable, sun- and rain-resistant genuine leathers, include solid RED or BLACK, or a choice of six two-tone color combinations in harmonizing or contrasting colors. The exceptionally trim appearance of the Convertible is enhanced by the use of genuine leather welts and smart French seams, bright and brushed chrome hardware and stainless steel moldings.

SERIES 62 CONVERTIBLE
COLOR AND UPHOLSTERY CHOICES

- **31.** GENUINE BLACK LEATHER throughout.
- **32.** LIGHT BLUE METALLIC LEATHER seat and seat back inserts with WHITE LEATHER trim.
- **33.** LIGHT BLUE METALLIC LEATHER seat and seat back inserts with DARK BLUE LEATHER trim.
- **35.** TANGIER TAN LEATHER seat and seat back inserts with LIGHT GRAY LEATHER trim.
- **36.** LIGHT GREEN METALLIC LEATHER seat and seat back inserts with WHITE LEATHER trim.
- **37.** LIGHT GREEN METALLIC LEATHER seat and seat back inserts with DARK GREEN LEATHER trim.
- **38.** RED LEATHER seat and seat back inserts with WHITE LEATHER trim.
- **39.** GENUINE RED LEATHER throughout.

TOP COLORS: 3. Blue 4. Cotan White 5. Beige 7. Green 9. Black

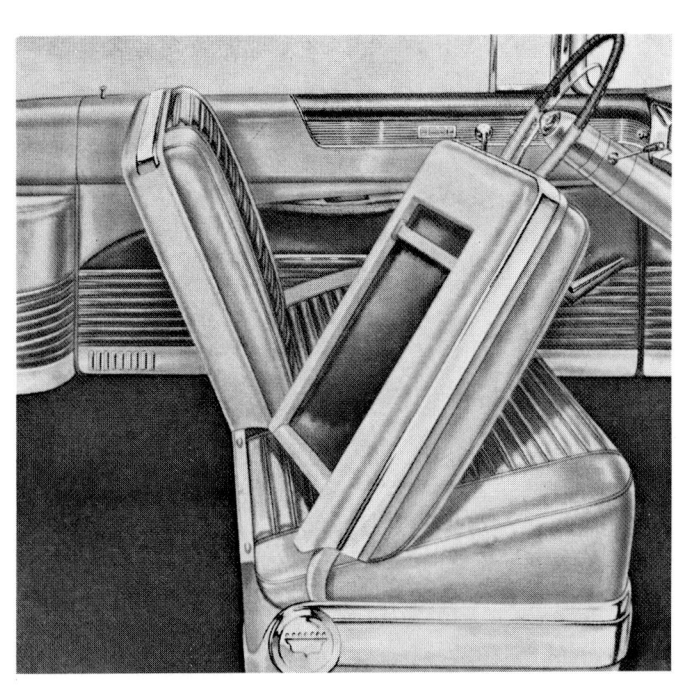

In comfort and convenience, the Series 62 Convertible provides the driver and passengers with every consideration. There is ample seating comfort. For example, the front seat offers some five feet of hip and shoulder room. There is the convenience of an electrically operated fore-and-aft front seat adjustment and electrically operated window lifts. Robe cords on the front seat backs, a visor vanity mirror, glove box light, map or courtesy light, an electric clock and, of course, cigarette lighter and ash receivers all add to the convenience and enjoyment of motoring in the glamorous Cadillac Series 62 Convertible Coupe.

1955   SERIES 62 COUPE DE VILLE

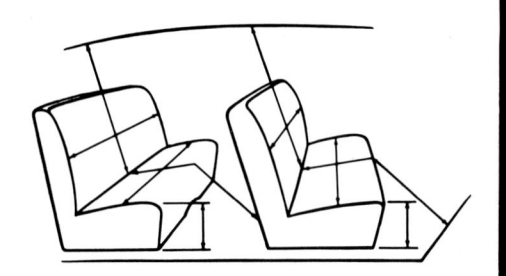

INTERIOR DIMENSIONS

	REAR	FRONT
Head room	34.3"	34.4"
Shoulder room	58.9"	59"
Hip room	56.3"	63.9"
Leg room	41.8"	42.8"
Seat height	12.6"	13.2"

STANDARD EQUIPMENT

Air Cleaner, oil-bath type
Armrest, center-rear
Cadillac Power Steering
Cigarette Lighters, front and rear
Clock, electric
Front Seat Adjustment (horizontal), electrically operated
Hydra-Matic Transmission
Lights, Back-up (dual)
Light, Courtesy or Map (automatic)
Lights, Directional Signal
Light, Glove Box (automatic)
Light, Luggage Compartment (automatic)
Mirror, glare-proof, rear-view, flip-type
Oil Filter
Outside Mirror, left side
Paint, two-tone
Parking Brake Warning Signal
Robe Cords on front seat backs
Visor Vanity Mirror
Visors, dual sun
Wheel Discs (set of four)
Window Lifts, electrically operated
Windshield Washer and Coordinator

OPTIONAL EQUIPMENT (EXTRA COST)

Cadillac Air Conditioner
Cadillac Power Brakes
E-Z-Eye Tinted Glass
Fog Lamps (pair)
Front Seat Adjustment (vertical), electrically operated
Headlight Dimmer, automatic
Heater
License Frames
Radio
Sabre-Spoke Wheels (set of five)
Spotlight(s)
Whitewall Tires, 8.20 x 15 (set of five)

In the glamorous beauty of its lavishly appointed interiors, there is literally nothing to approach the enchanting Cadillac Coupe de Ville. The elegant upholstery of its new button-and biscuit-fashioned seats and side walls is offered in a fabulous new array of patterns and colors. In fact, the choice of eleven color combinations in two patterns of metallic nylon fabrics, with genuine leather trim, enables the owner to personalize his Coupe de Ville to a greater extent than ever before. Included are three new glamour trim styles featuring Black V-Pattern Metallic Nylon with Tangier Tan Leather; Wedgewood Green V-Pattern Metallic Nylon with Green Leather and Gold V-Pattern Metallic Nylon with White Leather. Appointments and trim throughout the interior are color-harmonized to present a truly breath-taking appearance in 1955. Bright and brushed chrome hardware and stainless steel moldings add highlights of beauty in the Coupe de Ville.

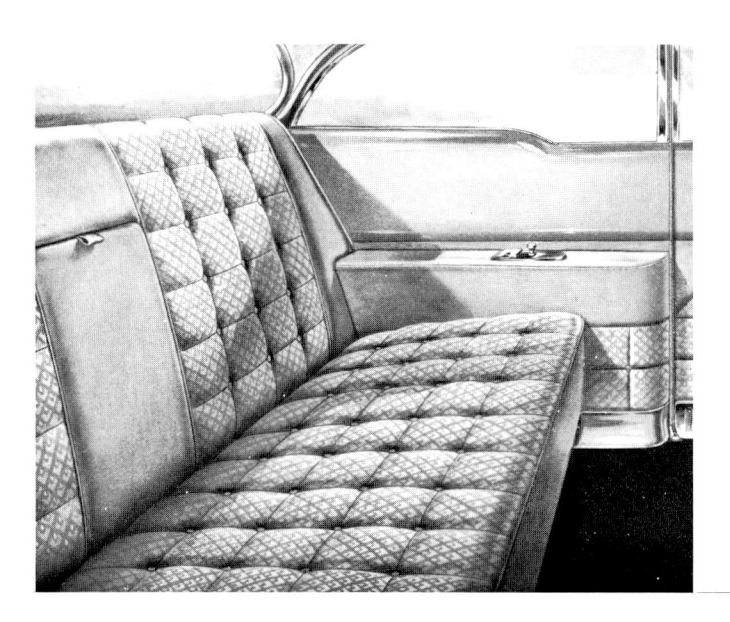

In keeping with the exceptional smartness and styling beauty of the de Ville is the unsurpassed comfort and convenience provided on every hand. Window lifts and fore-and-aft front seat adjustment are electrically operated at the touch of a button. And there are individual ash receivers and cigarette lighters in each side armrest of the rear compartment. These are in addition to such other Cadillac conveniences as the two robe cords, wide rear-seat center armrest, electric clock, visor vanity mirror, courtesy and map lights and glove box light. In fact, nothing has been overlooked in making the 1955 Coupe de Ville the most glamorous coupe ever offered in the history of Cadillac.

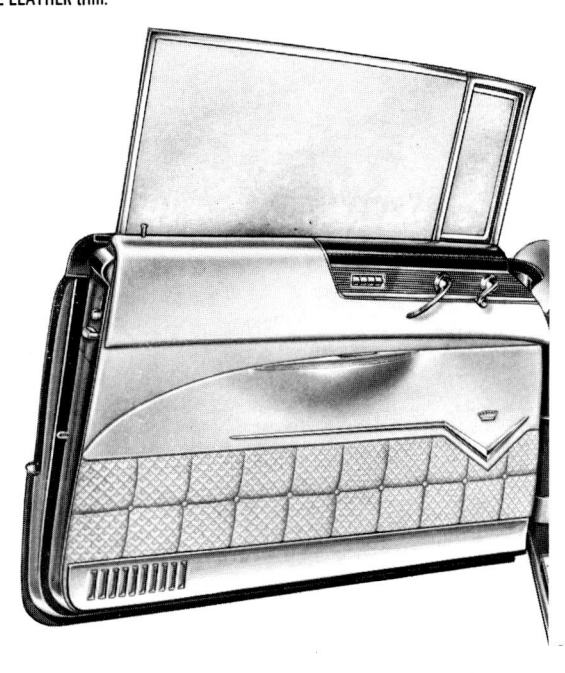

SERIES 62 COUPE DE VILLE
COLOR AND FABRIC CHOICES

50. LIGHT GRAY DIAGONAL-PATTERN METALLIC NYLON seat and seat back inserts with DARK GRAY LEATHER trim.
51. LIGHT GRAY V-PATTERN METALLIC NYLON seat and seat back inserts with DARK GRAY LEATHER trim.
52. LIGHT BLUE DIAGONAL-PATTERN METALLIC NYLON seat and seat back inserts with DARK BLUE LEATHER trim.
53. LIGHT BLUE V-PATTERN METALLIC NYLON seat and seat back inserts with DARK BLUE LEATHER trim.
54. LIGHT TAN DIAGONAL-PATTERN METALLIC NYLON seat and seat back inserts with DARK TAN LEATHER trim.
55. LIGHT TAN V-PATTERN METALLIC NYLON seat and seat back inserts with DARK TAN LEATHER trim.
56. LIGHT GREEN DIAGONAL-PATTERN METALLIC NYLON seat and seat back inserts with DARK GREEN LEATHER trim.
57. LIGHT GREEN V-PATTERN METALLIC NYLON seat and seat back inserts with DARK GREEN LEATHER trim.

GLAMOUR TRIM
61. BLACK V-PATTERN METALLIC NYLON seat and seat back inserts with TANGIER TAN LEATHER trim.
63. WEDGEWOOD GREEN V-PATTERN METALLIC NYLON seat and seat back inserts with GREEN LEATHER trim.
65. GOLD V-PATTERN METALLIC NYLON seat and seat back inserts with WHITE LEATHER trim.

ELDORADO SPECIAL CONVERTIBLE

1955

STANDARD EQUIPMENT

Air Cleaner, oil-bath type
Cadillac Power Brakes
Cadillac Power Steering
Cigarette Lighter, front
Clock, electric
Fog Lamps (pair)
Front Seat Adjustment (4-way), electrically operated
Heater
Hydra-Matic Transmission
License Frames
Lights, Back-up (dual)
Light, Courtesy or Map (automatic)
Lights, Directional Signal
Light, Glove Box (automatic)
Light, Luggage Compartment (automatic)
Mirror, glare-proof, rear-view, flip-type
Oil Filter
Outside Mirror, left side
Parking Brake Warning Signal
Radio
Robe Cords on front seat backs
Sabre-Spoke Wheels (set of five)
Visors, dual sun, translucent plastic, chrome frames
Window Lifts, electrically operated
Windshield Washer and Coordinator
Whitewall Tires 8.20 x 15 (4-ply)

In the Eldorado, for 1955, Cadillac stylists have created a motor car of such advanced styling . . . such perfected power and performance that it is certain to pace the industry for many years to come. Its sweeping lines, from the tip of the gracefully contoured gull-wing bumper guards in front to the twin-exhaust outlets in the rear, are climaxed by the daring design of the new rear fenders. Cadillac's famous rear fender fins are sharply accented on the Eldorado, while newly designed taillights, turn signals and back-up lights are contained in twin housings at the end of raised, tubular contours in the fenders. Interiors are distinctively tailored in genuine leathers in a wide choice of solid and two-tone colors. Improved Cadillac Hydra-Matic and the brilliant new 270-horsepower Eldorado engine combine to deliver breath-taking acceleration, or silent, effortless cruising with equal facility. Finally, in completeness of equipment (as listed on the following page) the Eldorado is unmatched by any other motor car, anywhere.

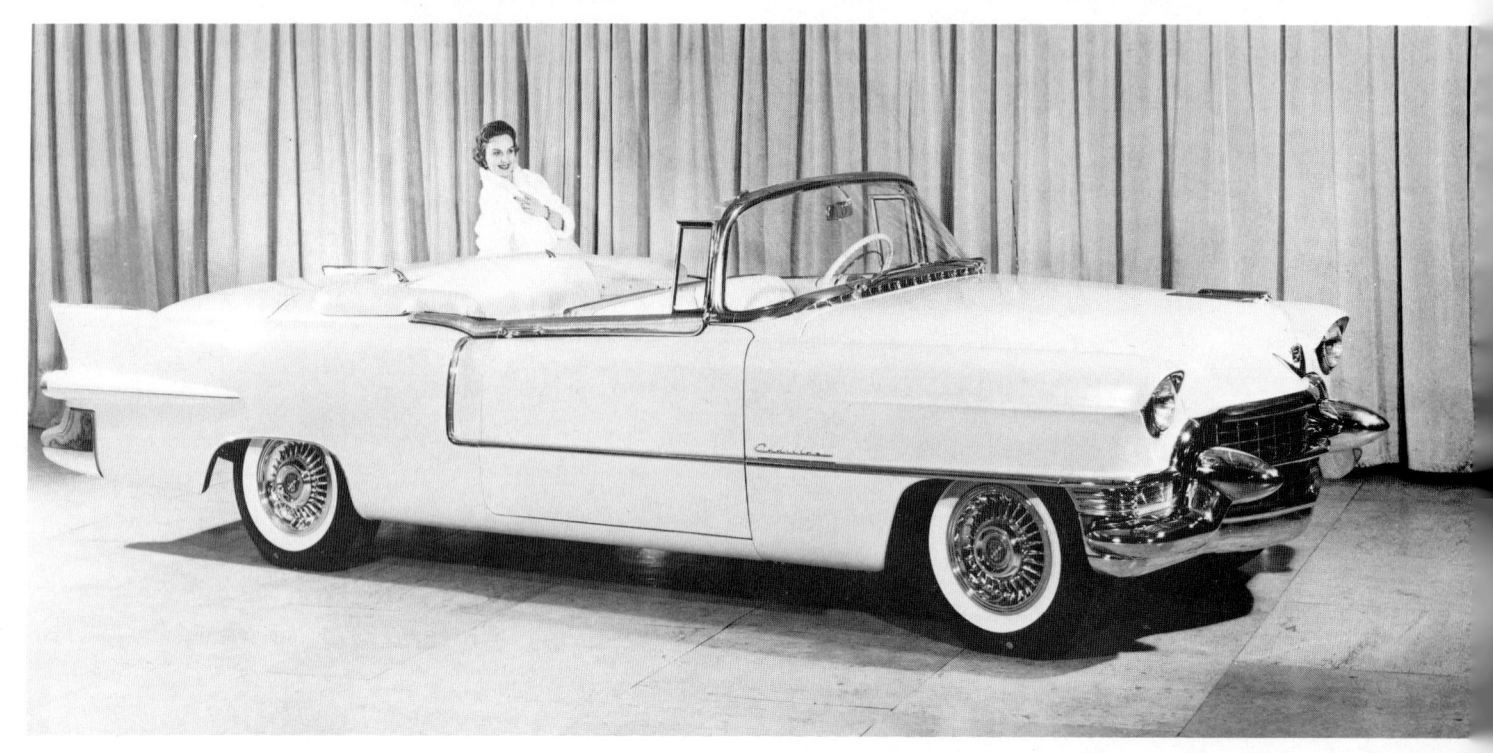

The Cadillac Eldorado Special Convertible offers ultra-smart interiors as distinctive in styling and trim as the modish exterior design of the car itself. Seat cushions and seat backs are fashioned in heavily padded biscuits with deeply recessed, beautifully chromed, concave buttons adding a bright new style note. Newly designed bolsters extend down into the seat back inserts to form a smart "V" pattern. Upholstery is of precisely tailored, genuine leathers, boasting such luxury details of the leather worker's art as French seams and raised leather welts. Choice of upholstery colors has been increased for 1955 and now includes five solid colors— BLACK, BLUE, BEIGE, GRAY or RED—and four combinations of BLACK, BLUE, GRAY or RED LEATHER combined with WHITE LEATHER trim. Top material is again sleek, durable Orlon in WHITE or BLACK. Floors are carpeted with luxurious, dark-toned, nylon loop pile inset with aluminum ribbed rubber floor pads, front and rear. New door panel styling in light- and dark-toned genuine leathers features a convenient pocket in each door with openings concealed beneath leather flaps with snap fasteners.

The exquisite beauty and sleek lines of the Eldorado are combined with every convenience to make driving an effortless pleasure. Steering, braking, seat adjustment forward and back, or up and down, raising or lowering the windows or the sleek Orlon top, are all power-assisted. All instrument panel control knobs, finished in bright or brushed chrome, are located for maximum convenience. Dual sun visors offer the beauty of translucent plastic panels framed in bright chrome. Here, indeed, is styling and beauty, comfort and convenience without compromise.

ELDORADO
COLOR AND UPHOLSTERY CHOICES

- **90.** BLACK LEATHER seat and seat back inserts with WHITE LEATHER trim.
- **91.** BLACK LEATHER throughout.
- **92.** BLUE LEATHER seat and seat back inserts with WHITE LEATHER trim.
- **93.** BLUE LEATHER throughout.
- **95.** BEIGE LEATHER throughout.
- **96.** GRAY LEATHER seat and seat back inserts with WHITE LEATHER trim.
- **97.** GRAY LEATHER throughout.
- **98.** RED LEATHER seat and seat back inserts with WHITE LEATHER trim.
- **99.** RED LEATHER throughout.

TOP MATERIAL: 1. WHITE ORLON.   2. BLACK ORLON.

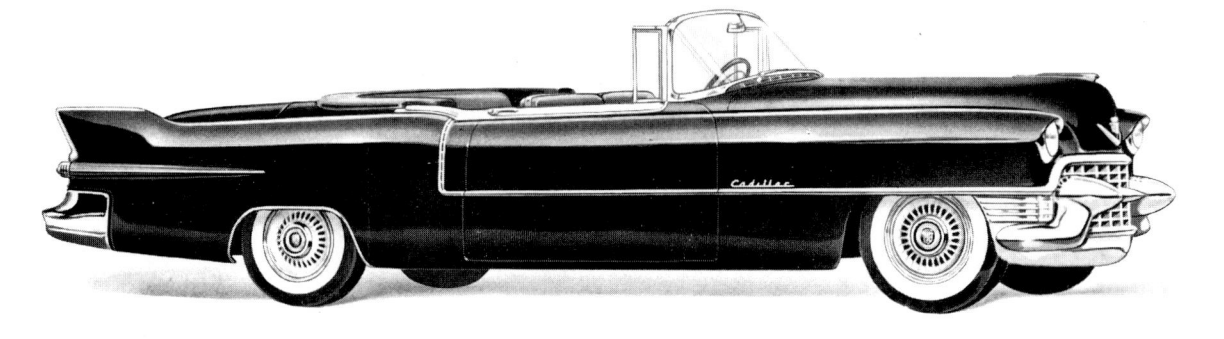

270 Horsepower   129" Wheelbase   223.3" Over-all Length   Shipping Weight ____ Lbs.

1955 SERIES 60 SPECIAL SEDAN

250 Horsepower   133" Wheelbase   227.3" Over-all Length   Shipping Weight ____ Lbs.

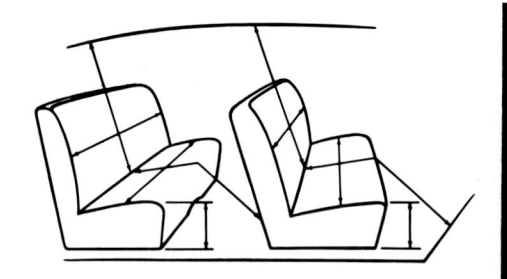

INTERIOR DIMENSIONS

	REAR	FRONT
Head room	35.6"	35.8"
Shoulder room	58.9"	59.4"
Hip room	65.2"	64.3"
Leg room	46.3"	43.3"
Seat height	12.8"	13.8"

STANDARD EQUIPMENT

Air Cleaner, oil-bath type
Armrest, center-rear
Assist Handles (2)
Cadillac Power Steering
Cigarette Lighters, front and rear
Clock, electric
Front Seat Adjustment (horizontal), electrically operated
Hydra-Matic Transmission
Lights, Directional Signal
Light, Courtesy or Map (automatic)
Lights, Back-up (dual)
Light, Glove Box (automatic)
Light, Luggage Compartment (automatic)
Mirror, glare-proof, rear-view, flip-type
Oil Filter
Outside Mirror, left side
Paint, two-tone
Parking Brake Warning Signal
Robe Cord on back of front seat
Visor Vanity Mirror
Visors, dual sun
Wheel Discs (set of four)
Window Lifts, electrically operated
Windshield Washer and Coordinator

OPTIONAL EQUIPMENT (EXTRA COST)

Cadillac Air Conditioner
Cadillac Power Brakes
E-Z-Eye Tinted Glass
Fog Lamps (pair)
Front Seat Adjustment (vertical) electrically operated
Headlight Dimmer, automatic
Heater
License Frames
Radio
Sabre-Spoke Wheels (set of five)
Spotlight(s)
Whitewall Tires, 8.20 x 15 (set of five)

118

The Cadillac Series 60 Special Sedan has long been the symbol of Cadillac's leadership in building America's finest luxury cars. And, in 1955, the 60 Special interiors offer even greater beauty. Light-toned seat cushions and seat back inserts are fashioned of smart piping with the dark-toned seat back bolster in the form of a large "V". Door panels, harmonious in styling and color, feature a lower panel of dark-toned horizontal risers, a center section of light-toned body cloth and an upper section of light-toned painted metal. Upholstery choices include colors of BLUE, GRAY, GREEN or TAN in plain broadcloth, or in smartly patterned nylon, all with bolsters and trim in harmonizing dark-toned broadcloth. A new special glamour trim features a Beige Square-Pattern Nylon with Tangier Tan Leather bolsters and trim. The full luxury of the 60 Special Sedan is further marked by deep nylon loop pile carpeting in rich harmonizing dark-tone shades.

The spacious interior of the 60 Special provides some five feet of shoulder room and hip room in both the front and rear compartments. And there are such convenience features as electrically operated window lifts and front seat adjustment, two assist handles plus a leather covered robe cord on the front seat back, cigarette lighters and ash receivers, front and rear, and electric clock, visor vanity mirror, courtesy, map and glove box lights, and a wide rear-seat center armrest. In every way, the Cadillac 60 Special merits the amazing allegiance of its owners who, year after year, refuse to compromise with lesser cars.

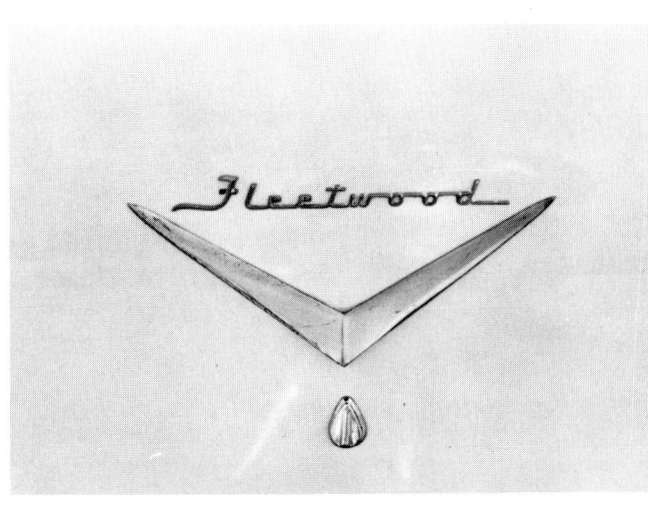

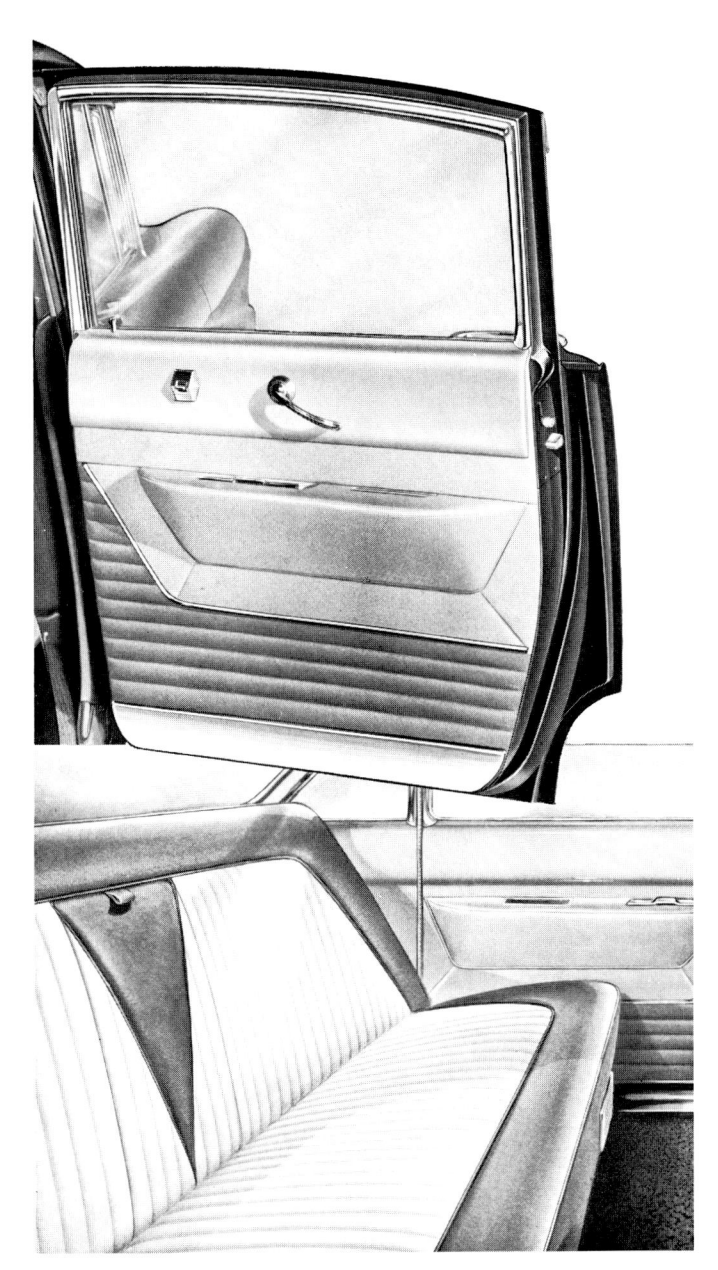

SERIES 60 SPECIAL
COLOR AND UPHOLSTERY CHOICES

70. LIGHT GRAY PATTERN NYLON seat and seat back inserts with DARK GRAY BROADCLOTH bolsters and trim.
71. LIGHT GRAY PLAIN BROADCLOTH seat and seat back inserts with DARK GRAY BROADCLOTH bolsters and trim.
72. LIGHT BLUE PATTERN NYLON seat and seat back inserts with DARK BLUE BROADCLOTH bolsters and trim.
73. LIGHT BLUE PLAIN BROADCLOTH seat and seat back inserts with DARK BLUE BROADCLOTH bolsters and trim.
74. LIGHT TAN PATTERN NYLON seat and seat back inserts with DARK TAN BROADCLOTH bolsters and trim.
75. LIGHT TAN PLAIN BROADCLOTH seat and seat back inserts with DARK TAN BROADCLOTH bolsters and trim.
76. LIGHT GREEN PATTERN NYLON seat and seat back inserts with DARK GREEN BROADCLOTH bolsters and trim.
77. LIGHT GREEN PLAIN BROADCLOTH seat and seat back inserts with DARK GREEN BROADCLOTH bolsters and trim.
81. LIGHT GRAY V-PATTERN METALLIC NYLON seat and seat back inserts with DARK GRAY BROADCLOTH bolsters and trim.
83. LIGHT BLUE V-PATTERN METALLIC NYLON seat and seat back inserts with DARK BLUE BROADCLOTH bolsters and trim.
85. LIGHT TAN V-PATTERN METALLIC NYLON seat and seat back inserts with DARK TAN BROADCLOTH bolsters and trim.
87. LIGHT GREEN V-PATTERN METALLIC NYLON seat and seat back inserts with DARK GREEN BROADCLOTH bolsters and trim.

GLAMOUR LINE TRIM

88. BEIGE SQUARE-PATTERN NYLON seat and seat back inserts with TANGIER TAN LEATHER bolsters and trim.

1955 SERIES 75
8-PASSENGER SEDAN AND LIMOUSINE

250 Horsepower   149.8" Wheelbase   237.1" Over-all Length   Shipping Weight ____ Lbs.

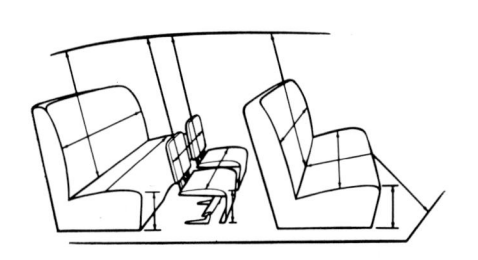

INTERIOR DIMENSIONS

	REAR	AUXILIARY	FRONT
Head room	35.1"	37.2"	36.5"
Shoulder room	58.4"	58.9"	59.3"
Hip room	59.1"	65.6"	64.4"
Leg room	—	—	43.4"
Seat height	14.4"	12.8"	13.8"

STANDARD EQUIPMENT

Air Cleaner, oil-bath type
Armrest, center-rear
Assist Handles (2)
Cadillac Power Steering
Cigarette Lighters, front and rear
Clocks, electric, front and rear compartments
Foot Rests, adjustable (2), rear compartment
Front Seat Adjustment (horizontal), electrically operated
Hydra-Matic Transmission
Lights, Back-up (dual)
Lights, Courtesy and Map (automatic)
Lights, Directional Signal
Light, Glove Box (automatic)
Light, Luggage Compartment (automatic)
Mirror, glare-proof, rear-view, flip-type
Oil Filter
Outside Mirror, left side
Package Compartments in Side Armrests, rear (2)
Paint, two-tone
Parking Brake Warning Signal
Robe Cord on back of front seat
Visor Vanity Mirror
Visors, dual sun
Wheel Discs (set of four)
Window Lifts, electrically operated
Windshield Washer and Coordinator

OPTIONAL EQUIPMENT (EXTRA COST)

Cadillac Air Conditioner
Cadillac Power Brakes
E-Z-Eye Tinted Glass
Fog Lamps (pair)
Heater, with two under-rear-seat units
Headlight Dimmer, automatic
License Frames
Spotlight(s)
Radio, remote control
Whitewall Tires, 8.20 x 15 (set of five)

The Cadillac Series 75 Imperial Limousine is the most luxurious chauffeur-driven car in America. It provides all of the comfort and conveniences of the 8-passenger sedan described on the previous pages, plus the added practicality of a specially leather-upholstered front seat and looped nylon pile floor carpeting in the front compartment. A glass partition, separating the front and rear compartments, may be raised or lowered electrically by automatic control buttons located on the rear seat armrests.

SERIES SEVENTY-FIVE LIMOUSINE COLOR AND UPHOLSTERY CHOICES

Same as for the EIGHT-PASSENGER SEDAN except that the front seat is upholstered as follows:

BLACK LEATHER when GRAY or TAN rear compartment upholstery is selected;
BLUE LEATHER when BLUE rear compartment upholstery is selected.

Impressively big and beautiful, the Cadillac Series 75 eight-passenger sedan is the ideal car for the large family, or for company executive use. Interior of the Series 75 sedan is completely new in 1955. Seat cushions and seat back inserts are designed with three large horizontal pipes. Smart style contrast is provided by a center panel of six narrower pipes, extending from the bolster to the bottom of the seat backs and then forward across the seat cushions. Door panels have a new four-section lower panel. Luxurious, deep-textured Kinkomo carpeting covers the floor in the front and rear compartments, as well as forming the scuff pads along the base of the doors and across the bottom of the rear seat. Six ultra-smart upholstery choices include Bedford cord or fine wool broadcloth in carefully selected two-toned shades of GRAY, TAN or BLUE.

The elegant interior of the 75 Series eight-passenger sedan provides every comfort and convenience. There are, for example, two assist handles on the rear door pillars as well as on each side of the robe cord on the rear of the front seat back; an electric clock, cigarette lighters and ash receivers, front and rear; a wide rear-seat center armrest, two side armrests containing package compartments; an adjustable, carpeted foot rest, and electrically operated window lifts and fore-and-aft front seat adjustment.

Series 75 cars retained the '54-type rear fender trim treatment. The 75s of the 1950s are among the most beautifully scaled automobiles ever built because the long wheelbase chassis allowed uncrowded integration of sheetmetal components and bright metal accents.

SERIES 75 EIGHT-PASSENGER SEDAN COLOR AND UPHOLSTERY CHOICES

20. LIGHT GRAY BEDFORD CORD seat and seat back inserts with DARK GRAY BEDFORD CORD bolsters and trim.
21. LIGHT GRAY BROADCLOTH seat and seat back inserts with DARK GRAY BROADCLOTH bolsters and trim.
22. LIGHT BLUE BEDFORD CORD seat and seat back inserts with DARK BLUE BEDFORD CORD bolsters and trim.
23. LIGHT BLUE BROADCLOTH seat and seat back inserts with DARK BLUE BROADCLOTH bolsters and trim.
24. LIGHT TAN BEDFORD CORD seat and seat back inserts with DARK TAN BEDFORD CORD bolsters and trim.
25. LIGHT TAN BROADCLOTH seat and seat back inserts with DARK TAN BROADCLOTH bolsters and trim.

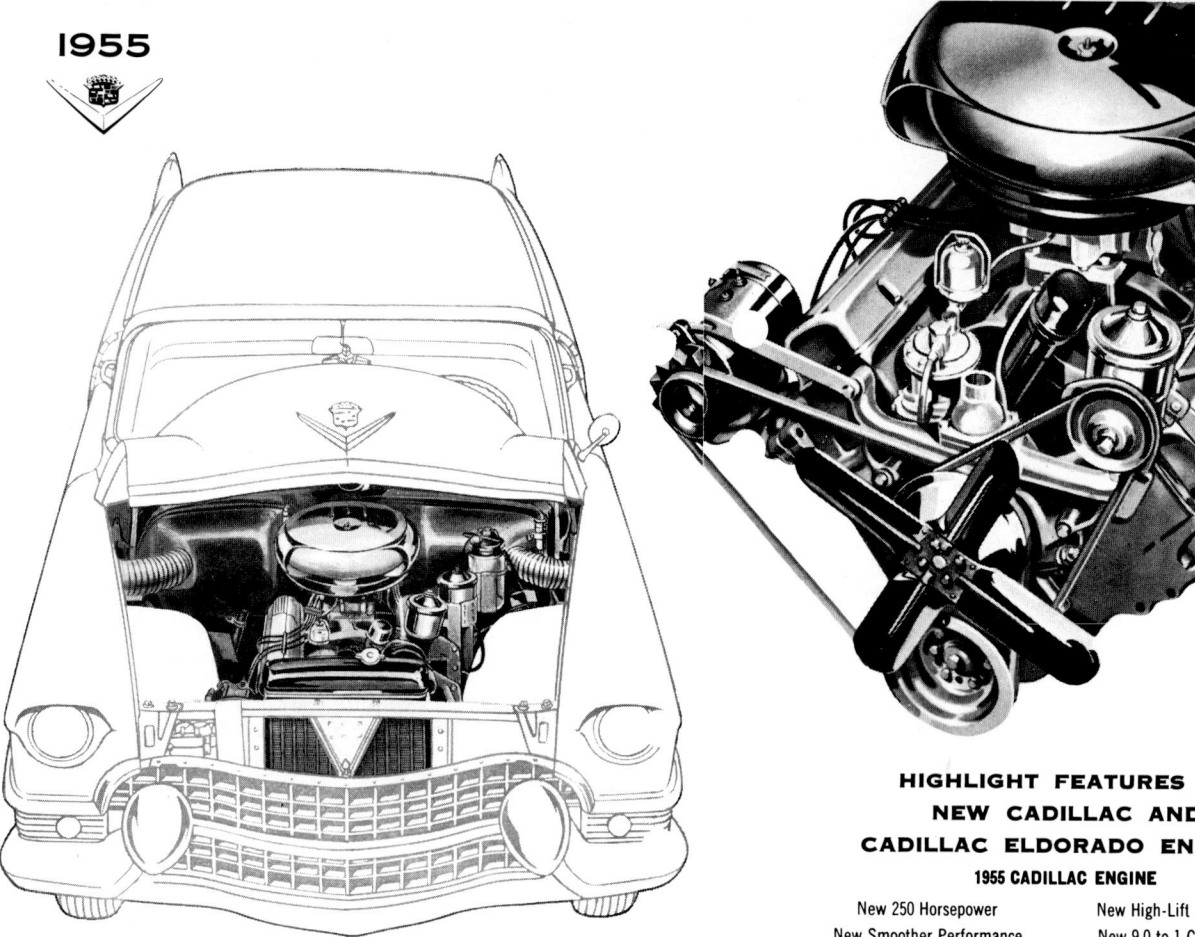

1955

In 1955, a new and brilliant chapter is added to the long and distinguished history of the Cadillac V-8 engine. In fact, Cadillac owners will find even more impressively, in 1955, that the power plant beneath the hood of a Cadillac necessitates no compromise with smaller bodies, lesser weight or the many other sacrifices made by competitors in their efforts to match Cadillac performance. The amazing new 250-horsepower Cadillac and 270-horsepower Eldorado V-8 engines literally leave nothing to be desired. Among their many features are a new combustion chamber, new higher compression ratio, new valve linkage for increased breathing efficiency, improved four-barrel carburetion and, above all, a tremendously increased output of torque or twisting force to drive the rear wheels.

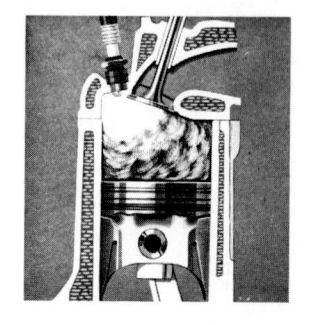

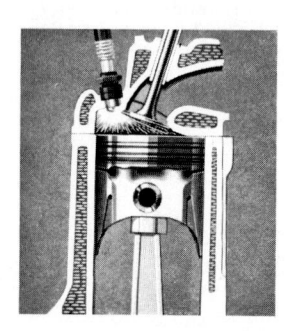

NEW COMBUSTION CHAMBER

The new combustion chamber in the 1955 Cadillac engine is designed to assure progressive and complete burning of each fuel-air charge. As a result, the force created by the expansion of the burning fuel is exerted on the piston head in the form of a smooth, powerful thrust. There is no undue strain or shock to pistons or other engine parts. Cadillac's combustion chamber design, combined with modern, high-octane fuels, permits high-compression power and performance without engine "ping".

HIGHLIGHT FEATURES OF NEW CADILLAC AND CADILLAC ELDORADO ENGINES

1955 CADILLAC ENGINE

- New 250 Horsepower
- New Smoother Performance
- New Higher Torque (345-foot pounds)
- New Quieter Operation
- Advanced 12-volt Ignition System
- New High-Lift Valve Mechanism
- New 9.0 to 1 Compression Ratio
- Cadillac Dual Exhaust System
- New Swifter Acceleration
- New Cadillac Four-Barrel Carburetor

1955 ELDORADO ENGINE

- New 270 Horsepower
- Two New Four-Barrel Carburetors
- New Intake Manifold
- New 350-foot pounds of Torque

NEW 9.0 TO 1 COMPRESSION RATIO

Cadillac's new 9.0 to 1 compression ratio is among the highest in the industry. Because the fuel-air mixture is even more tightly compressed at the moment it is ignited, more energy is obtained from each charge of fuel-air mixture into the cylinders, thus contributing to the increased power and economy of the engine. Use of a chromed top ring on the pistons minimizes wear on cylinder walls, thus assuring full compression for many additional thousands of miles. Piston oil rings are designed to minimize friction on cylinder walls.

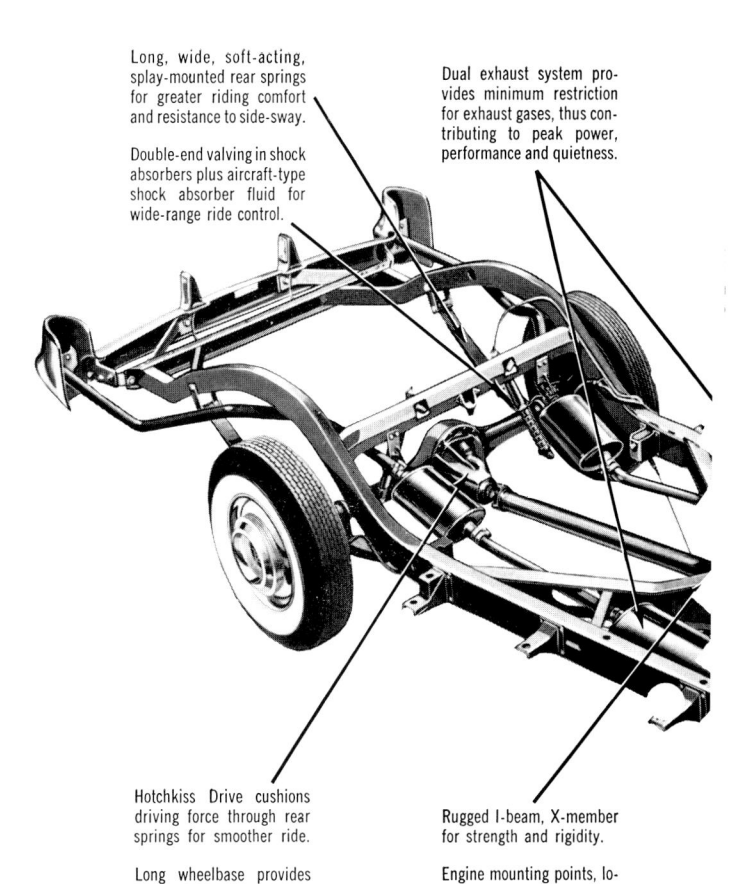

Long, wide, soft-acting, splay-mounted rear springs for greater riding comfort and resistance to side-sway.

Double-end valving in shock absorbers plus aircraft-type shock absorber fluid for wide-range ride control.

Dual exhaust system provides minimum restriction for exhaust gases, thus contributing to peak power, performance and quietness.

New tubeless tires, for greater puncture and blowout protection and for a smoother, safer ride.

Hydra-Matic transmission for completely automatic performance, economy, flexibility, convenience.

Cadillac Power Steering (standard at no extra cost) retains feel of the road while eliminating up to 75% of steering effort required.

Cadillac Power Brakes (an extra cost option) for sure, positive braking with minimum pedal pressure.

Large brake linings with grooved primary lining for smooth, easy brake application and longer lining life.

Hotchkiss Drive cushions driving force through rear springs for smoother ride.

Long wheelbase provides balanced ride, better weight distribution and roomier passenger compartments.

Rugged I-beam, X-member for strength and rigidity.

Engine mounting points, located low on the frame, straighten the drive line, thus minimizing vibration.

Wide front and rear tread for maximum stability and comfort... easier steering.

NEW TUBELESS TIRES

Among the features of the new tubeless tires, now standard equipment on 1955 Cadillac cars, is greater resistance to punctures, blowouts, and impact breaks. Whereas the ordinary tube tends to pull away from a puncturing object, the innerlining of a tubeless tire presses around the object, thus preventing escape of air. Tubeless tires give a smoother, safer ride with up to 400% longer trouble-free tire life.

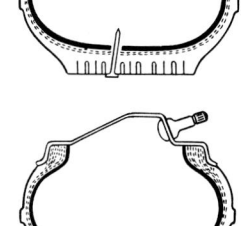

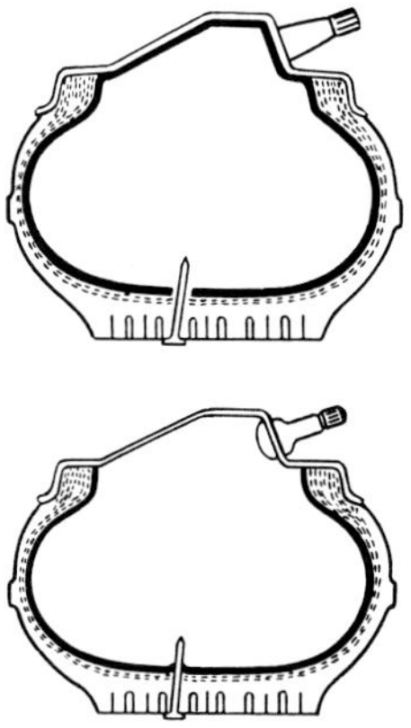

SELF-ENERGIZING BRAKES

Cadillac brakes are of the self-energizing type. In other words, the two brake shoes in each wheel are linked together at one end. As the first shoe is pressed against the revolving brake drum, the drum forces the first shoe to wedge the second shoe against the drum with increased force. Thus braking action is multiplied while the pressure required of the driver's foot on the brake pedal is minimized. The use of large 12" brakes further helps the Cadillac driver to bring the car to a safe, smooth stop with minimum effort.

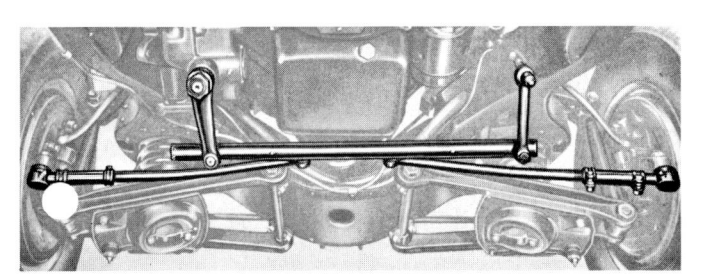

PARALLEL-LINK STEERING

The use of parallel-link steering in all Cadillac cars provides steering stability at all speeds and takes the "fight" out of the roughest roads. Additional features are a short turning radius and truly accurate steering geometry. In conjunction with its precision steering linkage, of course, Cadillac provides the many additional advantages of Cadillac Power Steering as standard equipment at no extra cost.

The benefits of Cadillac Power Steering are explained in detail on the following two pages.

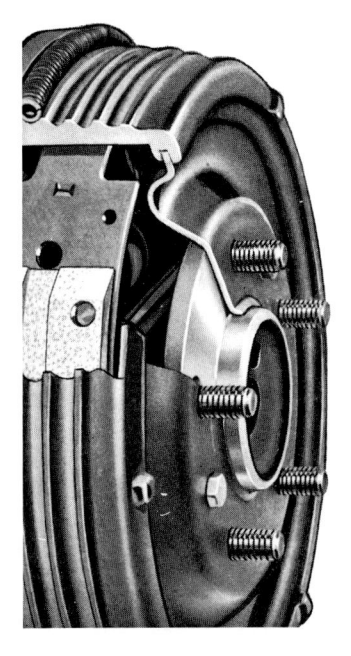

GROOVED BRAKE LINING

In addition to providing a large brake lining area, Cadillac furthers braking efficiency by use of a center groove running the length of the primary lining. This groove, at the point where greatest heat is normally generated when the brakes are applied, provides better cooling for the lining and drum.

1955

ACCESSORY GROUPS
(FACTORY-INSTALLED)

GROUP A $_____
White Sidewall Tires • Heater • Radio • Power Brakes • E-Z-Eye Glass

GROUP B $_____
White Sidewall Tires • Heater • Radio • Power Brakes

GROUP C $_____
Air Conditioner With Ducts—(Not Available on Coupes) • White Sidewall Tires • Heater • Radio • Power Brakes • E-Z-Eye Glass

GROUP N $_____
Air Conditioner Without Ducts—(Not Available on Series 75) • White Sidewall Tires • Heater • Radio • Power Brakes • E-Z-Eye Glass

GROUP 2 $_____
Autronic-Eye • Fog Lamps • Dor-Gards • License Frame (1)

GROUP 3 $_____
Autronic-Eye • Fog Lamps • Dor-Gards • License Frames (2)

GROUP 4 $_____
Fog Lamps • Dor-Gards • License Frame (1)

GROUP 5 $_____
Fog Lamps • Dor-Gards • License Frames (2)

Do not order any group for Eldorado Convertibles, as most of this equipment is standard.

ADDITIONAL CADILLAC ACCESSORIES

Rear-Compartment Radio Control . . . . $_____
Radio Foot-Control Switch . . . . $_____
Cadillac "Cushion Topper" . . . . $_____
Cadillac Twill Seat Covers . . . . $_____
Cadillac Nylon Seat Covers . . . . $_____
Cadillac Plastic Seat Covers . . . . . . $_____
Visor Vanity Mirror . . . . $_____
Cadillac Rubber Mats . . . . $_____
Fleetwood Robes . . . . $_____
Windshield Washer Solvent . . . . $_____
Cadillac Body Polish . . . . $_____
Cadillac Fabric Cleaner . . . . $_____
Cadillac Kar-Kleen . . . . $_____
Cadillac Blue Coral . . . . $_____
Cadillac Chrome Cleaner . . . . $_____
Cadillac Chrome Protector . . . . $_____
Cadillac Cooling System Inhibitor . . . . $_____
Cadillac Cooling System Cleaner . . . . $_____

NEW LICENSE PLATE FRAME

Cadillac License Plate Frames of gold-colored anodized aluminum, with a durable plastic window covering the plate, become an integral part of the car design. They eliminate the unsightliness and dangerous, rough, sharp edges of unframed license plates. Cadillac License Plate Frames are in sizes to fit license plates of any state.

E-Z-EYE TINTED GLASS

Cadillac E-Z-Eye Tinted Glass consists of a layer of gray tinted plastic between two layers of polished plate glass. It is available as an option at extra cost for all window areas in the 1955 Cadillac. E-Z-Eye glass presents all of the safety advantages of regular laminated Safety Plate Glass, but with the additional benefits of reducing glare and helping to keep the interior of the car cooler. The new gray tint does not alter colors of lights and traffic signals. Recommend Cadillac E-Z-Eye glass to your prospects before they place their order for the car.

SIGNAL-SEEKING PRE-SELECTOR RADIO

Cadillac's Signal-Seeking Pre-Selector Radio offers every tuning convenience. Five push buttons can be pre-set for immediate selection of favorite stations while the selector bar, just above the dial, selects the strongest signals in the area. Dual speakers (except in Convertible Coupes) permit the sound to be directed to the front or rear compartments, or balanced throughout the car. Other features include vacuum-powered raising or lowering of the antenna, and selective tone control.

An added feature, optional at slight extra cost, is a radio foot-control switch. It provides extra safety and convenience by permitting the driver to select any station within range without the necessity of taking his eyes off the road, or his hands off the steering wheel. On Series 75 models, remote-control tuning for rear compartment passengers is also available.

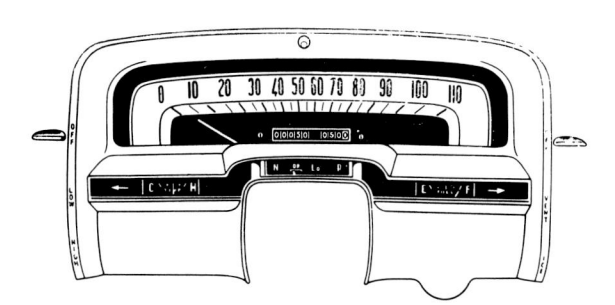

1955

The heater controls consist of two levers, one located on each side of the instrument cluster. The left-hand lever marked "HEATER" turns the heater on and off and also controls the temperature. To obtain heat, the engine is warmed up and this lever pushed down to the "LOW" position. If more heat is desired, the lever is pushed farther down until the desired temperature is obtained. The right-hand lever marked "DEFR" controls ventilating and defrosting air to the windshield. To obtain cool air for ventilation and defogging, the lever is moved down to the "VENT" position. For defrosting, the lever is pushed farther down to obtain air heated to the temperature setting of the "HEATER" lever. For maximum de-icing, *from a cold start*, push the "DEFR" lever all the way down to the "ICE" position while leaving the "HEATER" lever in the "OFF" position until windshield is cleared.

On Series 75 models, two under-seat heaters replace heater outlet grilles on front doors, thus assuring well-heated rear compartments in these larger models.

NEW CADILLAC SABRE-SPOKE WHEELS

New Cadillac Sabre-Spoke wheels, standard on Eldorado, are available as an extra cost option on all other models except the 75 Series. The fleet, low, graceful lines of the car are further enhanced by Sabre-Spoke wheels because they tend to keep the center of eye interest low. A note of practical value is the improved brake cooling with this type of wheel, similar to that obtained with wire wheels offered in 1954, but discontinued this year. The new Sabre-Spoke wheels are constructed of aluminum and steel and provide exceptional resistance to road mud and salt. Cadillac Sabre-Spoke wheels are available in sets of five.

ELECTRICALLY OPERATED VERTICAL FRONT SEAT ADJUSTER

For all Cadillac cars equipped with the electrically powered fore-and-aft seat adjuster, an automatic vertical adjuster is also available. It provides a four-inch range of vertical seat adjustment to accommodate any driver. The same control button is used to adjust the seat either horizontally or vertically.

CADILLAC AUTRONIC-EYE

Added safety and convenience is provided by the Cadillac Autronic-Eye. The headlights of oncoming cars automatically dim the lights of your owner's car. Thus the lights of the Cadillac owner's car avoid blinding other drivers. An overriding switch is provided to signal drivers who neglect to switch their own lights from bright to dim.

NEW FOG LAMPS

Cadillac fog lamps for 1955 are of rectangular design and fit into the grille extensions directly beneath the headlamps. They provide a penetrating beam of light close to the road surface and thus give better visibility than headlights under certain adverse weather conditions.

SPOTLIGHTS

Cadillac owners will enjoy the convenience of spotlights for either or both sides of their car. Motorists who travel a good deal by night find them almost indispensable for reading road signs or house numbers. Cadillac spotlights are smartly styled and are finished in bright chrome.

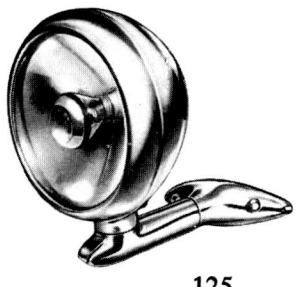

125

1955

CADILLAC HYDRA-MATIC

In the 1955 Cadillac, the famous Cadillac Hydra-Matic transmission has been modified to provide even smoother shifting and faster acceleration, both from a standing start and in the 3rd or "passing" gear. For your more technical-minded prospects, it can be pointed out that this faster acceleration is due to a change from a 1.45 to 1.55 to 1 third-gear ratio, and from a 3.82 to 4.08 to 1 first-gear ratio.

ONLY HYDRA-MATIC OFFERS CHOICE OF TWO DRIVE RANGES

A major advantage offered by Hydra-Matic, and no other automatic transmission, is the choice of two Drive Ranges. This permits the driver to select exactly the performance best suited to city traffic, or mountainous driving or for the open highway.

The first driving position is the one to be manually selected for all normal driving requirements. It provides four forward gear ratios. These are automatically selected for maximum efficiency and performance according to the pressure exerted on the accelerator and the speed of the car.

The second driving position locks out fourth gear up to about 75 miles per hour. This results in better acceleration in traffic and faster "stepdown" acceleration when the accelerator is put to the floor board, because advantage is taken of a lower gear ratio. It is the range best suited for ascending and descending steep grades, because the transmission will not "hunt" between third and fourth going up a hill and more engine braking is provided in going downhill.

The control lever may be moved at will between these two positions when traveling at any car speed. By providing the most efficient transmission ratio for any requirement, Cadillac provides sparkling performance with greater flexibility in traffic than ever before.

POWER BRAKES

Cadillac Power Brakes for 1955 have a new, larger control valve and reduced friction in the linkage. This enables you to offer your prospects greater safety and driving control with even less pedal pressure required. At the same time, the distance the pedal must travel in order to brake the car to a stop has been reduced, which results in faster braking in response to lighter pedal pressures. The height of the brake pedal has been shortened which reduces the time and adds to the convenience with which the driver swings his foot from the accelerator to the brake pedal. Unlike some systems, however, which use a very short pedal, the Cadillac Power Brake System provides sufficient pedal height to allow adequate leverage for operation of the regular hydraulic brake system in the event that the power brake unit should become inoperative. This is an important safety advantage for the Cadillac owner.

A step-down shift from 4th to 3rd gear can be made by depressing the accelerator pedal completely for passing or for extra bursts of speed at car speeds of between 25 and 75 miles per hour. This downshift can also be made by depressing the accelerator pedal about *halfway* at speeds between 15 and 25 miles per hour. A step-down shift from 3rd to 2nd can be made at any car speed below 20 miles per hour by pressing the accelerator pedal all the way down. Thus, valuable emergency acceleration is provided in the 12 to 20 miles per hour speed range.

For extremely steep grades, where speeds below 40 miles per hour are desirable, the gear selector lever can be placed in the Lo position where maximum engine braking is available.

CADILLAC'S LOW REAR AXLE RATIO

Because of the ideal combination of Cadillac's new, more powerful engine coupled with high-performance Hydra-Matic transmission, a lower rear axle ratio can be used than on most competitive cars.

Cadillac's low 3.36 to 1 axle means that the rear wheels make one complete revolution to only three and one-third revolutions of the engine. Slower engine speeds mean quieter engine operation, less fuel and oil consumption and less wear on engine parts. A 3.07 to 1 axle is optional at no extra cost.

CADILLAC AIR CONDITIONER

Cadillac owners can enjoy cool comfort during hottest summer temperatures with a Cadillac Air Conditioner installed on their cars. In addition, the car interior is dust-free, pollen-free and quiet. A new control lever used in 1955 permits selecting and holding the interior to the temperature desired without further adjustment since the compressor disengages from engine automatically when desired temperature is reached (also when Air Conditioner is turned off).

In operation, the Air Conditioner system functions as follows: The compressor draws refrigerant from the evaporator, where incoming air has been cooled, compresses and discharges the refrigerant in gaseous form into the condenser coils where it is changed back into liquid ready for recirculation back to the evaporator. Cooled and filtered air from the evaporator enters the interior through grilles on each side of the package shelf or, on Sedans only, if preferred by customer, through ducts mounted beneath the headlining with two adjustable outlets on each side of the front and rear compartments.

1955 CADILLAC GENERAL SPECIFICATIONS

	SERIES 62 SEDAN	SERIES 62 CONVERTIBLE COUPE	SERIES 62 COUPE DE VILLE	SERIES 62 COUPE	ELDORADO SPECIAL CONVERTIBLE	SERIES 60 FLEETWOOD SPECIAL	SERIES 75 8-PASSENGER SEDAN AND LIMOUSINE
Wheelbase	129"	129"	129"	129"	129"	133"	149 3/4"
Over-all Length	216 5/16"	223 5/16"	223 5/16"	223 5/16"	223 5/16"	227 5/16"	237
Over-all Width	79 13/16"	79 13/16"	79 13/16"	79 13/16"	79 13/16"	79 13/16"	79 13/16"
Over-all Height	62"	60"	59 5/8"	59 5/8"	60 3/16"	62"	63 15/16"
Frame-to-Road Clearance at Center of Wheelbase	6 1/2"	6 1/2"	6 1/2"	6 1/2"	6 1/2"	6 1/2"	7 1/2"
Steering Ratio—Over-all	21.3	21.3	21.3	21.3	21.3	21.3	21.3
Turning Radius	22.9'	22.9'	22.9'	22.9'	22.9'	23.7'	27.0'
Tread—Front	60"	60"	60"	60"	60"	60"	60"
Tread—Rear	63.10"	63.10"	63.10"	63.10"	63.10"	63.10"	63.10"
Tires, Tubeless—Size	8:00 x 15*	8:00 x 15*	8:00 x 15*	8:00 x 15*	8:20 x 15	8:00 x 15*	8:20 x 15
Tires—Ply Rating	4-ply	4-ply	4-ply	4-ply	4-ply	4-ply	6-ply

*8:20 x 15 ... ed in whitewc ... s (Standar ... Special Convertible)

Engine	250-horsepower Cadillac V-8	250-horsepower Cadillac V-8	250-horsepower Cadillac V-8	250-horsepower Cadillac V-8	270-horsepower Cadillac V-8	250-horsepower Cadillac V-8	250-horsepower Cadillac V-8
Compression Ratio	9.0:1	9.0:1	9.0:1	9.0:1	9.0:1	9.0:1	9.0:1
Piston Displacement	331 cu. in.	331 cu. in.	331 cu. in.	331 cu. in.	331 cu. in.	331 cu. in.	331 cu. in.
Valve Arrangement	Overhead	Overhead	Overhead	Overhead	Overhead	Overhead	Overhead
Carburetor	4-Barrel	4-Barrel	4-Barrel	4-Barrel	4-Barrel (Two)	4-Barrel	4-Barrel
Exhaust System	Dual	Dual	Dual	Dual	Dual	Dual	Dual
Transmission	Hydra-Matic	Hydra-Matic	Hydra-Matic	Hydra-Matic	Hydra-Matic	Hydra-Matic	Hydra-Matic
Steering	Hydraulic Power	Hydraulic Power	Hydraulic Power	Hydraulic Power	Hydraulic Power	Hydraulic Power	Hydraulic Power
Frame	I-Beam, X-Member	I-Beam, X-Member	I-Beam, X-Member	I-Beam, X-Member	I-Beam, X-Member	I-Beam, X-Member	I-Beam, X-Member
Springs	Coil front, semi-elliptic-leaf rear	Coil front, semi-elliptic-leaf rear	Coil front, semi-elliptic-leaf rear	Coil front, semi-elliptic-leaf rear	Coil front, semi-elliptic-leaf rear	Coil front, semi-elliptic-leaf rear	Coil front, semi-elliptic-leaf rear
Drive	Hotchkiss	Hotchkiss	Hotchkiss	Hotchkiss	Hotchkiss	Hotchkiss	Hotchkiss
Axle Ratio	3.36:1*	3.36:1*	3.36:1*	3.36:1*	3.36:1*	3.36:1*	3.77:1

*3.07:1 Optional

Right, a lovely 1955 Coupe de Ville at a gathering of Cadillac enthusiasts. One of the added pleasures of collecting Cadillacs is that every car is part of a continuing institution that dates back to the beginning of the automobile industry. And, as America's fourth most popular collector's car (only Ford, Chevrolet and Buick have larger followings) there is wide interest in the marque.

1955 CADILLAC DETAILED SPECIFICATIONS

ENGINE
Number of cylinders	8
Cylinder arrangement	90° V-type
Valve arrangement	Overhead
Bore and stroke	3 13/16" x 3 5/8"
Block and cylinder head material	Cast iron
Piston displacement	331 cu. in.
Taxable horsepower	46.5
Max. brake horsepower	250 @ 4600 r.p.m.
Eldorado engine	270 @ 4800 r.p.m.
Max. engine torque—lbs.-ft.	345 @ 2800 r.p.m.
Eldorado engine	350 @ 3000 r.p.m.
Compression ratio	9.0:1
Engine mounts	Vulcanized rubber
Number of points of suspension	3

PISTONS AND RINGS
Make	Alcoa—Bohn—Stearling
Material	Aluminum alloy
Type	T-slot, cam ground
Weight	20.00 oz.
Clearance	.0009
Number of oil rings per piston	1
Number of comp. rings per piston	2
Top compression ring	Chrome plated

RODS AND PINS
Wristpin length	3.093"
Wristpin material	Steel alloy
Type	Locked in rod
Connecting rod length	6.625"
Material—connecting rod	Forged steel alloy
Weight—connecting rod	23.04 oz.
Crankpin journal diameter	2 1/4"
Lower bearing material	Steel back aluminum
Connecting rod bearing clearance	.0005"-.0021"
Connecting rod bearing end play	.008"-.014" (total two rods)

CRANKSHAFT
Material	Forged alloy steel
Weight	70 pounds
Main bearing thrust	Rear main
Crankshaft end play	.001" to .005"
Main bearing type	Slip-on
Main bearing removable	Yes
Main bearing material	Steel back Durex
Main bearing clearance—rear	.0008" to .0025"
Main bearing journal Diameter x Length:	
Number 1	2.5" x 1"
Number 2	2.5" x 1.0625"
Number 3	2.5" x 1.0625"
Number 4	2.5" x 1.0625"
Number 5	2.5" x 1.875"

CAMSHAFT
Drive	Chain
Camshaft sprocket material	Steel
Timing chain—make	Link Belt
Timing chain—no. of links	46
Timing chain—width	.6875"
Timing chain—pitch	.500"

VALVES
Valve arrangement	Overhead
Intake opens	19° B.T.C. without ramp
Intake closes	70° A.B.C. without ramp
Exhaust opens	60° B.B.C. without ramp
Exhaust closes	30° A.T.C. without ramp

INTAKE
Material	Alloy steel
Over-all length	4.586" to 4.566"
Diameter of head	1.750"
Angle of seat	44°
Lift	.411"

EXHAUST
Material	Alloy steel
Over-all length	4.574" to 4.594"
Diameter of head	1.562"
Angle of seat	44°
Lift	.411"
Hydraulic valve lifters	Yes
Valve inserts	None
Valve seats cooled by	Direct water circulation

LUBRICATION
Type	Full pressure
Oil under pressure to:	
Main bearings	Yes
Connecting rods	Yes
Wristpins	Splash
Camshaft bearings	Yes
Tappets	Yes
Oil pump type	Gear
Normal oil pressure	30 to 35 lbs. @ 30 m.p.h.
Capacity of oil reservoir	Dry, 5 Qts.; Refill, 5 Qts.
Type of oil level gauge	Dip stick
Make of pressure gauge	AC—Tell-Tale Lite
Oil filter	Standard
Type	Partial flow

FUEL
Gasoline tank capacity	20 gallons
Type of fuel feed	Camshaft pump
Carburetor—make	Rochester & Carter
Carburetor—type	Four-barrel down draft*
Manifold heat control	Automatic
Type of air cleaner	Oil bath
Dual tail pipe diameters	2.094" to 2.099"

*Two 4-Barrel Carburetors on Eldorado.

COOLING
Water pump type	Centrifugal—dual outlet
Pressure relief valve	Yes
Choke for recirculation	Yes
Radiator core	Tube and center
Full-length cylinder water jacket	Yes
Water all around cylinders	Yes
Fan belt length	57"
Fan belt width	3/8"
Fan—No. of blades, Series 62 & 60	4
Fan—No. of blades, Series 75	5
Cooling system capacity	18.09 qts.
With heater	20.3 qts. (Series 75, 22.8 qts.)

GENERATOR
Make	Delco-Remy
Minimum charging speed	22 m.p.h. and up
Generator ventilation	Forced air

GENERATOR REGULATOR
Make	Delco-Remy
Voltage at cut-out closing	11.8–13.6 (adjust to 12.8)
Voltage regulator setting	14–15 (adjust to 14.5 at 90°)
Generator maximum charging rate	27–33 amp. (adjust to 30)

STARTING MOTOR
Make	Delco-Remy
Flywheel teeth, integral or ring	Steel integral

IGNITION
Spark advance	Centrifugal and vacuum
Ignition Unit: Make	Delco-Remy
Manual advance	None
Maximum centrifugal advance	Crankshaft (21.5°-25.5°)
Vacuum advance	Crankshaft (26°-29°)
Distributor breaker gap	.016"
Initial spark advance	2 1/2° B.T.C.
Firing order	1-8-4-3-6-5-7-2
Ignition Coil: Make	Delco-Remy
Spark Plugs:	
Make	AC
Model	44.5
Thread	14mm.
Gap	.035"

BATTERY
Make	Delco 3EM60W
Number of plates	9
Capacity (amp. hrs.)	70
Terminal grounded	Negative
Location of battery	Under hood on tray attached to right-hand body bracket front of dash

LIGHTS AND HORN
Headlight—make	Guide sealed-beam
Headlight cover glass, dia.	6 11/16"
Parking light—make	Guide
Taillight—make	Guide
Lighting switch—make	Delco-Remy
How are headlights dimmed?	Depressed beam—foot switch
Horn:	
Make	Delco-Remy
Type	Vibrator, seashell electric

HYDRA-MATIC DRIVE
Type	High efficiency fluid coupling and fully automatic transmission
Gearing	Planetary
No. of forward speeds	*4
No. of forward speeds in "City" DR range	3
No. of forward speeds in "Country" DR range	4
No. of forward speeds in Lo range	2
Transmission ratio, first	4.08:1
Transmission ratio, second	2.63:1
Transmission ratio, third	1.55:1
Transmission ratio, fourth	1:1
Transmission ratio, reverse	4.30:1
Oil capacity	11 qts.
Type of fluid	Hydra-Matic fluid

SHIFT POINTS:

With Rear Axle Ratio of:

Upshift DR- 4 Range	Throttle Opening	3.07:1 M.P.H.	3.36:1 M.P.H.	3.77:1 M.P.H.
1st to 2nd	Minimum	5.5-8.2	5-7.5	4.5-6.7
	Maximum	20-23	18-21	16.3-18.7
2nd to 3rd	Minimum	11.5-16	10.5-14.6	8.6-13
	Maximum	36-41	33-38	30-34
3rd to 4th	Minimum	21-26	19-24	17-21
	Maximum	73-79	67-72	60-64
Downshift DR- 4 Range				
4th to 3rd	Minimum	17.2-20.0	14.5-17.2	12-14
	Maximum	70-75	64-69	57-61
3rd to 2nd	Minimum	8.5-11	8-10.7	7-8.4
	Maximum	21-24	19-22	17-20
2nd to 1st	Minimum	4-6.6	3.6-6	3.3-5.4
	Maximum	8.5-11	7.8-10	7-9
DR- 3 Range Same as DR- 4 except				
Upshifts from 3rd to 4th only at:		73-79	67-72	60-64
Downshifts from 4th to 3rd only at:		70-79	64-72	57-64
LO Range 1st to 2nd Upshift and Downshift same as DR-4				
Upshifts from 2nd to 4th at:		42	39	34
Downshifts from 4th to 2nd at:		41	38	33

Note: Miles per hour at which shift is made is dependent on degree of throttle opening. Actually no gears shift. Term used for clarity of meaning.

FRAME

	SERIES 62	SERIES 60S	SERIES 75
Frame make	A. O. Smith	A. O. Smith	A. O. Smith
Frame depth, maximum	7 5/32"	7 3/16"	7 3/16"
Frame thickness, maximum	9/64"	5/32"	5/32"
Flange width, maximum	2 37/64"	2 19/32"	2 19/32"
Frame—Type	Channel side bars with I-beam X-member	Channel side bars with I-beam X-member	Channel side bars with I-beam X-member
Frame-to-road clearance at center of wheelbase	6 1/2"	6 1/2"	7 1/2"

FRONT END SUSPENSION
Front suspension, make	Own
Front suspension, type	Forked arms
Forked arm bearings, type	Threaded
Kingpin upper bearing, type	Bronze bushing
Kingpin lower bearing, type	Bronze bushing
Front wheel inner bearing, make and type	N. D. ball
Front wheel outer bearing, make and type	N. D. ball
Front spring, type	Helical coil
Front spring, material	Spring steel
Shock absorber, type	Hydraulic direct-acting type
Front stabilizer	Torsion rod

PROPELLER SHAFT
	SERIES 62-60	SERIES 75
Number used	1	2
Type	Exposed	Exposed

UNIVERSAL JOINTS
Make	Mechanics and Saginaw
Number used	2 3
Type	Cross and Trunnion
Bearing	Needle
Universal joints, lubricated	Permanently
Drive and torque taken through	Rear springs

REAR AXLE
	SERIES 62-60	SERIES 75
Rear axle, make	Own	
Rear axle, type	Semi-floating	
Differential gear, make	Own	
Rear axle:		
Oil capacity	5 pints	
Grade recommended: S.A.E. viscosity	90 hypoid	

DETAILED SPECIFICATIONS
CONTINUED

1955

REAR AXLE—CONTINUED	SERIES 62-60	SERIES 75
Type of final gearing	Hypoid	
Gear ratio:		
Standard	3.36:1	3.77:1
Optional	3.07:1	
Pinion adjustment (except 75)	None	
Pinion bearing adjustment	None (Preloaded)	
Are pinion bearings in sleeve?	No	
Backlash between pinion and ring gear	.003"-.010"	
Rear axle pinion shaft:		
Front bearing, type	Tapered roller	
Rear bearing, type	Tapered roller	

TIRES AND WHEELS
Tires:		
Make	U. S. Royal, Firestone and Goodrich	
Type	Tubeless	
Size	8.00 x 15*	8.20 x 15
Ply rating	4	6
Inflation pressure:		
Front	24 lbs.	28 lbs.
Rear	24 lbs.	28 lbs.

*8.20 x 15 when Whitewalls are ordered. Std. on Eldorado.

Wheels:		
Type	Slotted disc**	
Make	Kelsey-Hayes	
Rim, diameter	15"	15"
Rim, width	6.00"	6.00"
Tread:		
Front	60"	60"
Rear	63.10"	63.10"

**Aluminum spoke, steel rim wheels on Eldorado.

SPRINGS (REAR)	SERIES 62-60	SERIES 75
Rear Springs:		
Type	Semi-elliptic	
Material	Spring steel	
Length	56½"	
Width	2½"	
No. of leaves	5	6
Spring leaves lubricated with	Wax impregnated liners	
Spring bushings, type	Rubber	
Stabilizers	Rear—None	

SHOCK ABSORBERS (REAR)
Type	Direct Acting, Hydraulic

STEERING
Steering	Hydraulic power
Type	Bevel gear in rack
Make	Saginaw
Over-all steering ratio	21.3:1
Car turning radius (outside) bumper to bumper sweep	(62) 22.9' (75) 27.0' (60) 23.7'

BRAKES
Front and Rear		
Brake drum diameter	12"	12"
Brake drum, internal or external	Internal	Internal
Brake lining, length per wheel:		
Forward shoe	11.15"	11.15"
Reverse shoe	12.23"	12.23"
Total	23.38"	23.38"

BRAKES—CONTINUED	SERIES 62-60	SERIES 75
Brake lining width	2½"	2½"
Brake lining thickness	¼"	¼"
Brake lining effective area	211.55 sq. in.	
Brake clearance	.010" bottom; .015" top	
Hand brake location	Left side of dash	
Hand brake lever operates on	Rear service brakes	
Power brakes	Optional	

MISCELLANEOUS SPECIFICATIONS
Car lifting device, jack	Bumper type
Engine lubrication, type	Pressure
Chassis lubrication, type	High pressure
Axle lubrication, type	Splash

LUBRICANTS
Engine oil	5 qts.
Recommended viscosity	Min. anticipated temperature: +32°F. 20W or S.A.E. 20; +10°F. 20W; −10°F. 10W; Below −10°F. 5W
Drain	2000 miles (after initial 500-mile change)
Rear axle oil	5 pints
Recommended viscosity	90 hypoid
Auto trans. fluid type "A"	12 qts. dry
Gasoline	20 gals.

Above, the most talked about 1955 model was the plush 270 hp *Eldorado*. This distinctive convertible with exclusive interiors, sabre spoke wheels, fiber glass boot and newly styled fins was a preview of the exciting creations Cadillac was preparing for the future. MOTOR TREND tested one early in the year and concluded: *it might well be the "hottest-performing car" of 1955 – definitely as roadable as the best of the '55 crop.*

1956 styling features

The dignity and grace...the infinite attention to details which have long keynoted Cadillac styling were never more evident than in the brilliant 1956 Cadillac cars.

From the front...from the side...and from the rear there is exciting evidence that Cadillac is the Standard of the World in automotive styling as it is in engineering and mechanical excellence.

There is, for example, an impression of even greater strength and dignity in the new, more-massive front end ensemble and in the classic simplicity of the new rear bumper and exhaust outlet extensions.

And from the side, new lines of fleetness and grace are apparent in the slip-stream styling of the rear fenders, in the simulated air-scoop moldings and the new belt molding extending beneath the door windows.

New, deeply contoured wheel covers with radiating spokes add sparkling highlights of beauty.

From any view, the 1956 Cadillac looks longer, wider and lower than any previous car in Cadillac history. Point out to your prospects all of the new styling features of the 1956 Cadillac and you'll prove beyond contention that, in 1956, Cadillac again has set the pace in automotive styling elegance for the entire industry.

The illustration, above, shows several features typical of Cadillac's ability to combine pleasing style with the utmost in practical considerations for the comfort and convenience of the driver and passengers. There is, of course, the now widely imitated Panoramic windshield with its contributions to safe driver visibility. There is the smart overhanging roof visor on sedan models which prevents the accumulation of ice or snow on that portion of the windshield farthest from the defrosters. Finally, there is the newly designed, cowl air intake grid which assures safer, cleaner air than when air inlets are located behind the grille where exhaust fumes and dirt can enter more easily. A series of baffles traps rain water and permits it to drain through a tube to the ground.

Adding a gracious new style note is the gold-finish Cadillac script name plate on the grille.

Ribbed headlamp reflector shield adds new style note while enhancing the apparent width of front fenders.

In 1956, the magic of Cadillac styling genius has achieved a front end appearance of even more impressive strength, dignity and grace. Greater unity of design has been achieved through the use of smaller grille openings and by locating the parking lights at the extreme outside of the massive lower bumper bar just below the bumper guards. Other details of the new front end ensemble which serve to enhance the lower, wider look of the car itself are the flatter hood and fender contours, horizontal ribs in the headlamp reflector shields, wider spacing of the bumper guards, a new, wider, more-tapered V, wider crest and new hood ornament.

Newly available is a smart gold-finish grille optional at no extra cost on the Eldorados and at slight extra cost on all other models.

Graceful bullet-shaped bumper guards with gull wing extensions offer maximum protection where needed.

Newly located parking and fog lamp (optional at extra cost) location enhances low, wide look of car.

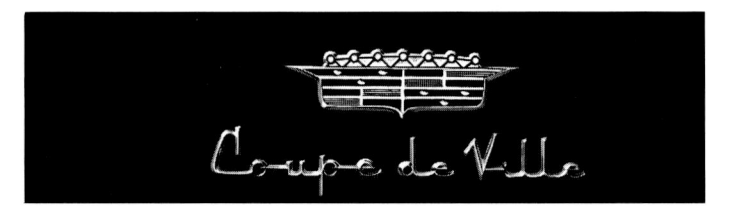

Cadillac crest and gold-finish name plate on the front fenders lend distinction and model identification to the Coupe de Ville, Sedan de Ville, Eldorados and 60 Special. Crest alone is used on the Series 62 Sedan, Coupe and Convertible and Series 75 models.

The 1956 Cadillac offers a longer, lower, smarter appearance than ever before in Cadillac history. Note particularly how the combination of the front fender molding and the new, slip-stream rear fender styling lend an air of motion even when the car is standing still. New horizontal ribs on the simulated air scoop molding enhance this impression still further. A new body belt molding extends along the sides of the car just beneath the door windows. On two-tone models, the top color is carried along the sides of the car between the belt molding and the windows.

Every detail of the rear end design accentuates the low, wide, road-hugging look of the 1956 Cadillac. Note here the clean, strong lines of the bumper, the low placement of the license plate mounting and the horizontal openings for the exhaust outlets. New deck ornamentation features a wider, more-tapered V and the name Cadillac, Eldorado or Fleetwood in gold-finish block letters.

The vertical windshield pillar posts on all Cadillac models eliminate the blind spot associated with old-style slanted pillars and permit use of smart rectangular ventwings. And, for safety and comfort, Cadillac provides overhanging door reveal moldings which permit leaving the windows slightly open for ventilation and to prevent window fogging, yet without permitting the entrance of rain or snow. Of special interest is the new outside rear-view mirror which is adjustable from inside the car, a particular convenience in adverse weather.

Certain to be copied by others is Cadillac's new, slip-stream, rear fender styling shown above as it appears on the Series 62 and below as it appears on the 60 Special. The distinguishing feature is the tubular contour tapering gracefully from near the forward edge of the rear fender and extending back to join the exhaust outlet extensions. On this raised fairing are chromed vertical ribs on the Series 62, while the entire fairing is covered with a ribbed chrome molding on the 60 Special Sedan. An additional new style note is the chromed molding outlining the top of the rear fender and the taillight.

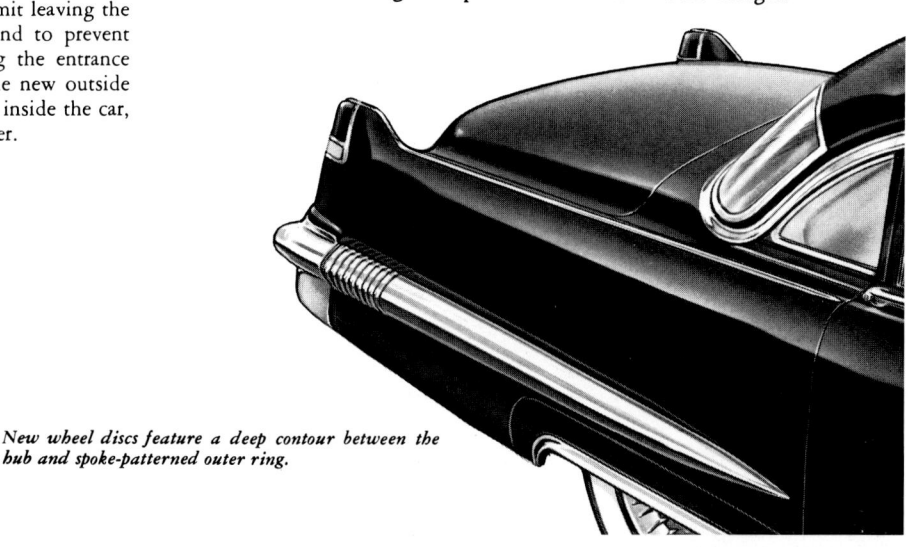

New wheel discs feature a deep contour between the hub and spoke-patterned outer ring.

1956

NEW MODELS
Series 62 Sedan de Ville (4-door hardtop)
Eldorado Seville (2-door, special hardtop)

NEW STYLING
New grille
New Cadillac script name plate on grille
New front bumper
New front bumper guards
New flatter hood contour
New hood "V" and crest
New flatter, wider fender contour
New ribbed headlamp reflector shield
New parking lights
New fog lamps
New hood ornaments
New cowl air-intake grille
New front fender name plate and/or crest
New wheel covers
New rear wheel opening moldings
New belt molding
Extension of top color between windows and belt molding
New slip-stream rear fender style
New rear fender top molding
New rear fender simulated air-scoop molding
New rear fender side molding
New rear deck "V"
New rear deck block letter name plate
New rear bumper
New license plate light
New exhaust outlet extensions
New rocker sill molding

NEW INTERIORS
New instrument panel styling
New instrument cluster
New control knobs and escutcheons
New centrally located glove compartment
Two new lighted front compartment ash receivers
Two new front compartment cigarette lighters
New remote control for outside rear-view mirror
New trim styles
New upholstery patterns and fabrics
Newly located electric window lift controls
New soft trim for upper door and sidewall panels
New flatter front compartment floor on driver's side
New three-spoke steering wheel
New horn ring
New turn signal lever
New hand brake handle
New Hydra-Matic quadrant
New wider accelerator pedal
New wider Power Brake pedal
New mechanically retained door seals

NEW CHASSIS FEATURES
New controlled-coupling Hydra-Matic
New Power Brake system
Improved Cadillac Power Steering
New 19.5 to 1 over-all steering ratio
New shock absorber valving
New standard 3.07 to 1 rear axle ratio
New stronger rear axle shaft
Newly located fuel intake in fuel tank
New five-inch longer mufflers

NEW ENGINE FEATURES
New 285-horsepower engine
New 305-horsepower Eldorado engine
New 400-foot pounds torque
New 9.75 to 1 compression ratio
Improved Cadillac Four-barrel Carburetor
New larger cylinder bore
New larger exhaust valve ports
New higher-lift valve linkage
New high-lift camshaft
New hydraulic valve lifters
New larger main bearing journals
New sturdier main bearing caps
New higher-torque starting motor
New sealed generator regulator
New distributor
New radiator fan
New 11-plate battery

NEW OPTIONAL EQUIPMENT FEATURES
New six-way front seat adjustment
New manual tuner on radio
New electrically operated radio antenna
New remote-controlled trunk opening lock
New gold-finish radiator grille
New gold-finish Sabre-Spoke wheels

Series 62 Sedan

285 Horsepower
129" Wheelbase
214.9" Over-all Length

1956

STANDARD EQUIPMENT

- Air Cleaner, oil-bath type
- Armrest, center-rear
- Cadillac Power Brakes
- Cadillac Power Steering
- Cigarette Lighters, front (two)
- Cigarette Lighter, rear
- Clock, electric
- Hydra-Matic Transmission
- Lights, front ash receivers
- Lights, Back-up (dual)
- Light, Courtesy or Map (automatic)
- Lights, Directional Signal
- Light, Glove Box (automatic)
- Light, Luggage Compartment (automatic)
- Mirror, glare-proof, rear-view, flip type
- Oil Filter
- Outside Mirror, left-side, remote-control
- Paint, two-tone
- Parking Brake Warning Signal
- Robe Cord on back of front seat
- Visor Vanity Mirror
- Visors, dual sun
- Wheel Discs (set of four)
- Windshield Washer and Coordinator

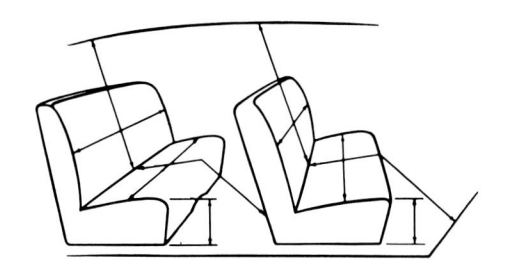

OPTIONAL EQUIPMENT (Extra Cost)

- Cadillac Air Conditioner
- E-Z-Eye Tinted Glass
- Fog Lamps (pair)
- Front Seat Adjustment (6-way) electrically operated
- Headlight Dimmer, automatic
- Heater
- License Frames
- Radiator Grille, gold-finish
- Radio
- Remote-control Trunk Lid Lock
- Sabre-Spoke Wheels (set of five), in aluminum or gold finish
- Spotlight(s)
- Window Lifts, electrically operated
- Whitewall Tires, 8.20 x 15 (set of five)

INTERIOR DIMENSIONS

	REAR	FRONT
Head room	35.1"	35.8"
Shoulder room	59.4"	59.5"
Hip room	65.2"	64.3"
Leg room	46.3"	43.3"
Seat height	12.8"	13.8"

62 Sedan Rear Compartment

Opposite page below, a 1956 Series 62 Sedan. Starting in 1956 Cadillac began to use elaborate indoor settings for backgrounds in promotional photographs. Throughout the balance of this volume a number of these have been inserted.

The glamorous new interiors of the 1956 Cadillac cars are marked by features of beauty, convenience and comfort which bespeak in every way the traditional luxury to be expected of the Standard of the World. There is new elegance, for example, and increased opportunity for individual owner expression in the wide range of upholstery and trim options. Here are glamorous, newly patterned nylon fabrics, many combined with gleaming Lurex thread; rich, all-wool gabardines in solid colors; plain, all-wool broadcloth; smart Bedford cord; and genuine leathers in natural and English grain. New appeal to the eye and to the touch is provided by the addition of a smart, leather-grained Elascofab covering on the upper panels of the doors and side walls. The use of bright and brushed chrome hardware adds highlights of gleaming beauty throughout the interior.

Owners are sure to appreciate the new convenience features of the 1956 Cadillac. In the front compartment, alone, for example, is the new centrally located glove compartment, a new, more conveniently located electric clock, two cigarette lighters, two lighted ash receivers, a new wider rear-view mirror, a new wider Power Brake pedal located for quick application by either foot, and new instrument cluster control knobs labeled for instant identification. Electric window controls are now located well forward and lower on the door panel for easier left-hand operation by the driver. Removal of the floor hump below the accelerator pedal prevents catching of high heels and improves floor appearance. In every way, the interiors of the 1956 Cadillac have been designed to further the affection felt by repeat Cadillac owners and to further the desire for Cadillac ownership by your first-time prospects.

1956 Series 62 Coupe

285 Horsepower
129" Wheelbase
221.9" Over-all Length

STANDARD EQUIPMENT

- Air Cleaner, oil-bath type
- Armrest, center-rear
- Cadillac Power Brakes
- Cadillac Power Steering
- Cigarette Lighters, front (two)
- Clock, electric
- Hydra-Matic Transmission
- Lights, front ash receivers
- Lights, Back-up (dual)
- Light, Courtesy or Map (automatic)
- Lights, Directional Signal
- Light, Glove Box (automatic)
- Light, Luggage Compartment (automatic)
- Mirror, glare-proof, rear-view, flip type
- Oil Filter
- Outside Mirror, left-side, remote-control
- Paint, two-tone
- Parking Brake Warning Signal
- Robe Cords on back of front seat
- Visor Vanity Mirror
- Visors, dual sun
- Wheel Discs (set of four)
- Windshield Washer and Coordinator

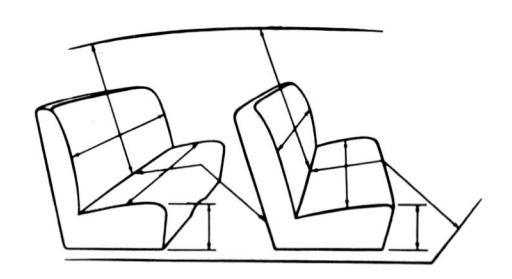

OPTIONAL EQUIPMENT (Extra Cost)

- Cadillac Air Conditioner
- E-Z-Eye Tinted Glass
- Fog Lamps (pair)
- Front Seat Adjustment (6-way) electrically operated
- Headlight Dimmer, automatic
- Heater
- License Frames
- Radiator Grille, gold-finish
- Radio
- Remote-control Trunk Lid Lock
- Sabre-Spoke Wheels (set of five), in aluminum or gold finish
- Spotlight(s)
- Window Lifts, electrically operated
- Whitewall Tires, 8.20 x 15 (set of five)

INTERIOR DIMENSIONS

	REAR	FRONT
Head room	34.3"	34.1"
Shoulder room	59.4"	59.2"
Hip room	56.4"	63.9"
Leg room	42.2"	42.8"
Seat height	12.5"	13.2"

As beautiful as it is functional, the new Cadillac instrument panel combines jewel-like appearance with the utmost convenience in the placement and design of controls and instruments. Note, in particular, the more central location of the glove compartment and the electric clock. Lending positive model-year identification are the words "nineteen fifty-six" in gleaming gold-finish script across the instrument panel grille on the right-hand side.

Interiors of the Cadillac Series 62 Sedan and Coupe are carefully tailored in smart two-tone combinations. There are four choices of Heather pattern nylon in light shades of Blue, Green, Gray or Beige combined with matching bolsters of all-wool gabardine, and three choices of gleaming, Lurex-threaded, Frost pattern nylon in shades of Light Gray, Green, or Blue with beautiful and durable White Elascofab bolsters. The entire seat cushions and seat backs are styled with heavily tufted biscuits and deeply recessed buttons on models where the Elascofab bolsters are selected. On models with all cloth trim, the upper half of the seat back has a smooth surfaced gabardine bolster. Furthering the smart appearance and lasting beauty of the Series 62 Sedan and Coupe interiors is the use of durable Elascofab at points of wear or stress such as on seat scuff pads, upper door and side wall panels and as seat welts. Floors are carpeted with thick, dark-toned nylon frieze.

62 Coupe Rear Compartment

62 Coupe Front Compartment

SERIES 62 SEDAN AND COUPE COLOR AND FABRIC CHOICES

30. LIGHT GRAY HEATHER PATTERN NYLON with LIGHT GRAY GABARDINE bolsters and trim.
31. LIGHT GRAY FROST PATTERN METALLIC NYLON with WHITE ELASCOFAB bolsters and trim.
32. LIGHT BLUE HEATHER PATTERN NYLON with LIGHT BLUE GABARDINE bolsters and trim.
33. LIGHT BLUE FROST PATTERN METALLIC NYLON with WHITE ELASCOFAB bolsters and trim.
34. BEIGE HEATHER PATTERN NYLON with BEIGE GABARDINE bolsters and trim.
36. LIGHT GREEN HEATHER PATTERN NYLON with LIGHT GREEN GABARDINE bolsters and trim.
37. LIGHT GREEN FROST PATTERN METALLIC NYLON with WHITE ELASCOFAB bolsters and trim.

1956 Series 62 Convertible Coupe

285 Horsepower
129" Wheelbase
221.9" Over-all Length

STANDARD EQUIPMENT

Air Cleaner, oil-bath type
Cadillac Power Brakes
Cadillac Power Steering
Cigarette Lighters, front (two)
Cigarette Lighters, rear (two)
Clock, electric
Front Seat Adjustment (horizontal), electrically operated
Hydra-Matic Transmission
Lights, front ash receivers
Lights, Back-up (dual)
Light, Courtesy or Map (automatic)
Lights, Directional Signal
Light, Glove Box (automatic)
Light, Luggage Compartment (automatic)
Mirror, glare-proof, rear-view, flip type
Oil Filter
Outside Mirror, left-side, remote-control
Parking Brake Warning Signal
Robe Cords on back of front seat
Visor Vanity Mirror
Visors, dual sun
Wheel Discs (set of four)
Window Lifts, electrically operated
Windshield Washer and Coordinator

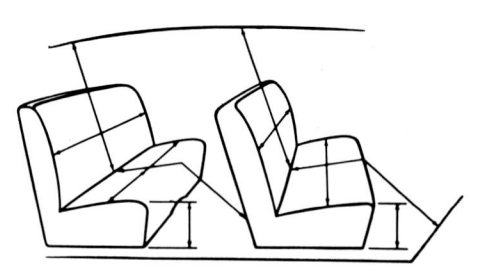

OPTIONAL EQUIPMENT (Extra Cost)

Cadillac Air Conditioner
E-Z-Eye Tinted Glass
Fog Lamps (pair)
Front Seat Adjustment (vertical and angle), electrically operated
Headlight Dimmer, automatic
Heater
License Frames
Radiator Grille, gold-finish
Radio
Remote-control Trunk Lid Lock
Sabre-Spoke Wheels (set of five), in aluminum or gold finish
Spotlight(s)
Whitewall Tires, 8.20 x 15 (set of five)

INTERIOR DIMENSIONS

	REAR	FRONT
Head room	34.2"	34.9"
Shoulder room	49.6"	59.2"
Hip room	52.9"	63.9"
Leg room	40.8"	42.6"
Seat height	12.5"	13.2"

The thrill of open-air motoring is truly reflected in the gay, colorful, durable interiors of the beautiful Cadillac Series 62 Convertible. Its new interior styling, for 1956, is immediately evident in the door panel, shown above. The upper section is covered with beautiful and durable Elascofab, relieved by a forward curving panel of light-tone painted metal, and by a satin-black and chromed-grid insert. The center area of the door panel, including the armrest, forms a massive "V" in dark-toned genuine leather. Smart, vertical pleats mark the Elascofab-covered lower section of the door panel. Kick pad combines the beauty and protection of a bright chrome molding against a dark-toned Elascofab background.

The beauty of the rich-looking, genuine leather upholstery in the Series 62 Convertible finds new lustre through the years. Completely restyled for 1956, the seat cushions and lower portion of the seat backs are fashioned of smart 2½" pipes. The upper half of the seat back is styled with a smooth-finish leather bolster inset with a rectangular design formed by exposed stitching. A final touch of beauty is added by a bright chrome molding extending around the ends of the seat cushion and up the sides and across the top of the front seat backs. Carpeting is beautiful and durable nylon frieze.

SERIES 62 CONVERTIBLE COLOR AND UPHOLSTERY CHOICES

- **20.** BLACK LEATHER seat and seat back inserts with WHITE LEATHER bolsters and trim.
- **21.** SOLID BLACK LEATHER throughout.
- **22.** LIGHT BLUE LEATHER seat and seat back inserts with WHITE LEATHER bolsters and trim.
- **23.** BLACK LEATHER seat and seat back inserts with AQUAMARINE LEATHER bolsters and trim.
- **25.** SOLID BEIGE LEATHER throughout.
- **26.** LIGHT GREEN LEATHER seat and seat back inserts with WHITE LEATHER bolsters and trim.
- **28.** RED LEATHER seat and seat back inserts with WHITE LEATHER bolsters and trim.
- **29.** SOLID RED LEATHER throughout.

VICODEC TOP COLORS: 1. White 2. Black 3. Light Blue 4. Beige 5. Light Green

1956 Series 62 Coupe de Ville

285 Horsepower
129" Wheelbase
221.9" Over-all Length

STANDARD EQUIPMENT

Air Cleaner, oil-bath type
Armrest, center-rear
Cadillac Power Brakes
Cadillac Power Steering
Cigarette Lighters, front (two)
Cigarette Lighters, rear (two)
Clock, electric
Front Seat Adjustment (horizontal), electrically operated
Hydra-Matic Transmission
Lights, front ash receivers
Lights, Back-up (dual)
Light, Courtesy or Map (automatic)
Lights, Directional Signal
Light, Glove Box (automatic)
Light, Luggage Compartment (automatic)
Mirror, glare-proof, rear-view, flip type
Oil Filter
Outside Mirror, left-side, remote-control
Paint, two-tone
Parking Brake Warning Signal
Robe Cords on back of front seat
Visor Vanity Mirror
Visors, dual sun
Wheel Discs (set of four)
Window Lifts, electrically operated
Windshield Washer and Coordinator

OPTIONAL EQUIPMENT (Extra Cost)

Cadillac Air Conditioner
E-Z-Eye Tinted Glass
Fog Lamps (pair)
Front Seat Adjustment (vertical and angle), electrically operated
Headlight Dimmer, automatic
Heater
License Frames
Radiator Grille, gold-finish
Radio
Remote-control Trunk Lid Lock
Sabre-Spoke Wheels (set of five), in aluminum or gold finish
Spotlight(s)
Whitewall Tires, 8.20 x 15 (set of five)

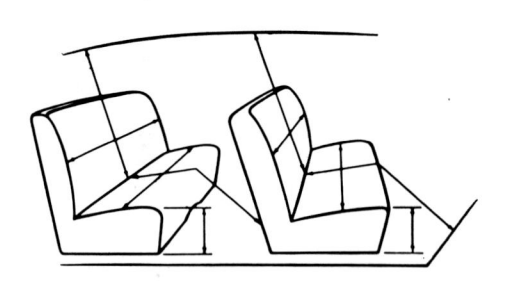

INTERIOR DIMENSIONS

	REAR	FRONT
Head room	34.3"	34.4"
Shoulder room	59.4"	59.2"
Hip room	56.4"	63.9"
Leg room	42.2"	42.8"
Seat height	12.5"	13.2"

The glamorous beauty of the Cadillac Coupe de Ville was never more evident than in the enchanting décor of its 1956 interiors. Door panel styling, for example, features smart vertical piping culminating in a massive "V" midway up the door. The area above the "V", up to and including the armrest, is covered in genuine leather in dark tones. Durable, leather-grained Elascofab and a satin-black and chromed-grid insert enhance the beauty of the upper door panel.

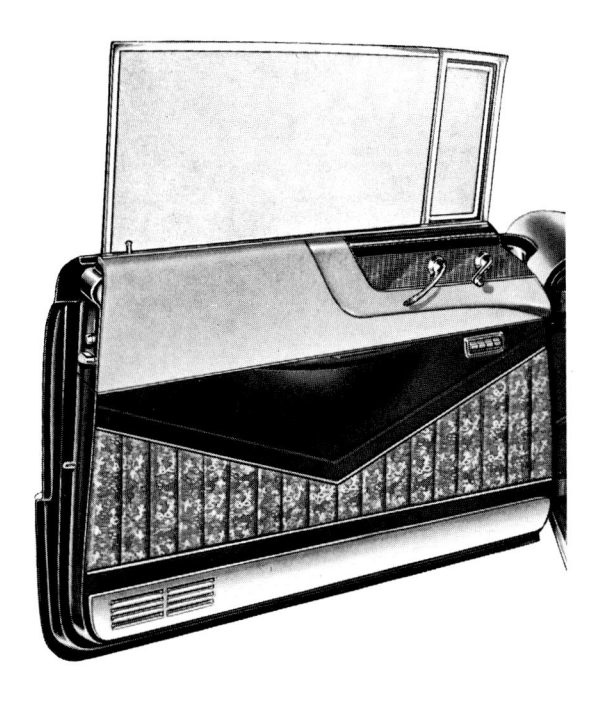

The upholstery, trim and appointments of the Coupe de Ville for 1956 present a truly breath-taking appearance. The glamorous array of fabrics and colors listed on the opposite page are designed to please the most discriminating of tastes. There is lustrous, black nylon, Stardust patterned with tiny colored stars or the bolder, Bombay pattern, metallic nylon with gleaming Lurex threads. Seat cushions and the lower half of the seat backs are newly fashioned in smart 2½" pipes. The leather-covered upper half of the seat back is designed with a rectangular pattern formed by smart, raised stitching. Lavish use of chrome for roof bows across the perforated headlining, for framing the seats and seat backs and for all other hardware and moldings, completes the air of modern elegance that marks the Cadillac Coupe de Ville. Carpeting is rich nylon frieze in dark tones.

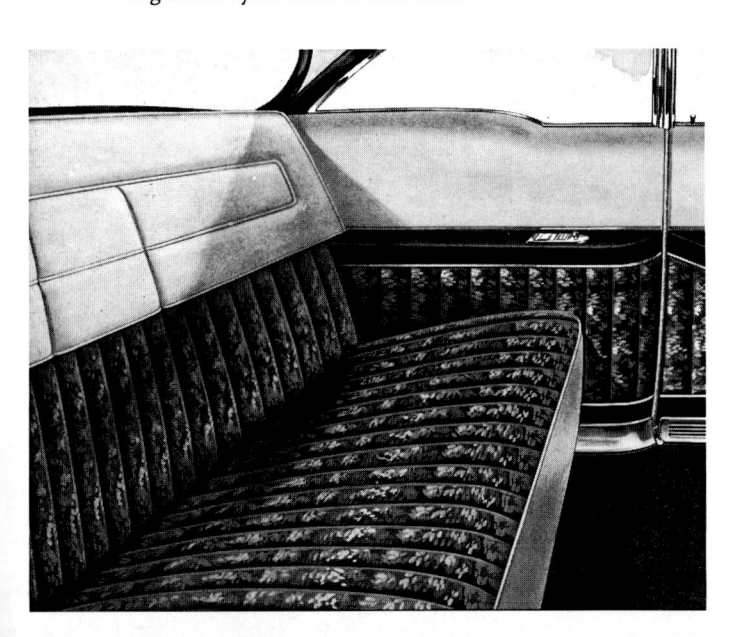

SERIES 62 COUPE de VILLE COLOR AND FABRIC CHOICES

40. GRAY BOMBAY PATTERN METALLIC NYLON with WHITE LEATHER bolsters and trim.
41. STARDUST PATTERN* NYLON with WHITE LEATHER bolsters and trim.
42. LIGHT BLUE BOMBAY PATTERN METALLIC NYLON with LIGHT BLUE LEATHER bolsters and trim.
43. STARDUST PATTERN* NYLON with LIGHT BLUE LEATHER bolsters and trim.
44. GOLD BOMBAY PATTERN METALLIC NYLON with WHITE LEATHER bolsters and trim.
45. STARDUST PATTERN* NYLON with YELLOW LEATHER bolsters and trim.
46. LIGHT GREEN BOMBAY PATTERN METALLIC NYLON with LIGHT GREEN LEATHER bolsters and trim.
47. STARDUST PATTERN** NYLON with LIGHT GREEN LEATHER bolsters and trim.
48. RED BOMBAY PATTERN METALLIC NYLON with WHITE LEATHER bolsters and trim.
49. STARDUST PATTERN** NYLON with MOUNTAIN LAUREL LEATHER bolsters and trim.

*White, Blue and Yellow stars against Black background.
**White, Green and Pink stars against Black background.

1956 Series 62 Sedan de Ville

285 Horsepower
129" Wheelbase
221.9" Over-all Length

STANDARD EQUIPMENT

Air Cleaner, oil-bath type
Armrest, center-rear
Cadillac Power Brakes
Cadillac Power Steering
Cigarette Lighters, front (two)
Cigarette Lighters, rear (two)
Clock, electric
Front Seat Adjustment (horizontal), electrically operated
Hydra-Matic Transmission
Lights, front ash receivers
Lights, Back-up (dual)
Light, Courtesy or Map (automatic)
Lights, Directional Signal
Light, Glove Box (automatic)
Light, Luggage Compartment (automatic)
Mirror, glare-proof, rear-view, flip type
Oil Filter
Outside Mirror, left-side, remote-control
Paint, two-tone
Parking Brake Warning Signal
Robe Cord on back of front seat
Visor Vanity Mirror
Visors, dual sun
Wheel Discs (set of four)
Window Lifts, electrically operated
Windshield Washer and Coordinator

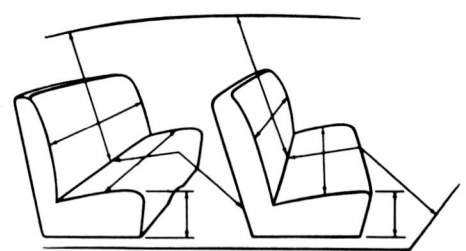

OPTIONAL EQUIPMENT (Extra Cost)

Cadillac Air Conditioner
E-Z-Eye Tinted Glass
Fog Lamps (pair)
Front Seat Adjustment (vertical and angle), electrically operated
Headlight Dimmer, automatic
Heater
License Frames
Radiator Grille, gold-finish
Radio
Remote-control Trunk Lid Lock
Sabre-Spoke Wheels (set of five), in aluminum or gold finish
Spotlight(s)
Whitewall Tires, 8.20 x 15 (set of five)

INTERIOR DIMENSIONS

	REAR	FRONT
Head room	34.6"	34.0"
Shoulder room	59.7"	59.4"
Hip room	65.6"	64.3"
Leg room	43.8"	42.8"
Seat height	11.2"	13.2"

140

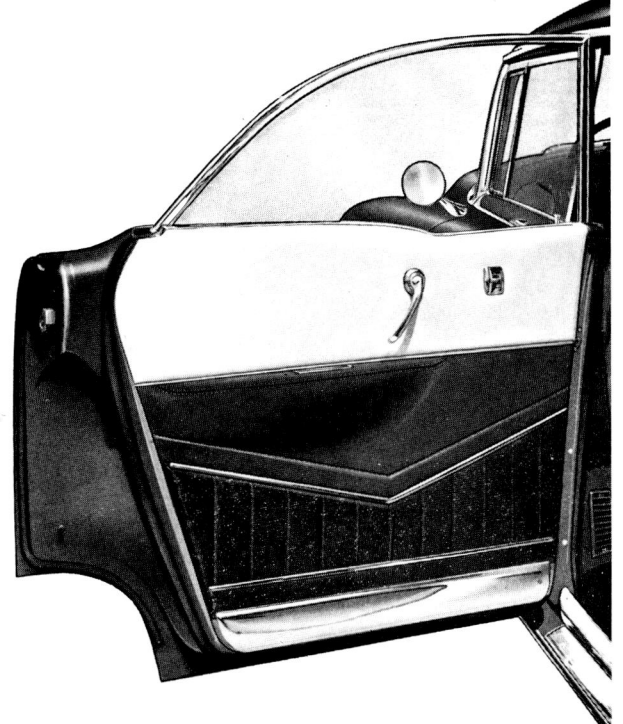

The brilliant new Cadillac Sedan de Ville, with its hardtop styling and four-door convenience, matches the Coupe de Ville in the modern elegance of its interior styling. A massive "V" covered in genuine dark-tone leather forms the center panel of the door up to and including the armrest. Durable, leather-grained Elascofab, used on parts of the upper door panel and around the chromed kick molding at the bottom, beautifies and protects points of wear. Ventwing and front door handle are mounted in a satin-black and chromed insert.

The carefully tailored interiors of the Sedan de Ville are marked by smart 2½" piping on the seat cushions, lower portion of the seat backs and on the side wall and door panels. Upper portion of the seat backs, forming full bolsters, are fashioned of rich, genuine leathers. Choices of upholstery include a bold, Bombay pattern, metallic nylon in any of five pastel colors, or a lustrous, black Stardust pattern nylon flecked with miniature colored stars. Bright and brushed chrome, used for all hardware, roof bows and door and seat moldings, adds alluring highlights to the interior of the Sedan de Ville. Handsome and durable Elascofab means lasting beauty for seat welts, seat scuff pads and many other points of wear or stress. Carpeting is luxurious dark-toned nylon frieze.

SERIES 62 SEDAN de VILLE COLOR AND FABRIC CHOICES

40. GRAY BOMBAY PATTERN METALLIC NYLON with WHITE LEATHER bolsters and trim.
41. STARDUST PATTERN* NYLON with WHITE LEATHER bolsters and trim.
42. LIGHT BLUE BOMBAY PATTERN METALLIC NYLON with LIGHT BLUE LEATHER bolsters and trim.
43. STARDUST PATTERN* NYLON with LIGHT BLUE LEATHER bolsters and trim.
44. GOLD BOMBAY PATTERN METALLIC NYLON with WHITE LEATHER bolsters and trim.
45. STARDUST PATTERN* NYLON with YELLOW LEATHER bolsters and trim.
46. LIGHT GREEN BOMBAY PATTERN METALLIC NYLON with LIGHT GREEN LEATHER bolsters and trim.
47. STARDUST PATTERN** NYLON with LIGHT GREEN LEATHER bolsters and trim.
48. RED BOMBAY PATTERN METALLIC NYLON with WHITE LEATHER bolsters and trim.
49. STARDUST PATTERN** NYLON with MOUNTAIN LAUREL LEATHER bolsters and trim.

*White, Blue and Yellow stars against Black background.
**White, Green and Pink stars against Black background.

1956 Eldorado Biarritz

305 Horsepower
129" Wheelbase
222.2" Over-all Length

STANDARD EQUIPMENT

Air Cleaner, oil-bath type
Cadillac Power Brakes
Cadillac Power Steering
Cigarette Lighters, front (two)
Cigarette Lighters, rear (two)
Clock, electric
Fog Lamps (pair)
Front Seat Adjustment (6-way), electrically operated
Heater
Hydra-Matic Transmission
License Frames
Lights, front ash receivers
Lights, Back-up (dual)
Light, Courtesy or Map (automatic)
Lights, Directional Signal
Light, Glove Box (automatic)
Light, Luggage Compartment (automatic)
Oil Filter
Outside Mirror, left-side, remote-control
Parking Brake Warning Signal
Pocket, flap type, each door
Radio
Rear-view Mirror, 3-way, E-Z-Eye
Robe Cords on back of front seat
Sabre-Spoke Wheels (set of five), aluminum finish
Visors, dual sun, translucent plastic, chrome frames
Whitewall Tires, 8.20 x 15 (4-ply)
Window Lifts, electrically operated
Windshield Washer and Coordinator

OPTIONAL EQUIPMENT (Extra Cost)

Cadillac Air Conditioner
E-Z-Eye Glass
Headlight Dimmer (automatic)
Remote-control Trunk Lid Lock
Spotlight(s)

OPTIONAL EQUIPMENT (No Extra Cost)

Gold-finish Radiator Grille
Gold-finish Sabre-Spoke Wheels

INTERIOR DIMENSIONS

	REAR	FRONT
Head room	34.2"	35.7"
Shoulder room	49.6"	59.2"
Hip room	52.9"	64.1"
Leg room	40.9"	42.6"
Seat height	12.5"	12.4"

In the Eldorado Biarritz, pictured here, and the Eldorado Seville, shown on page 145, the inspired magic of Cadillac styling and engineering enables you to offer your prospects the two most glamorous cars ever to bear the distinguished name "Cadillac". Eldorado exteriors are distinctively and exclusively styled from the tapered lines of the new twin hood ornaments to the sharply accented, stabilizer type, rear fender fins.

Noteworthy, too, are the Eldorados' gleaming Sabre-Spoke wheels, the lustrous and durable Vicodec top fabric (covering the all-steel Turret Top on the Seville) and the twin tubular housings for the taillights, turn signals and back-up lights. Interiors, precisely tailored in all genuine leather in English grain or these same fine leathers combined with smart, beautifully patterned nylon fabrics in the Eldorado Seville, offer such conveniences for driving pleasure as Power Steering, Power Brakes, Power Window Lifts and Six-way Power Seat Adjustment. And, for the unmatched performance to be expected of these glamour twins, here is a new 305-horsepower, special Eldorado engine, combined with the new "controlled-coupling" Cadillac Hydra-Matic transmission.

The exquisite beauty and sleek lines of the Eldorado Biarritz are matched by ultra-smart interiors as distinctive in styling and trim as the modish exterior of the car itself. Door panel design features a lower section of genuine leather deftly tailored in 1" pleats. A concealed snap fastener permits access to a convenient pocket within this pleated section. The center section of the door panel, containing the armrest and the electric window control button, is of dark-toned genuine leather framed by a bright chrome molding. Above the armrest, light-toned leathers combine with a light-tone painted panel in graceful, forward-swept lines. Ventwing and door handle are mounted in a satin-black and chromed insert.

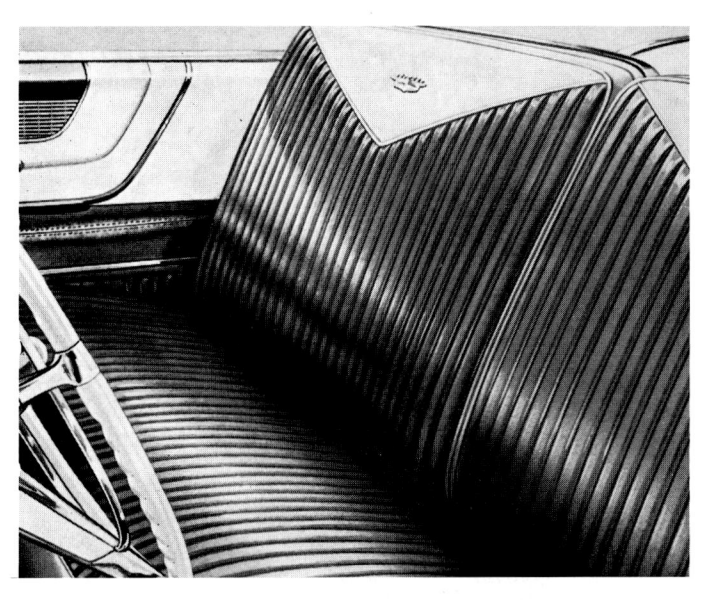

Seat cushions and seat backs in the Eldorado Biarritz are superbly tailored of luxurious genuine leathers in solid colors of Red, Black, Blue or Green, or with the added smartness of fine-grained, White leather bolsters. Here, too, are such luxury details of the leather workers' art as narrow 1" pleats, French seams and raised leather welts. At the top of each seat back, contrasting with the pleated portion, is a distinctive, smooth-leathered "V" inset with a miniature, chromed Cadillac crest. Carpeting is of dark-toned nylon and rayon with aluminum-ribbed, rubber floor pads in matching colors.

ELDORADO BIARRITZ COLOR AND UPHOLSTERY CHOICES

10. BLACK LEATHER seats and seat backs with WHITE LEATHER bolsters and trim.
11. Solid BLACK LEATHER throughout.
12. BLUE LEATHER seats and seat backs with WHITE LEATHER bolsters and trim.
13. Solid BLUE LEATHER throughout.
16. GREEN LEATHER seats and seat backs with WHITE LEATHER bolsters and trim.
17. Solid GREEN LEATHER throughout.
18. RED LEATHER seats and seat backs with WHITE LEATHER bolsters and trim.
19. Solid RED LEATHER throughout.

VICODEC TOP COLORS: 1. White 2. Black 3. Light Blue 4. Beige 5. Light Green

1956 Eldorado Seville

305 Horsepower
129" Wheelbase
222.2" Over-all Length

STANDARD EQUIPMENT

- Air Cleaner, oil-bath type
- Armrest, center-rear
- Cadillac Power Brakes
- Cadillac Power Steering
- Cigarette Lighters, front (two)
- Cigarette Lighters, rear (two)
- Clock, electric
- Fog Lamps (pair)
- Front Seat Adjustment (6-way), electrically operated
- Heater
- Hydra-Matic Transmission
- License Frames
- Lights, front ash receivers
- Lights, Back-up (dual)
- Light, Courtesy or Map (automatic)
- Lights, Directional Signal
- Light, Glove Box (automatic)
- Light, Luggage Compartment (automatic)
- Oil Filter
- Outside Mirror, left-side, remote-control
- Parking Brake Warning Signal
- Pocket, flap type, each door
- Radio
- Rear-view Mirror, 3-way, E-Z-Eye
- Robe Cords on backs of front seat
- Sabre-Spoke Wheels (set of five) aluminum finish
- Visors, dual sun, translucent plastic, chrome frames
- Whitewall Tires, 8.20 x 15 (4-ply)
- Window Lifts, electrically operated
- Windshield Washer and Coordinator

OPTIONAL EQUIPMENT (Extra Cost)

- Cadillac Air Conditioner
- E-Z-Eye Glass
- Headlight Dimmer (automatic)
- Remote-control Trunk Lid Lock
- Spotlight(s)

OPTIONAL EQUIPMENT (No Extra Cost)

- Gold-finish Radiator Grille
- Gold-finish Sabre-Spoke Wheels

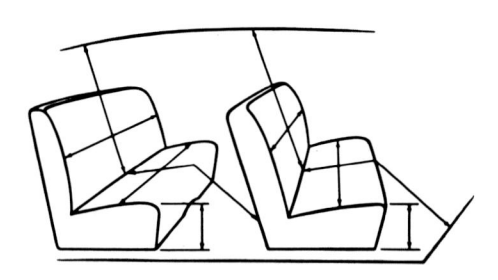

INTERIOR DIMENSIONS

	REAR	FRONT
Head room	34.3"	35.2"
Shoulder room	59.4"	59.1"
Hip room	56.3"	64.1"
Leg room	41.5"	42.7"
Seat height	12.5"	12.4"

The glamorous, new Eldorado Seville with its ultra-fashionable, fabric-covered, hardtop styling is a fitting companion to the famous Eldorado Biarritz. Its interiors, too, offer superbly tailored genuine leathers in two-tone colors, plus four additional choices of beautifully patterned, metallic nylon fabrics combined with genuine leather bolsters and trim. Where nylon fabric is selected, it replaces the pleated leather area on the door panel, as shown above. All other details of the door panel are the same as for the Eldorado Biarritz described on page *143*.

In keeping with the elegance of its exterior design, the new Eldorado Seville presents interiors of exquisite beauty. Seat cushions and seat backs of fine-grained genuine leathers or smart nylon fabrics are deftly tailored in fashionable 1″ pleats. All other areas of the seat and seat back are covered in light- or dark-toned genuine leather with highlights of bright chrome for moldings, hardware and ornamental Cadillac crests. From the top, with its perforated headlining and chromed roof bows, to the floor carpeting of rich, dark-toned nylon and rayon with aluminum-ribbed, rubber floor pads in matching colors, the Eldorado Seville sets a new standard of luxury in hardtop coupe styling for 1956.

ELDORADO SEVILLE COLOR AND UPHOLSTERY CHOICES

10. BLACK LEATHER seats and seat backs with WHITE LEATHER bolsters and trim.
12. BLUE LEATHER seats and seat backs with WHITE LEATHER bolsters and trim.
16. GREEN LEATHER seats and seat backs with WHITE LEATHER bolsters and trim.
18. RED LEATHER seats and seat backs with WHITE LEATHER bolsters and trim.
50. BLACK FLORENTINE PATTERN METALLIC NYLON with WHITE LEATHER bolsters and trim.
53. BLUE FLORENTINE PATTERN METALLIC NYLON with BLUE LEATHER bolsters and trim.
57. GREEN METALLIC NYLON CORD with GREEN LEATHER bolsters and trim.
58. RED METALLIC NYLON CORD with WHITE LEATHER bolsters and trim.
VICODEC TOP COLORS: 1. White 2. Black 3. Light Blue 4. Beige 5. Light Green

1956 Series 60 Special Sedan

285 Horsepower
133" Wheelbase
225.9" Over-all Length

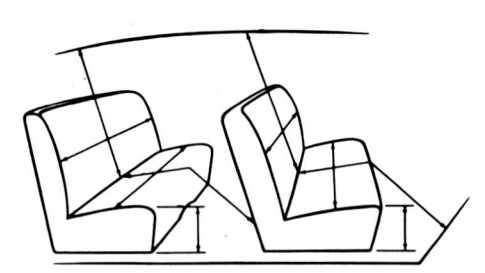

STANDARD EQUIPMENT

- Air Cleaner, oil-bath type
- Armrest, center-rear
- Assist Handles (two)
- Cadillac Power Brakes
- Cadillac Power Steering
- Cigarette Lighters, front (two)
- Cigarette Lighters, rear (two)
- Clock, electric
- Front Seat Adjustment (horizontal), electrically operated
- Hydra-Matic Transmission
- Lights, front ash receivers
- Lights, Back-up (dual)
- Light, Courtesy or Map (automatic)
- Lights, Directional Signal
- Light, Glove Box (automatic)
- Light, Luggage Compartment (automatic)
- Mirror, glare-proof, rear-view, flip type
- Oil Filter
- Outside Mirror, left-side, remote-control
- Paint, two-tone
- Parking Brake Warning Signal
- Pocket, back of front seat
- Robe Cord, back of front seat
- Visor Vanity Mirror
- Visors, dual sun
- Wheel Discs (set of four)
- Window Lifts, electrically operated
- Windshield Washer and Coordinator

OPTIONAL EQUIPMENT (Extra Cost)

- Cadillac Air Conditioner
- E-Z-Eye Tinted Glass
- Fog Lamps (pair)
- Front Seat Adjustment (vertical and angle), electrically operated
- Headlight Dimmer, automatic
- Heater
- License Frames
- Radiator Grille, gold-finish
- Radio
- Remote-control Trunk Lid Lock
- Sabre-Spoke Wheels (set of five), in aluminum or gold finish
- Spotlight(s)
- Whitewall Tires, 8.20 x 15 (set of five)

INTERIOR DIMENSIONS

	REAR	FRONT
Head room	35.1"	35.8"
Shoulder room	59.4"	59.5"
Hip room	65.2"	64.3"
Leg room	46.3"	43.3"
Seat height	12.8"	13.8"

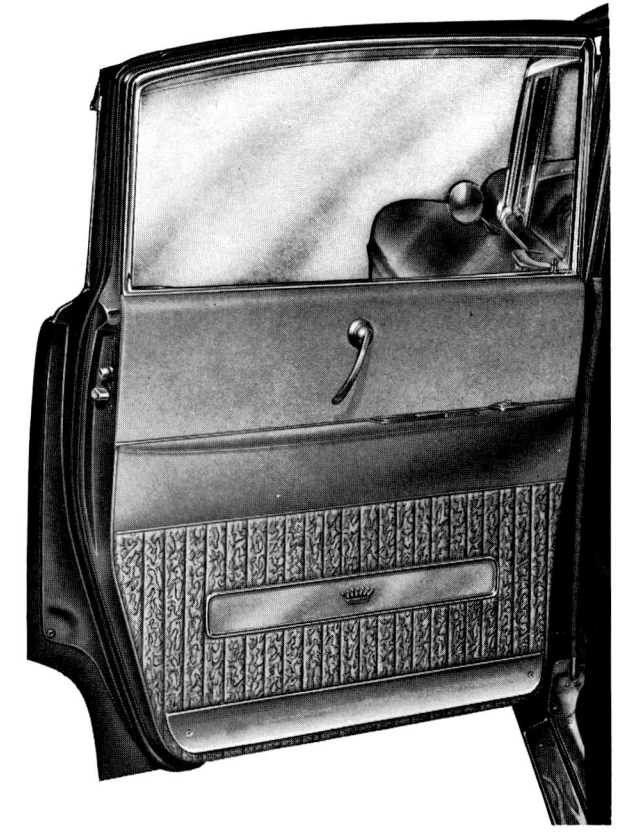

The inherent dignity and gracious beauty, which have earned for the 60 Special Sedan an exclusive niche in the hearts of luxury sedan owners, were never more evident than in 1956. From the distinctive 1¼" pleats and brushed chrome molding of the lower door panel to the richly grained leather and durable leather-grained Elascofab of the upper panel, there is full evidence of the quality and attention which make the 60 Special a car apart. Distinctively new is the bright and brushed chrome insert with gold-plated medallion, highlighting the pleated portion of the door trim.

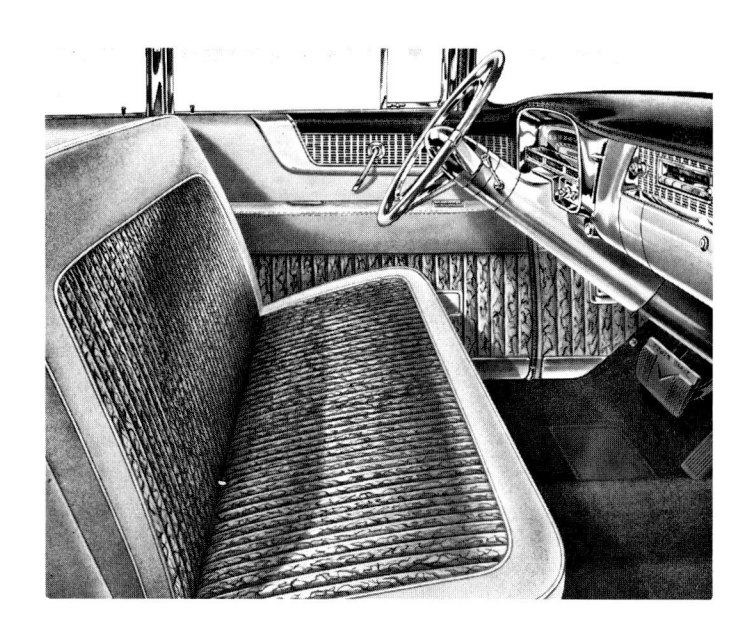

SERIES 60 SPECIAL COLOR AND UPHOLSTERY CHOICES

60. LIGHT GRAY ROSETTE PATTERN NYLON with LIGHT GRAY BROADCLOTH bolsters and trim.
61. LIGHT GRAY BROCADE PATTERN NYLON with LIGHT GRAY BROADCLOTH bolsters and trim.
62. LIGHT BLUE ROSETTE PATTERN NYLON with LIGHT BLUE BROADCLOTH bolsters and trim.
63. LIGHT BLUE BROCADE PATTERN NYLON with LIGHT BLUE BROADCLOTH bolsters and trim.
64. BEIGE ROSETTE PATTERN NYLON with BEIGE BROADCLOTH bolsters and trim.
65. BEIGE BROCADE PATTERN NYLON with BEIGE BROADCLOTH bolsters and trim.
66. LIGHT GREEN ROSETTE PATTERN NYLON with LIGHT GREEN BROADCLOTH bolsters and trim.
67. LIGHT GREEN BROCADE PATTERN NYLON with LIGHT GREEN BROADCLOTH bolsters and trim.
70. LIGHT GRAY BOMBAY PATTERN METALLIC NYLON with WHITE LEATHER bolsters and trim.
72. LIGHT BLUE BOMBAY PATTERN METALLIC NYLON with BLUE LEATHER bolsters and trim.
74. GOLD BOMBAY PATTERN METALLIC NYLON with WHITE LEATHER bolsters and trim.
76. LIGHT GREEN BOMBAY PATTERN METALLIC NYLON with GREEN LEATHER bolsters and trim.

Designed to please the most discerning eye, the interiors of the Cadillac 60 Special Sedan are impeccably tailored in a choice of three luxurious nylon fabrics combined with elegant all-wool broadcloth or smart, genuine-leather bolsters and trim. Seat cushions and seat backs are styled in fashionable 1¼" pleats, while raised seat welts provide the enduring beauty of light-toned, leather-grained Elascofab. A distinguishing feature of the 60 Special is the satin-black and chrome-lined molding around the sides and forward edge of front and rear seats, and the gold-plated "V" and crest on the rear of the front seat back. Carpeting is a luxurious blend of nylon- and rayon-loop pile.

147

1956 Series 75 8-passenger Sedan and Limousine

285 Horsepower
149.8" Wheelbase
235.7" Over-all Length

STANDARD EQUIPMENT

Air Cleaner, oil-bath type
Armrest, center-rear
Assist Handles (two)
Cadillac Power Brakes
Cadillac Power Steering
Cigarette Lighters, front (two)
Cigarette Lighters, rear (two)
Clocks, electric, front and rear compartments
Foot Rests, adjustable (2), rear compartment
Front Seat Adjustment (horizontal), electrically operated
Hydra-Matic Transmission
Lights, front ash receivers
Lights, Back-up (dual)
Light, Courtesy or Map (automatic)
Lights, Directional Signal
Light, Glove Box (automatic)
Light, Luggage Compartment (automatic)
Mirror, glare-proof, rear-view, flip type
Oil Filter
Outside Mirror, left-side, remote-control
Package Compartments in Side Armrests, rear (two)
Paint, two-tone
Parking Brake Warning Signal
Robe Cord on back of front seat
Visor Vanity Mirror
Visors, dual sun
Wheel Discs (set of four)
Window Lifts, electrically operated
Windshield Washer and Coordinator

OPTIONAL EQUIPMENT (Extra Cost)

Cadillac Air Conditioner
E-Z-Eye Tinted Glass
Fog Lamps (pair)
Headlight Dimmer, automatic
Heater, with two under-rear-seat units
License Frames
Radiator Grille, gold-finish
Radio, remote-control
Remote-control Trunk Lid Lock
Sabre-Spoke Wheels (set of five), in aluminum or gold finish
Spotlight(s)
Whitewall Tires, 8.20 x 15 (set of five)

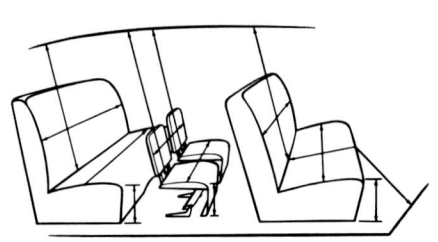

INTERIOR DIMENSIONS

	REAR	AUXILIARY	FRONT
Head room	35.1"	37.2"	36.5"
Shoulder room	58.4"	58.9"	59.5"
Hip room	59.1"	65.6"	64.4"
Leg room	—	—	43.4"
Seat height	14.4"	12.8"	13.8"

The most luxurious, chauffeur-driven car in America, the Cadillac Series 75 Imperial Limousine provides all the style, comfort and convenience of the eight-passenger sedan plus the added practicality of a genuine leather upholstered front seat and looped, nylon-pile carpeting in the front compartment. Separating the front and rear compartments is a glass partition which may be raised or lowered electrically by automatic control buttons located on the rear seat armrests.

SERIES SEVENTY-FIVE LIMOUSINE COLOR AND UPHOLSTERY CHOICES

Same selection of fabrics and colors as for the eight-passenger sedan except that the front seat is upholstered as follows:

BLACK LEATHER when BEIGE, BROWN or GRAY rear compartment upholstery is selected.

BLUE LEATHER when BLUE rear compartment upholstery is selected.

The Cadillac Series 75 eight-passenger Sedan, impressively big and beautiful, has long been recognized as the ideal car of unmatched distinction for the large family or for company executive use. Its interiors reflect in every way the dignity and character of the car itself. Luxurious, deep-textured, dark-toned Kinkomo carpeting, for example, covers not only the floor, but also the scuff-pad areas on the lower portions of the seats and sidewalls and the two adjustable rear compartment foot rests. Concealed in the beautifully appointed center partition are two fold-away seats upholstered in the same fine fabrics as the rest of the interior. Genuine leather is used for the robe cord, two assist handles and for all welted seams. A convenient electric clock and distinctive Cadillac crest are centered between two smartly grained insert panels on the front seat back.

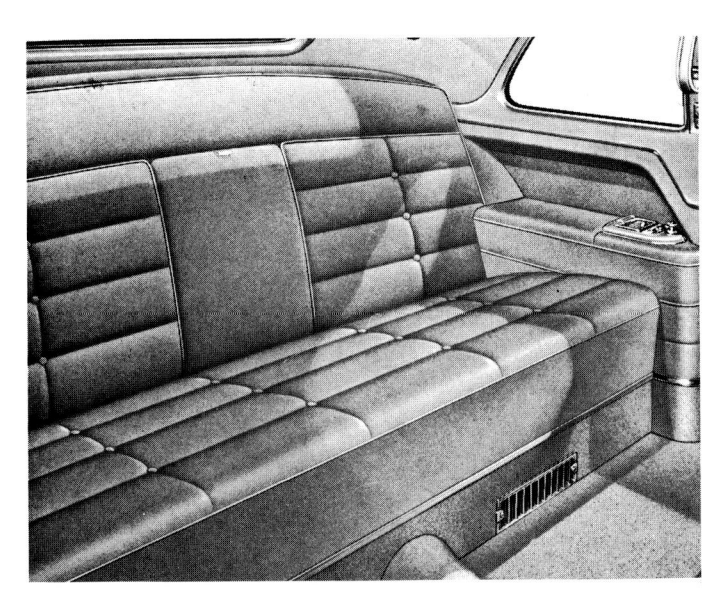

SERIES 75 EIGHT-PASSENGER SEDAN COLOR AND UPHOLSTERY CHOICES

The spacious front and rear seats of the Series 75 eight-passenger Sedan are elegantly tailored with stylish, heavily tufted biscuits and deeply recessed buttons. A smartly contrasting, smooth-surfaced panel extends across the upper portion and down the center of the seat backs to the seat cushion. Upholstery choices include ultra-smart Bedford cord in colors of Light Blue, Light Gray, Beige, Dark Gray or Brown combined with fine all-wool broadcloth bolsters and trim; or light Gray, Light Blue or Beige broadcloth throughout. Bright and brushed chrome finish of hardware and moldings adds gleaming highlights to the interior, while use of genuine leather or durable leather-grained Elascofab lends protective beauty at points of wear or stress.

80. **LIGHT GRAY BEDFORD CORD** seat and seat back inserts with **LIGHT GRAY BROADCLOTH** bolsters and trim.
81. **LIGHT GRAY BROADCLOTH** throughout.
82. **LIGHT BLUE BEDFORD CORD** seat and seat back inserts with **LIGHT BLUE BROADCLOTH** bolsters and trim.
83. **LIGHT BLUE BROADCLOTH** throughout.
84. **BEIGE BEDFORD CORD** seat and seat back inserts with **BEIGE BROADCLOTH** bolsters and trim.
85. **BEIGE BROADCLOTH** throughout.
90. **DARK GRAY BEDFORD CORD** seat and seat back inserts with **LIGHT GRAY BROADCLOTH** bolsters and trim.
94. **BROWN BEDFORD CORD** seat and seat back inserts with **BEIGE BROADCLOTH** bolsters and trim.

149

engine features

HIGHLIGHTS OF 1956 CADILLAC ENGINE

New 285 horsepower.
New 400 foot-pounds of torque.
New 9.75 to 1 compression ratio.
New high-lift valve mechanism.
New four-barrel carburetor.
New exhaust manifold.
New larger bore and piston displacement
New combustion chamber.
New larger exhaust ports.
New crankshaft rigidity and durability.
New more powerful starting motor.
New sealed voltage regulator.
New longer mufflers.
New distributor.
New 11-plate battery.

The 1956 285-horsepower Cadillac and 305-horsepower Eldorado engines are new in every important aspect that means increased satisfaction for the Cadillac owner. In fact, the new engines embody the greatest number of important advancements since the introduction of the famous short stroke, large bore Cadillac engine in 1949. The ability of Cadillac designers and engineers to continue, year after year, to set the pace in efficient engine design is a major reason why Cadillac cars deliver peak performance without resorting to such compromises as smaller bodies, lesser weight or other sacrifices necessitated in some competitive cars.

NEW 9.75 TO 1 COMPRESSION RATIO

The larger cylinder bore of the 1956 Cadillac engine permits a greater volume of fuel-air mixture to be drawn into the cylinders on each intake stroke of the pistons. Yet this larger volume of fuel-air mixture is compressed into an even smaller space before it is ignited, thus increasing the compression ratio to 9.75 to 1. Since the more tightly the fuel-air mixture is compressed the more energy is obtained from fuel consumed, the new higher compression ratio contributes to the more powerful, but continued economical performance, of the 1956 engine.

The efficiency of its lubrication system is a key factor in the long life and trouble-free performance provided by the Cadillac engine. Oil is pumped under pressure to the overhead valve assembly, crankshaft bearings, camshaft, connecting rods and rocker arm shafts. A jet of oil is directed to the cylinder walls and piston pins. Provided, at no extra cost, is an oil filter which minimizes wear by filtering abrasive particles from the oil. Linked to the oil pump is a vacuum pump which assures dependable windshield wiper operation.

NEW FUEL PICKUP IN GASOLINE TANK

In 1956, the flow of fuel from the fuel tank through the fuel line has been made more dependable through relocating the fuel pickup towards the rear of the fuel tank. Thus, during acceleration or uphill driving with a low fuel supply, any possibility of air being sucked into the fuel line has been minimized.

EFFICIENT ENGINE COOLING

Cadillac's large bore, short stroke engine design minimizes friction and exposes less cylinder wall to the flame from the burning fuel-air mixture. More heat energy from the burning fuel is utilized in driving the car and less heat must be absorbed by the cooling system. This enables Cadillac to achieve highly efficient cooling with a very compact radiator. A newly designed four-blade fan increases efficiency of the cooling system in 1956, as well as providing quieter operation. During warmup, water circulates only through the cylinder block and head, so that the engine quickly reaches its most efficient operating temperatures. Large water passages and a high-capacity water pump assure even temperature distribution in the cylinder head, thus minimizing any possibility of pre-ignition.

ADDITIONAL HIGHLIGHTS FOR 1956 ELDORADO ENGINE

New 305 horsepower.
Two new four-barrel carburetors.
Dual air cleaners.

IMPROVED CADILLAC HYDRA-MATIC TRANSMISSION

The 1956 Cadillac Hydra-Matic transmission incorporates many new engineering advancements. The result combines all of the efficiency and performance of previous Hydra-Matic transmissions, but with a new smoothness and greater durability.

In the previous Cadillac Hydra-Matic, changing of gear ratios either up or down through 1st, 2nd, 3rd and 4th, was accomplished through the intricate, finely timed engaging or disengaging of two multiple disc clutches and the tightening or releasing of two bands on revolving drums.

The smooth application of these various units required very precise timing, through extremely accurate adjustment.

In the 1956 Cadillac Hydra-Matic, the band and multiple disc clutch on the front gear set have been replaced by a simple one-way clutch, which requires no adjustment, and by the addition of a new controlled fluid coupling which is automatically filled with or emptied of oil in order to accomplish automatic shifting of gears.

The infinitely gradual and oil-smooth operation of the controlled fluid coupling not only cushions the mechanical forces involved in gear ratio changes, thus eliminating abrupt or erratic shifts, but minimizes stress and wear on parts as well.

Further improvements on the 1956 Cadillac Hydra-Matic include, on the rear gear set, a simple one-way clutch; and smoother, more consistent application of the rear multiple disc clutch through enlarging the clutch face area and through improved control of the oil pressure which applies the clutch.

New gear ratios, used in 1956, provide more even steps between 1st, 2nd, 3rd and 4th gears, thus further contributing to smoother, pleasanter shifts during acceleration or deceleration.

	1st	2nd	3rd	4th
1955 Gear Ratios:	4.1	2.63	1.55	1:1
1956 Gear Ratios:	3.97	2.55	1.55	1:1

IMPROVED "STEPDOWN" ACCELERATION

Because of the smoothness of gear ratio changes accomplished by the new controlled fluid coupling, stepdown shifts from fourth to third gear (by depressing the accelerator pedal completely) can be made with only the increased acceleration of the car, indicating that a downshift has been made. This new shift smoothness also permits *part-throttle* downshifts over a somewhat wider speed range than before. As a result, instead of the engine lugging at low speeds in fourth gear, the car can be smoothly downshifted to third, simply by depressing the accelerator pedal slightly, thus providing faster acceleration for safer passing. A further stepdown shift from third to second can be made at any car speed below 20 miles per hour, thus providing valuable emergency acceleration in the lower speed ranges, as well.

SAFE ENGINE BRAKING

The Cadillac Hydra-Matic provides engine braking in either of the two Drive Ranges or in LO Range. This permits selection of the right amount of engine braking to cope with the steepness of any downhill grade. Some competitive automatic transmissions provide engine braking only in a single Drive Range or, if this is insufficient, in LO Range which may provide more engine braking than is desirable or necessary.

NEW "PARK" POSITION

Another new feature of the 1956 Cadillac Hydra-Matic transmission is the addition of a "Park" position, designated as "P" on the Hydra-Matic quadrant. The new "Park" position engages a pawl within the gear teeth of a sprocket, thus locking the transmission. With the Hydra-Matic in the "Park" position, the car can be held on an incline or hill with the engine running, yet without using the foot or hand brake. The engine may be started with the Hydra-Matic in the "Park" position as well as in the "Neutral" position.

IMPROVED CADILLAC POWER STEERING

Cadillac, first to provide Power Steering as standard equipment on all of its passenger vehicles, offers even greater steering ease through improved Cadillac Power Steering in 1956.

The new Power Steering unit is lighter, more compact and even more efficient. It permits a new over-all steering ratio of 19.5 as against the previous 21.3 ratio. This means easier parking, since the number of turns of the steering wheel required to swing the road wheels from a full turn in one direction to a full turn in the opposite direction has been reduced 10%.

Parking is further simplified by a new parking valve and increased pump capacity which together reduce the maximum pull required on the steering wheel by 50%, from the previous 12 pounds to 6 pounds.

Steering on the highways or in city traffic has been made more effortless, too, since power assistance now comes to the driver's aid with only three instead of three and a half pounds pull on the steering wheel.

With all of these improvements, Cadillac Power Steering has retained its previous advantages. For example, the flexible coupling in the steering shaft, a feature sure to be copied by other makes of cars, has been retained. This type coupling prevents the transmission of vibration, road shock and noise from reaching the steering wheel. Also, since Cadillac Power Steering provides power assistance only when called for by the driver to negotiate curves or turns or to steer around some obstruction in the road, the driver retains the "feel of the road" as a guide in judging safe speeds for various road and weather conditions.

NEW CADILLAC POWER BRAKES

In 1956, Cadillac Power Brakes (now standard equipment) combine the master brake cylinder and the vacuum-power cylinder into a single, more compact and easily serviced unit. This eliminates the need of forcing brake fluid through the previous long hydraulic line between these two units, thus further reducing pedal pressure required for brake application. The new system also permits the use of a lower brake pedal, while still providing adequate mechanical braking control in the event of power failure.

The design and location of the new power brake foot pedal offer important advantages in safety, plus extra comfort and convenience for the driver. Note in the illustration, at right, how the extra-wide pedal is suspended by two brackets, one on each side of the steering column. This location, directly in front of the driver, enables him to use either his left or right foot for brake application. Since the pedal is lower to the floor, it takes less time for the driver to swing his toe to the brake pedal. In addition, it takes less pedal travel to apply the brakes effectively. All of these add up to important savings in fractional seconds, often a vital safety factor under modern motoring conditions.

151

1956

optional equipment

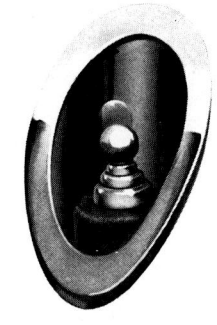

NEW ELECTRICALLY OPERATED ANTENNA

Cadillac's new electrically operated antenna provides advantages in function and appearance. Pushing the right-hand radio control knob raises the antenna to its full height for maximum range of reception. Pulling the knob lowers the antenna into a chromed fender recess.

NEW SIGNAL-SEEKING PRE-SELECTOR RADIO

For 1956, Cadillac's signal-seeking, pre-selector radio offers new tuning convenience. Retained are the five push buttons which can be pre-set for immediate selection of favorite stations, and the selector bar, just above the dial, which selects the strongest signals in the area. Now, however, the right-hand control knob provides the additional convenience of manual tuning of any station within range.

Operation of the 1956 radio control knobs is as follows: The left-hand knob turns the set off and on and regulates the volume. The ring on the left-hand knob adjusts tone from bass to treble. The right-hand knob, in addition to providing manual tuning, operates the new electrically powered antenna. Pushing the knob raises the antenna; pulling the knob lowers it. The ring around the right-hand knob directs the sound to either the front compartment speaker or the rear compartment speaker, or may be adjusted to provide balanced sound from both speakers. A sensitivity control in the center of the selector bar may be set in any of three positions to bring in only the strongest signals in the area or to reach out for weaker or more distant stations. Remote-control tuning for rear compartment passengers is available on Series 75 models.

CADILLAC SPOTLIGHTS

Cadillac Spotlights, finished in bright chrome, add a smart style note, as well as contributing to convenience and safety.

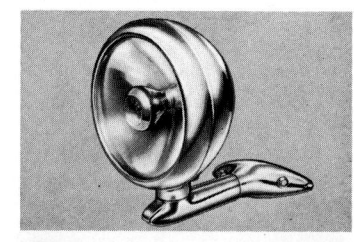

NEW FOG LAMPS

Cadillac Fog Lamps are designed to provide better visibility than headlamps under certain adverse weather conditions. For 1956, they are newly located beneath the outer wings of the bumper guards, closer to the road, for even greater effectiveness. Their rectangular design enhances the apparent width of the car.

CADILLAC AIR CONDITIONER

Ever increasing in popularity is the Cadillac Air Conditioner. It enables Cadillac owners to enjoy cool comfort during hottest summer temperatures, and keeps car interiors dust-free, pollen-free and quiet. A feature of the Cadillac Air Conditioner is that, when the desired temperature is reached, the compressor automatically disengages from the engine (it is also disengaged when the Air Conditioner is turned off). This eliminates unnecessary drain of engine power and minimizes wear of compressor parts.

The Cadillac Air Conditioner system functions as follows: The compressor draws refrigerant from the evaporator, where incoming air has been cooled, compresses and discharges the refrigerant in gaseous form into the condenser coils, where it is changed back into liquid ready for recirculation to the evaporator. Cooled and filtered air from the evaporator enters the interior through grilles on each side of the package shelf or, on the 62 and 60 Special Sedans (if preferred by customer), and on Series 75 models, through ducts mounted beneath the headlining with two adjustable outlets on each side of the front and rear compartments. The Cadillac Air Conditioner is also available for Convertible models, in 1956, with the air return and cool air outlets located on the rear wall of the convertible top well.

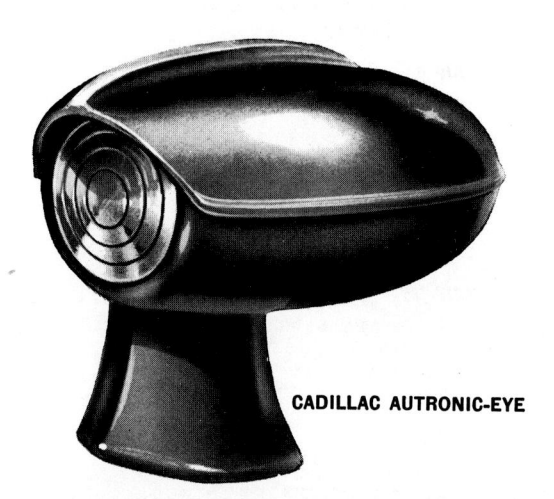

CADILLAC AUTRONIC-EYE

The Cadillac Autronic-Eye protects the Cadillac owner by causing the headlights of his car to switch to low beam when another car approaches from the opposite direction. Thus, the driver of the oncoming car is not blinded and both cars pass with greater safety. An overriding switch is provided to signal drivers who neglect to switch their own lights from bright to dim.

LICENSE PLATE FRAME

Cadillac License Plate Frames of gold-colored, anodized aluminum, with a durable plastic window covering the plate, are both beautiful and practical. They eliminate the unsightliness and dangerous rough, sharp edges of unframed license plates. Cadillac License Plate Frames are in sizes to fit license plates of any state.

E-Z-EYE TINTED GLASS

Available as an extra-cost option for all window areas in the 1956 Cadillac cars, E-Z-Eye glass presents all of the safety advantages of regular laminated Safety Plate glass, but with the additional benefits of reducing glare and helping to keep the interior of the car cooler. It consists of a layer of gray tinted plastic between two layers of polished plate glass. The gray tint does not alter colors of lights or traffic signals. Recommend Cadillac E-Z-Eye glass before your prospects place their order for the car.

accessory groups
(Factory-Installed)

GROUP A .... $_____
White Sidewall Tires • Heater • Radio • E-Z-Eye Glass

GROUP B .... $_____
White Sidewall Tires • Heater • Radio

GROUP C .... $_____
Air Conditioner with Ducts (Available for Series 75, 62 Sedan and 60 Special Sedan only) • White Sidewall Tires • Heater • Radio • E-Z-Eye Glass

GROUP N .... $_____
Air Conditioner without Ducts (Not Available on Series 75) • White Sidewall Tires • Heater • Radio • E-Z-Eye Glass

GROUP 2 .... $_____
Autronic-Eye • Fog Lamps • Dor-Gards • License Frame (1)

GROUP 3 .... $_____
Autronic-Eye • Fog Lamps • Dor-Gards • License Frames (2)

GROUP 4 .... $_____
Fog Lamps • Dor-Gards • License Frame (1)

CADILLAC SABRE-SPOKE WHEELS

Sabre-Spoke wheels, specially constructed of aluminum and steel, are standard on Eldorados and available in sets of five as an extra-cost option on all other models. They are also available in gold finish at no additional cost.

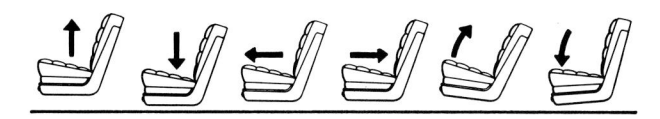

NEW ELECTRICALLY OPERATED SIX-WAY POWER SEAT

All 1956 Cadillac cars equipped with the electrically powered fore-and-aft seat adjuster may also be provided, as an extra-cost option, with a new electrically powered vertical and seat angle adjustment. It provides a four-inch range of vertical seat adjustment to accommodate any driver. At the same time, the seat may be tilted to exactly the angle required for greatest comfort. The complete six-way Power Seat adjustment is standard equipment on Eldorados, optional at extra cost on the Series 62 Sedan and Coupe.

NEW REMOTE-CONTROL TRUNK LID LOCK

Cadillac's Remote-control Trunk Lid Lock permits opening the deck lid with only the touch of a button located on the left-hand side within the glove compartment. This convenience feature will be particularly appreciated by Cadillac owners who live in areas where federal or local authorities must check trunk contents in compliance with law (such as when crossing an international boundary). It is equally convenient in enabling service station attendants to check spare tire inflation. A small warning light, just to the left of the instrument cluster, lets the driver know when his trunk lid is in an unlocked position.

additional CADILLAC ACCESSORIES

Rear-Compartment Radio Control ..... $_____

Radio Foot-Control Switch .... $_____

Cadillac "Cushion Topper" .... $_____

Cadillac Rubber Floor Mats .... $_____

Windshield Washer Solvent .... $_____

Cadillac Body Polish .... $_____

Cadillac Fabric Cleaner .... $_____

Cadillac Kar-Kleen .... $_____

Cadillac Blue Coral .... $_____

Cadillac Chrome Cleaner .... $_____

Cadillac Chrome Protector .... $_____

Cadillac Cooling System Inhibitor ..... $_____

Cadillac Whitewall Tire Cleaner .... $_____

1956

DETAILED SPECIFICATIONS

ENGINE

Number of cylinders	8
Cylinder arrangement	90° V-type
Valve arrangement	Overhead
Bore and stroke	4" x 3⅜"
Block and cylinder head material	Cast iron
Piston displacement	365 cu. in.
Taxable horsepower	51.2
Max. brake horsepower	285 @ 4600 r.p.m.
Eldorado engine	305 @ 4700 r.p.m.
Max. engine torque—lbs.-ft.	400 @ 2800 r.p.m.
Eldorado engine	400 @ 3200 r.p.m.
Compression ratio	9.75:1
Engine mounts	Vulcanized rubber
Number of points of suspension	3

PISTONS AND RINGS

Make	Alcoa—Bohn—Stearling
Material	Aluminum alloy
Type	T-slot, cam ground
Weight	22.72 oz.
Clearance	.0015
Number of oil rings per piston	1
Number of comp. rings per piston	2
Top compression ring	Chrome-plated

RODS AND PINS

Wristpin length	3.093"
Wristpin material	Steel
Type	Locked in rod
Connecting rod length	6.625"
Material—connecting rod	Forged steel
Weight—connecting rod	23.49 oz.
Crankpin journal diameter	2¼"
Lower bearing material	Steel back Moraine 400
Connecting rod bearing clearance	.0005"-.0021"
Connecting rod bearing end play	.008"-.014" (total two rods)

CRANKSHAFT

Material	Forged alloy steel
Weight	71 pounds
Main bearing thrust	Rear main
Crankshaft end play	.001" to .005"
Main bearing type	Slip-on
Main bearing removable	Yes
Main bearing material	Steel back Durex
Main bearing clearance—rear	.0008" to .0025"
Main bearing journal Diameter x Length:	
Number 1	2.625" x .907"
Number 2	2.625" x .907"
Number 3	2.625" x .907"
Number 4	2.625" x .907"
Number 5	2.625" x 1.622"

CAMSHAFT

Drive	Chain
Camshaft sprocket material	Steel
Timing chain—make	Link Belt
Timing chain—no. of links	46
Timing chain—width	.6875"
Timing chain—pitch	.500"

VALVES

Valve arrangement	Overhead
Intake opens	39° B.T.C. at .001 lift
Intake closes	105° A.B.C. at .001 lift
Exhaust opens	81° B.B.C. at .001 lift
Exhaust closes	63° A.T.C. at .001 lift

INTAKE

Material	Alloy steel
Over-all length	4.628" to 4.648"
Diameter of head	1.750"
Angle of seat	44°
Lift	.451"

EXHAUST

Material	Alloy steel
Over-all length	4.656"
Diameter of head	1.562"
Angle of seat	44°
Lift	.451"
Hydraulic valve lifters	Yes
Valve inserts	None
Valve seats cooled by	Direct water circulation

LUBRICATION

Type	Full pressure
Oil under pressure to:	
Main bearings	Yes
Connecting rods	Yes
Wristpins	Splash
Camshaft bearings	Yes
Tappets	Yes
Oil pump type	Gear
Normal oil pressure	30 to 35 lbs. @ 30 m.p.h.
Capacity of oil reservoir	Dry, 6 qts.; Refill, 6 qts.
Type of oil level gauge	Dip stick
Make of pressure gauge	AC—Tell-Tale Lite
Oil filter	Standard
Type	Partial flow

FUEL

Gasoline tank capacity	20 gallons
Type of fuel feed	Camshaft pump
Carburetor—make	Rochester & Carter
Carburetor—type	Four-barrel downdraft*
Manifold heat control	Automatic
Type of air cleaner	Oil bath
Dual tail pipe diameters	1.75"

*Two 4-Barrel Carburetors on Eldorado.

COOLING

Water pump type	Centrifugal—dual outlet
Pressure relief valve	Yes
Choke for recirculation	Yes
Radiator core	Tube and center
Full-length cylinder water jacket	Yes
Water all around cylinders	Yes
Fan belt length	57"
Fan belt width	⅜"
Fan—No. of blades, Series 62, 60 and 75	4
Cooling system capacity	17.5 qts.
With heater	19.5 qts. (Series 75, 22 qts.)

GENERATOR

Make	Delco-Remy
Minimum charging speed	22 m.p.h. and up
Generator ventilation	Forced air

GENERATOR REGULATOR

Make	Delco-Remy
Voltage at cut-out closing	11.8—13.6 (adjust to 12.8)
Voltage regulator setting	14—15 (adjust to 14.5 at 90°)
Generator maximum charging rate	27—33 amp. (adjust to 30)

STARTING MOTOR

Make	Delco-Remy
Flywheel teeth, integral or ring	Steel integral

IGNITION

Spark advance	Centrifugal and vacuum
Ignition Unit:	
Make	Delco-Remy
Manual advance	None
Maximum centrifugal advance	Crankshaft (18°-22°)
Vacuum advance	Crankshaft (33°-36°)
Distributor breaker gap	.016"
Initial spark advance	5° B.T.C.
Firing order	1-8-4-3-6-5-7-2
Ignition Coil:	
Make	Delco-Remy
Spark Plugs:	
Make	AC
Model	44.0
Thread	14mm.
Gap	.035"

BATTERY

Make	Delco 3EMR70-W
Number of plates	11
Capacity (amp. hrs.)	70
Terminal grounded	Negative
Location of battery	Under hood on tray attached to right-hand body bracket, front of dash

LIGHTS AND HORN

Headlight—make	Guide sealed-beam
Headlight cover glass, dia.	6 11/16"
Parking light—make	Guide
Taillight—make	Guide
Lighting switch—make	Delco-Remy
How are headlights dimmed?	Depressed beam—foot switch
Horn:	
Make	Delco-Remy
Type	*Vibrator, seashell electric (2)

*3 on Eldorados

HYDRA-MATIC DRIVE

Type	Fully automatic step-gear type with new controlled fluid coupling on forward gear set for smoother shifts.
Gearing	Planetary
No. of forward speeds	4
No. of forward speeds in "City" DR range	3
No. of forward speeds in "Country" DR range	4
No. of forward speeds in LO range	2
Transmission ratio, first	3.97:1
Transmission ratio, second	2.55:1
Transmission ratio, third	1.55:1
Transmission ratio, fourth	1:1
Transmission ratio, reverse	4.31:1
Oil capacity	13 qts.
Type of fluid	Hydra-Matic fluid

SHIFT POINTS:

		With Rear Axle Ratio of:	(Single Carburetor)	(Dual Carburetor)
		3.07:1	3.36:1	3.36:1
Upshift DR-4 Range	Throttle Opening	M.P.H.	M.P.H.	M.P.H.
1st to 2nd	Minimum	7-10	7-10	7-10
	Maximum	20-24	18-22	18-22
2nd to 3rd	Minimum	14-18	13-17	15-18
	Maximum	39-44	35-40	37-40
3rd to 4th	Minimum	20-24	18-22	18-22
	Maximum	68-75	62-69	62-69
Downshift DR-4 Range				
4th to 3rd	Minimum	14-18	12-16	12-16
	Maximum	61-68	56-62	56-62
3rd to 2nd	Minimum	11-15	10-18	12-15
	Maximum	23-27	21-25	22-25
2nd to 1st	Minimum	6-9	6-9	6-9
	Maximum	6-9	6-9	6-9
DR-3 Range				
Same as DR-4 except upshifts from 3rd to 4th at:		**68-75**	**62-69**	**62-69**
downshifts from 4th to 3rd at:		**61-68**	**56-62**	**56-62**
LO Range				
Same as DR-4 except upshifts to 3rd at:		**52-58**	**47-53**	**47-53**
upshifts to 4th at:		**68-75**	**62-69**	**62-69**
downshifts to 3rd at:		**61-68**	**56-64**	**56-64**
downshifts to 2nd at:		**41-47**	**37-43**	**37-43**

Note: Miles per hour at which shift is made is dependent on degree of throttle opening. Actually no gears shift. Term used for clarity of meaning.

FRAME

	Series 62	Series 60S	Series 75
Frame make	A. O. Smith	A. O. Smith	A. O. Smith
Frame depth, maximum	7 5/32"	7 3/16"	7 3/16"
Frame thickness, maximum	9/64"	5/32"	5/32"
Flange width, maximum	2 27/64"	2 19/32"	2 19/32"
Frame—Type	Channel side bars with I-beam, X-member	Channel side bars with I-beam, X-member	Channel side bars with I-beam, X-member
Frame-to-road clearance at center of wheelbase	6½"	6½"	7½"

FRONT END SUSPENSION

Front suspension, make	Own
Front suspension, type	Forked arms

DETAILED SPECIFICATIONS
CONTINUED

FRONT END SUSPENSION—Continued

Forked arm bearings, type	Threaded
Kingpin upper bearing, type	Bronze bushing
Kingpin lower bearing, type	Bronze bushing
Front wheel inner bearing, make and type	N. D. ball
Front wheel outer bearing, make and type	N. D. ball
Front spring, type	Helical coil
Front spring, material	Spring steel
Shock absorber, type	Hydraulic direct-acting type
Front stabilizer	Torsion rod

PROPELLER SHAFT

	Series 62-60	Series 75
Number used	1	2
Type	Exposed	Exposed

UNIVERSAL JOINTS

Make	Mechanics and Saginaw
Number used	2 3
Type	Cross and Trunnion
Bearing	Needle
Universal joints, lubricated	Permanently
Drive and torque taken through	Rear springs

REAR AXLE

Rear axle, make	Own
Rear axle, type	Semifloating
Differential gear, make	Own
Rear axle:	
Oil capacity	5 pints
Grade recommended:	
S.A.E. viscosity	90 hypoid
Type of final gearing	Hypoid
Gear ratio:	
Standard	3.07:1 3.36:1
Optional	3.36:1
Pinion adjustment (except 75)	None
Pinion bearing adjustment	None (Preloaded)
Are pinion bearings in sleeve?	No
Backlash between pinion and ring gear	.003"-.010"
Rear axle pinion shaft:	
Front bearing, type	Tapered roller
Rear bearing, type	Tapered roller

TIRES AND WHEELS

Tires:		
Make	U. S. Royal, Firestone and Goodrich	
Type	Tubeless	
Size	8.00 x 15*	8.20 x 15
Ply rating	4	6
Inflation pressure:		
Front	24 lbs.	28 lbs.
Rear	24 lbs.	28 lbs.
Wheels:		
Type	Slotted disc**	
Make	Kelsey-Hayes	
Rim, diameter	15"	15"
Rim, width	6.00"	6.00"
Tread:		
Front	60"	60"
Rear	63.16"	63.16"

*8.20 x 15 when whitewalls are ordered. Std. on Eldorado.
**Aluminum spoke, steel rim wheels on Eldorados.

SPRINGS (REAR)

	Series 62-60	Series 75
Rear Springs:		
Type	Semi-elliptic	
Material	Spring steel	
Length	56½"	
Width	2½"	
No. of leaves	5	6
Spring leaves lubricated with	Wax impregnated liners	
Spring bushings, type	Rubber	
Stabilizers	Rear—None	

SHOCK ABSORBERS (REAR)

Type	Direct Acting, Hydraulic

STEERING

Steering	Hydraulic power
Type	Concentric gear
Make	Saginaw
Over-all steering ratio	19.5:1
Car turning radius (outside) bumper to bumper sweep	(62) 21.7' (75) 25.8' (60) 22.5'

BRAKES

Front and Rear		
Brake drum diameter	12"	12"
Brake drum, internal or external	Internal	Internal
Brake lining, length per wheel:		
Forward shoe	11.52"	12.98"
Reverse shoe	12.98"	12.98"
Total	24.50"	25.96"
Brake lining width	2½"	2½"
Brake lining thickness	¼"	¼"
Brake lining effective area	221.96 sq. in.	233.64 sq. in.
Brake clearance	.010" top; .015" bottom	
Hand brake location	Left side of dash	
Hand brake lever operates on	Rear service brakes	
Power brakes	Standard all models	

MISCELLANEOUS SPECIFICATIONS

Car lifting device, jack	Bumper type
Engine lubrication, type	Pressure
Chassis lubrication, type	High pressure
Axle lubrication, type	Splash

LUBRICANTS

Engine oil	6 qts.
Recommended viscosity	Min. anticipated temperature:
	+32°F. 20W or S.A.E. 20
	+10°F. 20W
	−10°F. 10W
	Below −10°F. 5W
Drain	2000 miles (after initial 500-mile change)
Rear axle oil	5 pints
Recommended viscosity	90 hypoid
Auto trans. fluid type "A"	13 qts. dry
Gasoline	20 gals.

1956 CADILLAC GENERAL SPECIFICATIONS

	Series 62 Sedan	Series 62 Coupe	Series 62 Convertible Coupe	Series 62 Sedan and Coupe de Ville	Eldorado Biarritz and Eldorado Seville	Series 60 Special Sedan	Series 75 8-Passenger Sedan and Limousine
Wheelbase	129"	129"	129"	129"	129"	133"	149.8"
Over-all Length	214.9"	221.9"	221.9"	221.9"	222.2"	225.9"	235.7"
Over-all Width	80"	80"	80"	80"	80"	80"	80"
Over-all Height	62"	59.6"	60"	59.6"	59.8"**	62"	63.9"
Frame-to-Road Clearance at Center of Wheelbase	6.5"	6.5"	6.5"	6.5"	6.5"	6.5"	7.5"
Steering Ratio—Over-all	19.5	19.5	19.5	19.5	19.5	19.5	19.5
Turning Radius	21.7"	21.7"	21.7"	21.7"	21.7"	22.5"	25.8"
Tread—Front	60"	60"	60"	60"	60"	60"	60"
Tread—Rear	63.16"	63.16"	63.16"	63.16"	63.16"	63.16"	63.16"
Tires, Tubeless—Size	8.00 x 15*	8.00 x 15*	8.00 x 15*	8.00 x 15*	8.20 x 15	8.00 x 15*	8.20 x 15
Tires—Ply Rating	4-ply	4-ply	4-ply	4-ply	4-ply	4-ply	6-ply

* 8.20 x 15 supplied in whitewall tires (standard on Eldorado Biarritz and Seville)   ** 60" on Eldorado Biarritz

	Series 62 Sedan	Series 62 Coupe	Series 62 Convertible Coupe	Series 62 Sedan and Coupe de Ville	Eldorado Biarritz and Eldorado Seville	Series 60 Special Sedan	Series 75 8-Passenger Sedan and Limousine
Engine	285-horsepower Cadillac V-8	285-horsepower Cadillac V-8	285-horsepower Cadillac V-8	285-horsepower Cadillac V-8	305-horsepower Cadillac V-8	285-horsepower Cadillac V-8	285-horsepower Cadillac V-8
Compression Ratio	9.75:1	9.75:1	9.75:1	9.75:1	9.75:1	9.75:1	9.75:1
Piston Displacement	365 cu. in.	365 cu. in.	365 cu. in.	365 cu. in.	365 cu. in.	365 cu. in.	365 cu. in.
Valve Arrangement	Overhead	Overhead	Overhead	Overhead	Overhead	Overhead	Overhead
Carburetor	4-Barrel	4-Barrel	4-Barrel	4-Barrel	4-Barrel (Two)	4-Barrel	4-Barrel
Exhaust System	Dual	Dual	Dual	Dual	Dual	Dual	Dual
Transmission	Hydra-Matic	Hydra-Matic	Hydra-Matic	Hydra-Matic	Hydra-Matic	Hydra-Matic	Hydra-Matic
Steering	Hydraulic Power	Hydraulic Power	Hydraulic Power	Hydraulic Power	Hydraulic Power	Hydraulic Power	Hydraulic Power
Brakes	Power Brakes	Power Brakes	Power Brakes	Power Brakes	Power Brakes	Power Brakes	Power Brakes
Frame	I-Beam, X-Member	I-Beam, X-Member	I-Beam, X-Member	I-Beam, X-Member	I-Beam, X-Member	I-Beam, X-Member	I-Beam, X-Member
Springs	Coil front, semi-elliptic-leaf rear	Coil front, semi-elliptic-leaf rear	Coil front, semi-elliptic-leaf rear	Coil front, semi-elliptic-leaf rear	Coil front, semi-elliptic-leaf rear	Coil front, semi-elliptic-leaf rear	Coil front, semi-elliptic-leaf rear
Drive	Hotchkiss	Hotchkiss	Hotchkiss	Hotchkiss	Hotchkiss	Hotchkiss	Hotchkiss
Axle Ratio	3.07:1*	3.07:1*	3.07:1*	3.07:1*	3.36:1	3.07:1*	3.36:1

* 3.36:1 standard on Eldorado engine installations and Series 75, optional on other models.

1957

New front-end styling

The new front-end styling of the 1957 Cadillac is in perfect complement with the lower over-all height of the car itself. Not only is the hood considerably lower but note, too, how the massive lower bumper bar and gull-wing bumper guards draw eye-attention closer to the road. This effect is emphasized further by the lower grille and by the upper grille bar which if extended horizontally would pass well below the headlamps. Additional front-end styling features include the new, black, molded-rubber bumper guard tips, new ornamental grilles under each headlamp, new dual, circular parking and turn signal lamps in the outer extremities of the lower bumper bar, a new front license plate frame centered at the base of the radiator grille, and new extended headlamp bezels. Distinctive hood markings include a further refined version of the famous Cadillac "V" and Crest and new gracefully tapered twin hood-top ornaments.

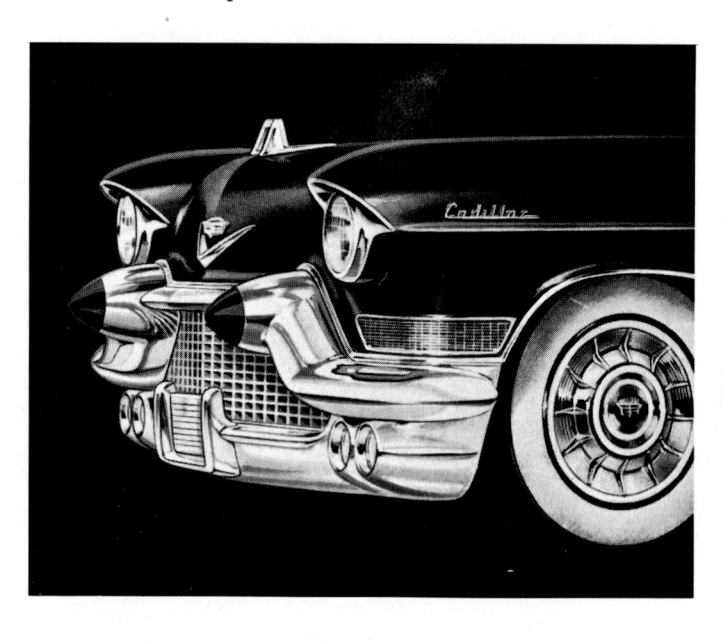

Entirely new for 1957 is the styling treatment accorded the glass areas of the car. Windshield pillars slant from the forward edge of the roof back into the sides of the car, while the rear window pillars have exactly the reverse slant. The result is not only one of more graceful lines, but improved visibility to the front, sides and rear. Note how, on sedan models, the rear window pillars are formed jointly by the roof supports and by extensions rising from the rear doors. On all models, except the Series 75, the beauty and unbroken visibility of hardtop styling is achieved through the use of stub center pillars. Of distinctively new design is the wider air-intake grille for the ventilation, heating and air-conditioning systems. It extends across the width of the hood, separated from the chromed windshield molding by a narrow band of body color. Additional styling features shown below are the flatter, lower hood with only a slight valley between hood and fender line and the new extended cadet visor headlamp bezels.

In the new 1957 Cadillac motor cars, every styling feature, from the lower, more-compact grille and bumper ensemble in front to the new twin, circular tail-, stop-, back-up and turn-signal lights in the rear, has been designed to make them the most beautiful motoring creations ever to bear the distinguished Cadillac name. The 1957 Cadillac cars present a new sleekness in every line. They are almost three inches lower in over-all height with the new lower hood, the new flush joining of the rear deck and quarter panels and the new slanting roof pillars adding further to the road-hugging appearance of the car. New swifter fender lines sweep back from extended headlamp bezels to culminate in new, smartly designed, stabilizer type versions of the famous Cadillac rear fender fins. Newly designed, chrome-framed wheel openings and extended contour lines in both front and rear fenders enhance the long, low look of the car. These are but a few of the many new styling features that lend distinction to the magnificent new Cadillac for 1957 . . . a car destined to set the trend in automotive styling for years to come.

New side and rear styling

The impressively lower height of the 1957 Cadillac is equally evident viewed from the side or the rear. What's more, this appearance is further emphasized by the new lines of the rear window which taper gracefully around into the sides of the rear quarter panels. Rear deck and fenders join in a clean, flush surface which adds to the sleek solidity of the car's appearance while enhancing its apparent width. From the side the 1957 Cadillac presents new lines of fleetness and beauty. The fender line flows back in a slight curve from the extended headlamp visors to a point midway across the rear door, forms a graceful arch at the junction of the roof pillar, then extends level with the rear deck to culminate in the sweeping beauty of the new stabilizer type rear fender fins. The raised contour lines in front and rear fenders are considerably longer. Wheel openings are higher and framed by chrome moldings. The rear wheel opening covers have been eliminated. A new stone shield between the rear fender contour molding and the rocker sill molding further tends to keep eye interest low. Fender identification markings are new for 1957 with a medallion mounted on the rear fender fins of 62 Series cars and the name "Cadillac" or model name, in the case of the Coupe and Sedan de Ville and the Eldorado Biarritz and Seville, appearing well-forward on the front fenders.

The lower and broader look of the 1957 Cadillac is emphasized by the flush joining of deck and fenders. Additional notes of rear-end styling are the new, upright, oval-shaped exhaust outlets in the rear bumper and twin circular lamps on each rear fender. The outer lamp housing contains the tail-, stop- and turn-signal lights. The inner lamp housing contains the back-up lights. On the 60 Special Sedan each pair of circular lamps provides dual tail-, stop- and turn-signal lights while separate rectangular back-up lights are mounted in the deck lid just above the bumper.

Rear fender styling of the Cadillac 60 Special Sedan is marked by greater length in keeping with the long rear deck and by the additional distinction of brush-finished stainless-steel lower fender panels with bright-finished horizontal grooves. Tapered rear fender fairing is highlighted by a chromed strip along its entire length.

Distinguishing the graceful rear fender lines of the Cadillac 62 Series is the long fender fairing extending from the tail lamp housing and tapering to a point just short of the front door opening. The upper half of the contour is in body color; the lower half finished in bright chrome. Note how the rear fender stone shield draws eye interest even lower by forming a connecting link between the contour molding and the rocker sill molding.

Always of eye-catching design, the sparkling wheel discs of the 1957 Cadillac feature a deep contour between the hub and spoke-patterned outer ring. Centered in the hub is a colorfully enameled Cadillac crest while the spoked outer ring is further highlighted by a series of concentric circles.

157

1957 SERIES 62 sedan and coupe

300 horsepower
129.5" wheelbase
215.9" over-all length

STANDARD EQUIPMENT

Air Cleaner, oil-bath type
Armrest, center-rear
Assist handles (two)
Cadillac Power Brakes
Cadillac Power Steering
Cigarette Lighters, front (two)
Cigarette Lighter, rear
Clock, Electric
Hydra-Matic Transmission

Lights, front ash receivers
Lights, Back-up (dual)
Light, Courtesy or Map (automatic)
Lights, Directional Signal
Light, Glove Box (automatic)
Light, Luggage Compartment, (automatic)
Mirror, glare-proof, rear-view, flip type

Oil Filter
Outside Mirror, left-side, remote-control
Paint, two-tone
Parking Brake Warning Signal
Visor Vanity Mirror
Visors, dual sun
Wheel Discs (set of four)
Windshield Washer and Coordinator

OPTIONAL EQUIPMENT (Extra Cost)

Cadillac Air Conditioner
E-Z-Eye Tinted Glass
Fog Lamps (pair)
Front Seat Adjustment (6-way), electrically operated

Headlight Dimmer, automatic
Heater
License Frames
Radiator Grille, gold-finish
Radio

Remote-control Trunk Lid Lock
Sabre-Spoke Wheels (set of five) in chrome finish
Window Lifts, electrically operated
Whitewall Tires, 8.20 x 15 (set of five)

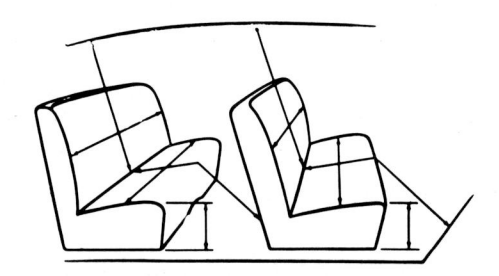

INTERIOR DIMENSIONS

	REAR	FRONT
Head room	34.9"	35.0"
Shoulder room	57.0"	59.0"
Hip room	65.0"	65.2"
Leg room	45.2"	45.0"
Seat height	12.7"	13.5"

62 Sedan Rear Compartment

62 Coupe Rear Compartment

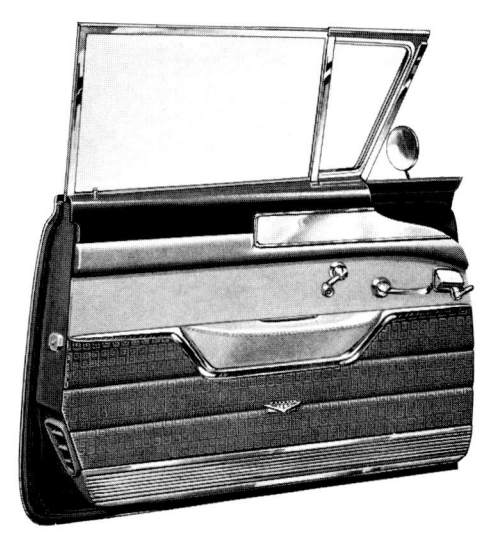

SERIES 62 SEDAN AND COUPE
COLOR AND UPHOLSTERY CHOICES

30. LIGHT GRAY NEPTUNE PATTERN METALLIC NYLON with LIGHT GRAY GLACIAL MIST METALLIC NYLON bolsters and trim.
31. LIGHT GRAY GRECIAN PATTERN METALLIC NYLON with WHITE ELASCOFAB bolsters and trim.
32. LIGHT BLUE NEPTUNE PATTERN METALLIC NYLON with LIGHT BLUE GLACIAL MIST METALLIC NYLON bolsters and trim.
33. LIGHT BLUE GRECIAN PATTERN METALLIC NYLON with LIGHT BLUE ELASCOFAB bolsters and trim.
34. BEIGE NEPTUNE PATTERN METALLIC NYLON with BEIGE GLACIAL MIST METALLIC NYLON bolsters and trim.
36. GREEN NEPTUNE PATTERN METALLIC NYLON with GREEN GLACIAL MIST METALLIC NYLON bolsters and trim.
37. LIGHT GREEN GRECIAN PATTERN METALLIC NYLON with GLADE GREEN ELASCOFAB bolsters and trim.

There are seven, beautiful two-tone color combinations available for the interiors of the Cadillac Series 62 Sedan and Coupe. There are bold-patterned Neptune-cloth nylons with rich, gleaming Lurex thread and tasteful, restrained Lurex-threaded Grecian-cloth nylons combined with modern, color-blended Elascofab. In Neptune and matching Glacial-cloth bolsters, color choices are blue, gray, green and beige. The available colors in Grecian-cloth nylon and Elascofab bolsters are light blue, light green and a gray Grecian cloth with a harmonizing white Elascofab bolster. The entire seat back, seat cushions and the lower portion of the door are styled with long, broad horizontal stitching and deeply recessed, nylon-covered buttons. Points throughout the interior that are subject to wear and stress such as the upper door and sidewall panels, seat scuff pads and seat welts are protected with smart, durable Elascofab. Carpeting is dark-toned, deep-pile nylon blend.

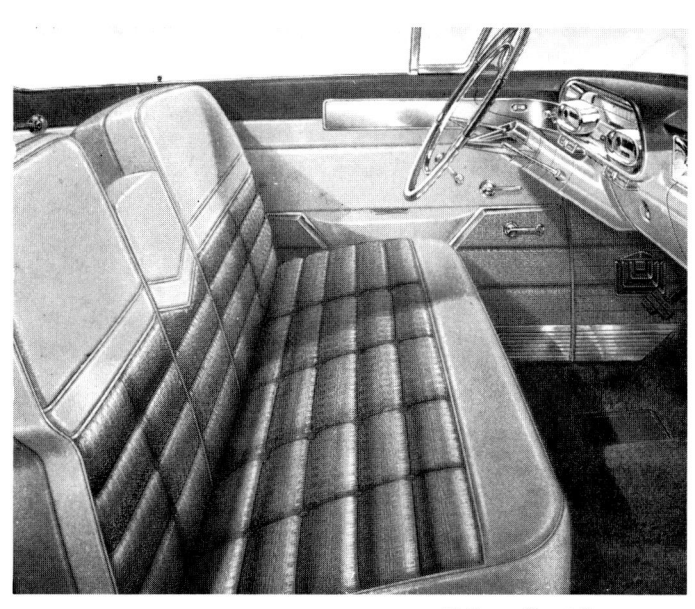

62 Coupe Front Compartment

300 horsepower
129.5" wheelbase
220.9" over-all length

Air Cleaner, oil-bath type
Armrest, center-rear
Cadillac Power Brakes
Cadillac Power Steering
Cigarette Lighters, front (two)
Clock, Electric
Hydra-Matic Transmission
Lights, front ash receivers

STANDARD EQUIPMENT

Lights, Back-up (dual)
Light, Courtesy or Map (automatic)
Lights, Directional Signal
Light, Glove Box (automatic)
Light, Luggage Compartment (automatic)
Mirror, glare-proof, rear-view, flip type
Oil Filter

Outside Mirror, left-side, remote-control
Paint, two-tone
Parking Brake Warning Signal
Visor Vanity Mirror
Visors, dual sun
Wheel Discs (set of four)
Windshield Washer and Coordinator

OPTIONAL EQUIPMENT (Extra Cost)

Cadillac Air Conditioner
E-Z-Eye Tinted Glass
Fog Lamps (pair)
Front Seat Adjustment (6-way), electrically operated

Headlight Dimmer, automatic
Heater
License Frames
Radiator Grille, gold-finish
Radio

Remote-control Trunk Lid Lock
Sabre-Spoke Wheels (set of five), in chrome finish
Window Lifts, electrically operated
Whitewall Tires, 8.20 x 15 (set of five)

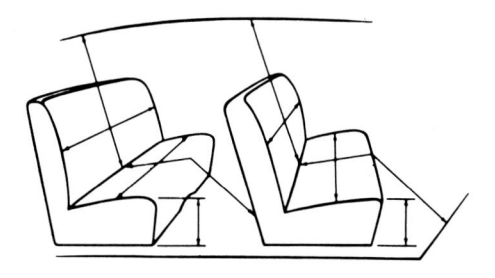

INTERIOR DIMENSIONS

	REAR	FRONT
Head room	34.0"	34.2"
Shoulder room	57.0"	59.1"
Hip room	57.3"	65.6"
Leg room	40.8"	44.6"
Seat height	13.7"	12.9"

1957 SERIES
62 convertible

300 horsepower
129.5" wheelbase
220.9" over-all length

STANDARD EQUIPMENT

Air Cleaner, oil-bath type
Armrest, center, front
Cadillac Power Brakes
Cadillac Power Steering
Cigarette Lighters, front (two)
Cigarette Lighters, rear (two)
Clock, electric
Front Seat Adjustment (horizontal), electrically operated
Hydra-Matic Transmission
Lights, front ash receivers
Lights, Back-up (dual)
Light, Courtesy or Map (automatic)
Lights, Directional Signal
Light, Glove Box (automatic)
Light, Luggage Compartment (automatic)
Mirror, glare-proof, rear-view, flip type
Oil Filter
Outside Mirror, left-side, remote-control
Parking Brake Warning Signal
Visor Vanity Mirror
Visors, dual sun
Wheel Discs (set of four)
Window Lifts, electrically operated
Windshield Washer and Coordinator

OPTIONAL EQUIPMENT (Extra Cost)

Cadillac Air Conditioner
E-Z-Eye Tinted Glass
Fog Lamps (pair)
Front Seat Adjustment (vertical and angle), electrically operated
Headlight Dimmer, automatic
Heater
License Frames
Radiator Grille, gold-finish
Radio
Remote-control Trunk Lid Lock
Sabre-Spoke Wheels (set of five), in chrome finish
Whitewall Tires, 8.20 x 15 (set of five)

The Cadillac Series 62 Convertible interiors are styled in keeping with the zest and the spirit of youth. The door panel, shown above, reveals the clean, functional design that spells beauty to the convertible buyer. Fine-grained, weather-resistant Elascofab entirely surrounds the pleated-leather door panel insert, the generously proportioned leather-covered armrest and a horizontal chrome molding with a stylized "V" and Crest. Gleaming chrome kick strip on the bottom edge of the door, chromed framing around the leather panel and the chromed insert on the upper section of the door add further to the distinctive and durable beauty of the Series 62 Convertible.

The genuine leather upholstery in the Series 62 Convertible imbues the prospective owner with the feeling that here is not only luxury, but enduring beauty as well. For there is nothing that connotes lasting quality as well as does fine leather. The seat cushions and seat back inserts are fashioned in smart biscuits and gleaming, concave, chromed buttons. The upper portion of the seat backs are marked by vertical 1″ pipes. Mounted in a recess in the center of the rear seat back is a chromed grille for the radio rear compartment speaker. A wide, center armrest in the front seat back contributes to greater comfort and motoring pleasure. Carpeting is a dark-toned, deep-tufted nylon blend.

SERIES 62 CONVERTIBLE
COLOR AND UPHOLSTERY CHOICES

20. BLACK LEATHER seat and seat back inserts with WHITE LEATHER bolsters and trim.
21. SOLID BLACK LEATHER throughout.
22. BLUE LEATHER seat and seat back inserts with ORION BLUE LEATHER bolsters and trim.
23. TURQUOISE GREEN LEATHER seat and seat back inserts with WHITE LEATHER bolsters and trim.
25. TAN LEATHER throughout.
26. LIGHT GREEN LEATHER seat and seat back inserts with GLADE GREEN bolsters and trim.
28. DAKOTA RED LEATHER seat and back inserts with WHITE LEATHER bolsters and trim.
29. DAKOTA RED LEATHER throughout.

TOP COLORS: 1. White   2. Black   3. Blue   4. Tan   5. Green

INTERIOR DIMENSIONS

	REAR	FRONT
Head room	34.7″	35.2″
Shoulder room	48.4″	59.1″
Hip room	52.2″	65.6″
Leg room	40.7″	44.6″
Seat height	13.7″	12.9″

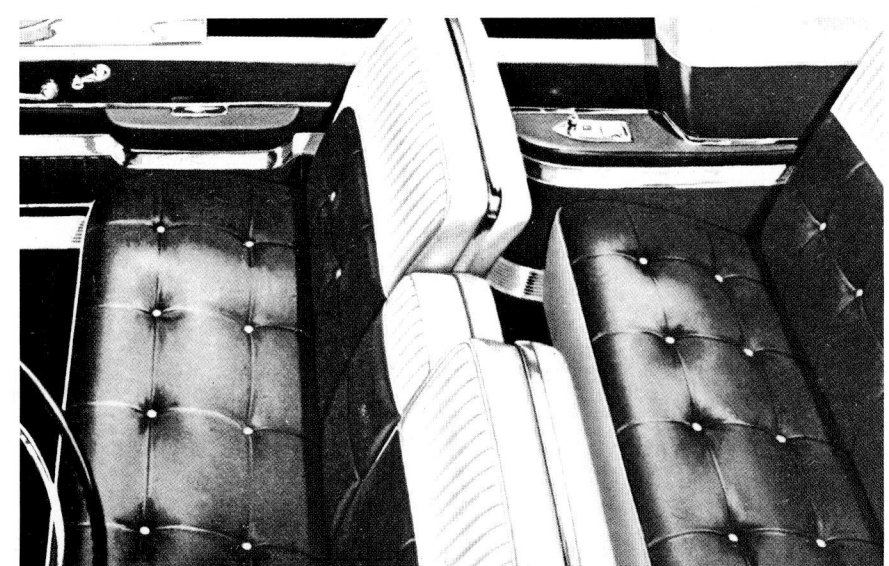

1957 SERIES
62 coupe de ville

300 horsepower
129.5" wheelbase
220.9" over-all length

STANDARD EQUIPMENT

Air Cleaner, oil-bath type
Armrest, center, front and rear
Cadillac Power Brakes
Cadillac Power Steering
Cigarette Lighters, front (two)
Cigarette Lighters, rear (two)
Clock, electric
Front Seat Adjustment (horizontal), electrically operated

Hydra-Matic Transmission
Lights, front ash receivers
Lights, Back-up (dual)
Light, Courtesy or Map (automatic)
Lights, Directional Signal
Light, Glove Box (automatic)
Light, Luggage Compartment (automatic)
Mirror, glare-proof, rear-view, flip type
Oil Filter

Outside Mirror, left-side, remote-control
Paint, two-tone
Parking Brake Warning Signal
Visor Vanity Mirror
Visors, dual sun
Wheel Discs (set of four)
Window Lifts, electrically operated
Windshield Washer and Coordinator

OPTIONAL EQUIPMENT (Extra Cost)

Cadillac Air Conditioner
E-Z-Eye Tinted Glass
Fog Lamps (pair)
Front Seat Adjustment (vertical and angle), electrically operated

Headlight Dimmer, automatic
Heater
License Frames
Radiator Grille, gold-finish
Radio

Remote-control Trunk Lid Lock
Sabre-Spoke Wheels (set of five), in chrome finish
Whitewall Tires, 8.20 x 15 (set of five)

INTERIOR DIMENSIONS

	REAR	FRONT
Head room	34.0"	34.7"
Shoulder room	57.0"	59.1"
Hip room	57.3"	65.6"
Leg room	40.1"	44.6"
Seat height	13.7"	12.9"

There is glamour and excitement in the appearance of the upholstery, trim and appointments of the Coupe de Ville for 1957. There are eight different choices of upholstery in breath-taking colors combined with rich leathers and gleaming, Lurex-threaded nylon. The buyer may select from four combinations of eye-pleasing Sahara cloth and leather or the delicately patterned Brocade with its design in soft relief combined with textured leather. The seat cushions and seat backs are styled with tufted biscuits and deeply recessed concave, chromed buttons. The leather-covered upper half of the seat back is designed with smart 1" pipes. Chromed roof bows enhance the beauty of the light-toned, perforated Elascofab headlining. All other moldings and metal appointments are finished in bright or brushed chrome, thus carrying out the elegant modernity of the Cadillac Coupe de Ville. Carpeting is a deep-pile nylon blend.

The Cadillac Coupe de Ville is truly an aristocrat and its interior conveys all the charm, taste and graciousness that the name implies. The door panel styling, for example, features harmonizing upholstery fabric surrounding a pleated and smooth leather, chrome-trimmed panel containing a large, functional armrest and a stylized "V" and Crest. A bright chrome kick strip across the bottom of the door provides gleaming highlights of protective beauty, while the upper section of the door panel is finished in beautiful, fine-grained Elascofab over a band of light-toned, painted metal.

IMPROVED PANORAMIC WINDSHIELD

The panoramic windshield, one of the most appreciated and copied of all Cadillac styling innovations, provides even better visibility for 1957. The windshield pillars, slanting backward from the forward edge of the roof, are designed to provide the driver with a wider arc of unobstructed visibility without need of turning his head to right or left. Safety Plate glass in the windshield and door windows and tempered plate glass in the rear window assure maximum safety for all car occupants.

SERIES 62 COUPE de VILLE
COLOR AND UPHOLSTERY CHOICES

40. GRAY SAHARA PATTERN METALLIC NYLON with WHITE LEATHER bolsters and trim.
41. GRAY BROCADE PATTERN METALLIC NYLON with WHITE LEATHER bolsters and trim.
42. BLUE SAHARA PATTERN METALLIC NYLON with BLUE LEATHER bolsters and trim.
43. BLUE BROCADE PATTERN METALLIC NYLON with BLUE LEATHER bolsters and trim.
44. BEIGE SAHARA PATTERN METALLIC NYLON with BEIGE LEATHER bolsters and trim.
46. GREEN SAHARA PATTERN METALLIC NYLON with LIGHT GREEN LEATHER bolsters and trim.
47. GREEN BROCADE PATTERN METALLIC NYLON with LIGHT GREEN LEATHER bolsters and trim.
49. MOUNTAIN LAUREL AND BLACK CORINTHIAN PATTERN METALLIC NYLON with MOUNTAIN LAUREL LEATHER bolsters and trim.

1957 SERIES
62 sedan de ville

300 horsepower
129.5" wheelbase
215.9" over-all length

STANDARD EQUIPMENT

Air Cleaner, oil-bath type
Armrest, center, front and rear
Assist handles (two)
Cadillac Power Brakes
Cadillac Power Steering
Cigarette Lighters, front (two)
Cigarette Lighters, rear (two)
Clock, electric
Front Seat Adjustment (horizontal), electrically operated

Hydra-Matic Transmission
Lights, front ash receivers
Lights, Back-up (dual)
Light, Courtesy or Map (automatic)
Lights, Directional Signal
Light, Glove Box (automatic)
Light, Luggage Compartment (automatic)
Mirror, glare-proof, rear-view, flip type
Oil Filter

Outside Mirror, left-side, remote-control
Paint, two-tone
Parking Brake Warning Signal
Visor Vanity Mirror
Visors, dual sun
Wheel Discs (set of four)
Window Lifts, electrically operated
Windshield Washer and Coordinator

OPTIONAL EQUIPMENT (Extra Cost)

Cadillac Air Conditioner
E-Z-Eye Tinted Glass
Fog Lamps (pair)
Front Seat Adjustment (vertical and angle), electrically operated

Headlight Dimmer, automatic
Heater
License Frames
Radiator Grille, gold-finish
Radio

Remote-control Trunk Lid Lock
Sabre-Spoke Wheels (set of five), in chrome finish
Whitewall Tires, 8.20 x 15 (set of five)

164

The Cadillac Sedan de Ville interiors are marked not only by luxurious materials, but by the manner in which the impeccable tailoring of these materials achieves a truly breath-taking elegance. Soft, textured leathers with smart 1" piping form full bolsters on the seat backs, while seat cushions and seat back inserts are fashioned of glamorous, Lurex-threaded, beautifully patterned nylon. Gleaming chrome finish highlights the concave buttons of the heavily tufted seat cushions and seat back inserts, as well as all other hardware throughout the interior. Headlining is durable and handsome, perforated Elascofab set off by chromed roof bows. Carpeting is a thick, dark-toned nylon blend.

The Cadillac Sedan de Ville, combining the verve of hardtop styling and the convenience of four doors, is in the vanguard of all that's new and exciting in the 1957 Cadillac line. The door panel is marked by a bold rectangular design of leather on cloth, trimmed with bright, gleaming chromium. The smooth, tapering design of the textured Elascofab molding at the top edge of the door panel is in keeping with the advanced design of modern fabrics and patterns. Gleaming chrome moldings tastefully frame the leather portion of the door panels and form the kick strip at the bottom edge of the door for protection against scuff marks.

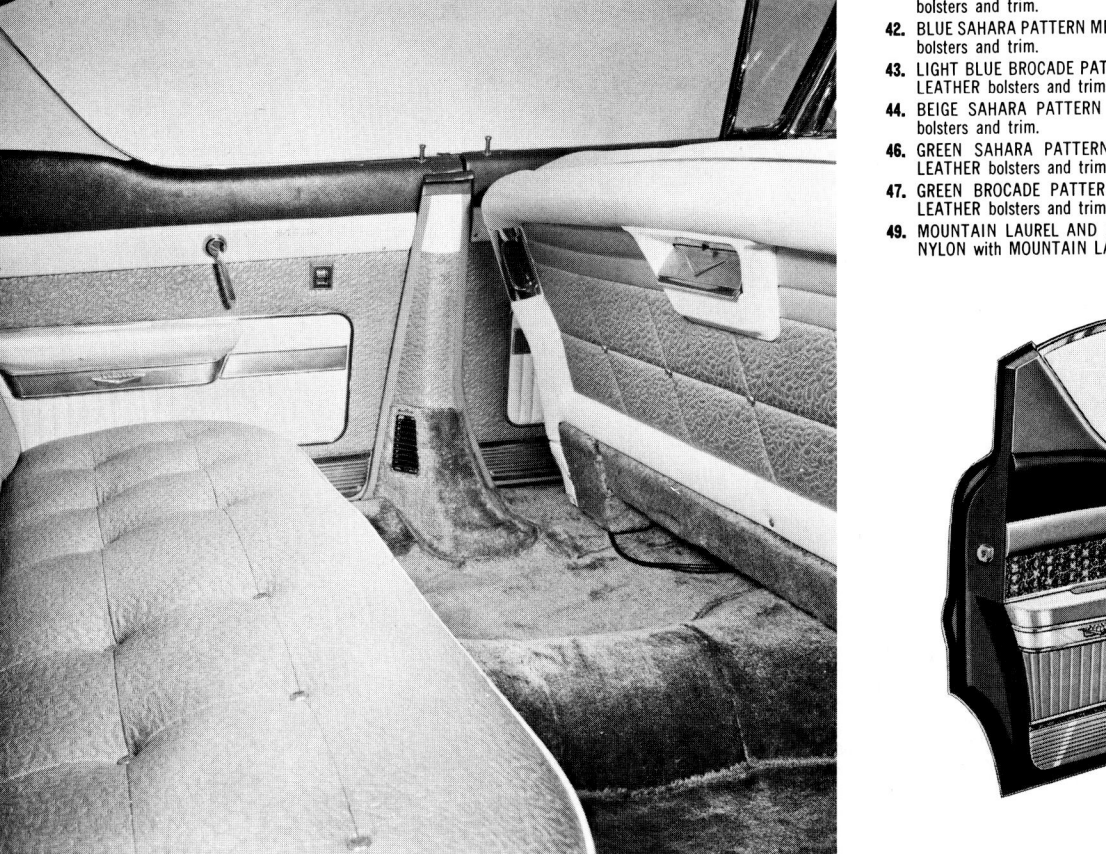

SERIES 62 SEDAN de VILLE
COLOR AND UPHOLSTERY CHOICES

40. GRAY SAHARA PATTERN METALLIC NYLON with WHITE LEATHER bolsters and trim.
41. GRAY BROCADE PATTERN METALLIC NYLON with WHITE LEATHER bolsters and trim.
42. BLUE SAHARA PATTERN METALLIC NYLON with LIGHT BLUE LEATHER bolsters and trim.
43. LIGHT BLUE BROCADE PATTERN METALLIC NYLON with LIGHT BLUE LEATHER bolsters and trim.
44. BEIGE SAHARA PATTERN METALLIC NYLON with BEIGE LEATHER bolsters and trim.
46. GREEN SAHARA PATTERN METALLIC NYLON with LIGHT GREEN LEATHER bolsters and trim.
47. GREEN BROCADE PATTERN METALLIC NYLON with LIGHT GREEN LEATHER bolsters and trim.
49. MOUNTAIN LAUREL AND BLACK CORINTHIAN PATTERN METALLIC NYLON with MOUNTAIN LAUREL LEATHER bolsters and trim.

165

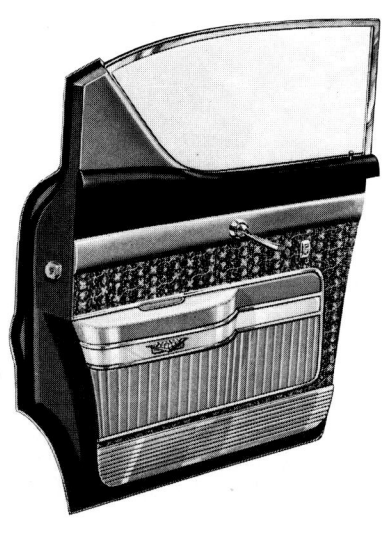

1957 eldorado biarritz

300 horsepower
129.5" wheelbase
222.1" over-all length

STANDARD EQUIPMENT

Air Cleaner, oil-bath type
Armrest, center, front
Cadillac Power Brakes
Cadillac Power Steering
Cigarette Lighters, front (two)
Cigarette Lighters, rear (two)
Clock, electric
Fog Lamps (pair)
Front Seat Adjustment (6-way), electrically operated
Heater
Hydra-Matic Transmission
License Frames
Lights, front ash receivers
Lights, Back-up (dual)
Light, Courtesy or Map (automatic)
Lights, Directional Signal
Light, Glove Box (automatic)
Light, Luggage Compartment (automatic)
Oil Filter
Outside Mirror, left-side, remote-control
Parking Brake Warning Signal
Pocket, flap type, each door
Radio
Rear-view Mirror, 3-way, E-Z-Eye
Remote-control Trunk Lid Lock
Sabre-Spoke Wheels (set of five), chrome finish
Visors, dual sun
Whitewall Tires, 8.20 x 15 (4-ply)
Window Lifts, electrically operated
Windshield Washer and Coordinator

OPTIONAL EQUIPMENT (Extra Cost)

Cadillac Air Conditioner
E-Z-Eye Glass
Gold-finish Radiator Grille (no extra cost)
Headlight Dimmer (automatic)

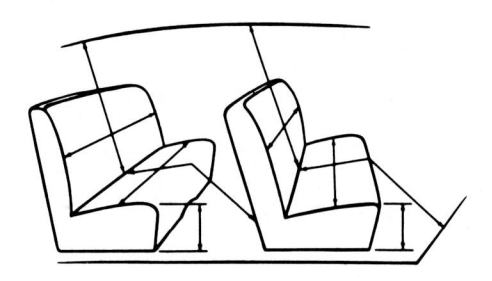

INTERIOR DIMENSIONS

	REAR	FRONT
Head room	34.7"	36.0"
Shoulder room	48.4"	59.3"
Hip room	52.2"	65.7"
Leg room	39.8"	44.5"
Seat height	13.4"	12.2"

The glamorous Eldorado Biarritz and Eldorado Seville, pictured here and on the following two pages, present even more distinctive and exclusive styling for 1957. They are more sleek-lined with an almost three-inch-lower silhouette achieved without sacrifice of important interior roominess. Emphasizing the lower over-all height is the lower hood without top ornamentation and the fleet, tapered lines of the rear deck and quarter panels. The Biarritz convertible top when in the "down" position is recessed beneath a fiber-glass, reinforced plastic top boot finished in the same color as the car body. The steel, Turret Top of the Eldorado Seville is covered with lustrous and durable Vicodec. Further distinguishing the 1957 Eldorados are new stabilizer type fins, flaring boldly rearward, and the new separate rear bumper sections which sweep around the sides of the rear quarter panels to join the heavy chrome molding of the rear wheel openings.

The distinctive exterior styling of the Eldorado Biarritz is matched by ultra-smart interiors combining full luxury with maximum durability. Lasting beauty, for example, is evident in every detail of the door panel shown above. Rich, Cape buffalo-grained leather is used for the pleated area of the door panel and also for the areas just above and below the molded-leather armrests. Behind the pleated area is a convenient map pocket held closed by a snap fastener. A wide kick molding finished in chrome protects the base of the door panel from scuff marks. The top section of the door panel is covered with rich and wear-resistant Elascofab in dark tones contrasting with a metallic band in light-toned painted finish. A chromed, rectangular inset on the upper part of the door and the chromed extensions from the armrest add further highlights of beauty to the distinctive interior of the Eldorado Biarritz.

Luxuriously upholstered in pliant, buffalo-grained leathers, the superbly tailored seat cushions and seat backs of the Biarritz are fashioned with smart pleats set off by an unpleated bolster of matching color or in white. A recessed center armrest in the front seat back and a recessed radio speaker grille in the center of the rear seat back achieve the appearance of two individual seats in both front and rear compartments. Centered in the bolster on each side of the armrest is a distinctive chromed Cadillac medallion. A front compartment radio speaker grille is mounted on the toeboard below the center of the instrument panel. Front and rear floor covering is of luxurious deep-pile, nylon-blend carpeting.

ELDORADO BIARRITZ
COLOR AND UPHOLSTERY CHOICES

10. BLACK LEATHER seats and seat backs with WHITE LEATHER bolsters and trim.
11. Solid BLACK LEATHER throughout.
13. SABRE BLUE METALLIC LEATHER throughout.
15. COPPER METALLIC LEATHER throughout.
17. ELYSIAN GREEN METALLIC LEATHER throughout.
18. KIOWA RED LEATHER seats and seat backs with WHITE LEATHER bolsters and trim.
19. Solid KIOWA RED LEATHER throughout.

VICODEC TOP COLORS: 1. White 2. Black 7. Sabre Blue
8. Copper 9. Elysian Green

Shown at the left in greater detail is the tapered, flush-surfaced rear side panel and deck treatment of the 1957 Eldorados, and the distinctive new tapered fins. Directly below each fin is a circular tail-, stop- and directional signal light with a reflector in the center of the lens. Set side by side in the individual rear bumper sections are a circular exhaust outlet on the outside and a circular back-up light on the inside. Sabre-Spoke forged aluminum wheels, shown below, further enhance the fleet lines of beauty which mark the Eldorados.

Viewed from the front, the new lower lines of the Eldorados are emphasized by the almost flush surface of hood and fenders, the lower grille, wide visors over the headlamps and the twin, circular lamps mounted in the outer extremities of the massive lower bumper bar. The outer lamps are parking and directional signals, the inner lamps are parking and fog lights. A final style note is the use of small twin ornaments atop each front fender. Tips of the gull-wing bumper guards are of black, molded rubber on all Cadillac models for 1957.

1957

1957 eldorado seville

300 horsepower
129.5" wheelbase
222.1" over-all length

STANDARD EQUIPMENT

Air Cleaner, oil-bath type
Armrest, center, front and rear
Cadillac Power Brakes
Cadillac Power Steering
Cigarette Lighters, front (two)
Cigarette Lighters, rear (two)
Clock, electric
Fog Lamps (pair)
Front Seat Adjustment (6-way), electrically operated
Heater
Hydra-Matic Transmission
License Frames
Lights, front ash receivers
Lights, Back-up (dual)
Light, Courtesy or Map (automatic)
Lights, Directional Signal
Light, Glove Box (automatic)
Light, Luggage Compartment (automatic)
Oil Filter
Outside Mirror, left-side, remote-control
Parking Brake Warning Signal
Pocket, flap type, each door
Radio
Rear-view Mirror, 3-way, E-Z-Eye
Remote-control Trunk Lid Lock
Sabre-Spoke Wheels (set of five), chrome finish
Visors, dual sun
Whitewall Tires, 8.20 x 15 (4-ply)
Window Lifts, electrically operated
Windshield Washer and Coordinator

OPTIONAL EQUIPMENT (Extra Cost)

Cadillac Air Conditioner
E-Z-Eye Glass
Gold-finish Radiator Grille (no extra cost)
Headlight Dimmer (automatic)

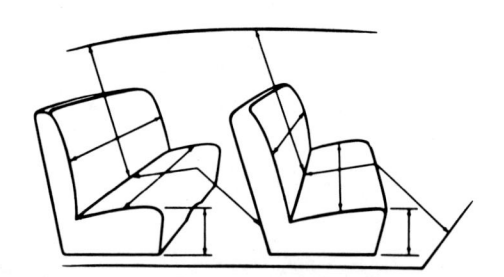

INTERIOR DIMENSIONS

	REAR	FRONT
Head room	34.0"	35.5"
Shoulder room	57.0"	59.3"
Hip room	57.3"	65.7"
Leg room	39.8"	44.5"
Seat height	13.4"	12.2"

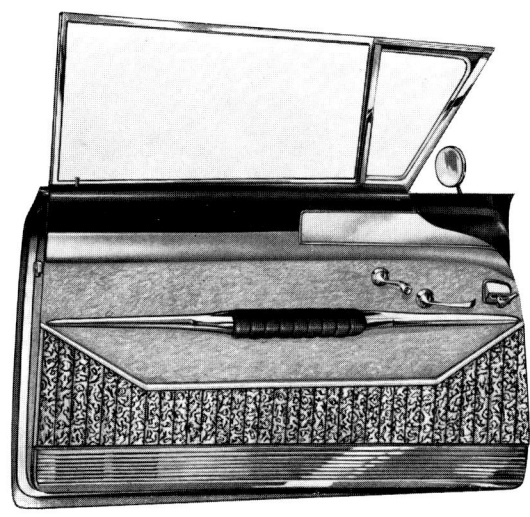

The exquisite interiors of the Eldorado Seville are marked by deftly tailored upholstery in a choice of many exclusive leathers or combinations of leather and glamorous metallic nylon fabrics in Paisley or fine-textured Versailles patterns. Chromed Cadillac medallions highlight the buffalo-grained leather of the seat back bolsters, while seat back inserts and seat cushions are fashioned of smart $1\frac{1}{4}''$ pipes. Floor covering of tufted, deep-pile, nylon-blend carpeting further enhances the luxury, elegance and comfort provided by the Eldorado Seville for 1957.

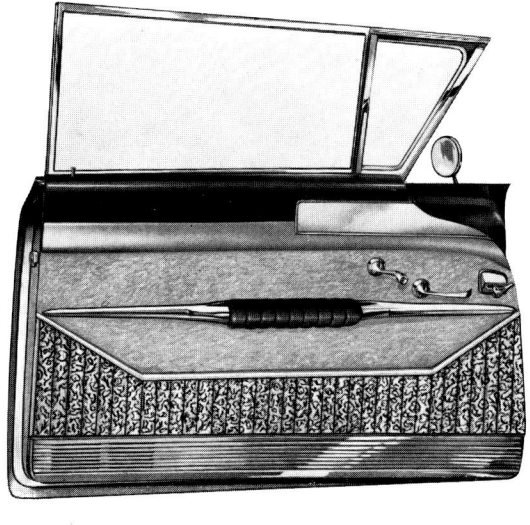

The sleek, Vicodec-covered, hardtop styling of the glamorous Eldorado Seville is fittingly complemented by its ultra-fashionable interiors. In styling detail the door panels and sidewalls of the Seville are similar to those of the Eldorado Biarritz described on page 67. However, when any of four additional Seville upholstery options of metallic nylon are ordered, this glamorous fabric replaces the leather-pleated sections of the door panel. Also, on the Seville, the radio speaker grille for the rear compartment is mounted beneath the package shelf rather than in the recess above the rear seat center armrest. Finally, enhancing the over-all beauty of the Seville interior décor is a headlining of durable, perforated Elascofab with gleaming chromed roof bows.

ELDORADO SEVILLE
COLOR AND UPHOLSTERY CHOICES

10. BLACK LEATHER seats and seat backs with WHITE LEATHER bolsters and trim.
13. SABRE BLUE METALLIC LEATHER throughout.
17. ELYSIAN GREEN METALLIC LEATHER throughout.
18. KIOWA RED seats and seat backs with WHITE LEATHER bolsters and trim.
50. SILVER AND BLACK PAISLEY CLOTH seats and seat backs with WHITE LEATHER bolsters and trim.
53. SABRE BLUE AND BLACK PAISLEY CLOTH seats and seat backs with SABRE BLUE LEATHER bolsters and trim.
57. ELYSIAN GREEN VERSAILLES CLOTH seats and seat backs with ELYSIAN GREEN METALLIC LEATHER bolsters and trim.
58. COPPER VERSAILLES CLOTH seats and seat backs with COPPER METALLIC LEATHER bolsters and trim.

VICODEC TOP COLORS: 1. White 2. Black 7. Sabre Blue
8. Copper 9. Elysian Green

1957 SERIES 60 special sedan

300 horsepower
133" wheelbase
224.4" over-all length

STANDARD EQUIPMENT

Air Cleaner, oil-bath type
Armrest, center, front and rear
Assist Handles (two)
Cadillac Power Brakes
Cadillac Power Steering
Cigarette Lighters, front (two)
Cigarette Lighters, rear (two)
Clock, electric
Front Seat Adjustment (horizontal), electrically operated

Hydra-Matic Transmission
Lights, front ash receivers
Lights, Back-up (dual)
Light, Courtesy or Map (automatic)
Lights, Directional Signal
Light, Glove Box (automatic)
Light, Luggage Compartment (automatic)
Mirror, glare-proof, rear-view, flip type
Oil Filter
Outside Mirror, left-side, remote-control

Paint, two-tone
Parking Brake Warning Signal
Pocket, back of front seat
Visor Vanity Mirror
Visors, dual sun
Wheel Discs (set of four)
Window Lifts, electrically operated
Windshield Washer and Coordinator

OPTIONAL EQUIPMENT (Extra Cost)

Cadillac Air Conditioner
E-Z-Eye Tinted Glass
Fog Lamps (pair)
Front Seat Adjustment (vertical and angle), electrically operated

Headlight Dimmer, automatic
Heater
License Frames
Radiator Grille, gold-finish
Radio

Remote-control Trunk Lid Lock
Sabre-Spoke Wheels (set of five) in chrome finish
Whitewall Tires, 8.20 x 15 (set of five)

Symbol of Cadillac leadership in the luxury-car field, the 60 Special Sedan interiors for 1957 will further enhance the enviable reputation of this truly elegant motor car. That there is no compromise with quality is evident in every detail. For example, its door-width armrests, each containing a large ash receiver and cigarette lighter; the wide, chromed kick moldings across the base of the doors, surmounted in vertical pleats by the most fashionable of modern fabrics; and the use of smart and durable Elascofab panels across the upper section of the door, divided by a glossy strip of light-toned lacquered metal. Lending further distinction is a chromed Cadillac crest set within the chromed armrest molding just above the door pull.

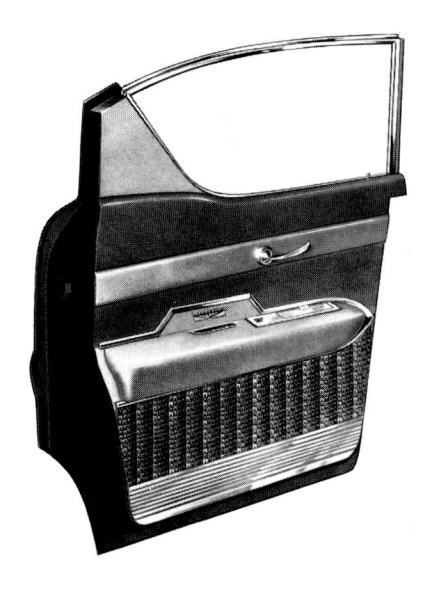

The interiors of the Cadillac 60 Special Sedan are designed to please the most discerning eye. Seat cushions and seat back inserts are impeccably tailored in two-inch pipes, while seat welts provide the enduring beauty of smart, leather-grained Elascofab. Upholstery choices include solid-color, all-wool broadcloth throughout or patterned nylons, many with gleaming Lurex threads, combined with bolsters of fine-textured metallic nylon or leather. Lending new distinction to the interior of the 60 Special for 1957 is the pleated headlining surrounded by a wide halo molding of light-toned lacquered metal. A final warm note of luxury and comfort is provided by the deep-pile, heavily tufted, nylon-blend carpeting in front and rear compartments.

The beautiful and functional instrument panel is a modern design in keeping with dynamic engineering inspired by the thought of individual comfort and convenience. The smooth, sleek, over-all design of the instrument panel incorporates many advanced features that make driving a Cadillac an effortless pleasure. Note, for example, the new location of the power window lift controls on the left-hand extension of the instrument panel—convenient to the driver's fingertips. Note, too, the new, conveniently placed radio controls—on the left of the dial where they can be easily operated by the driver. Even the lock on the glove compartment door has been located to the left for greater driver convenience.

SERIES 60 SPECIAL
COLOR AND UPHOLSTERY CHOICES

60. GRAY METALLIC SAHARA CLOTH seats and seat back inserts with GRAY METALLIC STRATA CLOTH bolsters and trim.
61. GRAY BROADCLOTH throughout.
62. BLUE METALLIC SAHARA CLOTH seats and seat back inserts with BLUE METALLIC STRATA CLOTH bolsters and trim.
63. BLUE CLASSIC CLOTH seats and seat back inserts with BLUE STRATA CLOTH bolsters and trim.
65. BEIGE BROADCLOTH throughout.
66. GREEN METALLIC SAHARA CLOTH seats and seat back inserts with GREEN METALLIC STRATA CLOTH bolsters and trim.
67. GREEN CLASSIC CLOTH seats and seat back inserts with GREEN METALLIC STRATA CLOTH bolsters and trim.
70. SILVER AND BLACK METALLIC CORINTHIAN CLOTH seats and seat back inserts with WHITE LEATHER bolsters and trim.
72. SABRE BLUE AND BLACK METALLIC CORINTHIAN CLOTH seats and seat back inserts with BLUE LEATHER bolsters and trim.
76. GREEN AND BLACK METALLIC CORINTHIAN CLOTH seats and seat back inserts with GREEN LEATHER bolsters and trim.

INTERIOR DIMENSIONS

	REAR	FRONT
Head room	34.7"	33.9"
Shoulder room	57.0"	59.0"
Hip room	65.0"	65.0"
Leg room	45.3"	45.2"
Seat height	12.7"	13.9"

1957 SERIES seventy-five

300 horsepower
149.75" wheelbase
236.2" over-all length

STANDARD EQUIPMENT

Air Cleaner, oil-bath type
Armrest, center, front and rear
Assist Handles (two)
Cadillac Power Brakes
Cadillac Power Steering
Cigarette Lighters, front (two)
Cigarette Lighters, rear (two)
Clocks, electric, front and rear compartments
Foot Rests, adjustable (two), rear compartment

Front Seat Adjustment (horizontal), electrically operated
Hydra-Matic Transmission
Lights, front ash receivers
Lights, Back-up (dual)
Light, Courtesy, Map (automatic)
Lights, Directional Signal
Light, Glove Box (automatic)
Light, Luggage Compartment (automatic)
Mirror, glare-proof, rear-view, flip type
Oil Filter

Outside Mirror, left-side, remote-control
Package Compartments in Side
Armrests, rear (two)
Paint, two-tone
Parking Brake Warning Signal
Robe Cord on back of front seat
Visor Vanity Mirror
Visors, dual sun
Wheel Discs (set of four)
Window Lifts, electrically operated
Windshield Washer and Coordinator

OPTIONAL EQUIPMENT (Extra Cost)

Cadillac Air Conditioner
E-Z-Eye Tinted Glass
Fog Lamps (pair)
Headlight Dimmer, automatic

Heater
License Frames
Radiator Grille, gold-finish
Radio, remote-control

Remote-Control Trunk Lid Lock
Sabre-Spoke Wheels (set of five) in chrome finish
Whitewall Tires, 8.20 x 15 (set of five)

INTERIOR DIMENSIONS

	REAR	AUXILIARY	FRONT
Head room	35.3"	37.4"	36.6"
Shoulder room	56.8"	57.7"	59.0"
Hip room	57.8"	64.6"	65.5"
Leg room	38.5"	36.1"	43.5"
Seat height	13.6"	12.3"	12.8"

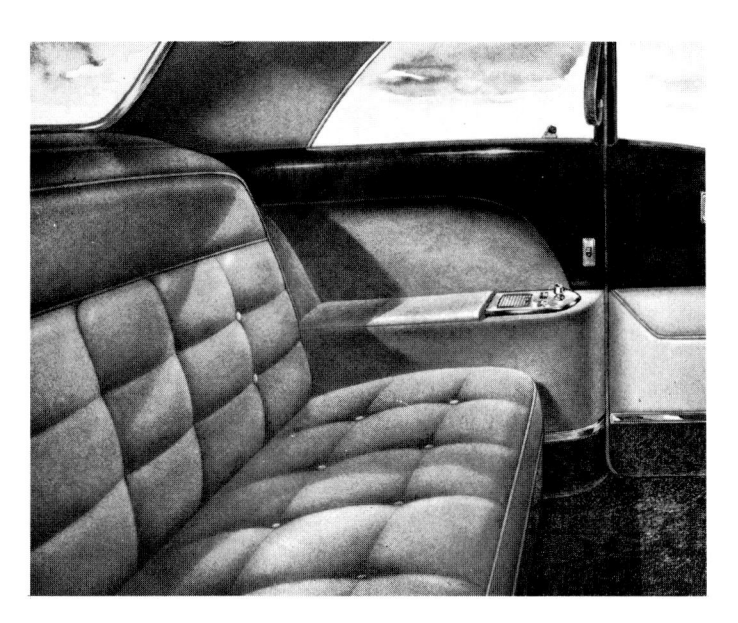

Interiors of the Series 75 Nine-Passenger Sedan are elegantly tailored in heavily tufted, rectangular biscuits and deeply recessed buttons. A smartly contrasting, smooth-surfaced panel extends across the upper portion of the seat backs. Upholstery options include fashionable Bedford cord in a choice of four colors with harmonizing all-wool broadcloth bolsters or two choices of solid-color, all-wool broadcloth throughout. The use of genuine leather or durable, leather-grained Elascofab lends protective beauty at all points of wear or stress. Adding gleaming highlights of beauty throughout the interior is the bright and brushed chrome finish of hardware and moldings.

Impressively big and beautiful, the Cadillac Series 75 Nine-Passenger Sedan provides unmatched dignity and distinction. Reflecting the inherent graciousness and luxury of its interior trim and appointments is the heavily tufted, deep-pile, nylon-blend carpeting covering not only the floor, but the scuff-pad areas of the doors and the lower portions of the seats and sidewalls, as well as the adjustable rear compartment foot rests. Two fold-away seats are concealed in the beautifully appointed center partition which also provides the conveniences of an electric clock, leather-covered robe cord and two leather-covered assist handles. Extending across the rear of the front seat back and on the upper sections of the doors and sidewalls is a beautiful teakwood-grained Dinoc panel.

The Cadillac Series 75 Limousine is the most luxurious chauffeur-driven car in America. It provides all of the style, comfort and convenience of the nine-passenger sedan but with the added practicality of a genuine leather-upholstered front compartment. A glass partition separating the front and rear compartments may be raised or lowered electrically by automatic control buttons located on the rear seat armrests, adjacent to the window control buttons.

SERIES SEVENTY-FIVE LIMOUSINE COLOR AND UPHOLSTERY CHOICES

Selection of fabrics and colors is the same as for the nine-passenger sedan except that the front compartment is upholstered throughout in genuine BLACK LEATHER. Seat cushions and seat backs are fashioned in two-inch piping without bolsters.

SERIES 75 NINE-PASSENGER SEDAN COLOR AND UPHOLSTERY CHOICES

80. LIGHT GRAY BEDFORD CORD seat and seat back inserts with LIGHT GRAY BROADCLOTH bolsters and trim.
81. LIGHT GRAY BROADCLOTH throughout.
84. BEIGE BEDFORD CORD seat and seat back inserts with BEIGE BROADCLOTH bolsters and trim.
85. BEIGE BROADCLOTH throughout.
90. DARK GRAY BEDFORD CORD seat and seat back inserts with LIGHT GRAY BROADCLOTH bolsters and trim.
94. BROWN BEDFORD CORD seat and seat back inserts with BEIGE BROADCLOTH bolsters and trim.

1957

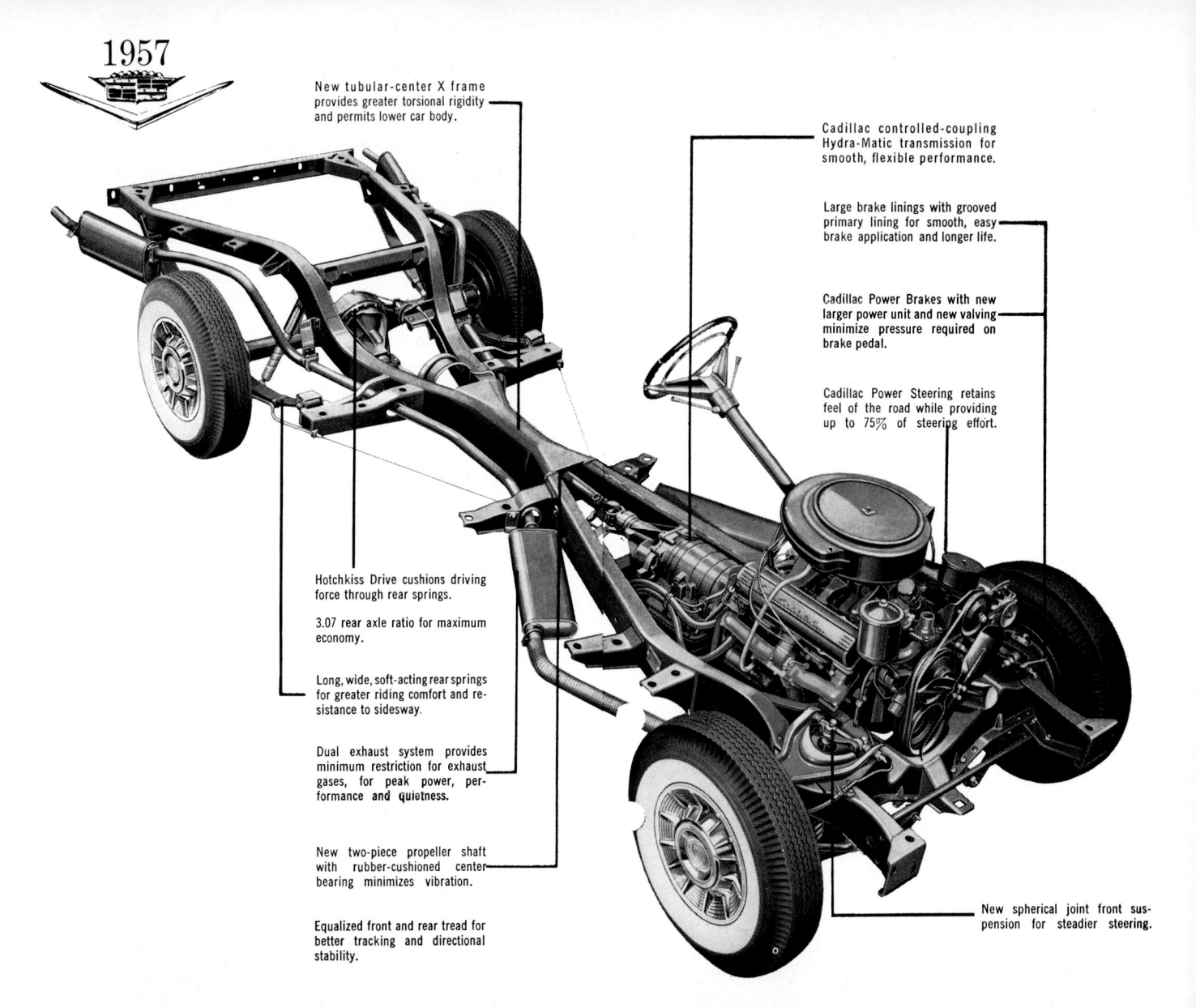

New tubular-center X frame provides greater torsional rigidity and permits lower car body.

Cadillac controlled-coupling Hydra-Matic transmission for smooth, flexible performance.

Large brake linings with grooved primary lining for smooth, easy brake application and longer life.

Cadillac Power Brakes with new larger power unit and new valving minimize pressure required on brake pedal.

Cadillac Power Steering retains feel of the road while providing up to 75% of steering effort.

Hotchkiss Drive cushions driving force through rear springs.

3.07 rear axle ratio for maximum economy.

Long, wide, soft-acting rear springs for greater riding comfort and resistance to sideway.

Dual exhaust system provides minimum restriction for exhaust gases, for peak power, performance and quietness.

New two-piece propeller shaft with rubber-cushioned center bearing minimizes vibration.

Equalized front and rear tread for better tracking and directional stability.

New spherical joint front suspension for steadier steering.

NEW CADILLAC TUBULAR-CENTER X FRAME

The tubular-center X frame without side rails is a new and exclusive Cadillac feature for 1957. It provides greater torsional rigidity and less vertical deflection than conventional frames. At the same time it permits lowering the floor and the over-all height of the car for smarter appearance, without sacrificing interior roominess. Lowering the body brings the car's center of gravity closer to the road for greater stability and safer cornering. The new more-rigid frame is joined to new reinforced body sill panels with pre-loaded, rubber-insulated body mountings. Since there is no metal-to-metal-contact between body and frame the transmission of road noise and vibration is virtually eliminated for a quieter, smoother, more comfortable ride.

IMPROVED SHOCK ABSORBER ACTION

Cadillac shock absorbers serve to control spring flexing to the degree required by various road surfaces. For example, on roads with minor irregularities they offer only slight resistance to spring action, while on rough roads they tend to keep the car level by providing the firmer resistance necessary to minimize pitching. For 1957, shock absorber valves have been modified for a softer ride. The high-viscosity fluid used in Cadillac shock absorbers is impervious to temperature changes, thus assuring uniformly good shock absorber action in any season of the year.

IMPROVED REAR SUSPENSION

Cadillac's long, wide, leaf rear springs have been moved outward, closer to the wheels for 1957. As a result of thus broadening the base upon which the weight of the car is supported, the 1957 Cadillac provides greater roll stability on curves or when cornering. Cadillac's rear springs not only cushion vertical motion of the car, but absorb thrusts of starting and stopping motion as well.

NEW FRONT SUSPENSION

The addition of ball joints to replace kingpins on Cadillac's individual coil-spring front suspension units permits positioning the control arms of the suspension system to provide greater resistance to front-end dive during braking. This minimizes any possibility of locking bumpers should impact with a car ahead occur. The new suspension also contributes to more positive control, less free play and easier, steadier steering.

NEW, TWO-PIECE PROPELLER SHAFT

For 1957, Cadillac has provided a new, two-piece propeller shaft with three Universal joints and a new, rubber-cushioned center bearing. Its design permits a lower rear floor tunnel and deeper rear seat cushions.

QUIETER DIFFERENTIAL GEARS

Typical of the many constant refinements which Cadillac seeks to embody in its cars is a change in the angle of the differential gear teeth from a 45° to a 50° helix. The result is smoother engagement of the gear teeth and quieter performance.

MORE RUGGED AXLE SHAFTS AND HOUSING

The value of a Cadillac car in the resale market is in large part due to the recognized dependability and durability of its mechanical components. On 1957 models an even stronger rear axle shaft, now made of induction hardened carbon steel, thicker rear axle housings and larger rear axle bearings provide additional strength and durability in keeping with the increased output of the new Cadillac engine.

ECONOMY REAR AXLE RATIO

Cadillac's powerful engine combined with the efficient performance of the Cadillac Hydra-Matic transmission makes possible the use of an economical 3.07 to 1 rear axle ratio. This means that the rear wheels make one complete revolution to just a little over three revolutions of the engine. On some competitive cars the engine may be required to make three and a half to nearly four revolutions with a resulting increase in fuel consumption. An optional 3.36 to 1 rear axle is available on the Series 62, 60 Special and the Eldorado Biarritz and Seville, and standard on the Series 75 and all air-conditioned models. A 3.77 rear axle is optional on the 75 Series.

HIGHLIGHTS OF THE 1957 CADILLAC ENGINE

New, 300 horsepower.

New, 10.0 to 1 compression ratio.

New combustion chambers.

New, larger intake valves and ports.

New, lower four-barrel carburetor with larger secondary barrels.

New, lower air cleaner.

New rocker arms.

New piston design.

New camshaft.

New intake manifold.

New motor mountings.

New starting motor.

New exhaust manifold.

New, higher output generator.

New battery and battery box.

New, higher capacity fuel pump.

ADDITIONAL HIGHLIGHTS OF OPTIONAL ENGINE FOR ELDORADO BIARRITZ AND SEVILLE ONLY

New, 325 horsepower.

Two new four-barrel carburetors.

New dual air cleaners.

NEW CADILLAC AIR CONDITIONER

Cadillac owners can enjoy cool comfort during hottest summer temperatures with a Cadillac Air Conditioner installed on their cars. In addition, the car interior is dust-free, pollen-free and quiet. The 1957 Cadillac Air Conditioner uses 100% outside air which enters through the wide cowl air intake, cools it in the cooling unit now located in the cowl, and circulates it within the car from three outlets on top of the instrument panel. Cool air is also directed to the floor from outlets on the dash panel. A complete change of air takes place every 40 seconds with no recirculation of air from within the car. Air direction is controlled by individual doors on each of the instrument panel air outlets. (On Series 75 models the cooling unit, located in the trunk compartment, circulates air through ducts in the car roof.)

Also new for 1957 is a compressor with increased operating speed for improved operation at low car speeds. As before, the compressor disengages from the engine when desired temperature is reached or when the Air Conditioner is turned OFF, thus eliminating unnecessary drain of engine power and minimizing wear on compressor parts. Two simple control levers are located to the right of the steering column just below the instrument cluster. The upper lever turns on the Air Conditioner and controls the volume of air discharged into the car. The lower lever controls the temperature of the air being discharged. For ventilation without air cooling the upper lever alone is used.

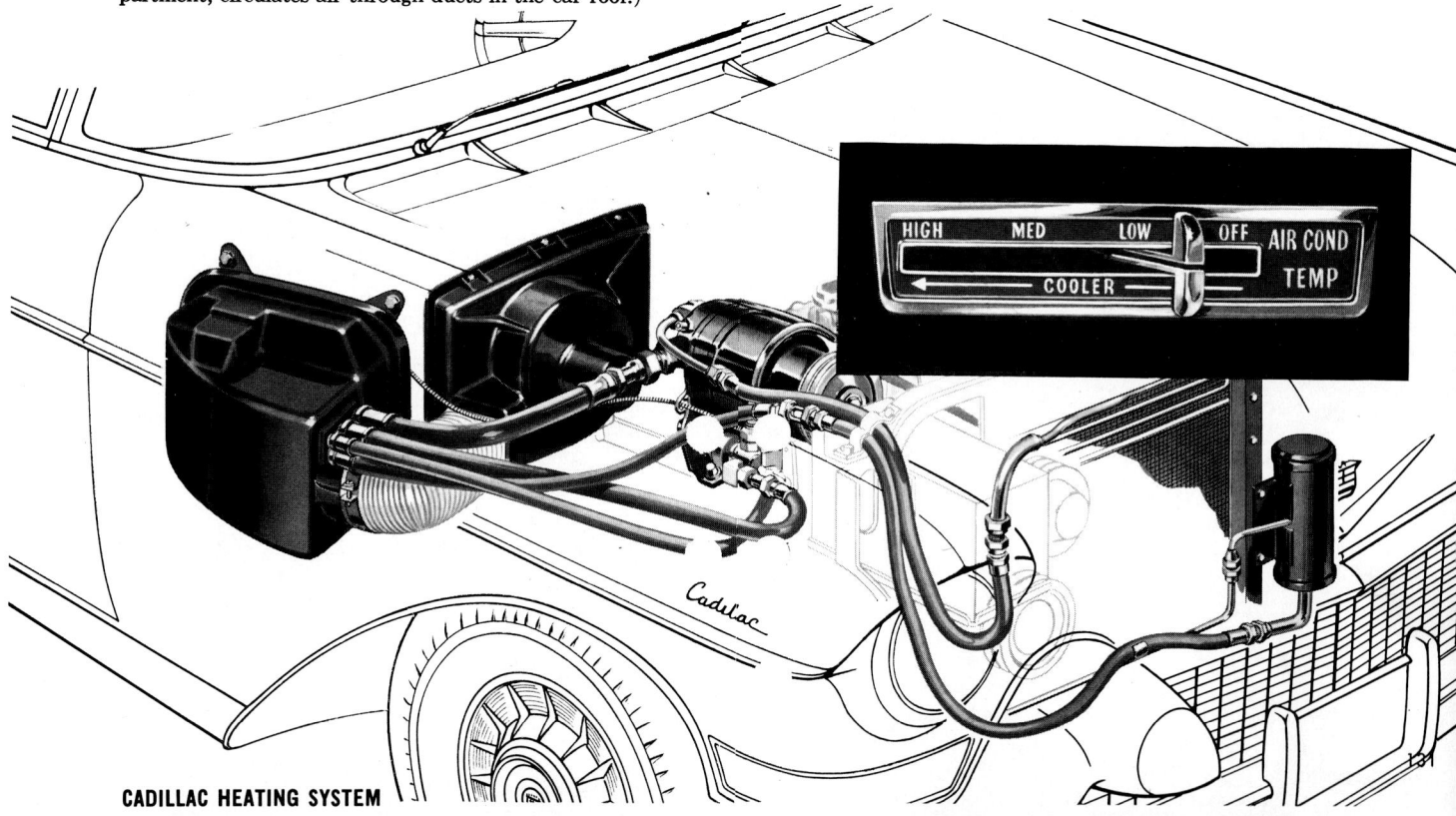

CADILLAC HEATING SYSTEM

The Cadillac Automatic Heating System is designed to provide full comfort in the coldest weather. It assures an ample supply of fresh air, heated and held to a constant temperature . . . seals out dust and moisture . . . rapidly defrosts and defogs windows and has a low noise level. Outside air is drawn into the system through the wide cowl air intake; warmed by the heating unit, located at the left side of the cowl; then circulated into the front compartment, through grilles in the cowl side panels and through an opening beneath the instrument panel, and into the rear compartment through door ducts with outlet grilles located on the kick moldings of coupes and on the center pillar posts of sedan models. (The Series 75 models have a second heating unit under the right-hand cowl to provide additional heated air for the larger rear compartment.)

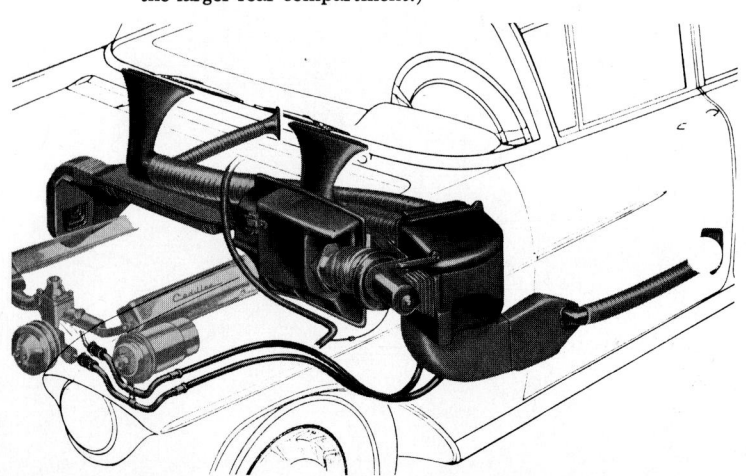

Heater controls consist of two levers located just below the instrument cluster to the left of the steering column. The lower lever turns the heater on and controls the amount and temperature of the air being discharged into the passenger compartments. The upper lever permits directing cool air to the windshield for ventilation or defogging or warmed air, to the temperature of the heater setting, for defrosting. When maximum heating of the windshield is desired for removal of ice, the entire output of the heater may be directed to the windshield by moving the lower, or heater lever full to the left and the upper lever full to the right.

ELECTRICALLY OPERATED ANTENNA

Providing advantages in both function and appearance is the electrically operated antenna located at the rear of the right front fender. It may be fully lowered into a chromed recess or raised to any degree of its maximum height simply by pulling or pushing the right-hand radio control knob.

CADILLAC "AUTRONIC-EYE"

The Cadillac "Autronic-Eye" protects the Cadillac owner by causing the headlights of his car to switch from high to low beam when another car approaches from the opposite direction. Since the driver of the oncoming car is not blinded, both cars pass with greater safety. An overriding switch is provided to signal drivers who neglect to switch their own lights from bright to dim.

NEW FOG LAMPS

Cadillac Fog Lamps are designed to provide illumination low to the surface of the road and thus provide better visibility under certain adverse weather conditions. When ordered, they are installed on the lower bumper bar in place of the inner pair of parking lights.

accessory groups
(Factory-Installed)

GROUP A . . . . $_____
   White Sidewall Tires • Heater • Radio • E-Z-Eye Glass

GROUP B . . . . $_____
   White Sidewall Tires • Heater • Radio

GROUP C . . . . $_____
   Air Conditioner • White Sidewall Tires • Heater • Radio • E-Z-Eye Glass

GROUP 2 . . . . $_____
   Autronic-Eye • Fog Lamps • Dor-Gards • License Frame (1)

GROUP 3 . . . . $_____
   Autronic-Eye • Fog Lamps • Dor-Gards • License Frames (2)

GROUP 4 . . . . $_____
   Fog Lamps • Dor-Gards • License Frame (1)

GROUP 5 . . . . $_____
   Fog Lamps • Dor-Gards • License Frames (2)

Do not order any group for Eldorados, as most of this equipment is standard.

CADILLAC SABRE-SPOKE WHEELS

Especially constructed of aluminum and steel, Sabre-Spoke wheels are standard on the Eldorado Biarritz and Seville and available in sets of five as an extra-cost option on all other models. Sabre-Spoke wheels are finished in chromium.

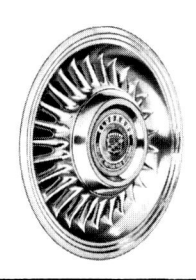

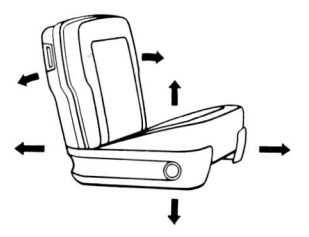

CADILLAC SIX-WAY POWER SEAT

For all 1957 Cadillac cars equipped with the electrically powered fore-and-aft seat adjuster, an electrically powered vertical and seat-angle adjustment is also available as an extra-cost option. It provides a four-inch range of vertical seat adjustment and also permits the seat to be tilted to the best angle required by the driver for maximum comfort. The complete Six-Way Power Seat is standard equipment on the Eldorado Biarritz and Seville, optional at extra cost on the Series 62 Coupe and Sedan. A new control switch, on left side of front seat, provides simplified adjustment for 1957.

REMOTE-CONTROL TRUNK LID LOCK

The Cadillac Remote-Control Trunk Lid Lock is a convenience feature which will be particularly appreciated by owners who live in areas where federal or local authorities must check trunk contents in compliance with law (such as when crossing an international boundary). The deck lid can be automatically unlocked at a touch of a button located within the glove compartment on the left side. A small warning light, just to the left of the instrument cluster, lets the driver know when the trunk is in the unlocked position.

Additional Cadillac accessories

Rear-Compartment Radio Control	$_____
Radio Foot-Control Switch	$_____
Cadillac "Cushion Topper"	$_____
Cadillac Rubber Floor Mats	$_____
Windshield Washer Solvent	$_____
Cadillac Body Polish	$_____
Cadillac Fabric Cleaner	$_____
Cadillac Kar-Kleen	$_____
Cadillac Blue Coral	$_____
Cadillac Chrome Cleaner	$_____
Cadillac Cooling System Inhibitor	$_____
Cadillac Whitewall Tire Cleaner	$_____
Cadillac Seat Belts	$_____

1957

The conceptual styling changes for 1957 were the most revolutionary since 1948. Perhaps the most interesting result of the dramatically lowered bodies — made possible by the new frame — was the blending of fenders and hood in an almost uniform horizontal plane. Above left, the 1957 Series 62 Sedan. Center left, the 1957 Series 62 Coupe. Bottom, the 1957 Sedan de Ville. Opposite page bottom, the 1957 *Eldorado Biarritz*.

1957 CADILLAC GENERAL SPECIFICATIONS

	Series 62 Sedan and Sedan de Ville	Series 62 Coupe and Coupe de Ville	Series 62 Convertible Coupe	Eldorado Biarritz and Eldorado Seville	Series 60 Special Sedan	Series 75 9-Passenger Sedan and Limousine
Wheelbase	129.5"	129.5"	129.5"	129.5"	133"	149.8"
Over-all Length	215.9"	220.9"	220.9"	222.1"	224.4"	236.2"
Over-all Width	80"	80"	80"	80"	80"	80"
Over-all Height	59.1"	57.7"	58.2"	57.9"**	59.1"	61.6"
Frame-to-Road Clearance at Center of Wheelbase	6.5"	6.5"	6.5"	6.5"	6.5"	7.5"
Steering Ratio—Over-all	19.5"	19.5"	19.5"	19.5"	19.5"	19.5"
Turning Radius	21.7"	21.7"	21.7"	21.7"	22.5"	25.8"
Tread—Front	61"	61"	61"	61"	61"	61"
Tread—Rear	61"	61"	61"	61"	61"	61"
Tires, Tubeless—Size	8:00 x 15*	8:00 x 15*	8:00 x 15*	8:20 x 15	8:00 x 15*	8:20 x 15
Tires—Ply Rating	4-ply	4-ply	4-ply	4-ply	4-ply	6-ply

*8:20 x 15 supplied in whitewall tires (standard on Eldorado Biarritz and Seville)   **58.4" on Eldorado Biarritz

	Series 62 Sedan and Sedan de Ville	Series 62 Coupe and Coupe de Ville	Series 62 Convertible Coupe	Eldorado Biarritz and Eldorado Seville	Series 60 Special Sedan	Series 75 9-Passenger Sedan and Limousine
Engine	300-horsepower Cadillac V-8	300-horsepower Cadillac V-8	300-horsepower Cadillac V-8	300-horsepower Cadillac V-8	300-horsepower Cadillac V-8	300-horsepower Cadillac V-8
Compression Ratio	10.0:1	10.0:1	10.0:1	10.0:1	10.0:1	10.0:1
Piston Displacement	365 cu. in.	365 cu. in.	365 cu. in.	365 cu. in.	365 cu. in.	365 cu. in.
Valve Arrangement	Overhead	Overhead	Overhead	Overhead	Overhead	Overhead
Carburetor	4-barrel	4-barrel	4-barrel	4-barrel	4-barrel	4-barrel
Exhaust System	Dual	Dual	Dual	Dual	Dual	Dual
Transmission	Hydra-Matic	Hydra-Matic	Hydra-Matic	Hydra-Matic	Hydra-Matic	Hydra-Matic
Steering	Hydraulic Power	Hydraulic Power	Hydraulic Power	Hydraulic Power	Hydraulic Power	Hydraulic Power
Brakes	Power Brakes	Power Brakes	Power Brakes	Power Brakes	Power Brakes	Power Brakes
Frame	Tubular-center X	Tubular-center X	Tubular-center X	Tubular-center X	Tubular-center X	Tubular-center X
Springs	Coil front, semi-elliptic-leaf rear	Coil front, semi-elliptic-leaf rear	Coil front, semi-elliptic-leaf rear	Coil front, semi-elliptic-leaf rear	Coil front, semi-elliptic-leaf rear	Coil front, semi-elliptic-leaf rear
Drive	Hotchkiss	Hotchkiss	Hotchkiss	Hotchkiss	Hotchkiss	Hotchkiss
Axle Ratio	3.07:1*	3.07:1*	3.07:1*	3.07:1*	3.07:1*	3.36:1**

*3.36:1 standard on Eldorados with the 325-h.p. engine, on Series 75 and air-conditioned models, optional on other models.
**3.77 optional on Series 75.

1957 specifications

ENGINE
Number of cylinders	8
Cylinder arrangement	90° V-type
Valve arrangement	Overhead
Bore and stroke	4" x 3⅝"
Block and cylinder head material	Cast iron
Piston displacement	365 cu. in.
Taxable horsepower	51.2
Max. brake horsepower	300 @ 4800 r.p.m.
Optional engine Eldorado only	325 @ 4800 r.p.m.
Max. engine torque—lbs.-ft.	400 @ 2800 r.p.m.
Optional engine Eldorado only	400 @ 3300 r.p.m.
Compression ratio	10.0:1
Engine mounts	Vulcanized rubber
Number of points of suspension	3

PISTONS AND RINGS
Make	Alcoa—Bohn—Stearling
Material	Aluminum alloy
Type	T-slot, cam ground
Weight	22.72 oz.
Clearance	.0015
Number of oil rings per piston	1
Number of comp. rings per piston	2
Top compression ring	Chrome-plated

RODS AND PINS
Wristpin length	3.093"
Wristpin material	Steel
Type	Locked in rod
Connecting rod length	6.625"
Material—connecting rod	Forged steel
Weight—connecting rod	23.49 oz.
Crankpin journal diameter	2¼"
Lower bearing material	Steel back Moraine 400
Connecting rod bearing clearance	.0005"-.0021"
Connecting rod bearing end play	.008"-.014" (total two rods)

CRANKSHAFT
Material	Forged alloy steel
Weight	71 pounds
Main bearing thrust	Rear main
Crankshaft end play	.001" to .005"
Main bearing type	Slip-on
Main bearing removable	Yes
Main bearing material	Steel back Durex
Main bearing clearance—rear	.0008" to .0025"
Main bearing journal Diameter x Length:	
Number 1	2.625" x .907"
Number 2	2.625" x .907"
Number 3	2.625" x .907"
Number 4	2.625" x .907"
Number 5	2.625" x 1.622"

CAMSHAFT
Drive	Chain
Camshaft sprocket material	Steel
Timing chain—make	Link Belt
Timing chain—no. of links	46
Timing chain—width	.6875"
Timing chain—pitch	.500"

VALVES
Valve arrangement	Overhead
Intake opens	36° B.T.C. at .001 lift
Intake closes	108° A.B.C. at .001 lift
Exhaust opens	86° B.B.C. at .001 lift
Exhaust closes	58° A.T.C. at .001 lift

INTAKE
Material	Alloy steel
Over-all length	4.675"
Diameter of head	1.875"
Angle of seat	44°
Lift	.451"

EXHAUST
Material	Alloy steel
Over-all length	4.692"
Diameter of head	1.437"
Angle of seat	44°
Lift	.451"
Hydraulic valve lifters	Yes
Valve inserts	None
Valve seats cooled by	Direct water circulation

LUBRICATION
Type	Full pressure
Oil under pressure to:	
Main bearings	Yes
Connecting rods	Yes
Wristpins	Splash
Camshaft bearings	Yes
Tappets	Yes
Oil pump type	Gear
Normal oil pressure	30 to 35 lbs. @ 30 m.p.h.
Capacity of oil reservoir	Dry, 6 qts.; Refill, 6 qts.
Type of oil level gauge	Dip stick
Make of pressure gauge	AC—Tell-Tale Lite
Oil filter	Standard
Type	Partial flow

FUEL
Gasoline tank capacity	20 gallons
Type of fuel feed	Camshaft pump
Carburetor—make	Rochester & Carter
Carburetor—type	Four-barrel downdraft*
Manifold heat control	Automatic
Type of air cleaner	Oil bath
Dual tailpipe diameters	1.75"

*Two 4-Barrel Carburetors on 325-h.p. engine optional on Eldorados only.

COOLING
Water pump type	Centrifugal—dual outlet
Pressure relief valve	Yes
Choke for recirculation	Yes
Radiator core	Tube and center
Full-length cylinder water jacket	Yes
Water all around cylinders	Yes

COOLING—Continued
Fan belt length	57"
Fan belt width	⅜"
Fan—No. of blades, Series 62, 60 and 75	4
Cooling system capacity	17.5 qts.
With heater	18.7 qts. (Series 75, 19.8 qts.)

GENERATOR
Make	Delco-Remy
Minimum charging speed	22 m.p.h. and up
Generator ventilation	Forced air

GENERATOR REGULATOR
Make	Delco-Remy
Voltage at cut-out closing	11.8—13.6 (adjust to 12.8)
Voltage regulator setting	14—15 (adjust to 14.5 at 90°)
Generator maximum charging rate	32—37 amp. (adjust to 35)

STARTING MOTOR
Make	Delco-Remy
Flywheel teeth, integral or ring	Steel integral

IGNITION
Spark advance	Centrifugal and vacuum
Ignition Unit: Make	Delco-Remy
Manual advance	None
Maximum centrifugal advance	Crankshaft (22°-26°)
Vacuum advance	Crankshaft (22.5°-25.5°)
Distributor breaker gap	.016"
Initial spark advance	5° B.T.C.
Firing order	1-8-4-3-6-5-7-2
Ignition Coil: Make	Delco-Remy
Spark Plugs:	
Make	AC
Model	44.0
Thread	14mm.
Gap	.035"

BATTERY
Make	Delco 3EMR70-W
Number of plates	11
Capacity (amp. hrs.)	70
Terminal grounded	Negative
Location of battery	Under hood on tray atta to right-hand side of ator cradle.

LIGHTS AND HORN
Headlight—make	Guide sealed-beam
Headlight cover glass, dia.	6¹¹⁄₁₆"
Parking light—make	Guide
Taillight—make	Guide
Lighting switch—make	Delco-Remy
How are headlights dimmed?	Depressed beam—foot sw
Horn:	
Make	Delco-Remy
Type	*Vibrator, seashell electr

*3 on Eldorados

HYDRA-MATIC DRIVE
Type	Fully automatic step-type with controlled coupling on forward set for smoother shifts
Gearing	Planetary
No. of forward speeds	4
No. of forward speeds in "City" DR range	3
No. of forward speeds in "Country" DR range	4
No. of forward speeds in LO range	2
Transmission ratio, first	3.97:1
Transmission ratio, second	2.55:1
Transmission ratio, third	1.55:1
Transmission ratio, fourth	1:1
Transmission ratio, reverse	3.74:1
Oil capacity	13 qts.
Type of fluid	Hydra-Matic fluid

SHIFT POINTS:

		With Rear Axle Ratio		
		(Single Carburetor)		(Dua Carbure
		3.07:1	3.36:1	3.36:
	Throttle			
Upshift DR-4 Range	Opening	M.P.H.	M.P.H.	M.P.H
1st to 2nd	Minimum	6-9	6-9	6-9
	Maximum	20-24	18-22	18-2
2nd to 3rd	Minimum	13-16	12-15	13-1
	Maximum	39-44	35-40	37-4
3rd to 4th	Minimum	20-24	18-22	17-2
	Maximum	68-75	62-69	62-6
Downshift DR-4 Range				
4th to 3rd	Minimum	14-18	12-16	12-1
	Maximum	61-68	56-62	60-6
3rd to 2nd	Minimum	11-15	10-18	12-1
	Maximum	23-27	21-25	22-2
2nd to 1st	Minimum	0-5	0-5	0-5
	Maximum	0-5	0-5	0-5
DR-3 Range Same as DR-4 except upshifts from 3rd to 4th at:		68-75	62-69	62-
downshifts from 4th to 3rd at:		61-68	56-62	56-
LO Range Same as DR-4 except upshifts to 3rd at:		52-58	47-53	47-
upshifts to 4th at:		68-75	62-69	62-
downshifts to 3rd at:		61-68	56-64	56-
downshifts to 2nd at:		41-47	37-43	37-

Note: Miles per hour at which shift is made is depende degree of throttle opening. Actually no gears shift. used for clarity of meaning.

FRAME

	Series 62	Series 60S	Series 75
Frame make	A. O. Smith	A. O. Smith	A. O. S
Frame depth, maximum	7"	7"	7"
Frame thickness, maximum	⁹⁄₆₄"	⁵⁄₃₂"	⁵⁄₃₂"
Widths of flange, maximum	3¹⁷⁄₃₂"	3¹⁷⁄₃₂"	3¹⁷⁄₃₂"
Frame—Type	Tubular-center X frame	Tubular-center X frame	Tub cente fra
Frame-to-road clearance at center of wheelbase	6½"	6½"	7½"

180

1957 CADILLAC Detailed Specifications
CONTINUED

FRONT END SUSPENSION

Front suspension, make	Own
Front suspension, type	Forked arms
Forked arm bearings	Inner threaded
Knuckle support bearing	Spherical
Front wheel inner bearing, make and type	N.D. ball
Front wheel outer bearing, make and type	N. D. ball
Front spring, type	Helical coil
Front spring, material	Spring steel
Shock absorber, type	Hydraulic direct-acting type
Front stabilizer	Torsion rod

PROPELLER SHAFT

Number used	2
Type	Exposed

UNIVERSAL JOINTS

Make	Mechanics and Saginaw
Number used	3
Type	Cross and Trunnion
Bearing	Needle
Universal joints, lubricated	Permanently
Drive and torque taken through	Rear springs

REAR AXLE

Rear axle, make	Own	
Rear axle, type	Semifloating	
Differential gear, make	Own	
Rear axle:		
Oil capacity	5 pints	
Grade recommended		
S.A.E. viscosity	90 hypoid	
Type of final gearing	Hypoid	
Gear ratio:		
Standard	3.07:1	3.36:1*
Optional	3.36:1	3.77
Pinion adjustment (except 75)	None	
Pinion bearing adjustment	None (Preloaded)	
Are pinion bearings in sleeve?	No	
Backlash between pinion and ring gear	.003"–.010"	
Rear axle pinion shaft:		
Front bearing, type	Tapered roller	
Rear bearing, type	Tapered roller	

*Standard on Eldorados with 325-h.p. engine and on air-conditioned models.

TIRES AND WHEELS

Tires:		
Make	U. S. Royal, Firestone and Goodrich	
Type	Tubeless	
Size	8.00 x 15*	8.20 x 15
Ply rating	4	6
Inflation pressure:		
Front	24 lbs.	28 lbs.
Rear	24 lbs.	28 lbs.
Wheels:		
Type	Slotted disc**	
Make	Kelsey-Hayes	
Rim, diameter	15"	
Rim, width	6.00"	
Tread:		
Front	61"	
Rear	61"	

*8.20 x 15 when whitewalls are ordered. Standard on Eldorados.
**Aluminum spoke, steel rim wheels on Eldorados.

SPRINGS (REAR)

	Series 62-60	Series 75
Rear Springs:		
Type	Semi-elliptic	
Material	Spring steel	
Length	56½"	
Width	2½"	
No. of leaves	5	6
Spring leaves lubricated with	Wax impregnated liners	
Spring bushings, type	Rubber	
Stabilizers	Rear—None	

SHOCK ABSORBERS (REAR)

Type	Direct Acting, Hydraulic

STEERING

Steering	Hydraulic power	
Type	Concentric gear	
Make	Saginaw	
Over-all steering ratio	19.5:1	
Car turning radius (outside) bumper to bumper sweep	(62) 21.7' (60) 22.5'	(75) 25.8'

BRAKES

Front and Rear:		
Brake drum diameter	12"	12"

BRAKES—Continued

	Series 62-60	Series 75
Brake lining width	2½"	2½"
Brake lining thickness	¼"	¼"
Brake lining effective area	210.32 sq. in.	233.72 sq. in.
Brake clearance	.010" top; .015" bottom	
Foot emergency brake location	Left side below dash	
Operates on	Rear service brakes	
Power brakes	Standard all models	
Brake drum, internal or external	Internal	Internal
Brake lining, length per wheel:		
Forward shoe	10.05"	12.98"
Reverse shoe	12.98"	12.98"
Total	23.03	25.96"

MISCELLANEOUS SPECIFICATIONS

Car lifting device, jack	Bumper type
Engine lubrication, type	Pressure
Chassis lubrication, type	High pressure
Axle lubrication, type	Splash

LUBRICANTS

Engine crankcase capacity	5 qts.
With oil filter (Std.)	6 qts.
Recommended viscosity	Min. anticipated temperature: +32°F. 20W or S.A.E. 20 +10°F. 20W −10°F. 10W Below −10°F. 5W
Drain	2000 miles (after initial 500-mile change)
Rear axle oil	5 pints
Recommended viscosity	90 hypoid
Auto trans. fluid type "A"	13 qts. dry
Gasoline	20 gals.

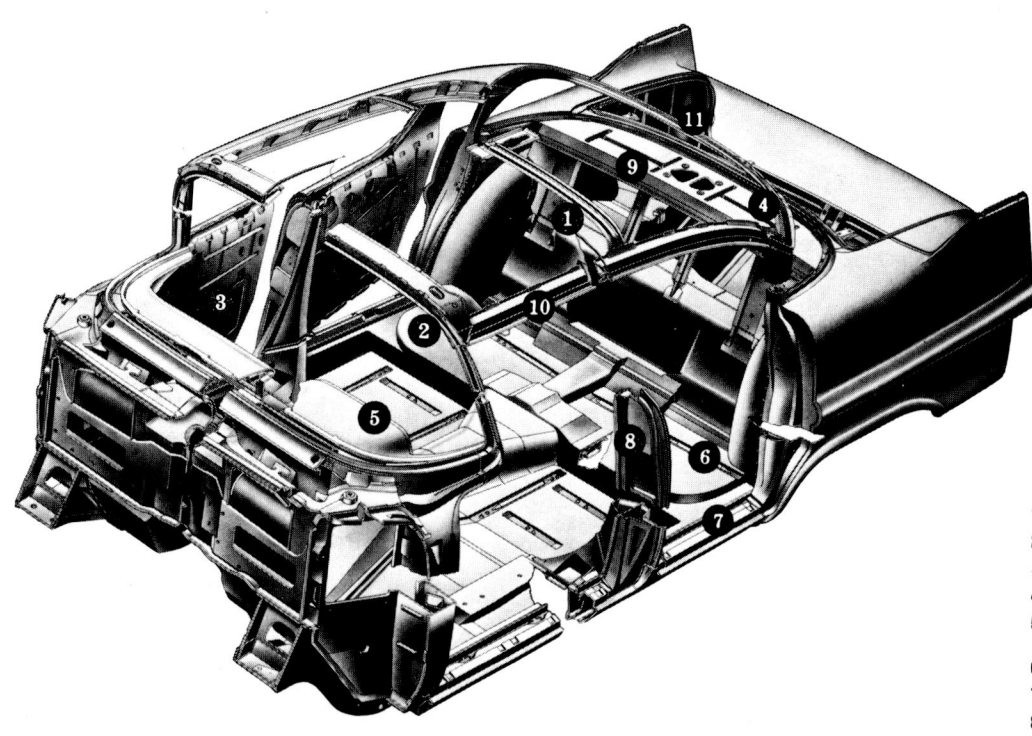

1. Double-ribbed U-shaped roof bow.
2. Solid steel Turret Top.
3. Genuine Safety Plate glass.
4. Box-girder header assembly.
5. Steel cowl and dash with box-girder cross member.
6. Steel floor, ribbed, braced and welded to body.
7. Box-girder rocker panels.
8. Box-section steel pillars.
9. Box-section braces at back of rear seat.
10. Box-girder roof rails.
11. Box-girder reinforced rear quarter panels with integrally welded-on rear fenders.
12. Specially reinforced floor sections around stub center posts.

the magnificent Eldorado Brougham
by Cadillac

The elegant beauty of the Eldorado Brougham ... its superb comfort and handling ease ... are always at their best through an air suspension system which keeps the car at its showroom height even with a full complement of passengers.

The Eldorado Brougham was conceived, developed and carefully custom crafted with but one objective in mind ... to provide the finest limited-production luxury motor car possible for the world's most discriminating motorists.

The Eldorado Brougham is sleek and road hugging in appearance, graceful and balanced in every line of contour and chrome. Its low silhouette styling, the Brougham is only 55½" in over-all height, was achieved with a proportionate lowering of the hood, rear deck and fenders. The result is a pleasingly balanced beauty, as contrasted with the squat look of cars whose lowness is achieved by arbitrary lowering of the roof line alone. What's more, since the Eldorado Brougham's sleek design begins with a special frame which permits a lower floor, the interiors provide the spacious comfort expected of the world's finest luxury sedan.

From the front or rear the Eldorado Brougham looks much wider than its actual width of 78.5". This appearance is further enhanced by the flat deck and hood, which are actually lower than the fender lines.

The lower rear fender panel and rocker sill molding are of beautiful and durable stainless steel.

The top is of brushed stainless steel, a feature adding to the strength and durability of the Brougham as well as enhancing its appearance.

The interior of the Brougham is luxurious to a high degree with 44 choices of trim and color combinations. Carpeting is available in either high-pile nylon Karakul or mouton, a specially processed lambskin. There are wide center armrests front and rear. The rear armrest contains a small compartment with such convenience items as a note pad and pencil, portable vanity mirror and a perfume bottle atomizer containing Arpège Extrait de Lanvin.

Front fenders and cross-over panel, above grille, are a one-piece unit. Hood is forward-hinged on cross-over panel.

Three-section rear bumper is flush mounted to the body.

Rear-end styling includes dramatically swept-back rear fender fins edged in gleaming chrome. Vertical tail lamps are inset at the base of the tail fin. Outer rear bumper sections each contain a louvered exhaust outlet and twin circular lamps. The outer lamps with red lenses are stop lights and turn signals; the inner lamps are for back-up lighting. Centered between the outer bumper sections is a heavy, chromed, recessed mounting for the license plate.

The Eldorado Brougham's parallel dual headlamps, introduced at the 1954 General Motors Motorama, utilize the upper beam of the outer pair of headlamps plus the bright inner headlamps for country driving. The lower beams of the outer lamps only are used in passing an approaching car or in city driving. Centered below each pair of dual headlamps is a sound-outlet grille for the Eldorado Brougham's four specially tuned horns.

A highlight of the Brougham's exclusive styling is the new, deep-fluted wheels of forged aluminum and steel. They combine strength and lightness with lasting beauty of appearance. High-speed, low-profile tires have a distinguishing 1-inch-wide whitewall stripe.

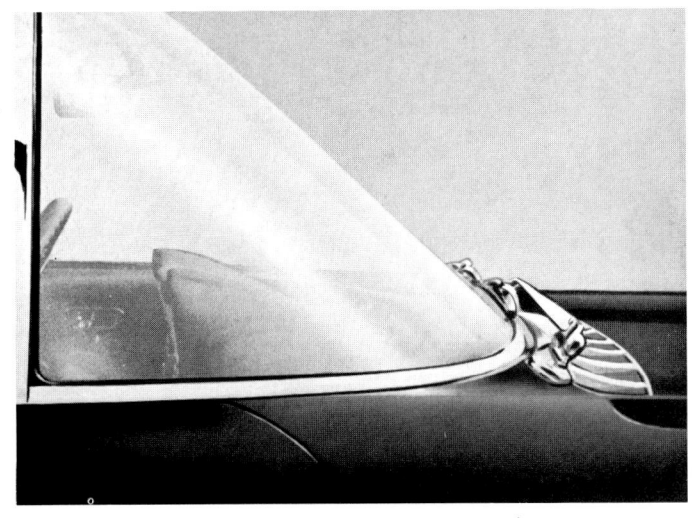

At the base of the windshield is a stainless steel air intake grille for ventilation, heating and air conditioning units.

Recessed into the crown of each front fender is an air outlet grille which acts as a vent for the engine compartment.

183

COMPLETE STANDARD EQUIPMENT

- Air Cleaner, dry-pack type
- Armrest, center, front
- Armrest, center, rear, custom fitted
- Cadillac Air Conditioner
- Cadillac Power Brakes
- Cadillac Power Steering
- Cigarette Lighters, front (two)
- Cigarette Lighters, rear (two)
- Clock, electric, drum type
- E-Z-Eye Glass
- Fog Lamps (pair)
- Front Seat Adjustment (6-way), Favorite Position, electrically operated
- Glove Compartment, custom fitted
- Headlight Dimmer (automatic)
- Heater, front
- Heater, rear, under seat
- Hydra-Matic Transmission
- License Frames
- Light, courtesy or map (automatic)
- Light, glove box (automatic)
- Light, luggage compartment (automatic)
- Lights, back-up (dual)
- Lights, directional signal
- Lights, front ash receivers
- Oil Filter
- Outside Mirror, left-side, remote-control
- Parking Brake Warning Signal
- Radio, transistor
- Rear-View Mirror, 3-way, E-Z-Eye
- Remote-Control Trunk Lid Lock
- Special Wheels (set of five), forged aluminum and steel
- Visors, dual sun, translucent tinted plastic
- Whitewall Tires, high-speed, low-profile type, 8:40-8:20 x 15 (4 ply)
- Window Lifts (including ventipanes), electrically operated
- Windshield Washer and Coordinator

Complete safety is assured through the use of electric door locks controlled from the front seat. When the button in the center of either front door locking control lever is depressed, the locks on all doors move to the locked position.

Fashioned with jeweler's precision, the neat, compact dash panel has everything arranged for maximum driver convenience. Indicator lights warn of low oil pressure, low fuel level, high water temperature and battery discharge. The glove compartment is centered in the dash panel with the lock located left of center for easier driver accessibility. Radio controls, too, are located for maximum convenience. To the right of the radio dial is an easily read, drum type electric clock.

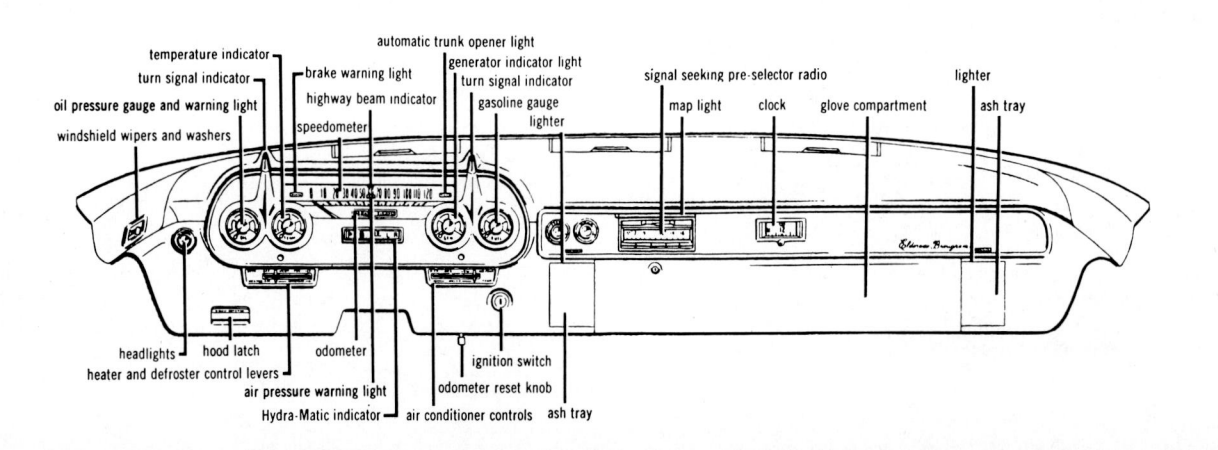

184

The rear seat of the Brougham is designed for maximum comfort for two passengers. Dividing the two individual seating sections is a wide center armrest containing a compartment with note pad and pencil, portable vanity mirror and a perfume atomizer containing Arpège Extrait de Lanvin. Above the armrest is the radio rear speaker grille. An underseat heater warms the rear compartment through grilles at the base of the rear seats. An individual heat control lever is provided on each of the two grilles.

The front seat of the Brougham accommodates three passengers when the center armrest is in its recessed position in the seat back. Electric power controls permit adjustment of the seat forward or back, up or down and also permit tilting the seat cushion and seat back to the desired angle for most comfortable posture. Thus, even the tallest or shortest person will find driving the Brougham a restful experience.

"Favorite Position Seat" controls are located on the front door on the driver's side of the car. Once the three dials have been set to the driver's preferred seating position no further adjustments are necessary. For maximum convenience in entering or leaving the car the front seat moves fully back and down when a front door is opened. When the doors are closed the seat automatically returns to the position preset by the driver. For two-driver families, separate seat settings may be selected on the control dials, using the red arrows for one driver and the green arrows for the other.

The glove compartment is custom fitted with cigarette case, tissue dispenser, vanity compact and lipstick, stick cologne, six metal magnetized silver-finish drinking cups and full-length, metal-back, acrylic vanity mirror which folds out to form a horizontal metal shelf.

Exceptionally easy entrance and exit to the Brougham are provided by ball bearing hinged doors which latch securely to a central steel pillar only 14" high. Thus, there is nothing to obstruct the passengers in entering or leaving either the front or rear compartments.

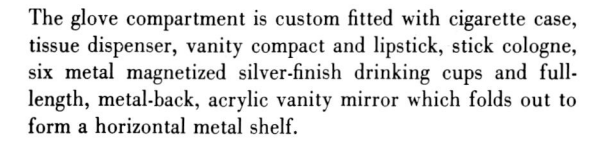

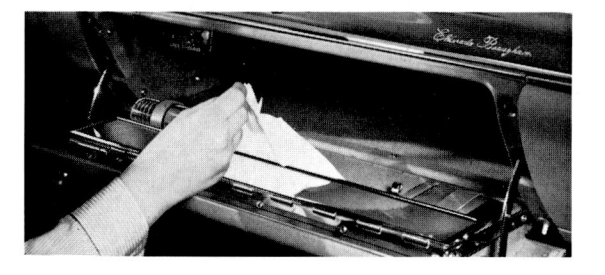

Each rear door lock incorporates a safety switch which prevents shifting the transmission selector lever into any drive position when either rear door is open while the ignition is turned "ON". Also, whenever the transmission selector lever is in any drive position the inside rear door handles are disengaged.

In the event an electrical failure should occur, the door locks may be operated manually, and the inside rear door handles will engage to permit opening rear doors from the inside.

185

Advantages which result from this air suspension system are many.

1. The Eldorado Brougham is always level and at the same height from the road whether carrying only the driver or fully loaded with passengers and luggage.

Same clearance loaded or unloaded.

2. The maintained clearance between the rear axle and the frame, regardless of load, assures consistent quality of ride over smooth or rough road surfaces.

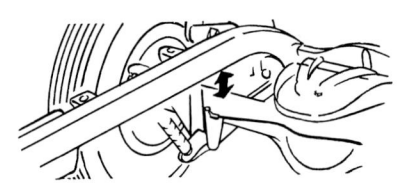

3. Softer cushioning action is permitted, since any possibility of excessive bottoming is overcome by the constant maintenance of adequate clearance between the rear axle and the frame.

Average car.
① Higher center of gravity.
② Low roll center.

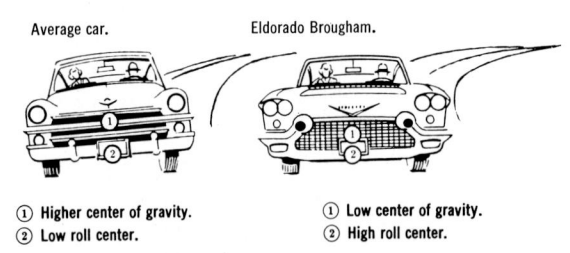

Eldorado Brougham.
① Low center of gravity.
② High roll center.

4. The normal outward lean of a car body on curves is minimized on the Eldorado Brougham. First, because the center of the Eldorado Brougham's weight distribution (center of gravity) is much closer to the road than in ordinary cars. Second, because the Eldorado Brougham's new rear suspension permits location of the roll center near the top of the rear axle housing, higher than in cars with conventional leaf springs.

5. Side sway, too, is minimized on the Eldorado Brougham since the new rear suspension holds the frame and body in firm alignment with the rear axle at all times.

THE ELDORADO BROUGHAM IS POWERED BY THE FINEST ENGINE IN CADILLAC HISTORY

In keeping with its elegant beauty, the luxury of its air ride and the wonderful comforts and conveniences which it provides, the Eldorado Brougham leaves nothing to be desired in the smooth, powerful and quiet responsiveness of its 335-horsepower engine.

Here are all of the advanced engine features discussed in the regular engine section of the Cadillac Data Book plus the extra power and performance provided by three dual-barrel carburetors, larger capacity air intake and air cleaner and larger free-flow intake manifold.

The transmission of power from the engine to the rear wheels is accomplished with maximum smoothness and efficiency through the finest Cadillac Hydra-Matic Transmission ever developed. The changing of gear ratios as the car accelerates or decelerates, for example, is accomplished smoothly, quietly, almost imperceptibly through the automatic filling and emptying of a small fluid coupling with oil.

ELDORADO BROUGHAM GENERAL SPECIFICATIONS*

Wheelbase	126"
Over-all Length	216.3"
Over-all Width	78.5"
Over-all Height	55.5"
Tread, front and rear	61.0"
Min. Ground Clearance	5.3"
Adjustable to	6.3"
Steering Ratio, over-all	19.5
Turning Diameter, curb to curb	42 ft.
Rear Axle Ratio	3.36 to 1
Tire Size (tubeless, low profile)	8.40-8.20 x 15 (4-ply)
Wheels	Forged aluminum and steel
Suspension, front and rear	Air springs
Drive	Cadillac Four-link
Frame	Tubular-center X frame
Engine	335 horsepower at 4800 rpm
Compression Ratio	10.25 to 1
Torque	405 ft. lbs. at 3400 rpm
Carburetor	Three, dual-barrel
Oil Filter	Full-flow
Oil Capacity with Filter	6 qts.
Cooling System Capacity	22.6 qts.
Fuel Pump	Electric
Fuel Capacity	20 gals.
Headlights	Four lamp system
Inner pair	High beam
Outer pair	High and low beam
Horns	3 seashell, 1 trumpet
Battery	12 volt, 11 plate, 72 watt
Location	Trunk
Generator	55 amp.
Regulator	55 amp.

INTERIOR DIMENSIONS

	front	rear
Head Room	35.5"	34.8"
Leg Room	43.7"	39.7"
Hip Room	61.3"	60.7"
Shoulder Room	59.2"	56.9"
Seat Height	(Adjustable height)	13.3"

For additional information or specifications on the engine, transmission, frame, brakes, steering, heating or air conditioning, refer to the regular sections of the 1958 Cadillac Data

FABULOUS AIR SUSPENSION ON AMERICA'S MOST ADVANCED LIMITED-PRODUCTION MOTOR CAR

Riding on air is a reality for the driver and passengers of the Eldorado Brougham. Four air springs, one at each wheel, replace the steel springs found on conventional production automobiles.

The Brougham's air suspension system was developed on the principle that air is compressible, offers outstanding ability to dampen out shocks or jolts and may be easily controlled to provide the variable pressures in the air suspension units necessary to keep the car always at the same height whether loaded or unloaded.

Basic components of the Eldorado Brougham's air suspension system are the individual air springs at each wheel and an electric powered compressor which operates only as required to maintain an air pressure of from 100 to 120 pounds per square inch in an air accumulator or storage tank. From this storage tank air is metered to the individual air springs at each wheel as required to keep the car level. Passage of air from the storage tank to or from the individual air springs occurs only when a car door is open or the ignition is "ON". When the car doors are closed and the ignition is "OFF", there is no passage of air and the leveling system is locked out. This prevents loss of air from the air storage tank while the car is jacked up, while parked or during shipment.

When any door is opened, whether the ignition is "ON" or "OFF", an unrestricted flow of air to the leveling valves at each wheel quickly compensates for any change in car height due to entrance or exit of passengers. During all driving there is a restricted flow of air which permits constant adjustment of car height to compensate for any loss of weight (as with consumption of gas) or a gain in weight (as with an accumulation of snow or ice).

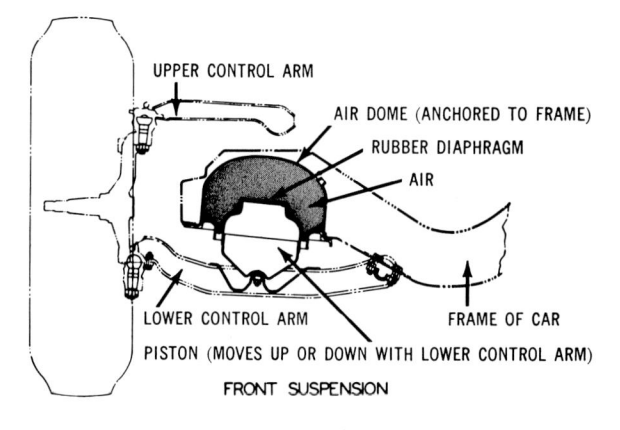

The air springs themselves consist of a metal dome or cup mounted to the frame, a rubber diaphragm which seals the air within the dome and a piston which maintains constant contact with the diaphragm. As any wheel of the car rises and falls as it passes over road irregularities the piston increases or lessens pressure against the diaphragm, thus letting the air within the dome absorb the jolts or shocks.

Individual leveling valves, one at each rear air spring and a third leveling valve which serves both front air springs, are mounted on the frame and connected to the wheel control arms with a mechanical linkage. Any change in the height of the frame actuates the valve so that air is admitted to, or exhausted from, the air spring to restore the normal height of the car. Manual adjustment at each levelizer valve permits raising or lowering the normal height of the car approximately one inch to suit individual owner preference for increased or lessened ground clearance. The quality of the ride is not affected by these changes in height.

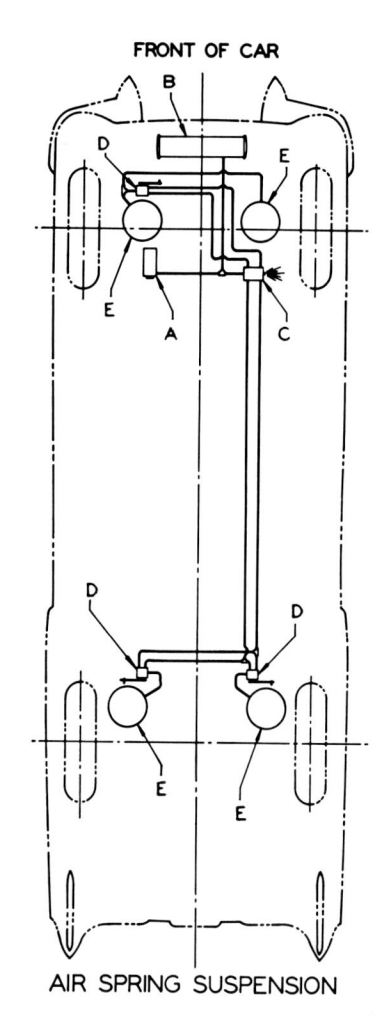

FRONT SUSPENSION

AIR SPRING SUSPENSION

A COMPRESSOR
B AIR RESERVOIR
C MAIN AIR CONTROL UNIT
D WHEEL LEVELING VALVES
E AIR SPRINGS

THE MAGNIFICENT ELDORADO BROUGHAM... MOST COMPLETELY EQUIPPED MOTOR CAR IN PRODUCTION TODAY

POWER STEERING

Famous Cadillac Power Steering relieves the driver of all but the minimum steering effort required as an aid in judging safe speed on curves or slippery road surfaces. Additional advantages are explained in the Cadillac Data Book.

POWER BRAKES

Cadillac Power Brakes provide smooth, safe, sure braking with a minimum of pressure on the brake pedal.

POWER WINDOWS

All door windows, including the ventipanes, are electrically powered on the Eldorado Brougham.

POWER SEATS

As explained in detail on the previous pages, the front seat is power adjusted to exactly the position desired by the driver . . . then always returns to that preselected position once the driver is seated.

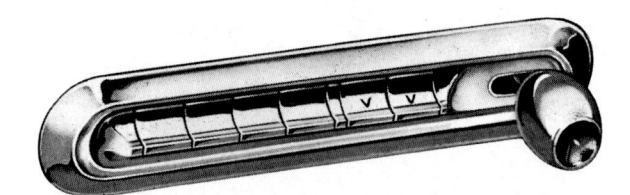

AUTOMATIC STARTING

With the transmission selector lever in either Neutral or Park positions the Eldorado Brougham engine is automatically started simply by *turning* the ignition key to the right. It is not necessary to *hold* the key to the right unless additional engine cranking is required as with a flooded engine.

POWER DECK LID

Even the deck lid on the Eldorado Brougham is power operated. Buttons located within the glove compartment permit unlocking, raising, then lowering and locking the deck lid . . . all without the driver having to leave the car.

AUTOMATIC RADIO ANTENNA

Rises to a height level with the roof of the car when the radio is turned on . . . automatically recesses when radio is turned off. It may also be raised to its maximum height for country driving or for best reception of distant stations.

TRANSISTOR RADIO

Cadillac's new transistor radio uses tiny but powerful transistors rather than the previous bulky radio tubes. Transistors put less drain on the battery, provide longer, more reliable performance and are unaffected by the normal stress to which a car radio is subjected as the car traverses rough roads.

HEATING AND AIR CONDITIONING

Complete all-weather comfort is provided by separate front and rear compartment heaters and by the Cadillac Air Conditioning System.

All window controls on the Brougham including the ventipanes are electrically powered. A master control panel on the front door on the driver's side permits opening or closing of all windows by the driver. On the right-hand front door are controls for the right door window and ventipane. Each rear door has a control for operating that individual window.

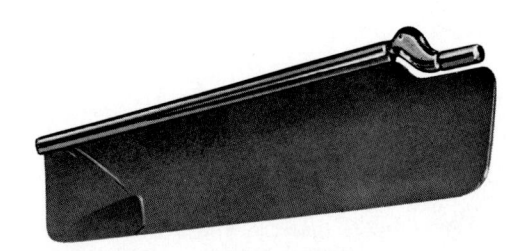

Another exclusive Brougham feature is the use of laminated tinted plastic for the sun visors. In addition to their beauty of appearance they shield against the sun without cutting off the driver's visibility.

An automatic headlamp beam control, Cadillac's "Autronic-Eye", is mounted at the extreme left on the instrument panel. It causes the headlights of the Brougham to switch from high to low beam when a car approaches from the opposite direction. Since the oncoming driver is not blinded both cars pass with greater safety. An overriding switch permits signaling oncoming drivers who forget to dim their lights.

The *Eldorado Brougham* is among the most exotic and exciting automobiles built anywhere, anytime. 1957 and 1958 models were assembled at Fleetwood in Detroit and little difference exists between the two editions. Prototype *Broughams* had sabre-spoke wheels, as seen in the lower photo, but subsequent production had the special fluted wheels seen above. Interior variations were limited primarily to door panel areas — painted metal upper panels in 1957, covered with leather in 1958.

styling

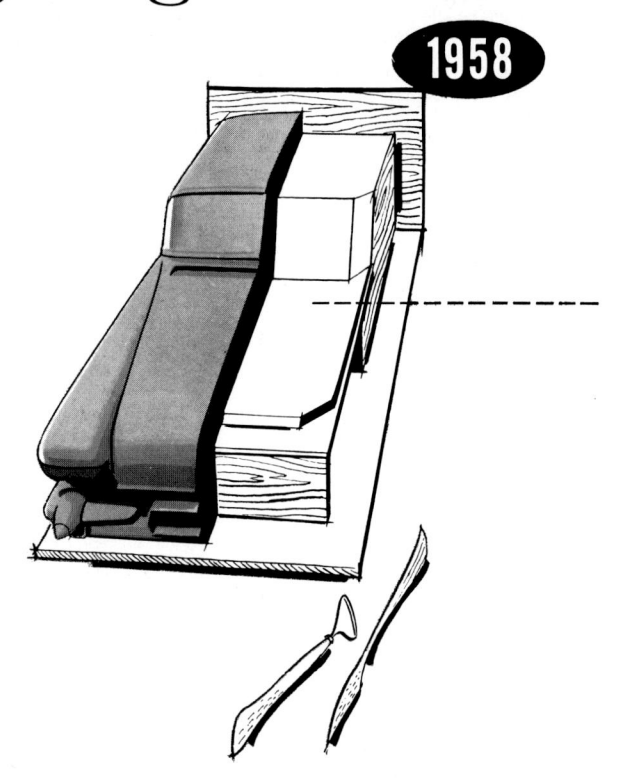

1958

In calling the latest Cadillac creation "Motordom's Masterpiece for 1958", the phrase makers could have been swayed by the magnificent appearance of the car alone. For, even without experiencing the comfort of its newly engineered ride and the wonderful performance which it provides, your prospects are certain to agree that this brilliant Cadillac has advanced the standards of automotive beauty to spectacular new heights for 1958.

Every sculptured-in-steel contour . . . every application of chrome, stainless steel or brushed aluminum has been skillfully designed to achieve an even longer, lower and wider appearance while enhancing the quiet elegance and distinctive beauty inherent in Cadillac styling through the years.

For 1958 . . . the most beautiful Cadillac ever conceived dramatically illustrates why Cadillac continues to reign as the Standard of the World . . . in beauty of design as well as in engineering excellence.

SERIES SIXTY-TWO SEDAN EXTENDED DECK

Representative of the beautiful Cadillac Series Sixty-Two styling for 1958 is the new extended-deck sedan shown on the opposite page. Long horizontal lines in contour and chrome combine with a longer hood and front fender line to accentuate its length of 225.3" over-all. In addition to the styling details illustrated on the previous pages, the Series Sixty-Two Sedans have a new chrome-framed ventipane in each rear door which provides improved visibility as well as individual ventilation for rear compartment passengers.

Viewed from the rear, the Series Sixty-Two models present, in addition to the new sweptback rear fender fins, a newly styled "V" and Crest and parallel, circular tail and back-up lights over simulated exhaust outlets.

THE ELDORADO BIARRITZ

The sleek, long lines of the Eldorado Biarritz, shown at right, and Seville are enhanced by the new longer hood and front fenders plus the individual treatment of rear quarter panels and fins. Lending further distinction to Eldorados, as viewed from the side, is the single-winged chrome molding on the front fender crown, the ten vertical chromed bars of the simulated stone-shield, the broad chromed molding around the rear wheel opening and the Cadillac crest insignia on the tapered rear quarter panel fins.

The Eldorado Biarritz and Seville deck lid is distinguished by a stylized "V" and the word "Eldorado" in gold, block letters. New bumper impact bars of steel construction have a horizontal chromed grille opening containing the back-up lights. Added protection and beauty are provided by five vertical bars on each side of the license plate holder.

FLEETWOOD SIXTY SPECIAL SEDAN

This illustrious, long-wheelbase sedan bears many distinguishing features which emphasize its exclusive character. Lower rear fender panel, wheel cover and stone-guard, for example, are styled as a single panel of grooved anodized aluminum with stainless-steel molding.

Distinctive rear-end styling of the Sixty Special Sedan is marked by a textured molding across the lower deck lid between two horizontal back-up lights; vertical ribs within the concave contour of the bumper; and twin taillights.

NEW STYLING

New grille

New headlamp-driving lamps and bezels

New twin-blade hood ornament on all Sixty-Two Series except Eldorados

New longer hood with formed windsplit on centerline

New longer front fenders

New single-blade front fender ornaments on Eldorados and Sixty Special Sedan

New front bumper guards

New fresh air inlet grille on cowl

New front fender side molding

New front fender crown molding

New front fender name plates or medallion (except Sixty Special Sedan)

New front fender wheel opening molding

New chrome-framed simulated front fender air scoop

New hood "V" and Crest

New parking lamps

New fog lamps

New windshield wiper escutcheon

New rocker sill molding

New stone guard moldings

New rear wheel opening cover on Sixty Special Sedan

New wheel discs

New rear quarter vent windows on sedan models only (brushed chrome panels with bright chrome crest on coupes)

New rear fender fins

New rear fender fin model identification

New rear window molding

New rear deck "V" and Crest on Series Sixty-Two models

New classic "V" and name "Eldorado" on rear deck of Eldorado Biarritz and Seville

New outside rear-view mirror (two on Sixty Special Sedan)

New back-up lights

New taillights

New simulated bumper exhaust outlets

New rear bumpers

New larger luggage compartment

NEW INTERIORS

New trim styles and materials

New inserts for instrument panel and upper door panel

New front compartment radio speaker located next to radio dial on instrument panel

New instrument panel emblem with word "Cadillac" or "Eldorado"

Newly styled control buttons and knobs

New rectangular dome lights

New power seat controls

New narrow chromed rear window molding

New molded headlining on Coupe and Sedan de Ville and Seville

New electrically operated front ventipanes (standard on Eldorados and Sixty Special Sedan, optional on others)

New clock located within instrument cluster

Newly styled emergency brake foot release

NEW CHASSIS FEATURES

New two-plate transmission oil cooler

Newly designed Cadillac tubular-center X frame

New four-link rear suspension

New optional air suspension system

New power braking system

NEW ENGINE FEATURES

New 10.25 to 1 compression ratio

New combustion chambers

New contoured head pistons

New camshaft

New larger exhaust valves and ports

New three, dual-barrel carburetors (standard on Eldorados—optional on all other models)

New dry-pack air cleaner

New engine accessory drive arrangement

New high-capacity generator

New battery location

New plastic-covered battery hold-down

New radiator air shroud on air-conditioned cars

New larger capacity compressor and condenser on air-conditioned cars

NEW OPTIONAL EQUIPMENT FEATURES

New air-conditioning system

New electrically powered ventipanes (standard on Eldorados and Sixty Special Sedan)

New fog lamps (standard on Eldorados)

New electric safety door locks

New gold-finish radiator grille (extra cost except on Eldorados)

New electric deck lid lock

New auxiliary wheel carrier (not available for Eldorados)

New license plate frame (for rear plate only)

New six-way power seat controls

New three, dual-barrel-carburetor engine (standard on Eldorados)

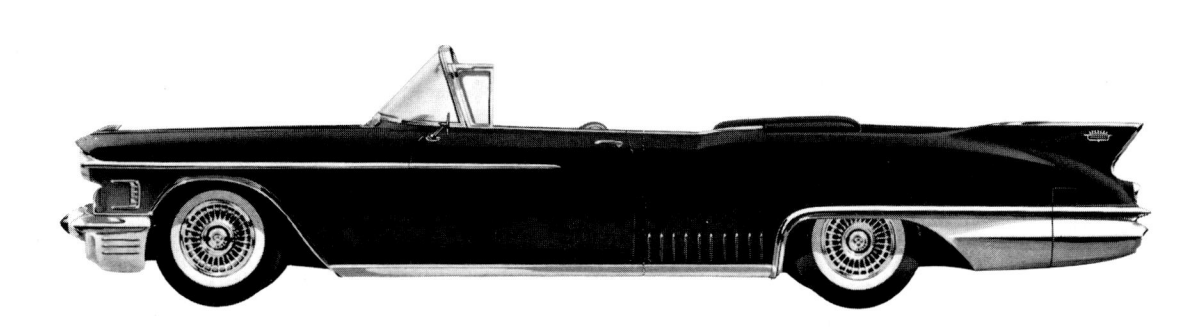

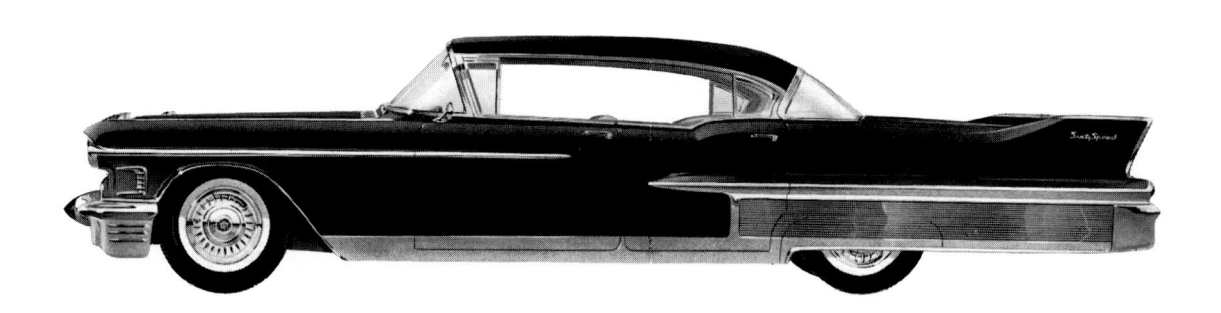

Gleaming new grille of anodized aluminum has wide-spaced fins with bright, concave, bullet-like projectiles at each intersection. Entire grille, encompassing the black rubber-tipped bumper guards, extends full width of the car thus accentuating the car's lower, wider appearance.

Dual, parallel headlamp-driving lamps further enhance the broad, massive front-end appearance while providing brilliant, far-reaching, four-lamp illumination for country driving or the shielded beam of the outer lamps only for city driving or for safety in passing oncoming cars.

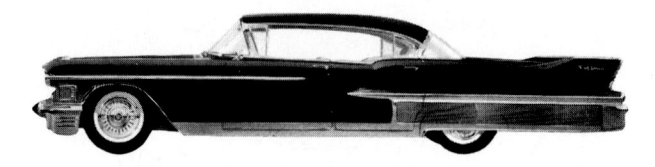

Seldom is the yearly introduction of any motor car greeted with such enthusiastic welcome as that habitually accorded the introduction of a new Cadillac. This is a tribute to the basic quality of a Cadillac, and to the constant and genuine efforts to improve it.

Occasionally a motor car manufacturer attempts to capitalize unduly on a minor style trend or unimportant feature, which may, for the moment, capture the public's fancy. Yet time and again it has been proved that success does not endure through these random attempts to excite the motoring public.

Many years ago, Cadillac set its sights on a *single goal*—to be the Standard of the World. It is this standard that promises and rewards Cadillac owners with the finest possible design, materials and craftsmanship. Because of this standard the Cadillac motor car enjoys a demand and prestige unprecedented in motor car history, proving, once again, that there is no real or lasting substitute for quality.

The 1958 Cadillac, like all others before it, offers refreshing new style and mechanical advancements that will be copied in years to come. But above and beyond this, Cadillac offers superior quality—that all-important ingredient that so many of our competitors have, in their haste to succeed, overlooked.

Swept-back, twin-blade hood ornaments and tapered chrome moldings on the front fender crowns are distinguishing front-end markings on the Series Sixty-Two sedans, coupes and the convertible.

On the Eldorado Biarritz and Seville, the hood top bears no ornamentation. However, the front fender crown moldings on these models are further distinguished by a single-blade, swept-back ornament.

The Sixty Special Sedan in addition to the single-blade front-fender crown moldings has chromed engine compartment ventilator grilles on the rear of each front fender crown.

Stylized, chromed Cadillac crest and the name "Cadillac" in block letters appear at the rear of the front fenders just beneath the chromed windsplit molding on the Series Sixty-Two Sedans, Coupe, and Convertible; "Fleetwood" on Series Seventy-Five.

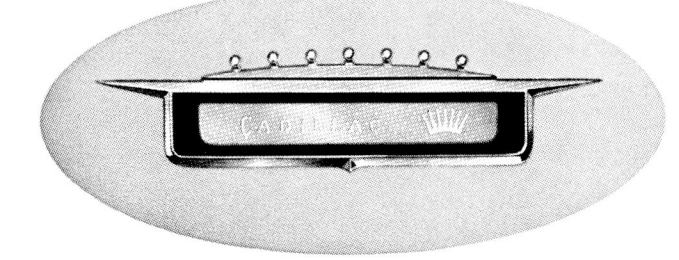

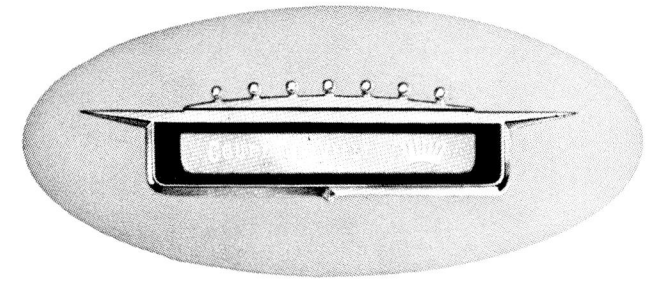

The Sedan de Ville and Coupe de Ville front fender insignia is styled the same as the Series Sixty-Two models but bears the individual name "Sedan de Ville" or "Coupe de Ville" instead of the word "Cadillac".

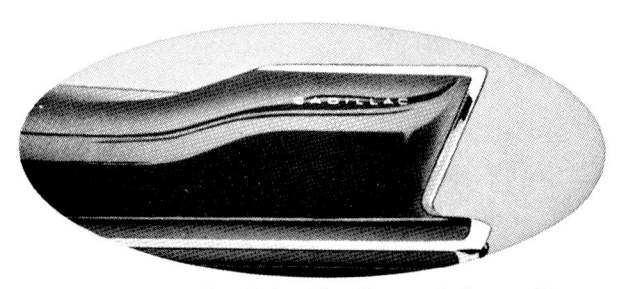

On Series Sixty-Two and Seventy-Five models rear fender fins with a chromed molding on the top and trailing edges bear the name CADILLAC in gold, block letters.

On the Series Sixty-Two models horizontal, chromed bars of the simulated stone-guards serve to enhance the long, sleek appearance of the cars themselves. Newly styled wheel discs add highlights of gleaming beauty.

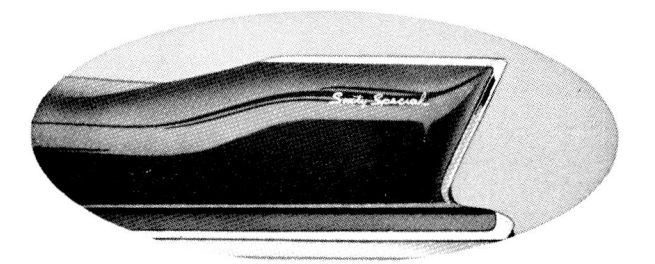

The Sixty Special Sedan rear fender fins have the same profile as the Sixty-Two Series but are further distinguished by the words "Sixty Special" in gold script.

The Sixty Special Sedan lower rear fender panel, wheel opening cover and stone-guard are designed into a single rectangular panel of grooved anodized aluminum with a molding of stainless steel.

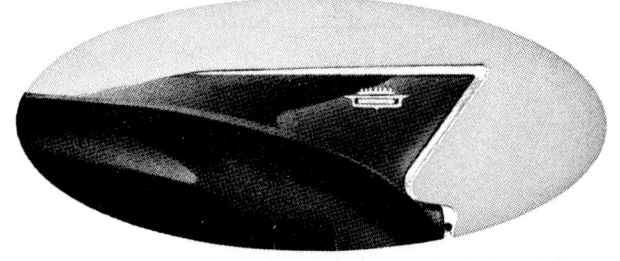

The Eldorado Biarritz and Seville have their own exclusive rear quarter panel fin design, chrome edged and with the famous Cadillac crest its only ornamentation.

The Eldorado Biarritz and Seville feature special Sabre-Spoke wheels, broad chromed moldings around the rear wheel openings and a distinctive simulated stone-guard of ten chromed vertical bars.

series sixty-two sedan

1958

series sixty-two sedan
EXTENDED DECK

STANDARD EQUIPMENT

Air Cleaner, dry-pack	Hydra-Matic Transmission	Oil Filter
Armrest, center-rear	Lights, front ash receivers	Outside Mirror, left-side, remote-control
Assist Handles (two)	Lights, back-up (dual)	Paint, two-tone
Cadillac Power Brakes	Light, courtesy or map (automatic)	Parking Brake Warning Signal
Cadillac Power Steering	Lights, directional signal	Visor Vanity Mirror
Cigarette Lighters, front (two)	Light, glove box (automatic)	Visors, dual sun
Cigarette Lighter, rear	Light, luggage compartment (automatic)	Wheel Discs (set of four)
Clock, electric	Mirror, glare-proof, rear-view, flip type	Windshield Washer and Coordinator

OPTIONAL EQUIPMENT (Extra Cost)

Cadillac Air Conditioner	Front Seat Adjustment	Remote-Control Trunk Lid Lock
Cadillac Air Suspension	(6-way), power operated	Sabre-Spoke Wheels (set of five)
Door Locks, electric	Headlight Dimmer, automatic	in chrome finish
Dor-Gards	Heater	Vent Window Regulators, front, power operated
Eldorado Engine (3 dual-barrel carburetors)	License Frame	
E-Z-Eye Tinted Glass	Radiator Grille, gold-finish	Window Lifts, power operated
Fog Lamps (pair)	Radio	Whitewall Tires, 8.20 x 15 (set of five)

series sixty-two coupe

STANDARD EQUIPMENT

Air Cleaner, dry-pack	Lights, back-up (dual)	Paint, two-tone
Armrest, center-rear	Light, courtesy or map (automatic)	Parking Brake Warning Signal
Cadillac Power Brakes	Lights, directional signal	Visor Vanity Mirror
Cadillac Power Steering	Light, glove box (automatic)	Visors, dual sun
Cigarette Lighters, front (two)	Light, luggage compartment (automatic)	Wheel Discs (set of four)
Clock, electric	Mirror, glare-proof, rear-view, flip type	Windshield Washer and Coordinator
Hydra-Matic Transmission	Oil Filter	
Lights, front ash receivers	Outside Mirror, left-side, remote-control	

OPTIONAL EQUIPMENT (Extra Cost)

Cadillac Air Conditioner	Front Seat Adjustment	Radio
Cadillac Air Suspension	(6-way), power operated	Remote-Control Trunk Lid Lock
Door Locks, Electric	Front Seat Back Lock, right side	Sabre-Spoke Wheels (set of five)
Dor-Gards	Headlight Dimmer, automatic	in chrome finish
Eldorado Engine (3 dual-barrel carburetors)	Heater	Vent Window Regulators, power operated
E-Z-Eye Tinted Glass	License Frame	Window Lifts, power operated
Fog Lamps (pair)	Radiator Grille, gold-finish	Whitewall Tires, 8.20 x 15 (set of five)

SERIES SIXTY-TWO

COUPE, SEDAN AND SEDAN
(extended deck)

Here are glamorous newly patterned nylon fabrics, many combined with gleaming Lurex threads; fine, all-wool broadcloth; fashionable Bedford cord; and richly grained natural and metallic leathers in single or two-tone colors or combined with fabric seat and seat back inserts. Beauty and convenience are combined in the smart new design and studied placement of all control knobs and instrument dials. Completing the aura of warmth and well-being reflected throughout the interiors of the 1958 Cadillac is the luxurious floor covering of heavily tufted, deep-pile nylon blend carpeting.

SERIES SIXTY-TWO SEDAN • FRONT COMPARTMENT

SERIES SIXTY-TWO SEDAN • REAR COMPARTMENT

SERIES SIXTY-TWO COUPE • REAR COMPARTMENT

The interiors of the Series Sixty-Two Sedan, Coupe and extended deck Sedan are smartly styled and deftly tailored. Upholstery choices include seven two-tone combinations, three of nylon Moroccan cloth with its fine pattern of Turquoise, Bronze or White threads against a black background combined with harmonizing bolsters of smart and durable Elascofab; four choices are offered in block-patterned, Lurex-threaded nylon Venetian cloth in pastel colors of Green, Blue, Beige and Gray combined with bolsters of fine-textured nylon Victoria cloth in harmonizing shades.

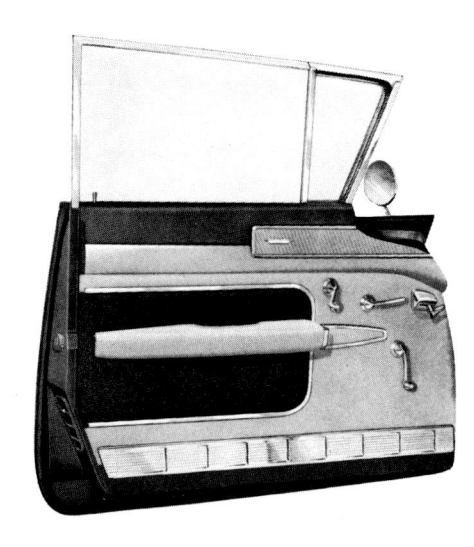

30. White and Black Moroccan Pattern Nylon with White Elascofab bolsters and trim.
31. Light Gray Venetian Pattern Metallic Nylon with Light Gray Victoria Pattern Metallic Nylon bolsters and trim.
33. Light Blue Venetian Pattern Metallic Nylon with Light Blue Victoria Pattern Metallic Nylon bolsters and trim
34. Bronze and Black Moroccan Pattern Nylon with Bronze Metallic Elascofab bolsters and trim.
35. Beige Venetian Pattern Metallic Nylon with Beige Victoria Pattern Metallic Nylon bolsters and trim.
36. Turquoise and Black Moroccan Pattern Nylon with Turquoise Metallic Elascofab bolsters and trim.
37. Light Green Venetian Pattern Metallic Nylon with Light Green Victoria Pattern Metallic Nylon bolsters and trim.

series sixty-two convertible coupe

1958

STANDARD EQUIPMENT

Air Cleaner, dry-pack
Armrest, center, front
Cadillac Power Brakes
Cadillac Power Steering
Cigarette Lighters, front (two)
Cigarette Lighters, rear (two)
Clock, electric
Front Seat Adjustment (horizontal), power operated

Hydra-Matic Transmission
Lights, front ash receivers
Lights, back-up (dual)
Light, courtesy or map (automatic) front and rear compartment
Lights, courtesy, on front seat sides
Lights, directional signal
Light, glove box (automatic)
Light, luggage compartment (automatic)

Mirror, glare-proof, rear-view, flip type
Oil Filter
Outside Mirror, left-side, remote-control
Parking Brake Warning Signal
Visor Vanity Mirror
Visors, dual sun
Wheel Discs (set of four)
Window Lifts, power operated
Windshield Washer and Coordinator

OPTIONAL EQUIPMENT (Extra Cost)

Cadillac Air Conditioner
Cadillac Air Suspension
Door Locks, Electric
Dor-Gards
Eldorado Engine (3 dual-barrel carburetors)
E-Z-Eye Tinted Glass
Fog Lamps (pair)

Front Seat Adjustment (vertical and angle), power operated
Front Seat-Back Lock, right side
Headlight Dimmer, automatic
Heater
License Frame
Radiator Grille, gold-finish

Radio
Remote-Control Trunk Lid Lock
Sabre-Spoke Wheels (set of five) in chrome finish
Vent Window Regulators, power operated
Whitewall Tires, 8.20 x 15 (set of five)

SERIES SIXTY-TWO CONVERTIBLE

Long-lasting luxury is inherent in the genuine leather upholstery provided in the Cadillac Series Sixty-Two Convertible Coupe. Selections for 1958 include four solid and four two-tone combinations as described on the opposite page. Completely restyled seat back bolsters are fashioned of three horizontal panels with the lower panel forming a wide-spread "V". Seat back inserts and seat cushions have large rectangular biscuits with deeply recessed buttons. A newly designed rear compartment radio speaker grille is centered in a recessed position at the top of the rear seat back bolster.

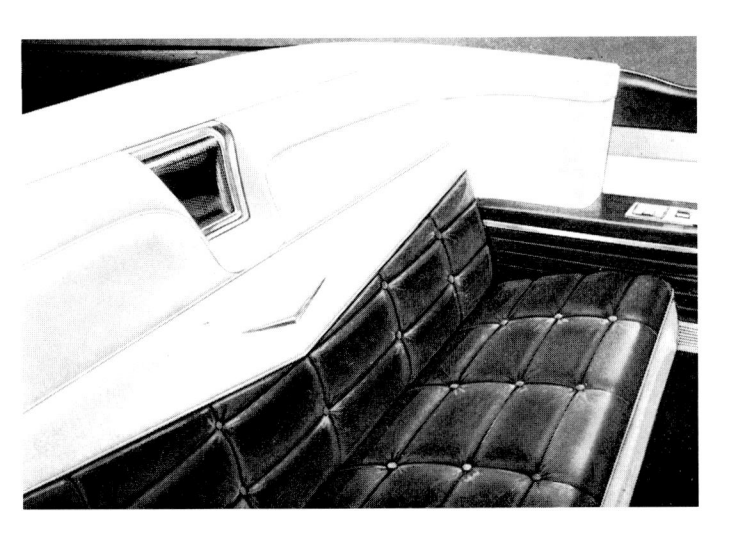

The interiors of the Cadillac Series Sixty-Two Convertible are designed to combine the smart appearance desired in a motor car whose beauty is often open to view, and the durability requisite to the all-weather exposure it receives. Coupled with the Convertible's beauty and durability is a full complement of comfort and convenience features which adds to the carefree motoring pleasure this car so ably provides.

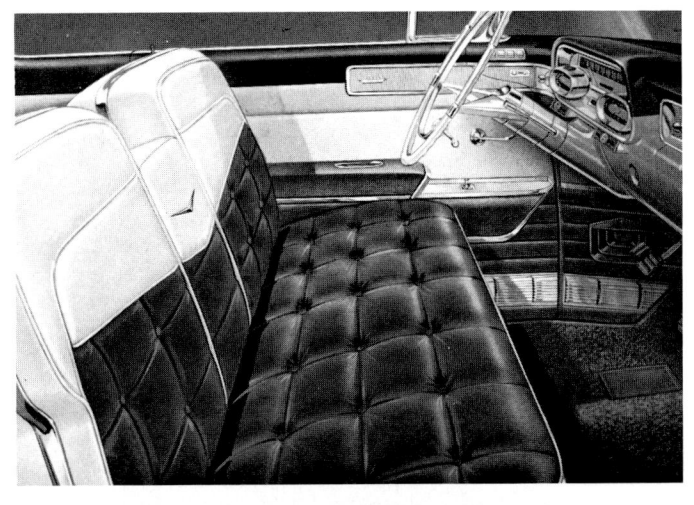

20. Black Leather seat and seat back inserts with Ivory Leather bolsters and trim.
21. Genuine Black Leather throughout.
22. Light Blue Metallic Leather seat and seat back inserts with Ivory Leather bolsters and trim.
24. Genuine Bronze Leather throughout.
25. Genuine Saddle Tan Leather throughout.
26. Light Green Metallic Leather seat and seat back inserts with Ivory Leather bolsters and trim.
28. Red Leather seat and seat back inserts with Ivory Leather bolsters and trim.
29. Genuine Red Leather throughout.

TOP COLORS: 1. White 2. Black 3. Blue 4. Tan 5. Green

coupe de ville

STANDARD EQUIPMENT

Air Cleaner, dry-pack
Armrest, center, front and rear
Cadillac Power Brakes
Cadillac Power Steering
Cigarette Lighters, front (two)
Cigarette Lighters, rear (two)
Clock, electric
Front Seat Adjustment (horizontal), power operated

Hydra-Matic Transmission
Lights, front ash receivers
Lights, back-up (dual)
Light, courtesy or map (automatic)
Lights, directional signal
Light, glove box (automatic)
Light, luggage compartment (automatic)
Mirror, glare-proof, rear-view, flip type
Oil Filter

Outside Mirror, left-side, remote-control
Paint, two-tone
Parking Brake Warning Signal
Visor Vanity Mirror
Visors, dual sun
Wheel Discs (set of four)
Window Lifts, power operated
Windshield Washer and Coordinator

OPTIONAL EQUIPMENT (Extra Cost)

Cadillac Air Conditioner
Cadillac Air Suspension
Door Locks, Electric
Dor-Gards
Eldorado Engine (3 dual-barrel carburetors)
E-Z-Eye Tinted Glass
Fog Lamps (pair)

Front Seat Adjustment
(vertical and angle), power operated
Front Seat-Back Lock, right side
Headlight Dimmer, automatic
Heater
License Frame
Radiator Grille, gold finish

Radio
Remote-Control Trunk Lid Lock
Sabre-Spoke Wheels (set of five)
in chrome finish
Vent Window Regulators, power operated
Whitewall Tires, 8.20 x 15 (set of five)

sedan de ville

STANDARD EQUIPMENT

Air Cleaner, dry-pack
Armrest, center, front and rear
Assist Handles (two)
Cadillac Power Brakes
Cadillac Power Steering
Cigarette Lighters, front (two)
Cigarette Lighter rear
Clock, electric
Front Seat Adjustment (horizontal), power operated

Hydra-Matic Transmission
Lights, front ash receivers
Lights, back-up (dual)
Light, courtesy or map (automatic)
Lights, directional signal
Light, glove box (automatic)
Light, luggage compartment (automatic)
Mirror, glare-proof, rear-view, flip type
Oil Filter

Outside Mirror, left-side, remote-control
Paint, two-tone
Parking Brake Warning Signal
Visor Vanity Mirror
Visors, dual sun
Wheel Discs (set of four)
Window Lifts, power operated
Windshield Washer and Coordinator

OPTIONAL EQUIPMENT (Extra Cost)

Cadillac Air Conditioner
Cadillac Air Suspension
Door Locks, Electric
Dor-Gards
Eldorado Engine (3 dual-barrel carburetors)
E-Z-Eye Tinted Glass
Fog Lamps (pair)

Front Seat Adjustment (vertical and angle),
power operated
Headlight Dimmer, automatic
Heater
License Frame
Radiator Grille, gold-finish
Radio

Remote-Control Trunk Lid Lock
Sabre-Spoke Wheels (set of five)
in chrome finish
Vent Window Regulators, front, power operated
Whitewall Tires, 8.20 x 15 (set of five)

SEDAN DE VILLE AND COUPE DE VILLE

The brilliant array of fabrics and colors for the glamorous Sedan and Coupe de Ville were designed to please the most discriminating of tastes. Nine selections in all, they include choices of five exquisitely patterned nylons in a range of nine colors with genuine leather bolsters in harmonizing shades. Every detail of interior décor from door panels to new vinyl-covered molded fiber glass headlining in the Coupe and Sedan de Ville has been designed to make these two glamour twins of the Cadillac family even more outstanding for 1958.

COUPE DE VILLE • REAR COMPARTMENT

40. Silver and Black Calcutta Pattern Metallic Nylon with Ivory Leather bolsters and trim.
41. Silver Westminster Pattern Metallic Nylon with Silver Metallic Leather bolsters and trim.
42. Light Gray Mojave Pattern Nylon with Light Gray Leather bolsters and trim.
43. Light Blue Westminster Pattern Metallic Nylon with Light Blue Metallic Leather bolsters and trim.
44. Bronze and Black Sierra Pattern Nylon with Bronze Metallic Leather bolsters and trim.
45. Beige Tunisian Pattern Metallic Nylon with Beige Metallic Leather bolsters and trim.
46. Turquoise and Black Calcutta Pattern Metallic Nylon with Turquoise Metallic Leather bolsters and trim.
47. Light Green Tunisian Pattern Metallic Nylon with Light Green Metallic Leather bolsters and trim.
48. Taupe and Black Sierra Pattern Nylon with Taupe Metallic Leather bolsters and trim.

SEDAN DE VILLE • FRONT COMPARTMENT

SEDAN DE VILLE • REAR COMPARTMENT

199

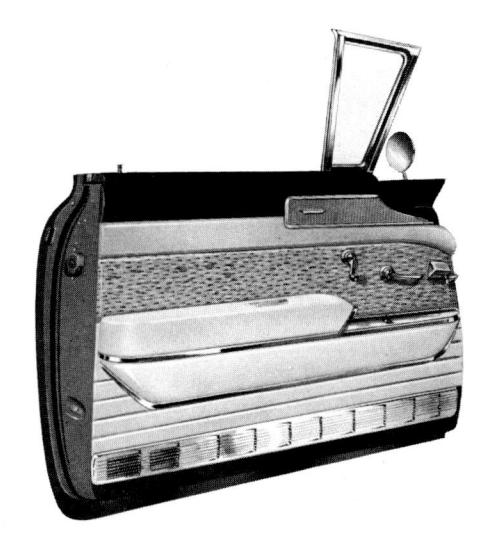

eldorado biarritz

1958

STANDARD EQUIPMENT

Air Cleaner, dry-pack
Armrest, center, front
Cadillac Power Brakes
Cadillac Power Steering
Cigarette Lighters, front (two)
Cigarette Lighters, rear (two)
Clock, electric
Eldorado Engine (3 dual-barrel carburetors)
Fog Lamps (pair)
Front Seat Adjustment (6-way), power operated
Heater
Hydra-Matic Transmission

License Frame
Lights, front ash receivers
Lights, back-up (dual)
Light, courtesy or map (automatic) front and rear compartment
Lights, courtesy, front seat sides
Lights, directional signal
Lights, door panel, safety warning
Light, glove box (automatic)
Light, luggage compartment (automatic)
Oil Filter
Outside Mirror, left-side, remote-control
Parking Brake Warning Signal

Radio
Rear-View Mirror, 3-way, E-Z-Eye
Remote-Control Trunk Lid Lock
Sabre-Spoke Wheels (set of five), chrome finish
Vent Window Regulators, power operated
Visor Vanity Mirror
Visors, dual sun
Whitewall Tires, 8.20 x 15 (set of five)
Window Lifts, power operated
Windshield Washer and Coordinator

OPTIONAL EQUIPMENT (Extra Cost)

Cadillac Air Conditioner
Cadillac Air Suspension

Door Locks, Electric
E-Z-Eye Glass
Front Seat-Back Lock, right side

Gold-Finish Radiator Grille (no extra cost)
Headlight Dimmer (automatic)

ELDORADO BIARRITZ

The glamorous beauty of the Eldorado Biarritz is the result of distinctive design combined with the superb quality of all upholstery, hardware and trim. Seat cushions and seat back inserts, for example, fashioned with narrow, finely tailored pleats are of special-grained Cape buffalo leather in a selection of solid colors or in two-toned colors as described on the opposite page. Bolsters at the sides of the seat back are joined by an unpleated panel containing two embossed Cadillac crests. Carpeting is a deep-pile nylon blend.

The magnificent luxury and individual distinction of the Eldorado Biarritz interiors were never more evident than for 1958. Typical of the functional beauty of the Eldorado is the newly styled door panel shown below. Note, for example, the long expanse of the armrest and the recessed forward portion with power seat and power vent window controls at the driver's finger tips. A new feature adding to beauty of appearance and contributing to safer nighttime driving is provided by a concealed light within the recessed, pleated portion of the door panel. When a door is opened a red glow illuminates the door panel as a warning to cars approaching from the rear and as an aid for passengers entering or leaving the car.

10. Black Cape Buffalo Grained Leather seat cushion and seat back inserts with White Leather bolsters and trim.
11. Black Cape Buffalo Grained Leather throughout.
12. Silver Metallic Cape Buffalo Grained Leather throughout.
13. Blue Metallic Cape Buffalo Grained Leather throughout.
15. Copper Metallic Cape Buffalo Grained Leather throughout.
17. Green Metallic Cape Buffalo Grained Leather throughout.
18. Vermilion Cape Buffalo Grained Leather seat cushion and seat back inserts with White Leather bolsters and trim.
19. Vermilion Cape Buffalo Grained Leather throughout.

VICODEC TOP COLORS: 1. White 2. Black 6. Gleneagles Green
7. Argyle Blue 8. Copper

ADDITIONAL HIGHLIGHTS OF THE ELDORADO ENGINE

(Standard on Eldorado Brougham, Biarritz and Seville; optional at extra cost on all other models.)

New three, dual-barrel carburetor
New 335 horsepower
New 405 foot pounds of torque
New dry-pack air cleaner
New manifold design

eldorado seville

1958

STANDARD EQUIPMENT

Air Cleaner, dry-pack
Armrest, center, front and rear
Cadillac Power Brakes
Cadillac Power Steering
Cigarette Lighters, front (two)
Cigarette Lighters, rear (two)
Clock, electric
Eldorado Engine (3 dual-barrel carburetors)
Fog Lamps (pair)
Front Seat Adjustment (6-way), power operated
Heater

Hydra-Matic Transmission
License Frame
Lights, front ash receivers
Lights, back-up (dual)
Light, courtesy or map (automatic)
Lights, directional signal
Lights, door panel, safety warning
Light, glove box (automatic)
Light, luggage compartment (automatic)
Oil Filter
Outside Mirror, left-side, remote-control
Parking Brake Warning Signal

Radio
Rear-View Mirror, 3-way, E-Z-Eye
Remote-Control Trunk Lid Lock
Sabre-Spoke Wheels (set of five), chrome finish
Vent Window Regulators, power operated
Visor Vanity Mirror
Visors, dual sun
Whitewall Tires, 8.20 x 15 (set of five)
Window Lifts, power operated
Windshield Washer and Coordinator

OPTIONAL EQUIPMENT (Extra Cost)

Cadillac Air Conditioner
Cadillac Air Suspension

Door Locks, electric
E-Z-Eye Glass
Front Seat-Back Lock, right side

Gold-Finish Radiator Grille (no extra cost)
Headlight Dimmer (automatic)

ELDORADO SEVILLE

The distinctive styling of the Eldorado Seville is evident in every way, from its smart exterior with Vicodec covered steel top, to its fabulous interiors with new molded fiber glass headlining and a stunning array of glamorous upholstery choices in fine fabrics and leather. Upholstery selections for 1958 include a new "V" and Crest pattern nylon in Green, Blue, Copper or Black and Silver combined with bolsters and trim of harmonizing Cape buffalo grained metallic leather or a choice of four all-leather combinations. Floor covering of heavily tufted, deep-pile nylon blend carpeting further enhances the beauty of the Eldorado Seville interior décor.

The Eldorado Seville presents the ultra-smart interior décor one might expect of America's most distinctive hard-top coupe. A new feature of beauty, safety and convenience is the recessed pleated portion of the door panel containing a concealed light. When a door is opened the pleated area is illuminated with a red glow as a warning to approaching cars and as an aid for passengers entering or alighting from the car. As in the Biarritz, the Seville has a full-length armrest with its recessed chromed forward portion containing the controls for the power seat and power vent windows.

NEW THREE, DUAL-BARREL CARBURETOR

A three, dual-barrel carburetor is provided as standard equipment on the Eldorado Biarritz, Seville and Brougham and is optional on all other models. Only the center or primary dual-barrel carburetor is used for all normal operation, including starting, idling and at cruising speeds, thus assuring maximum efficiency and dependability because of the relative simplicity of single carburetor adjustment. The two secondary dual-barrel carburetors are used only when the driver depresses the accelerator pedal beyond 75% of its travel. Then they open simultaneously releasing a vast increase in power for extra safety in passing another car or for accelerating up steep grades.

50. Black and Silver V-Crest Patterned Nylon with Silver Metallic Leather bolsters and trim.
51. Black Cape Buffalo Grained Leather with White Leather bolsters and trim.
52. Blue and Silver V-Crest Patterned Nylon with Blue Metallic Leather bolsters and trim.
53. Blue Cape Buffalo Grained Leather throughout.
54. Copper and Silver V-Crest Patterned Nylon with Copper Metallic Leather bolsters and trim.
56. Green and Silver V-Crest Patterned Nylon with Green Metallic Leather bolsters and trim.
57. Green Cape Buffalo Grained Leather throughout.
58. Vermilion Cape Buffalo Grained Leather with White Leather bolsters and trim.

VICODEC TOP COLORS: 1. White   2. Black   6. Gleneagles Green
                       7. Argyle Blue   8. Copper

fleetwood sixty special sedan

1958

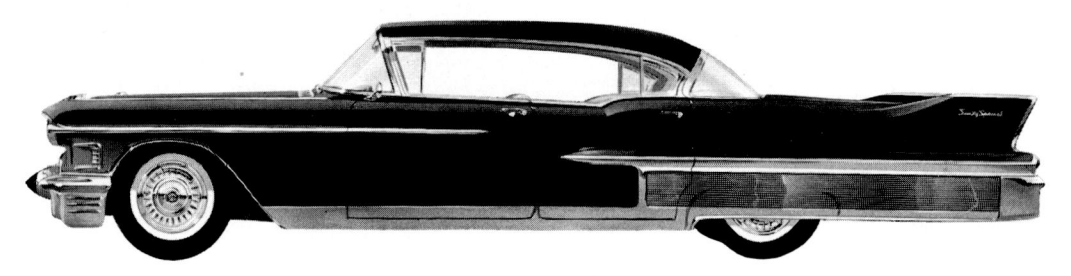

STANDARD EQUIPMENT

Air Cleaner, dry-pack
Armrest, center, front and rear
Assist Handles (two)
Cadillac Power Brakes
Cadillac Power Steering
Cigarette Lighters, front (two)
Cigarette Lighter, rear
Clock, electric
Front Seat Adjustment (horizontal), power operated

Hydra-Matic Transmission
Lights, front ash receivers
Lights, back-up (dual)
Light, courtesy or map (automatic)
Lights, directional signal
Light, glove box (automatic)
Light, luggage compartment (automatic)
Mirror, glare-proof, rear-view, flip type
Oil Filter
Outside Mirror, left-side, remote-control
Outside Mirror, right side

Paint, two-tone
Parking Brake Warning Signal
Pocket, back of front seat
Vent Window Regulators, front, power operated
Visor Vanity Mirror
Visors, dual sun
Wheel Discs (set of four)
Window Lifts, power operated
Windshield Washer and Coordinator

OPTIONAL EQUIPMENT (Extra Cost)

Cadillac Air Conditioner
Cadillac Air Suspension
Door Locks, Electric
Dor-Gards
Eldorado Engine (3 dual-barrel carburetors)
E-Z-Eye Tinted Glass

Fog Lamps (pair)
Front Seat Adjustment (vertical and angle), power operated
Headlight Dimmer, automatic
Heater
License Frame

Radiator Grille, gold-finish
Radio
Remote-Control Trunk Lid Lock
Sabre-Spoke Wheels (set of five) in chrome finish
Whitewall Tires, 8.20 x 15 (set of five)

FLEETWOOD SIXTY SPECIAL SEDAN

The impeccably tailored interiors of the Fleetwood Sixty Special Sedan are offered in a new wide range of luxurious upholstery selections for 1958. There are, for example, choices of soft, fine-textured Mojave cloth or rich, all-wool broadcloth in Light Gray, Light Blue or Beige, styled as shown above in rectangular biscuits with deeply recessed buttons. Seven choices of exquisitely patterned nylon fabrics with gleaming metallic threads are available with leather bolsters in harmonizing colors. When nylon and leather upholstery is selected, seat cushions and seat backs are fashioned in two-inch piping with full bolsters of smooth leather.

The magnificent Fleetwood Sixty Special Sedan has long epitomized Cadillac leadership in the luxury car field. What is more, its inherent dignity and gracious beauty, enhanced still further for 1958, are certain to increase its hold on the affections of America's luxury sedan owners. Nothing has been overlooked in interior design, appointments, upholstery and trim which could add to the beauty, comfort and convenience provided by the Sixty Special. Door panel, below, shows the new power vent window controls and the power seat controls on the recessed forward portion of the new, more massive armrest.

60. Silver and Black Calcutta Patterned Metallic Nylon with Ivory Leather bolsters and trim.
61. Silver and Black Calcutta Patterned Metallic Nylon with Silver Metallic Leather bolsters and trim.
63. Light Blue Tunisian Pattern Metallic Nylon with Light Blue Metallic Leather bolsters and trim.
65. Beige Tunisian Patterned Metallic Nylon with Beige Metallic Leather bolsters and trim.
66. Turquoise and Black Calcutta Patterned Metallic Nylon with Turquoise Metallic Leather bolsters and trim.
67. Green Tunisian Patterned Metallic Nylon with Light Green Metallic Leather bolsters and trim.
68. Light Gray Tunisian Patterned Metallic Nylon with Silver Metallic Leather bolsters and trim.
70. Light Gray Mojave Cloth throughout.
71. Light Gray Broadcloth throughout.
72. Light Blue Mojave Cloth throughout.
73. Light Blue Broadcloth throughout.
74. Beige Mojave Cloth throughout.
75. Beige Broadcloth throughout.

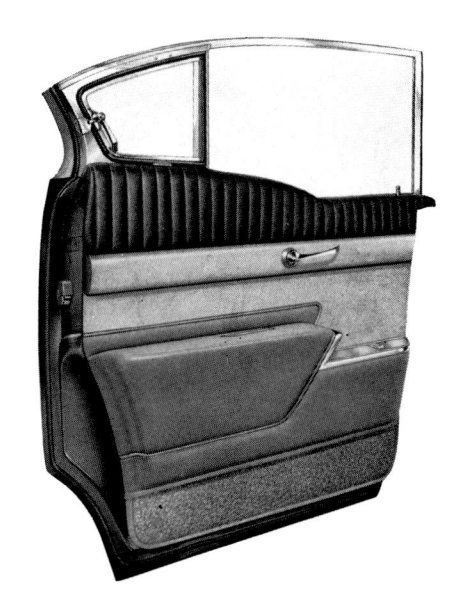

NEW EMERGENCY BRAKE FOOT RELEASE

The emergency brake is located for quick and easy application by the driver's left foot. Extra safety is provided by locating the emergency brake release pedal to the left side of the emergency brake pedal. Thus the release pedal is less likely to be tripped accidentally.

fleetwood series seventy-five 9 passenger sedan and limousine

1958

STANDARD EQUIPMENT

- Air Cleaner, dry-pack
- Armrest, center, front and rear
- Assist Handles (two)
- Cadillac Power Brakes
- Cadillac Power Steering
- Cigarette Lighters, front (two)
- Cigarette Lighters, rear (two)
- Clocks, electric, front and rear compartments
- Foot Rests, adjustable (two), rear compartment
- Front Seat Adjustment (horizontal), power operated
- Hydra-Matic Transmission
- Lights, front ash receivers
- Lights, back-up (dual)
- Lights, courtesy, map (automatic)
- Lights, directional signal
- Light, glove box (automatic)
- Light, luggage compartment (automatic)
- Mirror, glare-proof, rear-view, flip type
- Oil Filter
- Outside Mirror, left-side, remote-control
- Package Compartments in Side Armrests, rear (two)
- Paint, two-tone
- Parking Brake Warning Signal
- Robe Cord, back of front seat
- Visor Vanity Mirror
- Visors, dual sun
- Wheel Discs (set of four)
- Window Lifts, power operated
- Windshield Washer and Coordinator

OPTIONAL EQUIPMENT (Extra Cost)

- Cadillac Air Conditioner
- Cadillac Air Suspension
- E-Z-Eye Tinted Glass
- Eldorado Engine (3 dual-barrel carburetors)
- Fog Lamps (pair)
- Headlight Dimmer, automatic
- Heater
- License Frame
- Radiator Grille, gold-finish
- Radio, front compartment controls
- Radio, rear compartment controls
- Remote-Control Trunk Lid Lock
- Sabre-Spoke Wheels (set of five) in chrome finish
- Vent Window Regulators, front, power operated
- Whitewall Tires, 8.20 x 15 (set of five) 6-ply

FLEETWOOD SEVENTY-FIVE

The Fleetwood Seventy-Five Nine-Passenger Sedan lends unmatched distinction and dignity to any occasion or any place it appears. Impressively big and beautiful, it has long been recognized as the ideal car for company executive use, for public dignitaries or the man with a large family. Its interiors reflect in every way the distinguished character of the car itself. Concealed in the beautifully appointed center partition are two fold-away seats upholstered in the same fine fabrics used throughout the interior. Just above the fold-away seats is a leather covered robe cord while across the top portion of the center partition are such conveniences as two assist handles, two ash receivers and an easily read, beautifully framed electric clock.

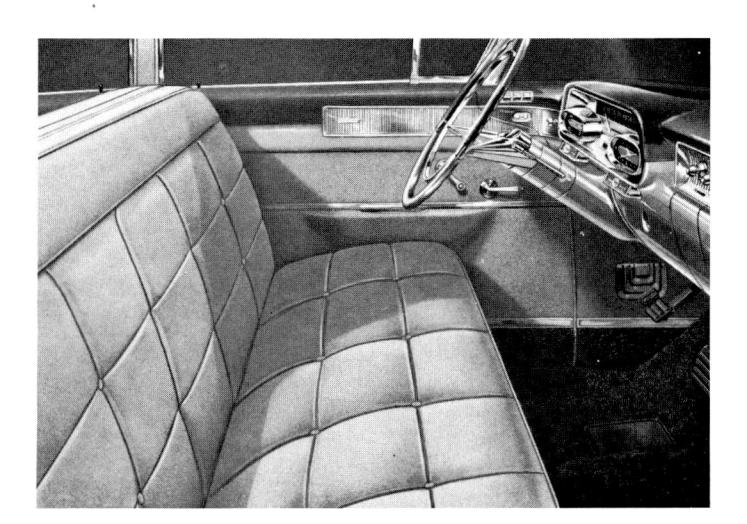

80. Light Gray Bedford Cord seat cushions and seat backs with Gray Broadcloth bolsters and trim.
81. Light Gray Broadcloth throughout.
84. Beige Bedford Cord seat cushions and seat backs with Beige Broadcloth bolsters and trim.
85. Beige Broadcloth throughout.
90. Dark Gray Bedford Cord seat cushions and seat backs with Light Gray Broadcloth bolsters and trim.
94. Brown Bedford Cord seat cushions and seat backs with Beige Broadcloth bolsters and trim.

Front and rear seats of the spacious Fleetwood Seventy-Five 9-Passenger Sedan are impeccably tailored with heavily tufted rectangular biscuits and deeply recessed buttons. A smartly contrasting, smooth-surfaced panel extends across the upper portion of the seat backs. Upholstery selections of fashionable Bedford cord or fine, all-wool broadcloth in the colors and combinations described on the opposite page are in full keeping with the inherent dignity and grace of this sedan's interior décor. A final note of luxury is provided by the heavily tufted, deep-pile nylon blend carpeting which covers not only the floor and adjustable foot rests, but the scuff pad areas of the side walls, doors and center partition.

FLEETWOOD SEVENTY-FIVE LIMOUSINE

The Fleetwood Seventy-Five Limousine, the most luxurious, chauffeur-driven car in America, provides all the style, comfort and conveniences of the nine-passenger sedan plus the added practicality of an all-leather upholstered front compartment. Separating the front and rear compartments is a glass dividing partition which may be raised or lowered electrically by automatic control buttons located on the rear seat armrests.

Fabrics and color selections for the limousine are the same as for the nine-passenger sedan. In each case, however, the front compartment of the limousine is upholstered throughout with genuine BLACK LEATHER, styled in two-inch piping without bolsters.

1958 optional equipment

CADILLAC SIX-WAY POWER SEAT

For all 1958 Cadillac cars equipped with the electrically powered fore-and-aft seat adjuster, an electrically powered vertical and seat-angle adjustment is also available as an extra-cost option. The complete Six-Way Power Seat is standard equipment on the Eldorado Biarritz and Seville, optional at extra cost on the Series Sixty-Two Coupe, Sedan and extended-deck Sedan. Control switch is on left side of front seat on the Series Sixty-Two Sedan, Coupe and extended-deck Sedan; on the front top portion of the armrest on all other models.

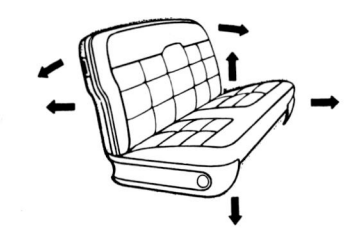

CADILLAC SABRE-SPOKE WHEELS

Especially constructed of aluminum and steel, Sabre-Spoke wheels are standard on the Eldorado Biarritz and Seville and available in sets of five as an extra-cost option on all other models. Sabre-Spoke wheels are finished in chromium.

REMOTE-CONTROL TRUNK LID LOCK

The Cadillac Remote-Control Trunk Lid Lock is a convenience feature particularly appreciated by owners in areas where federal or local authorities must check trunk contents in compliance with law. The deck lid can be automatically unlocked at a touch of a button located within the glove compartment on the left side. A warning light on the instrument cluster indicates when trunk is unlocked.

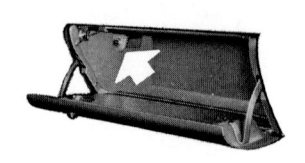

E-Z-EYE TINTED GLASS

Cadillac E-Z-Eye Glass, available as an extra-cost option on all 1958 Cadillac cars, presents all of the safety advantages of regular laminated Safety Plate glass, but with the additional benefits of reducing glare and helping keep the interior of the car cooler. It consists of tinted plastic between two layers of polished plate glass. The tint does not alter colors of lights or traffic signals.

CADILLAC "AUTRONIC-EYE"

The Cadillac "Autronic-Eye" protects the Cadillac owner by causing the headlights of his car to switch from high to low beam when another car approaches from the opposite direction. Since the driver of the oncoming car is not blinded, both cars pass with greater safety. An overriding switch is provided to signal drivers who neglect to switch their own lights from bright to dim.

LICENSE PLATE FRAME

The new Cadillac License Plate Frame for rear only adds protective beauty to the license plates of any state. Frame is made of gold-colored, anodized aluminum with a durable plastic window.

NEW ELECTRIC DOOR LOCKS

Electric door locks are available at extra cost on all models except the Series 75. An electric door locking switch is provided on each door of coupes, front doors of sedans. Pushing the switch down on either door locks all doors. Pushing the switch up unlocks all doors. Individual doors may be unlocked by pulling up the standard door lock button.

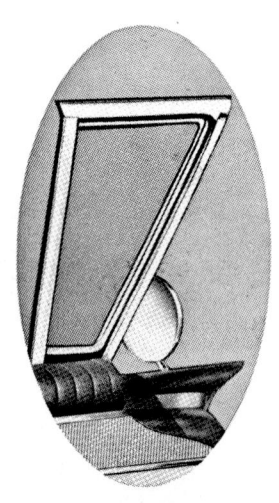

NEW POWER VENT WINDOWS

Electrically powered front ventipanes are standard equipment on the Eldorado Biarritz and Seville and the Sixty Special Sedan and optional at extra cost on all other power window equipped models. Two controls marked "V" are located on the driver's door just below the four door window controls. A single control is located on the right-hand door for operation by the front compartment passenger.

NEW FOG LAMPS

Cadillac Fog Lamps are designed to provide illumination low to the surface of the road and thus provide better visibility under certain adverse weather conditions. When ordered, they are installed on the lower bumper bar in place of the parking lights.

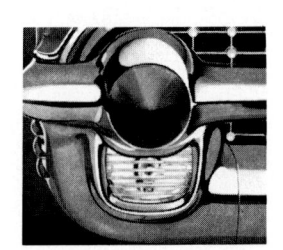

1958 CADILLAC GENERAL SPECIFICATIONS

	Series 62 Sedan, Sedan (extended deck) and Sedan de Ville	Series 62 Coupe and Coupe de Ville	Series 62 Convertible Coupe	Eldorado Biarritz and Eldorado Seville	Series 60 Special Sedan	Series 75 9-Passenger Sedan and Limousine
Wheelbase	129.5"	129.5"	129.5"	129.5"	133"	149.8"
Over-all Length	225.3"***	221.8"	221.8"	223.4"	225.3"	237.1"
Over-all Width	80"	80"	80"	80"	80"	80"
Over-all Height	59.1"	57.7"	58.2"	57.9"**	59.1"	61.6"
Minimum Road Clearance	6.4"	6.4"	6.4"	6.6"	6.4"	7.2"
Steering Ratio—Over-all	19.5"	19.5"	19.5"	19.5"	19.5"	19.5"
Turning Diameter	47'3"	47'3"	47'3"	47'3"	48'3"	52'9"
Tread—Front	61"	61"	61"	61"	61"	61"
Tread—Rear	61"	61"	61"	61"	61"	61"
Tires, Tubeless—Size	8.00 x 15*	8.00 x 15*	8.00 x 15*	8.20 x 15	8.00 x 15*	8.20 x 15
Tires—Ply Rating	4-ply	4-ply	4-ply	4-ply	4-ply	6-ply

*8.20 x 15 supplied in whitewall tires (standard on Eldorado Biarritz and Seville).
**58.4" on Eldorado Biarritz.   ***Standard Sedan 216.8".

Engine	310-horsepower Cadillac V-8	310-horsepower Cadillac V-8	310-horsepower Cadillac V-8	335-horsepower Cadillac V-8	310-horsepower Cadillac V-8	310-horsepower Cadillac V-8
Compression Ratio	10.25:1	10.25:1	10.25:1	10.25:1	10.25:1	10.25:1
Piston Displacement	365 cu. in.	365 cu. in.	365 cu. in.	365 cu. in.	365 cu. in.	365 cu. in.
Valve Arrangement	Overhead	Overhead	Overhead	Overhead	Overhead	Overhead
Carburetor	4-barrel	4-barrel	4-barrel	Three dual-barrel	4-barrel	4-barrel
Exhaust System	Dual	Dual	Dual	Dual	Dual	Dual
Transmission	Hydra-Matic	Hydra-Matic	Hydra-Matic	Hydra-Matic	Hydra-Matic	Hydra-Matic
Steering	Hydraulic Power	Hydraulic Power	Hydraulic Power	Hydraulic Power	Hydraulic Power	Hydraulic Power
Brakes	Power Brakes	Power Brakes	Power Brakes	Power Brakes	Power Brakes	Power Brakes
Frame	Tubular-center X	Tubular-center X	Tubular-center X	Tubular-center X	Tubular-center X	Tubular-center X
Springs	Helical coil, front and rear	Helical coil, front and rear	Helical coil, front and rear	Helical coil, front and rear	Helical coil, front and rear	Helical coil, front and rear
Drive	Cadillac Four-Link	Cadillac Four-Link	Cadillac Four-Link	Cadillac Four-Link	Cadillac Four-Link	Cadillac Four-Link
Axle Ratio	3.07:1*	3.07:1*	3.07:1*	3.36:1**	3.07:1*	3.36:1**

*3.36:1 standard with Eldorado engine; on Series 75 and air-conditioned models and optional on other models.
**3.77 optional on Series 75.

NEW CADILLAC AIR SUSPENSION

Air suspension, introduced on the limited-production Eldorado Brougham in 1957, is now available as an extra-cost option on all Cadillac models. It offers the ultimate in consistent quality of ride and roadability in addition to maintaining the same pre-determined car height and road clearance irrespective of whether the car is empty or carrying a full complement of passengers and luggage.

The new air suspension system was developed through years of research and refinement by Cadillac engineers working closely with the General Motors Engineering Staff. Exhaustive tests determined the design of a compressor capable of maintaining adequate pressure even at Pikes Peak altitudes; rubber bellows durable enough to withstand over a million flexings and an air-tight seal at the wheels and through the lines. The result for your 1958 Cadillac owners who choose air suspension is a new high degree of riding comfort and roadability of consistently high quality regardless of road or load.

FULLY CONTROLLED RIDE

- Air suspension gives a damping quality unobtainable with conventional springs and shock absorbers.
- The ride is of slower frequency with slower body motions which make a far more pleasant ride for passengers.
- Air springs adjust automatically to provide softer or firmer cushioning as required to maintain best quality ride regardless of load.
- Maintained clearance between the rear axle and frame regardless of load keeps car always at showroom height.
- Maintained normal height of car assures consistent steering without over- or under-steering sometimes resulting from variations in car loading.

1958 specifications

ENGINE

Number of cylinders	8
Cylinder arrangement	90° V-type
Valve arrangement	Overhead
Bore and stroke	4″ x 3⅝″
Block and cylinder head material	Cast iron
Piston displacement	365 cu. in.
Taxable horsepower	51.2
Max. brake horsepower	310 @ 4800 r.p.m.
Eldorado engine	335 @ 4800 r.p.m.
Max. engine torque—lbs.-ft.	405 @ 3100 r.p.m.
Eldorado engine	405 @ 3400 r.p.m.
Compression ratio	10.25:1
Engine mounts	Vulcanized rubber
Number of points of suspension	3

PISTON AND RINGS

Make	Alcoa—Bohn—Sterling
Material	Aluminum alloy
Type	T-slot, cam ground
Weight	22.72 oz.
Clearance	.0015
Number of oil rings per piston	1
Number of comp. rings per piston	2
Top compression ring	Chrome-plated

RODS AND PINS

Wristpin length	3.093″
Wristpin material	Steel
Type	Locked in rod
Connecting rod length	6.625″
Material—connecting rod	Forged steel
Weight—connecting rod	23.49 oz.
Crankpin journal diameter	2¼″
Lower bearing material	Steel-back Moraine 400
Connecting rod bearing clearance	.0005″-.0021″
Connecting rod bearing end play	.008″-.014″ (total two rods)

CRANKSHAFT

Material	Forged alloy steel
Weight	71 pounds
Main bearing thrust	Rear main
Crankshaft end play	.002″ to .007″
Main bearing type	Slip-on
Main bearing removable	Yes
Main bearing material	Steel-back Durex
Main bearing clearance—rear	.0008″ to .0025″
Main bearing journal Diameter x Length:	
Number 1	2.625″ x .907″
Number 2	2.625″ x .907″
Number 3	2.625″ x .907″
Number 4	2.625″ x .907″
Number 5	2.625″ x 1.622″

CAMSHAFT

Drive	Chain
Camshaft sprocket material	Steel
Timing chain—make	Link Belt
Timing chain—no. of links	46
Timing chain—width	.6875″
Timing chain—pitch	.500″

VALVES

Valve arrangement	Overhead
Intake opens	39° B.T.C. at .001 lift
Intake closes	113° A.B.C. at .001 lift
Exhaust opens	85° B.B.C. at .001 lift
Exhaust closes	59° A.T.C. at .001 lift

INTAKE

Material	Alloy steel
Over-all length	4.794″
Diameter of head	1.875″
Angle of seat	44°
Lift	.451″

EXHAUST

Material	Alloy steel
Over-all length	4.815″
Diameter of head	1.500″
Angle of seat	44°
Lift	.451″
Hydraulic valve lifters	Yes
Valve inserts	None
Valve seats cooled by	Direct water circulation

LUBRICATION

Type	Full pressure
Oil under pressure to:	
Main bearings	Yes
Connecting rods	Yes
Wristpins	Splash
Camshaft bearings	Yes
Tappets	Yes
Oil pump type	Gear
Normal oil pressure	30 to 35 lbs. @ 30 m.p.h.
Capacity of oil reservoir	Dry, 6 qts.; Refill, 6 qts.
Type of oil level gauge	Dip stick
Make of pressure gauge	AC—Tell-Tale Lite
Oil filter	Standard
Type	Partial flow

FUEL

Gasoline tank capacity	20 gallons
Type of fuel feed	Camshaft pump
Carburetor—make	Rochester & Carter
Carburetor—type	Four-barrel downdraft*
Manifold heat control	Automatic
Type of air cleaner	Dry-pack
Dual tailpipe diameters	1.75″

*Three, Dual-barrel Carburetors on 335 h.p. engine, standard on Eldorados and optional on all other models.

COOLING

Water pump type	Centrifugal—dual outlet
Pressure relief valve	Yes
Choke for recirculation	Yes
Radiator core	Tube and center
Full-length cylinder water jacket	Yes
Water all around cylinders	Yes
Fan belt length	57″
Fan belt width	⅜″
Fan—no. of blades	4
(Series 75 and air-conditioned cars)	6
Cooling system capacity	19.56 qts.
With heater	20.7 qts. (Series 75, 21.8 qts.)

GENERATOR

Make	Delco-Remy
Minimum charging speed	22 m.p.h. and up
Generator ventilation	Forced air
(Series 75 and air-conditioned cars)	Directed outside air

GENERATOR REGULATOR

Make	Delco-Remy
Voltage at cut-out closing	11.8—13.6 (adjust to 12.8)
(Series 75 and air-conditioned cars)	11.8—13.0 (adjust to 12.4)
Voltage regulator setting	14—15 (adjust to 14.5 at 90°)
(Series 75 and air-conditioned cars)	13.8—14.8 (adjust to 14.0 at 90°)
Generator max. charging rate	32—37 amp. (adjust to 35)
(Series 75 and air-conditioned cars)	42—47 amp. (adjust to 45)

STARTING MOTOR

Make	Delco-Remy
Flywheel teeth, integral or ring	Steel integral

LIGHTS AND HORN

Headlight—make	Guide sealed-beam (Dual)
Headlight cover glass, dia.	5¾″
Parking light—make	Guide
Taillight—make	Guide
Lighting switch—make	Delco-Remy
How are headlights dimmed?	Depressed beam—foot switch
Horn:	
Make	Delco-Remy
Type	Vibrator, seashell electric (2)*

*3 on Eldorados.

IGNITION

Spark advance	Centrifugal and vacuum
Ignition unit:	
Make	Delco-Remy
Manual advance	None
Maximum centrifugal advance	Crankshaft (14°-18°)
Vacuum advance	Crankshaft (22.5°-25.5°)
Distributor breaker gap	.016″
Initial spark advance	5° B.T.C. (Nominal)
(on Eldorado engine)	10° B.T.C. (Nominal)
Firing order	1-8-4-3-6-5-7-2
Ignition coil:	
Make	Delco-Remy
Spark Plugs:	
Make	AC
Model	44.0
Thread	14 mm.
Gap	.035″

BATTERY

Make	Delco 3EMR70-W
Number of plates	11
Capacity (amp. hrs.)	70
Terminal grounded	Negative
Location of battery	Under hood on tray attached to front right-hand side of radiator cradle

HYDRA-MATIC DRIVE

Type	Fully automatic step-gear type with controlled fluid coupling on forward gear set for smoother shifts.
Gearing	Planetary
No. of forward speeds	4
No. of forward speeds in "City" DR range	3
No. of forward speeds in "Country" DR range	4
No. of forward speeds in LO range	2
Transmission ratio, first	3.97:1
Transmission ratio, second	2.55:1
Transmission ratio, third	1.55:1
Transmission ratio, fourth	1:1
Transmission ratio, reverse	3.74:1
Oil capacity	11½ qts. dry (check dip stick)
Type of fluid	Hydra-Matic fluid

SHIFT POINTS:

		With Rear Axle Ratio of: 3.07:1	3.36:1	3.77:1
Upshift DR-4 Range	**Throttle Opening**	**M.P.H.**	**M.P.H.**	**M.P.H.**
1st to 2nd	—Minimum	3-9	3-8	3-7
	—Maximum	18-21	16-19	16-18
2nd to 3rd	—Minimum	13-17	12-15	11-14
	—Maximum	40-43	37-39	35-37
3rd to 4th	—Minimum	22-25	20-23	19-21
	—Maximum	76-81	69-74	65-70
Downshift DR-4 Range				
4th to 3rd	—Minimum	17-14	16-13	15-12
	—Maximum	74-68	67-62	64-59
3rd to 2nd	—Minimum	12-8	11-7	10-7
	—Maximum	26-22	24-20	22-19
2nd to 1st	—Minimum	7-3	7-3	6-2
	—Maximum	13-9	12-8	11-8
DR-3 Range				
Same as DR-4 except upshifts from 3rd to 4th at:		76-81	69-74	65-70
downshifts from 4th to 3rd at		74-68	67-62	64-59
LO Range				
Same as DR-4 except upshifts to 3rd at		48-54	44-49	42-47
upshifts to 4th at		76-81	69-74	65-70
downshifts to 3rd at		74-68	67-62	64-59
downshifts to 2nd at		47-44	43-40	41-38

NOTE: Miles per hour at which shift is made is dependent on degree of throttle opening. Actually no gears shift. Term used for clarity of meaning.

FRAME

	Series 62	Series 60S	Series 75
Frame make	A. O. Smith	A. O. Smith	A. O. Smith
Frame depth, maximum	7″	7″	7″
Frame thickness, maximum	9/64″	5/32″	5/32″
Width of flange, maximum	3 17/32″	3 17/32″	3 17/32″
Frame—Type	Tubular-center X frame	Tubular-center X frame	Tubular-center X frame

1958

FRONT-END SUSPENSION

Front suspension, make	Own
Front suspension, type	Forked arms
Forked arm bearings	Inner threaded
Knuckle support bearing	Spherical
Front wheel inner bearing, make and type	N.D. ball
Front wheel outer bearing, make and type	N.D. ball
Front spring, type	Helical coil*
Front spring, material	Spring steel
Shock absorber, type	Hydraulic direct-acting type
Front stabilizer	Torsion rod

REAR SUSPENSION

Type	Cadillac four-link
Springs	Helical coil*
Material	Spring steel
Spring bushings, type	Rubber
Shock absorbers	Hydraulic direct-acting, inverted "V" mounting

*Air suspension optional at extra cost.

PROPELLER SHAFT

Number used	2
Type	Exposed

UNIVERSAL JOINTS

Make	Mechanics and Saginaw
Number used	3
Type	Cross and Trunnion
Bearing	Needle
Universal joints, lubricated	Permanently
Drive and torque taken through	Four-link rear suspension

TIRES AND WHEELS

Tires:	
Make	U. S. Royal, Firestone and Goodrich
Type	Tubeless

*Standard with 335-h.p. Eldorado engine and on air-conditioned models.

SERIES 62 COUPE DE VILLE

TIRES AND WHEELS—Continued

	Series 62-60	Series 75
Size	8.00 x 15*	8.20 x 15
Ply rating	4	6
Inflation pressure:		
Front	24 lbs.	28 lbs.
Rear	24 lbs.	28 lbs.
Wheels:		
Type	Slotted disc**	
Make	Kelsey-Hayes	
Rim, diameter	15"	
Rim, width	6.00"	
Tread:		
Front	61"	
Rear	61"	

*8.20 x 15 when whitewalls are ordered. Standard on Eldorados.
**Aluminum spoke, steel rim wheels on Eldorados.

REAR AXLE

Rear axle, make	Own	
Rear axle, type	Semifloating	
Differential gear, make	Own	
Rear axle:		
Oil capacity	5 pints	
Grade recommended:		
S.A.E. viscosity	90 hypoid	

	Series 62-60	Series 75
Type of final gearing	Hypoid	
Gear ratio:		
Standard	3.07:1	3.36:1
Optional	3.36:1*	3.77
Pinion adjustment (except 75)	None	
Pinion bearing adjustment	None (preloaded)	
Are pinion bearings in sleeve?	No	
Backlash between pinion and ring gear	.003"-.010"	
Rear axle pinion shaft:		
Front bearing, type	Tapered roller	
Rear bearing, type	Tapered roller	

STEERING

Steering	Hydraulic power
Type	Concentric gear
Make	Saginaw
Over-all steering ratio	19.5:1
Car turning radius (outside) bumper to bumper sweep	(62) 23'7" (75) 26'5" (60) 24'2"

BRAKES

	Series 62-60	Series 75
Brake lining width	2½"	2½"
Brake lining thickness	¼"	¼"
Brake lining effective area	210.32 sq. in.	233.72 sq. in.
Brake clearance	.010" top; .015" bottom	
Foot emergency brake location	Left side below dash	
Operates on	Rear service brakes	
Power brakes	Standard, all models	
Front and Rear:		
Brake drum diameter	12"	12"
Brake drum, internal or external	Internal	Internal
Brake lining, length per wheel:		
Forward shoe	10.05"	12.98"
Reverse shoe	12.98"	12.98"
Total	23.03"	25.96"

MISCELLANEOUS SPECIFICATIONS

Car lifting device, jack	Bumper type
Engine lubrication, type	Pressure
Chassis lubrication, type	High pressure
Axle lubrication, type	Splash

LUBRICANTS

Engine crankcase capacity	5 qts.
With oil filter (Std.)	6 qts.
Recommended viscosity	Min. anticipated temperature: +32°F. 20W or S.A.E. 20 +10°F. 20W −10°F. 10W Below −10°F. 5W
Drain	2000 miles (after initial 500-mile change)
Rear axle oil	5 pints
Recommended viscosity	90 hypoid
Auto trans. fluid type "A"	11½ qts. dry (check dip stick)
Gasoline	20 gals.

Cadillac

1959

The inherent dignity and grace and beauty which have become a hallmark of Cadillac styling take a giant stride forward for 1959.

There is, for example, all of the impressive stature which only a motor car of adequate length and wheelbase can offer. There is the appearance of solid, enduring beauty imparted by the massive bumper and grille design, front and rear. And, of course, from any angle there is the unmistakable mantle of quality which marks each new Standard of the World.

But here, too, are a new lower silhouette, as much as five and one-half inches lower, and new sweeping lines of motion set off by the extended visors of the headlamp bezels and culminating in new sharply defined, swept-back rear quarter fins with twin, projectile-shaped taillight nacelles.

There is new elegance, too, in the tastefully restrained applique of fine chrome mouldings in their sweeping flow from front to rear and in the gracefully curved extension of front and rear glass areas well into the roof line.

Even the finish of the 1959 Cadillac offers a new and enduring beauty. For here are all-new acrylic lacquers whose composition is such that only normal washing is required to maintain the car's showroom splendor.

Cadillac's new Vista-Panoramic windshield provides unsurpassed visibility with its 1740.1 square inches of Safety Plate glass . . . more than that of any competitive car. Though slightly smaller on Cadillac coupe and four-window sedan models, at 1711.8 square inches, the advantage is still Cadillac's.

The four-headlamp system and the four parking lamps continue the strong horizontal motif of the front-end ensemble while providing ideal illumination. All four headlamps are lighted on upper beam while the shielded filament of outer lamps only is lighted on low beam. The outer parking lamps also serve as directional signal lights. The inner pair may be replaced with fog lamps at extra cost.

Highlighting the elegance and refinement of the 1959 Cadillac as viewed from the front are the reflective beauty of concave projectiles at each intersecting line of the wide aluminum grille. The use of straight horizontal lines, from the leading edge of hood and headlamp bezels through the top and center grille bars to the massive lower bumper bar, add a feeling of strength and rigidity while enhancing the apparent width of the car. Traditional identification and graceful ornamentation are provided by the tapered, widespread silver-toned "V" and new, wider, slimmer crest. The new, lower, wider hood extends to the front fender crown mouldings thus virtually eliminating any visible juncture of hood and fenders.

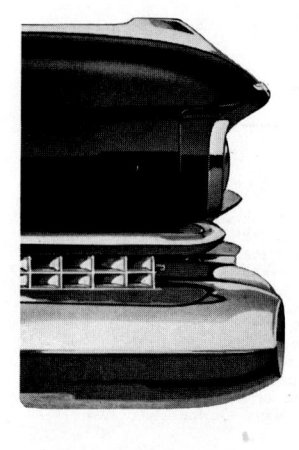

Blending of front ensemble into front fender sides is achieved through gracefully curved extensions of bumper, grille and headlamp bezels. The tapering projection of headlamp bezels and extended front bumper continue the air of motion imparted throughout Cadillac's new styling. A single, swept-back, chromed blade front fender ornament enhances their fleet look for 1959.

The rear styling, as viewed in profile, further emphasizes the sweeping, tapered contours of the rear fenders, fender fins and taillight nacelles. Projectile-like red taillight lenses are easily seen from the side for extra safety. Furthering the uninterrupted continuity of lines and enhancing the road hugging appearance of the car itself are new demountable rear wheel-opening covers.

The sweeping lines of beauty of the 1959 Cadillac culminate in gracefully tapered, chrome-edged rear fender fins with twin, nacelle-like contours containing the projectile-shaped red lenses of the tail, stop and turn signal lamps. At the outer extremities of the massive rear bumper, with its grilled upper portion, are large chrome-framed back-up lamps. The deck lid itself slopes smoothly from the rear window base moulding to the top grille bar relieved only by a graduated center crease line surmounted by a slim, widespread chromed "V" and crest.

CADILLAC FEATURES

NEW ENGINE FEATURES
New larger displacement • New higher compression ratio • New intake manifold with larger passages • New fuel filters • New automatic choke control • New automatic temperature compensator for improved idle operation • New lower air cleaner • New high-capacity fuel pump • New radiator and fan • New tapered exhaust valves • New lighter pistons and connecting rods • New crankshaft

NEW OPTIONAL EQUIPMENT FEATURES
New air conditioning system • New heating system • Newly refined air suspension • New "Q" engine • New shaded and tinted glass options • New radio and electrically operated antenna • New Cruise Control • New power deck lid lock • New fog lamps • New Autronic-Eye (automatic headlamp beam control) with sensitivity adjustment knob

NEW CHASSIS FEATURES
New frame with increased rigidity • New shock absorbers • New quieter rear axle gear-tooth design • New lower rear axle ratios • New direct-acting power brake booster • New power steering with rotary valve for improved response • New power steering pump with increased capacity • New 18.9 to 1 over-all steering ratio • New radiator with increased cooling capacity • Newly refined Hydra-Matic for greater efficiency • New, more efficient transmission oil cooler • New propeller shaft center-bearing • New modifications to air suspension for improved ride

NEW STYLING
New lower silhouette • New lower, wider hood • New hood "V" and crest • New grille • New grille header moulding • New headlamp bezels • New winged crest on headlamp bezels • New front bumper • New parking and directional signal lamps • New front fenders • New front fender crown mouldings • New front fender side mouldings • New front fender name plates and medallions • New Vista-Panoramic windshield • New wheel discs • New body side mouldings • New rocker sill moulding • New fixed rear quarter windows on 6-window sedans • New sliding-type rear quarter windows on the Fleetwood 75 sedan and limousine • New rear quarter panels • New rear quarter panel fins • New rear wheel opening covers • New larger rear windows (shaded and tinted standard on all coupe models) • New tapered rear deck • New rear deck "V" and crest • New rear bumper • New fuel tank filler location in rear bumper • New taillights • New directional signal lights • New back-up lights with reflectors

NEW INTERIORS
New trim styles and materials • New seat cushions and seat backs with rubber-dipped springs (Marshall type springs on Fleetwood Sixty Special sedan and Seventy-Five models) • New instrument panel • New instrument cluster • New control knobs and levers • New 17-inch steering wheel • New horn ring and medallion • New courtesy and map lights • New narrower, corrugated door sill plates with medallion • New lighters and ash receivers • New vinyl coated luggage compartment lining • New assist handles (sedans) • New power brake pedal • New emergency brake pedal and release • New accelerator pedal • New 3-speed electric windshield wiper-washer controls • New electric clocks

1959

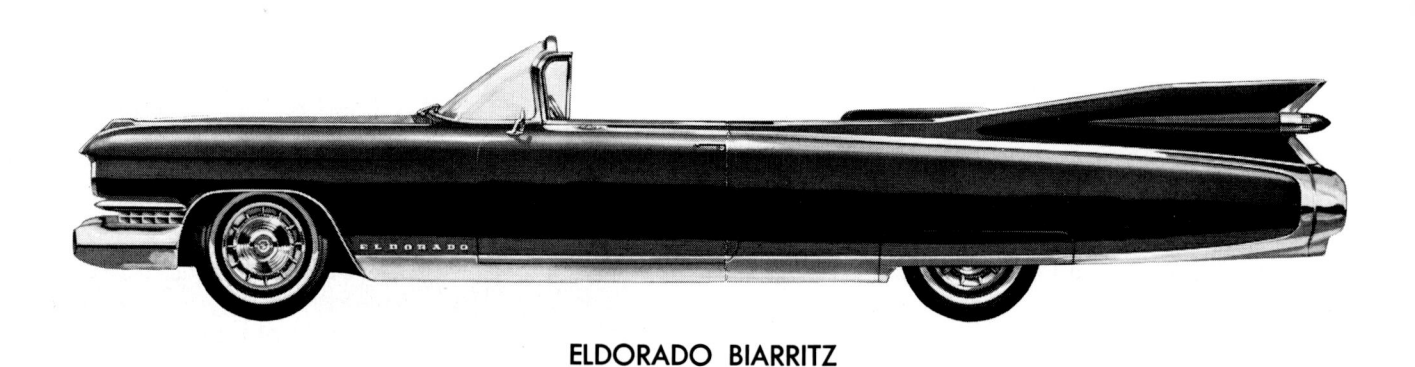

SIXTY-TWO SEDAN (six window)

ELDORADO BIARRITZ

FLEETWOOD SIXTY SPECIAL SEDAN

As beautiful as it is functional, the new compound-curved Vista-Panoramic windshield extends well around into the sides of the car as well as curving well up into the roof lines. As a further aid to good visibility the windshield pillars slant rearward from the roof line thus eliminating the customary blind spot associated with forward slanting windshield pillars.

Four headlamp lighting, as pioneered by Cadillac, provides ideal illumination for city or country driving. Mounted in a single horizontal line, all four lamps are at a height for the most effective, far reaching illumination. On lower beam, for city driving or for safety in passing oncoming cars, the shielded filament of outer lamps only are lighted. On upper beam, the inner lamps provide a wide, far reaching beam of light which combines with the upper beam of the outer lamps to provide unexcelled highway visibility.

The gas filler cap, for 1959, is concealed behind a pivoted, center section of the decorative panel just above the rear bumper. Readily accessible from either side it minimizes the possibility of a pump hose being rubbed against the car finish.

CADILLAC SIX-WINDOW SEDANS (see Body Styles Section) provide the glamorous beauty and unexcelled visibility of the largest rear window glass area of any sedan in the luxury car field. As in every other window, including the fixed rear quarter windows, the 1553.7 square inch rear window is Safety Plate glass, a quality feature which virtually eliminates annoying distortion found in ordinary safety glass.

CADILLAC FOUR-WINDOW SEDANS (see Body Styles Section) provide an entirely new Cadillac rear window styling in which the glass area extends completely around into the sides of the car thus eliminating the rear quarter panel windows. Adding further distinction to the sweeping expanse of the rear window is the visor-like rearward extension of the roof line on these Cadillac sedan models.

FLEETWOOD SEVENTY-FIVE SEDAN AND LIMOUSINE rear window treatment fully complements the traditional exclusiveness and dignity associated with these magnificent motor cars. A note of classic simplicity and increased privacy for rear compartment passengers is achieved through the restrained, rectangular design of the rear window. Further distinction is provided by the sharply sculptured drop at the rear of the roof line and by the rear quarter windows contoured to match the roof line and rear window.

Cadillac wheel discs feature a ribbed concave outer ring circling a raised hub inset with a new silver and white Cadillac medallion. They provide flashing highlights of beauty accenting flowing lines of the car.

The Fleetwood Sixty Special sedan and Eldorado models have their own distinctive wheel discs. Of an exclusive deep-fluted styling, they feature more prominent spokes and a ribbed perimeter on the hub.

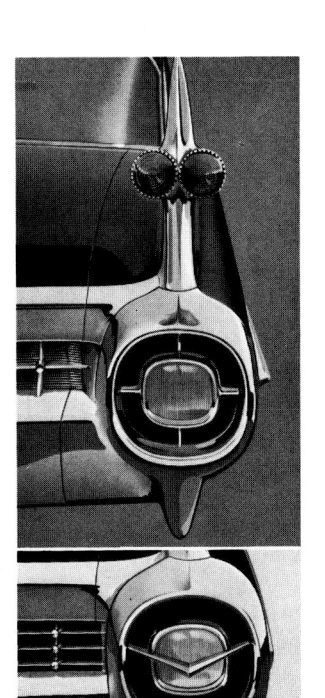

Detail at left shows back-up light encircled by red reflective area set within the outer extremities of the massive rear bumper. Decorative panel just above bumper contains a single row of concave projectiles at the intersection of cross bars. The Fleetwood Sixty Special sedan and the Eldorado models have three rows shown, below.

The Fleetwood Sixty Special sedan, the Fleetwood Seventy-Five sedan and limousine and the Eldorados have a chromed "V" instead of the four sectional bars on the back-up light. In addition, the name FLEETWOOD or ELDORADO, as applicable, is superimposed in block letters on a brushed chrome panel at the base of the deck lid replacing the deck lid "V" and crest used on all other models.

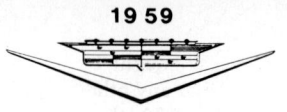

1959 SIXTY-TWO SEDAN | FOUR WINDOW

SIXTY-TWO SEDAN | SIX WINDOW

SIXTY-TWO SEDAN

STANDARD EQUIPMENT

- Air Cleaner, dry-pack
- Armrest, center-rear
- Assist Handles (two)
- Cadillac Power Brakes
- Cadillac Power Steering
- Cigarette Lighters, front (two)
- Cigarette Lighters, rear (two)
- Clock, electric
- Hydra-Matic Transmission
- Lights, front ash receivers
- Lights, back-up (dual)
- Lights, courtesy and map (automatic)
- Lights, directional signal
- Light, glove box (automatic)
- Light, luggage compartment (automatic)
- Mirror, glareproof, rear-view, flip type
- Oil Filter
- Outside Mirror, left side, remote-control
- Paint, two-tone
- Parking Brake Warning Signal
- Visor Vanity Mirror
- Visors, dual sun
- Wheel Discs (set of four)
- Windshield Washer and Coordinator

OPTIONAL EQUIPMENT (Extra Cost)

- Cadillac Air Conditioner
- Cadillac Air Suspension
- Cadillac Cruise Control
- Door Locks, electric
- Dor-Gards
- Fog Lamps (pair)
- Front Seat Adjustment (6-way), power operated
- Headlight Dimmer, automatic
- Heater
- License Frames
- "Q" Engine (3 dual-barrel carburetors)
- Radio
- Remote-Control Trunk Lid Lock
- Shaded and/or Tinted Glass
- Vent Window Regulators, front, power operated
- Window Regulators, power operated
- Whitewall Tires, 8.20 x 15 (set of five)

BASIC SPECIFICATIONS*

Wheelbase	130"
Length, over-all	225"
Width, over-all	80.2"
Height, over-all	56.2" (53.7")
Engine Horsepower	325

INTERIOR DIMENSIONS*

	FRONT	REAR
Head room	35.2" (33.1")	33.2"
Shoulder room	60.1" (60.5")	59.1"
Hip room	64.6"	64.4" (65.7")
Leg room	45.9"	45" (42.6")
Seat height	9.8" (9.3")	13.3" (11.4")

*Figures in parentheses for four-window sedan.

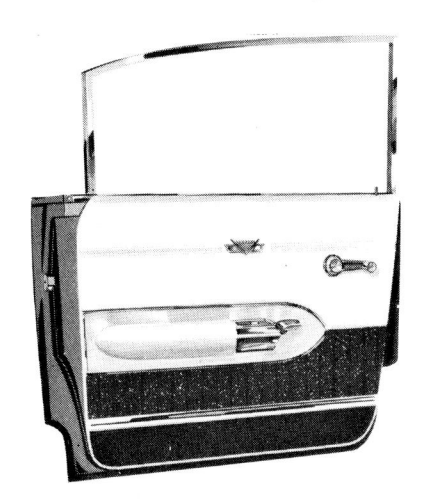

The Cadillac Sixty-Two sedan is bought by more luxury motor car buyers than any other motor car in the world. And for 1959, they, too, will find their favorite Cadillac model offering an even higher degree of quality throughout. The interiors, for example, offer five selections of black, nylon Carlisle cloth finely interwoven with bright Lurex metallic threads in a choice of Silver, Blue, Rose, Turquoise or Green as well as two, velvet-soft upholstery selections in Fawn or Gray Mojave cloth. Seat cushions and seat backs are fashioned in elegant 1¼" piping with smooth-surfaced Elascofab bolsters in harmonizing colors. Carpeting of a deep, loop-pile, nylon blend continues the luxurious interior treatment of the Sixty-Two sedans. Certain to win favor are the many new interior details such as the pull-to-open door handles recessed into the armrests and the new rear compartment lighters, one located in each stub pillar.

UPHOLSTERY SELECTIONS

30. SILVER-BLACK CARLISLE PATTERN METALLIC NYLON with WHITE ELASCOFAB bolsters and trim.

31. GRAY MOJAVE PATTERN NYLON with GRAY ELASCOFAB bolsters and trim.

32. BLUE-BLACK CARLISLE PATTERN METALLIC NYLON with BLUE METALLIC ELASCOFAB bolsters and trim.

34. ROSE-BLACK CARLISLE PATTERN METALLIC NYLON with ROSE METALLIC ELASCOFAB bolsters and trim.

35. FAWN MOJAVE PATTERN NYLON with FAWN ELASCOFAB bolsters and trim.

36. TURQUOISE-BLACK CARLISLE PATTERN METALLIC NYLON with TURQUOISE METALLIC ELASCOFAB bolsters and trim.

37. GREEN-BLACK CARLISLE PATTERN METALLIC NYLON with GREEN METALLIC ELASCOFAB bolsters and trim.

1959

SIXTY-TWO | COUPE

SIXTY-TWO COUPE

STANDARD EQUIPMENT

- Air Cleaner, dry-pack
- Armrest, center-rear
- Cadillac Power Brakes
- Cadillac Power Steering
- Cigarette Lighters, front (two)
- Clock, electric
- Hydra-Matic Transmission
- Lights, front ash receivers
- Lights, back-up (dual)
- Lights, courtesy and map (automatic)
- Lights, directional signal
- Light, glove box (automatic)
- Light, luggage compartment (automatic)
- Mirror, glareproof, rear-view, flip type
- Oil Filter
- Outside Mirror, left side, remote-control
- Paint, two-tone
- Parking Brake Warning Signal
- Shaded and Tinted Rear Window
- Visor Vanity Mirror
- Visors, dual sun
- Wheel Discs (set of four)
- Windshield Washer and Coordinator

OPTIONAL EQUIPMENT (Extra Cost)

- Cadillac Air Conditioner
- Cadillac Air Suspension
- Cadillac Cruise Control
- Door Locks, electric
- Dor-Gards
- Fog Lamps (pair)
- Front Seat Adjustment (6-way), power operated
- Headlight Dimmer, automatic
- Heater
- License Frames
- "Q" Engine (3 dual-barrel carburetors)
- Radio
- Remote-Control Trunk Lid Lock
- Shaded and/or Tinted Glass (windshield and side windows)
- Vent Window Regulators, front, power operated
- Window Regulators, power operated
- Whitewall Tires, 8.20 x 15 (set of five)

BASIC SPECIFICATIONS

Wheelbase	130"
Length, over-all	225"
Width, over-all	80.3"
Height, over-all	54.1"
Engine Horsepower	325

INTERIOR DIMENSIONS

	FRONT	REAR
Head room	32.7"	33.8"
Shoulder room	60.5"	58.8"
Hip room	66.1"	57.0"
Leg room	45.9"	39.4"
Seat height	9.1"	11.7"

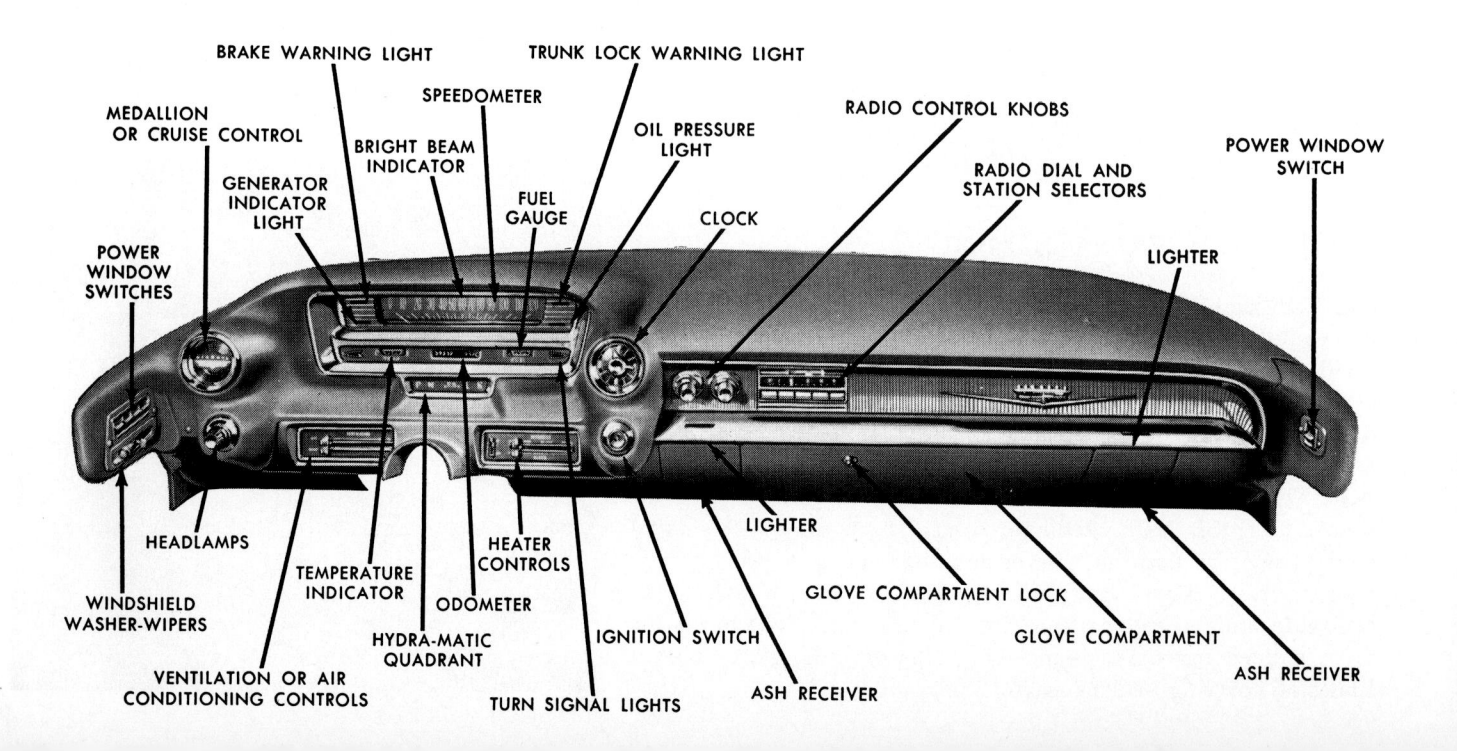

The Cadillac Sixty-Two coupe, most modestly priced of all Cadillac models, offers interiors of new refinement for 1959. There are, for example, new fabrics of superb good taste including black nylon Carlisle cloth highlighted by gleaming Lurex threads in a choice of Silver, Blue, Rose, Turquoise or Green; or fine-patterned, soft-textured Mojave cloth in the more subdued colors of Fawn or Gray. Seat cushion and seat back styling offer new elegance with narrow 1¼" piping. Color-harmonized, Elascofab side bolsters provide pleasing design contrast. Door panels continue this piped and plain motif completing the unity of design apparent throughout every Cadillac motor car. Furthering the aura of luxury and warmth imparted by the Sixty-Two coupe interior is the thick loop-pile, nylon blend carpeting, covering not only the floor but also the scuff-pad areas of the seat cushions, door panels and cowl sidewalls.

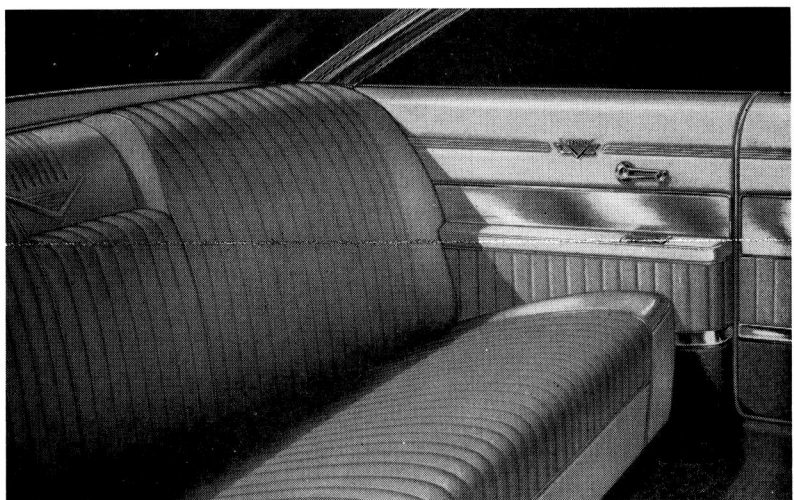

UPHOLSTERY SELECTIONS

30. **SILVER-BLACK CARLISLE PATTERN METALLIC NYLON** with **WHITE ELASCOFAB** bolsters and trim.

31. **GRAY MOJAVE PATTERN NYLON** with **GRAY ELASCOFAB** bolsters and trim.

32. **BLUE-BLACK CARLISLE PATTERN METALLIC NYLON** with **BLUE METALLIC ELASCOFAB** bolsters and trim.

34. **ROSE-BLACK CARLISLE PATTERN METALLIC NYLON** with **ROSE METALLIC ELASCOFAB** bolsters and trim.

35. **FAWN MOJAVE PATTERN NYLON** with **FAWN ELASCOFAB** bolsters and trim.

36. **TURQUOISE-BLACK CARLISLE PATTERN METALLIC NYLON** with **TURQUOISE METALLIC ELASCOFAB** bolsters and trim.

37. **GREEN-BLACK CARLISLE PATTERN METALLIC NYLON** with **GREEN METALLIC ELASCOFAB** bolsters and trim.

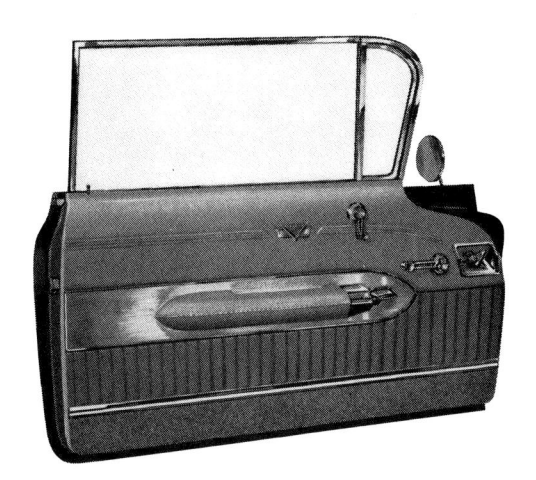

INSTRUMENT PANEL STYLING

The Cadillac instrument panel with its bright and brushed chrome and satin-black inserts achieves a jewel-like appearance while providing maximum legibility of all instruments and controls. The more compact instrument cluster, for 1959, is located in a recessed housing directly ahead of, and at a sufficient distance from, the driver to permit instant reference without conscious readjustment of vision. A new convenience feature permits lighting the interior of the car simply by turning the headlamp control knob to the left. Equal convenience for both the driver and passengers is provided by separate front compartment ash receivers and lighters and by the central location of the spacious glove compartment. The top of the safety-padded instrument panel has a fine-grained, glare-resistant Elascofab covering—color harmonized to the interior.

1959 SIXTY-TWO CONVERTIBLE

SIXTY-TWO CONVERTIBLE

STANDARD EQUIPMENT

- Air Cleaner, dry-pack
- Armrest, center, front
- Cadillac Power Brakes
- Cadillac Power Steering
- Cigarette Lighters, front (two)
- Cigarette Lighters, rear (two)
- Clock, electric
- Front Seat Adjustment (horizontal), power operated
- Hydra-Matic Transmission
- Lights, front ash receivers
- Lights, back-up (dual)
- Lights, courtesy and map (automatic)
- Lights, directional signal
- Light, glove box (automatic)
- Light, luggage compartment (automatic)
- Mirror, glareproof, rear-view, flip type
- Oil Filter
- Outside Mirror, left side, remote-control
- Paint, two-tone
- Parking Brake Warning Signal
- Pockets, back of front seat
- Visor Vanity Mirror
- Visors, dual sun
- Wheel Discs (set of four)
- Window Regulators, power operated
- Windshield Washer and Coordinator

OPTIONAL EQUIPMENT (Extra Cost)

- Cadillac Air Conditioner
- Cadillac Air Suspension
- Cadillac Cruise Control
- Door Locks, electric
- Dor-Gards
- Fog Lamps (pair)
- Front Seat Adjustment (vertical and angle), power operated
- Headlight Dimmer, automatic
- Heater
- License Frames
- "Q" Engine (3 dual-barrel carburetors
- Radio
- Remote-Control Trunk Lid Lock
- Shaded and/or Tinted Glass (windshield and side windows)
- Vent Window Regulators, power operated
- Whitewall Tires, 8.20 x 15 (set of five)

BASIC SPECIFICATIONS

Wheelbase	130"
Length, over-all	225"
Width, over-all	80.3"
Height, over-all	53.7"
Engine Horsepower	325

INTERIOR DIMENSIONS

	FRONT	REAR
Head room	33.3"	33.6"
Shoulder room	60.5"	51.8"
Hip room	66.1"	52.4"
Leg room	45.9"	39.4"
Seat height	9.1"	11.5"

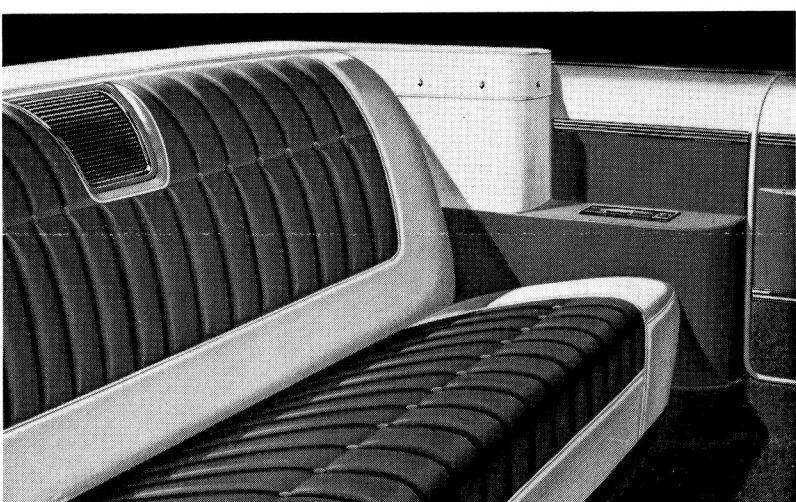

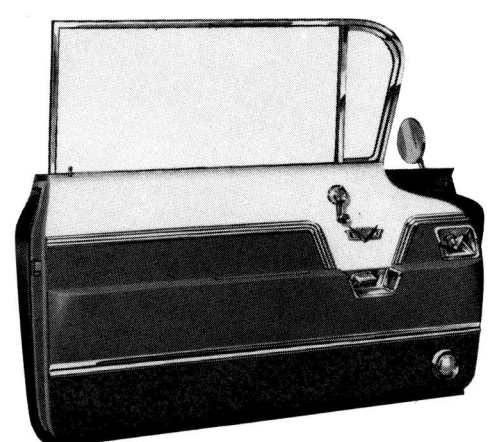

The Cadillac Sixty-Two convertible interiors are styled in keeping with the spirit of its brilliant exterior design. Enduring beauty and evident quality are fully expressed in the fine, Leeds grain leathers offered in eight selections including solid colors, two-tone combinations and metallic finishes. Exemplifying the boldness and zest of open air motoring is the wide, 2½" smartly tailored piping with a single row of recessed buttons on the seat cushion and seat back. Adding to the carefree motoring enjoyment provided by the Sixty-Two convertible are its many conveniences such as power seats, power windows, individual cigarette lighters and ash receivers and courtesy lights, front and rear. The sleek, power operated convertible top is available in five colors to complement the beautiful acrylic lacquer finish of the car itself.

UPHOLSTERY SELECTIONS

20. BLACK LEEDS GRAIN LEATHER with WHITE LEEDS GRAIN LEATHER bolsters and trim.

21. BLACK LEEDS GRAIN LEATHER throughout.

23. BLUE LEEDS GRAIN METALLIC LEATHER throughout.

25. SADDLE TAN LEEDS GRAIN LEATHER throughout.

26. TURQUOISE LEEDS GRAIN METALLIC LEATHER throughout.

27. GREEN LEEDS GRAIN METALLIC LEATHER throughout.

28. RED LEEDS GRAIN LEATHER with WHITE LEEDS GRAIN LEATHER bolsters and trim.

29. RED LEEDS GRAIN LEATHER throughout.

TOP COLORS: 1. IVORY 2. BLACK
4. GREEN 6. BUCKSKIN 8. BLUE

NEW FUEL SYSTEM PROTECTION

For even greater dependability, Cadillac engines for 1959 have a new, more efficient fuel pump to assure an even more positive flow of fuel from the fuel tank to the carburetor and minimize any possible likelihood of vapor lock in the fuel lines. Double protection against dirt particles or water entering the fuel system is provided by a new fuel filter located in the fuel tank itself. Its finely woven, 2-ply, saran plastic filtering element is self-cleansed by the sloshing action of the gasoline. Any remaining impurities are removed by the sediment bowl filter in the engine compartment.

1959 COUPE DE VILLE

COUPE DE VILLE

STANDARD EQUIPMENT

- Air Cleaner, dry-pack
- Armrest, center, front and rear
- Cadillac Power Brakes
- Cadillac Power Steering
- Cigarette Lighters, front (two)
- Cigarette Lighters, rear (two)
- Clock, electric
- Front Seat Adjustment (horizontal), power operated
- Hydra-Matic Transmission
- Lights, front ash receivers
- Lights, back-up (dual)
- Lights, courtesy and map (automatic)
- Lights, directional signal
- Light, glove box (automatic)
- Light, luggage compartment (automatic)
- Mirror, glareproof, rear-view, flip type
- Oil Filter
- Outside Mirror, left side, remote-control
- Paint, two-tone
- Parking Brake Warning Signal
- Pockets, back of front seat
- Shaded and Tinted Rear Window
- Visor Vanity Mirror
- Visors, dual sun
- Wheel Discs (set of four)
- Window Regulators, power operated
- Windshield Washer and Coordinator

OPTIONAL EQUIPMENT (Extra Cost)

- Cadillac Air Conditioner
- Cadillac Air Suspension
- Cadillac Cruise Control
- Door Locks, electric
- Dor-Gards
- Fog Lamps (pair)
- Front Seat Adjustment (vertical and angle), power operated
- Headlight Dimmer, automatic
- Heater
- License Frames
- "Q" Engine (3 dual-barrel carburetors)
- Radio
- Remote-Control Trunk Lid Lock
- Shaded and/or Tinted Glass (windshield and side windows)
- Vent Window Regulators, power operated
- Whitewall Tires, 8.20 x 15 (set of five)

BASIC SPECIFICATIONS

Wheelbase	130"
Length, over-all	225"
Width, over-all	80.3"
Height, over-all	54.1"
Engine Horsepower	325

INTERIOR DIMENSIONS

	FRONT	REAR
Head room	32.7"	33.8"
Shoulder room	60.5"	58.8"
Hip room	66.1"	57.0"
Leg room	45.9"	39.4"
Seat height	9.1"	11.7"

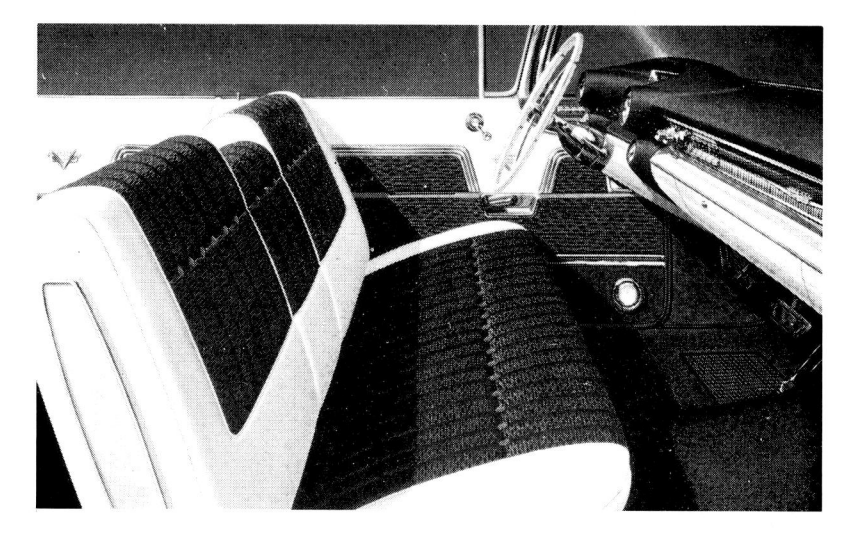

There is glamour and excitement in the new upholstery, trim and appointments of the Coupe de Ville for 1959. Upholstery selections include a new nylon Coronado cloth with a ribbed pattern of gleaming Lurex threads in a choice of Silver or Turquoise against a Black background or in Rose or Green metallic threads with a harmonizing Coronado cloth background. There is also a new block-patterned Camden cloth, softer in finish and in its tones of Fawn, Gray or Blue. Bolsters and trim of fine-grained leathers are color harmonized to the fabrics. Seat cushions and seat backs with their ten-inch wide center armrests are styled in smart 2½" piping with a single row of recessed buttons. The accoutrements of the Coupe de Ville provide a full measure of luxury and convenience for the driver and passengers while the bright and brushed chrome for control knobs and trim add highlights of gleaming beauty. Completing this elegant interior decor is Trieste carpeting of loop-pile nylon blend, covering the lower portions of the cowl sidewall, door panels and seat cushions as well as the floor.

UPHOLSTERY SELECTIONS

- **40. SILVER-BLACK CORONADO PATTERN METALLIC NYLON** with **WHITE LEATHER** bolsters and trim.

- **41. GRAY CAMDEN PATTERN NYLON** with **GRAY LEATHER** bolsters and trim.

- **43. BLUE CAMDEN PATTERN NYLON** with **BLUE LEATHER** bolsters and trim.

- **45. FAWN CAMDEN PATTERN NYLON** with **FAWN LEATHER** bolsters and trim.

- **46. GREEN CORONADO PATTERN METALLIC NYLON** with **GREEN METALLIC LEATHER** bolsters and trim.

- **47. TURQUOISE-BLACK CORONADO PATTERN METALLIC NYLON** with **TURQUOISE METALLIC LEATHER** bolsters and trim.

- **48. ROSE CORONADO PATTERN METALLIC NYLON** with **ROSE METALLIC LEATHER** bolsters and trim.

NEW SPARE TIRE MOUNTING

Spare tire, mounted horizontally on the floor, is covered by a flat metal disc. An additional carpeted covering, shown above, for wheel and tire is standard on the Fleetwood Sixty Special sedan and Eldorados, optional at extra cost on all other models.

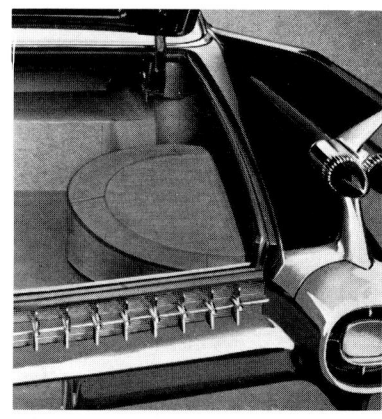

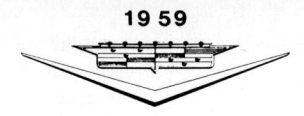

1959 SEDAN DE VILLE — FOUR WINDOW

SEDAN DE VILLE — SIX WINDOW

SEDAN DE VILLE

STANDARD EQUIPMENT

- Air Cleaner, dry-pack
- Armrest, center, front and rear
- Assist Handles (two)
- Cadillac Power Brakes
- Cadillac Power Steering
- Cigarette Lighters, front (two)
- Cigarette Lighters, rear (two)
- Clock, electric
- Front Seat Adjustment (horizontal), power operated
- Hydra-Matic Transmission
- Lights, front ash receivers
- Lights, back-up (dual)
- Lights, courtesy and map (automatic)
- Lights, directional signal
- Light, glove box (automatic)
- Light, luggage compartment (automatic)
- Mirror, glareproof, rear-view, flip type
- Oil Filter
- Outside Mirror, left side, remote-control
- Paint, two-tone
- Parking Brake Warning Signal
- Pockets, back of front seat
- Visor Vanity Mirror
- Visors, dual sun
- Wheel Discs (set of four)
- Window Regulators, power operated
- Windshield Washer and Coordinator

OPTIONAL EQUIPMENT (Extra Cost)

- Cadillac Air Conditioner
- Cadillac Air Suspension
- Cadillac Cruise Control
- Door Locks, electric
- Dor-Gards
- Fog Lamps (pair)
- Front Seat Adjustment (vertical and angle), power operated
- Headlight Dimmer, automatic
- Heater
- License Frames
- "Q" Engine (3 dual-barrel carburetors)
- Radio
- Remote-Control Trunk Lid Lock
- Shaded and/or Tinted Glass
- Vent Window Regulators, power operated
- Whitewall Tires, 8.20 x 15 (set of five)

BASIC SPECIFICATIONS*

Wheelbase	130"
Length, over-all	225"
Width, over-all	80.2"
Height, over-all	53.7" (56.2")
Engine Horsepower	325

INTERIOR DIMENSIONS*

	FRONT	REAR
Head room	33.1" (35.2")	33.2"
Shoulder room	60.5" (60.1")	59.1"
Hip Room	64.6"	65.7" (64.4")
Leg room	45.9"	42.6" (45")
Seat height	9.3" (9.8")	11.4" (13.3")

*Figures in parentheses for six-window sedan.

Sedan de Ville interiors combine an air of enchantment with their full complement of luxury and convenience features. Wide, center armrests, front and rear, power windows, power seat, courtesy lights and individual lighters and ash receivers are but a few of the interior features of this elegant sedan. Distinctive new upholstery fabrics are tailored in 2½" piping with leather bolsters and trim. These fabrics are available with metallic Lurex threads in Silver and Turquoise against a Black background, or Rose and Green with a harmonizing background of nylon Coronado cloth or in soft and supple, block-patterned Camden cloth in Gray, Blue or Fawn. Combinations of bright and brushed chrome for hardware and metal trim provide pleasing variations in the intensity of highlights throughout the interior. Trieste quality, loop-pile, nylon blend carpeting covering the entire floor is carried up into the lower portions of the seats and sidewalls protecting these areas from unsightly scuff marks.

UPHOLSTERY SELECTIONS

40. SILVER-BLACK CORONADO PATTERN METALLIC NYLON with WHITE LEATHER bolsters and trim.

41. GRAY CAMDEN PATTERN NYLON with GRAY LEATHER bolsters and trim.

43. BLUE CAMDEN PATTERN NYLON with BLUE LEATHER bolsters and trim.

45. FAWN CAMDEN PATTERN NYLON with FAWN LEATHER bolsters and trim.

46. GREEN CORONADO PATTERN METALLIC NYLON with GREEN METALLIC LEATHER bolsters and trim.

47. TURQUOISE-BLACK CORONADO PATTERN METALLIC NYLON with TURQUOISE METALLIC LEATHER bolsters and trim.

48. ROSE CORONADO PATTERN METALLIC NYLON with ROSE METALLIC LEATHER bolsters and trim.

SMOOTHER, STEADIER IDLING

The smooth, steady idling performance provided by Cadillac has been further improved for 1959 by the addition of a heat-sensitive air control valve. As engine heat increases during any period of sustained idling, the valve begins to open permitting additional air flow through the carburetor. This maintains the correct ratio of air to fuel by compensating for any excess fuel vapors forced into the carburetor by boiling fuel in the float chamber. The result is consistently smooth, stable idling even under the most severe conditions.

1959 FLEETWOOD | SIXTY SPECIAL SEDAN

FLEETWOOD SIXTY SPECIAL SEDAN

STANDARD EQUIPMENT

- Air Cleaner, dry-pack
- Armrest, center, front and rear
- Assist Handles (two)
- Cadillac Power Brakes
- Cadillac Power Steering
- Cigarette Lighters, front (two)
- Cigarette Lighters, rear (two)
- Clock, electric
- Fluted Wheel Discs (set of four)
- Front Seat Adjustment (2-way), power operated
- Hydra-Matic Transmission
- Lights, front ash receivers
- Lights, back-up (dual)
- Lights, courtesy and map (automatic)
- Lights, directional signal
- Light, glove box (automatic)
- Light, luggage compartment (automatic)
- Mirror, glareproof, rear-view, flip type
- Oil Filter
- Outside Mirror, left side, remote-control
- Outside Mirror, right side
- Paint, two-tone
- Parking Brake Warning Signal
- Pockets, back of front seat
- Vent Window Regulators, front, power operated
- Visor Vanity Mirror
- Visors, dual sun
- Window Regulators, power operated
- Windshield Washer and Coordinator

OPTIONAL EQUIPMENT (Extra Cost)

- Cadillac Air Conditioner
- Cadillac Air Suspension
- Cadillac Cruise Control
- Dor-Gards
- Door Locks, electric
- Fog Lamps (pair)
- Front Seat Adjustment (6-way), power operated
- Headlight Dimmer, automatic
- Heater
- License Frames
- "Q" Engine (3 dual-barrel carburetors)
- Radio
- Remote-Control Trunk Lid Lock
- Shaded and/or Tinted Glass
- Whitewall Tires, 8.20 x 15 (set of five)

BASIC SPECIFICATIONS

Wheelbase	130"
Length, over-all	225"
Width, over-all	81.1"
Height, over-all	56.2"
Engine Horsepower	325

INTERIOR DIMENSIONS

	FRONT	REAR
Head room	35.5"	34.2"
Shoulder room	60.1"	59.1"
Hip room	64.6"	64.4"
Leg room	45.9"	44.0"
Seat height	9.3"	13.3"

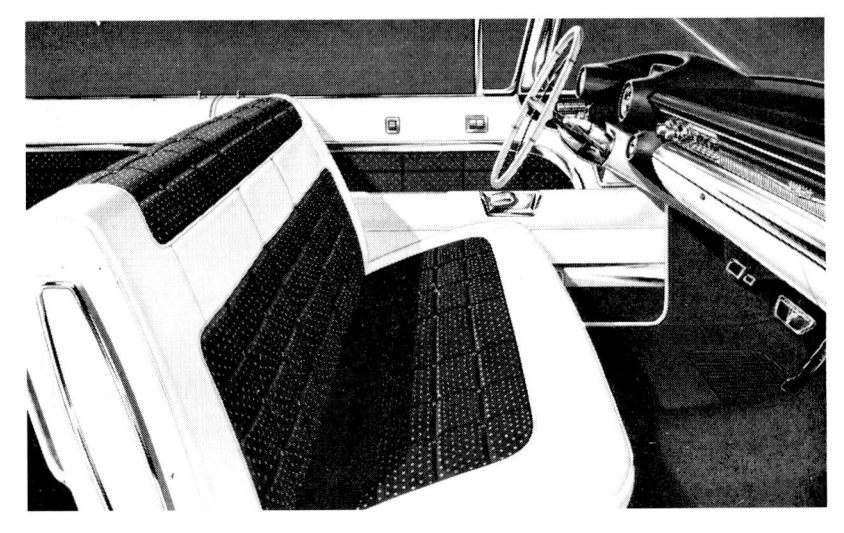

Perhaps the most beloved of all Cadillac motor cars in the hearts of its owners is the Fleetwood Sixty Special sedan. And this deep affection is well earned, not only by the distinctive exterior styling of this magnificent motor car, but by the gracious atmosphere and elegant decor of its tastefully appointed interiors. Seat cushions and seat backs are of Marshall type construction providing the unsurpassed comfort of full coil springs. Equally exclusive are the heavily tufted biscuits and deeply recessed buttons of the superbly tailored upholstery. Fleetwood Sixty Special sedan fabrics include a swiss dot patterned Black or Blue Colony cloth, with, respectively, White leather or Blue metallic leather bolsters; Gray, Blue, Green or Fawn shantung weave Clarion cloth with harmonizing Concord nylon broadcloth bolsters; or Gray, Blue or Fawn Concord cloth throughout. Another option, there are ten in all, is a beautiful Light Gray all-wool broadcloth. Even the nylon blend carpeting in the Fleetwood Sixty Special sedan is of special quality, extra-deep, looped pile for maximum warmth and luxury.

UPHOLSTERY SELECTIONS

- **60.** BLACK COLONY PATTERN METALLIC NYLON with WHITE LEATHER bolsters and trim.
- **61.** GRAY CLARION PATTERN NYLON with GRAY CONCORD NYLON BROADCLOTH bolsters and trim.
- **62.** BLUE COLONY PATTERN METALLIC NYLON with BLUE METALLIC LEATHER bolsters and trim.
- **63.** BLUE CLARION PATTERN NYLON with BLUE CONCORD NYLON BROADCLOTH bolsters and trim.
- **65.** FAWN CLARION PATTERN NYLON with FAWN CONCORD NYLON BROADCLOTH bolsters and trim.
- **67.** GREEN CLARION PATTERN NYLON with GREEN CONCORD NYLON BROADCLOTH bolsters and trim.
- **70.** GRAY CONCORD NYLON BROADCLOTH throughout.
- **71.** GRAY WOOL BROADCLOTH throughout.
- **72.** BLUE CONCORD NYLON BROADCLOTH throughout.
- **74.** FAWN CONCORD NYLON BROADCLOTH throughout.

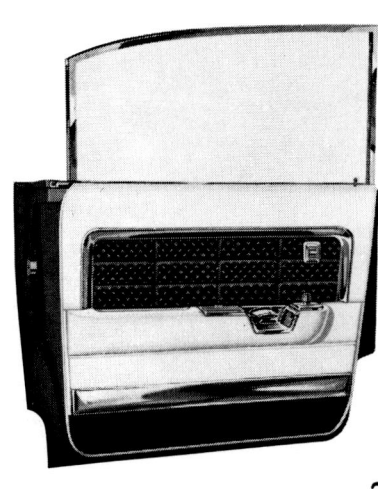

1959

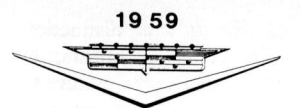

SEVENTY-FIVE SEDAN AND LIMOUSINE

FLEETWOOD SEVENTY-FIVE SEDAN AND LIMOUSINE

STANDARD EQUIPMENT

- Air Cleaner, dry-pack
- Armrest, center, front and rear
- Assist Handles (two)
- Cadillac Power Brakes
- Cadillac Power Steering
- Cigarette Lighters, front (two)
- Cigarette Lighters, rear (two)
- Clocks, electric, front and rear compartments
- Foot Rests, adjustable (two), rear compartment
- Front Seat Adjustment (horizontal), power operated
- Hydra-Matic Transmission
- Lights, front ash receivers
- Lights, back-up (dual)
- Lights, courtesy and map (automatic)
- Lights, directional signal
- Light, glove box (automatic)
- Light, luggage compartment (automatic)
- Mirror, glareproof, rear-view, flip type
- Oil Filter
- Outside Mirror, left side, remote-control
- Package Compartments in side armrests, rear (two)
- Paint, two-tone
- Parking Brake Warning Signal
- Robe Cord, back of front seat
- Visor Vanity Mirror
- Visors, dual sun
- Wheel Discs (set of four)
- Window Regulators, power operated
- Windshield Washer and Coordinator

OPTIONAL EQUIPMENT (Extra Cost)

- Cadillac Air Conditioner
- Cadillac Air Suspension
- Cadillac Cruise Control
- Fog Lamps (pair)
- Headlight Dimmer, automatic
- Heater
- License Frames
- "Q" Engine (3 dual-barrel carburetors)
- Radio, front compartment controls
- Radio, rear compartment controls
- Remote-Control Trunk Lid Lock
- Shaded and/or Tinted Glass
- Whitewall Tires, 8.20 x 15 (set of five) 6 ply

BASIC SPECIFICATIONS

Wheelbase	149.8"
Length, over-all	244.8"
Width, over-all	80.2"
Height, over-all	59.3"
Engine Horsepower	325

INTERIOR DIMENSIONS

	FRONT	AUX.	REAR
Head room	36.2"*	36.4"***	34.8"**
Shoulder room	60.5"	58.6"	58.8"
Hip room	65.4"	64.5"	60.1"
Leg Room	43.9"	—	—
Seat height	8.5"	12.0"	13.1"

*Limousine—35.9"
**Limousine—33.8"
***Limousine—35.7"

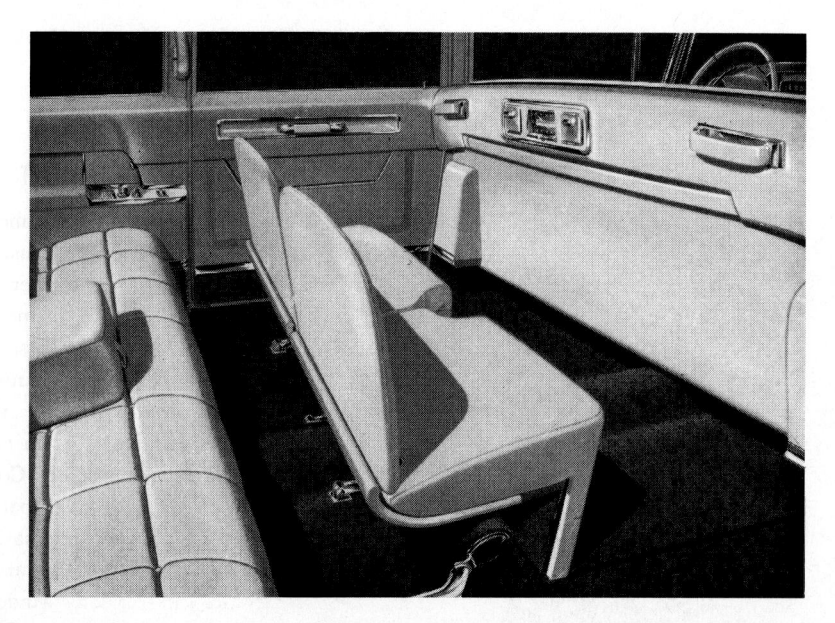

AUXILIARY SEATS

Auxiliary seats in the Fleetwood Seventy-Five sedan and limousine are designed to provide maximum comfort as well as full seating capacity. They are upholstered in the same fine fabrics as the rest of the rear compartment so that when folded forward into the recessed base at the front seat back they blend harmoniously into the seat back panel. Just above the fold-away auxiliary seats is a leather covered robe cord, while centered in the seat back panel is a handsome, chrome-framed electric clock flanked by two ash receivers for the convenience of auxiliary seat passengers. At the extremities of the rear of the front seat back panel are two, woven-fabric, leather-bound assist handles retained by escutcheons of bright and brushed chrome.

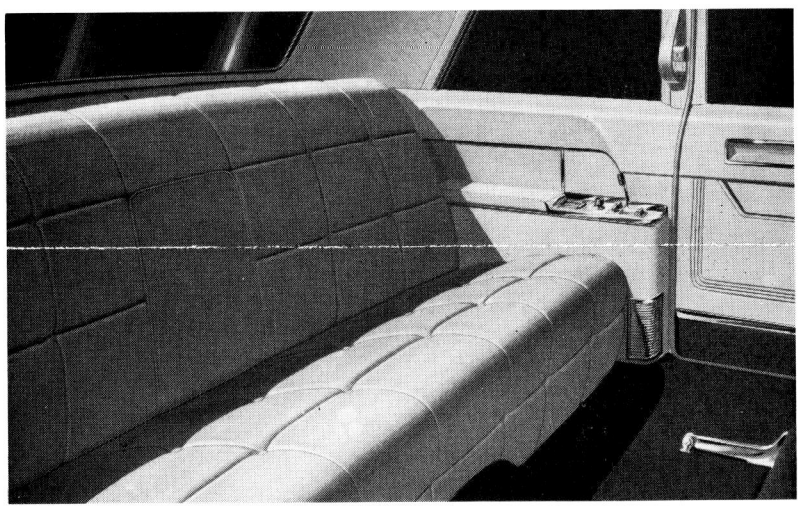

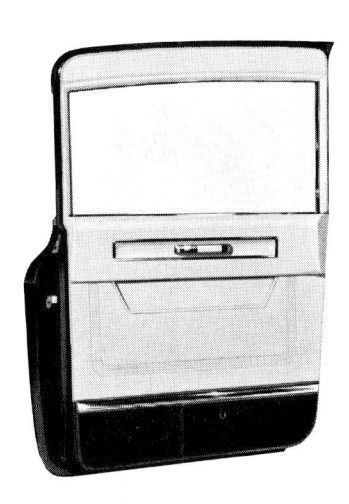

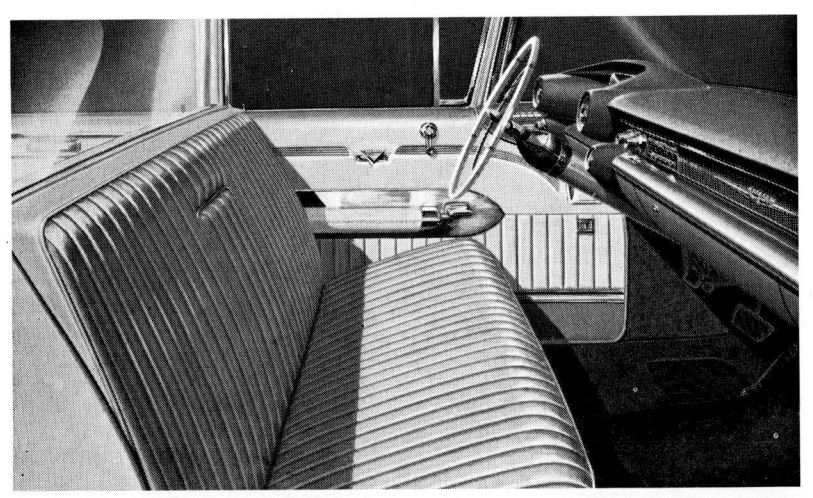

Lending unmatched dignity and distinction to any occasion or any place it appears, no other motor car so truly reflects the stature of its owners as the magnificent Fleetwood Seventy-Five sedan and limousine. Impressive in its exterior styling, it is equally so in the spaciousness and elegance of its superbly appointed interiors. For example, even the heater and air conditioner controls are concealed in the right-hand rear quarter armrest behind a sliding cover finished in satin-smooth enamel. Upholstery selections fully reflect the tone of the many state, business and social functions at which the Fleetwood Seventy-Five is so often in attendance. There are, for example, choices of all-wool broadcloth in solid colors of Fawn or Gray and choices of nylon Bedford Cord in Fawn, Light Gray or Dark Gray with harmonizing trim of all-wool broadcloth. Seat cushions and seat backs, excepting auxiliary seats, feature Marshall type construction with full coil springs for maximum comfort. For chauffeur driven use, the limousine front compartment is upholstered in genuine leather as shown and described on the following two pages.

UPHOLSTERY SELECTIONS

80. LIGHT GRAY NYLON BEDFORD CORD with LIGHT GRAY WOOL BROADCLOTH trim.

81. LIGHT GRAY WOOL BROADCLOTH throughout.

84. FAWN NYLON BEDFORD CORD with FAWN WOOL BROADCLOTH trim.

85. FAWN WOOL BROADCLOTH throughout.

90. DARK GRAY NYLON BEDFORD CORD with LIGHT GRAY WOOL BROADCLOTH trim.

CHAUFFEUR COMPARTMENT (Limousine)

GRAY SOLID LEATHER when GRAY trims are selected, above.

FAWN SOLID LEATHER when FAWN trims are selected, above.

BLACK LEATHER available with any of above trims if so ordered.

CHAUFFEUR COMPARTMENT

The glass partitioned chauffeur's compartment of the Fleetwood Seventy-Five limousine is upholstered in Gray or Fawn leather to match the rear compartment color scheme or in Black leather if the owner so prefers. In contrast to the tufted biscuit and button tailoring of the rear compartment, the chauffeur's compartment is fashioned in two inch wide piping without bolster effect. Controls for lowering or raising the center partition glass are located on a bright and satin-finish escutcheon on each rear quarter armrest which also houses the rear door window controls, cigarette lighters and ash receivers.

1959 ELDORADO SEVILLE

ELDORADO BIARRITZ ——— ELDORADO SEVILLE

STANDARD EQUIPMENT

- Air Cleaner, dry-pack
- Armrest, center, front and rear
- Cadillac Air Suspension
- Cadillac Power Brakes
- Cadillac Power Steering
- Cigarette Lighters, front (two)
- Cigarette Lighters, rear (two)
- Clock, electric
- Door Locks, electric
- Fluted Wheel Discs (set of four)
- Fog Lamps (pair)
- Front Seat Adjustment (6-way), power operated
- Heater
- Hydra-Matic Transmission
- License Frames
- Lights, front ash receivers
- Lights, back-up (dual)
- Lights, courtesy and map (automatic) front and rear compartment
- Lights, courtesy, front door panels
- Lights, directional signal
- Lights, door panel, safety warning
- Light, glove box (automatic)
- Light, luggage compartment (automatic)
- Oil Filter
- Outside Mirror, left side, remote-control
- Parking Brake Warning Signal
- Pockets, back of front seat
- "Q" Engine (3 dual-barrel carburetors)
- Radio
- Rear-View Mirror, 3-way, E-Z-Eye
- Remote-Control Trunk Lid Lock
- Shaded and Tinted Rear Window
- Vent Window Regulators, power operated
- Visor Vanity Mirror
- Visors, dual sun
- Whitewall Tires, 8.20 x 15 (set of five)
- Window Regulators, power operated
- Windshield Washer and Coordinator

OPTIONAL EQUIPMENT (Extra Cost)

- Cadillac Air Conditioner
- Cadillac Cruise Control
- Headlight Dimmer (automatic)
- Shaded and/or Tinted Glass (windshield and side windows)

BASIC SPECIFICATIONS

Wheelbase	130"
Length, over-all	225"
Width, over-all	80.3"
Height, over-all	54.8"
Engine Horsepower	345

INTERIOR DIMENSIONS

	FRONT	REAR
Head room	33.2"	33.8"
Shoulder room	60.5"	58.8"
Hip room	66.3"	57.0"
Leg room	45.7"	38.8"
Seat height	8.6"	11.7"

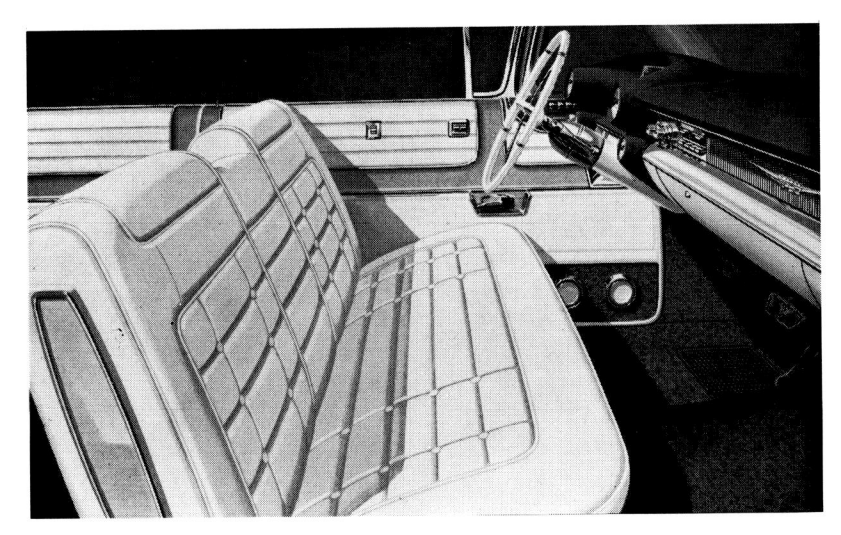

The Eldorado Seville is not only one of the most completely equipped motor cars in the world but one of the most lavishly bestowed motor cars in every styling detail. From the smartly textured, vinyl-coated fabric covering its steel top, to its deep, looped-pile, nylon blend, Tangier quality carpeting, nothing has been overlooked in making the Eldorado Seville the world's most luxurious coupe. Seat cushion and seat back inserts are distinctively styled in deep-grained Cardiff leathers in White or Red with fine-grained White Florentine leather bolsters or in Light Blue metallic Cardiff leather with Light Blue metallic Florentine leather bolsters. In addition, there are four choices of sleek nylon Clarion cloth with its fine, random-ribbed pattern in Gray, Blue, Bronze or Slate Green with harmonizing metallic leather bolsters. There is, in fact, no other coupe which can match the Eldorado Seville in glamour, in lasting beauty and in the comfort and convenience it provides.

UPHOLSTERY SELECTIONS

50. WHITE CARDIFF GRAIN LEATHER with WHITE FLORENTINE LEATHER bolsters and trim.

51. GRAY NYLON CLARION CLOTH with GRAY CARDIFF GRAIN LEATHER bolsters and trim.

52. BLUE NYLON CLARION CLOTH with BLUE METALLIC CARDIFF GRAIN LEATHER bolsters and trim.

53. BLUE METALLIC CARDIFF GRAIN LEATHER with BLUE METALLIC FLORENTINE LEATHER bolsters and trim.

56. SLATE GREEN NYLON CLARION CLOTH with SLATE GREEN METALLIC LEATHER bolsters and trim.

58. BRONZE NYLON CLARION CLOTH with BRONZE METALLIC LEATHER bolsters and trim.

59. RED CARDIFF GRAIN LEATHER with WHITE FLORENTINE LEATHER bolsters and trim.

TOP COLORS: 1. IVORY 2. BLACK 3. BRONZE 7. SLATE GREEN 8. BLUE

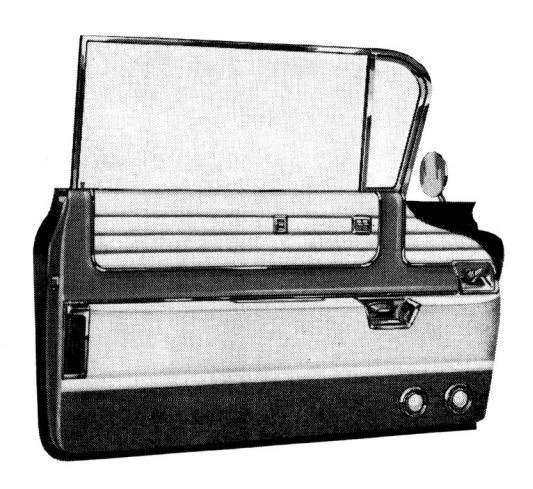

The 345-horsepower Cadillac engine, standard equipment on the Eldorado Biarritz, Seville and Brougham, and optional at extra cost on all other models. It provides all of the dependability, durability, smoothness and quietness expected of Cadillac engine performance but with additional benefits for the owner through use of a three, dual-barrel carburetor.

The central dual-barrel unit, used for all normal operation including starting, idling and cruising speeds, assures maximum efficiency and dependability because of the relative simplicity of single carburetor adjustment.

However, when the driver depresses the accelerator pedal beyond 75% of its travel, both secondary dual-barrel carburetors open simultaneously releasing a vast increase in power for maximum safety in passing another car, for fast emergency acceleration or for traveling up very steep grades.

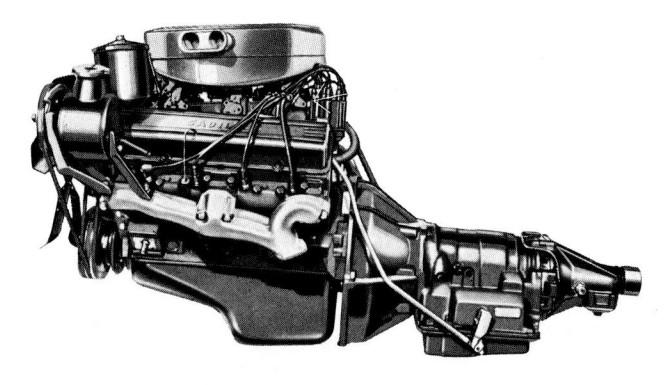

345-HORSEPOWER CADILLAC "Q" ENGINE

ELDORADO BIARRITZ

The Eldorado Biarritz is for many the ultimate dream machine of the finned generation of American automobiles. Here is the zenith of nostalgia envoking 1950's design, the supreme example of the era's futuristic styling. Below, the captivating 1959 rear ensemble; bold, windsplitting and illuminated fins towering above simulated jet exhaust ports, connected by a provacative brightmetal grille stretching high and wide above the bumper.

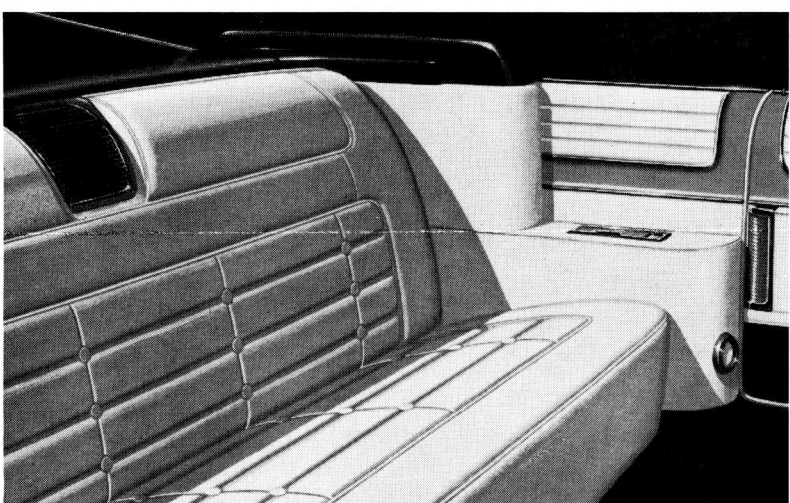

The fabulous Eldorado Biarritz brings the glamour and zest of open-car motoring to heights of comfort, convenience and luxury never before attained. Completely equipped with air suspension, the 345-horsepower "Q" engine and every power and convenience accessory, it affords unique motoring enjoyment in a setting of interiors unmatched for lasting luxury and beauty. All-leather upholstery selections are offered in a choice of solid Red, solid White, solid Black, Gray metallic, Blue metallic, Slate Green metallic or Bronze metallic with contrasting deep-grained Cardiff leather for seat and seat back inserts and fine-grained Florentine leather for bolsters and trim. In addition to the conventional front seat styling with its wide center armrest, the Eldorado Biarritz is available with full bucket-type front seats for the more sports-minded and for those who appreciate the extra support provided by the contoured back rest.

UPHOLSTERY SELECTIONS*

10. **WHITE CARDIFF GRAIN LEATHER** with **WHITE FLORENTINE LEATHER** bolsters and trim.
11. **BLACK CARDIFF GRAIN LEATHER** with **BLACK FLORENTINE LEATHER** bolsters and trim.
12. **GRAY METALLIC CARDIFF GRAIN LEATHER** with **GRAY METALLIC FLORENTINE LEATHER** bolsters and trim.
13. **BLUE METALLIC CARDIFF GRAIN LEATHER** with **BLUE METALLIC FLORENTINE LEATHER** bolsters and trim.
17. **SLATE GREEN METALLIC CARDIFF GRAIN LEATHER** with **SLATE GREEN METALLIC FLORENTINE LEATHER** bolsters and trim.
18. **BRONZE METALLIC CARDIFF GRAIN LEATHER** with **BRONZE METALLIC FLORENTINE LEATHER** bolsters and trim.
19. **RED CARDIFF GRAIN LEATHER** with **RED FLORENTINE LEATHER** bolsters and trim.

TOP COLORS: 1. IVORY 2. BLACK 3. BRONZE 7. SLATE GREEN 8. BLUE

*Add B after upholstery code number when selecting Bucket Seats.

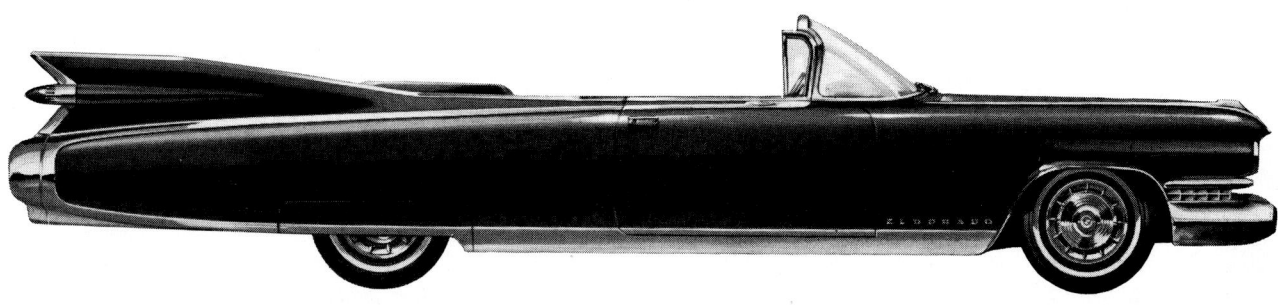

Eldorado Brougham

Dramatically and classically beautiful, the Eldorado Brougham presents an entirely new concept of motor car excellence. Its exclusive design and construction offer the highest expression of luxurious Fleetwood custom coachcrafting. The poise and bearing of the Eldorado Brougham . . . its elegance and refinement are certain to place it among man's most prideful of all material possessions. Here, indeed, is a motor car with distinction, grace and dignity that reflects . . . far more powerfully than words . . . the stature of those for whom it was created.

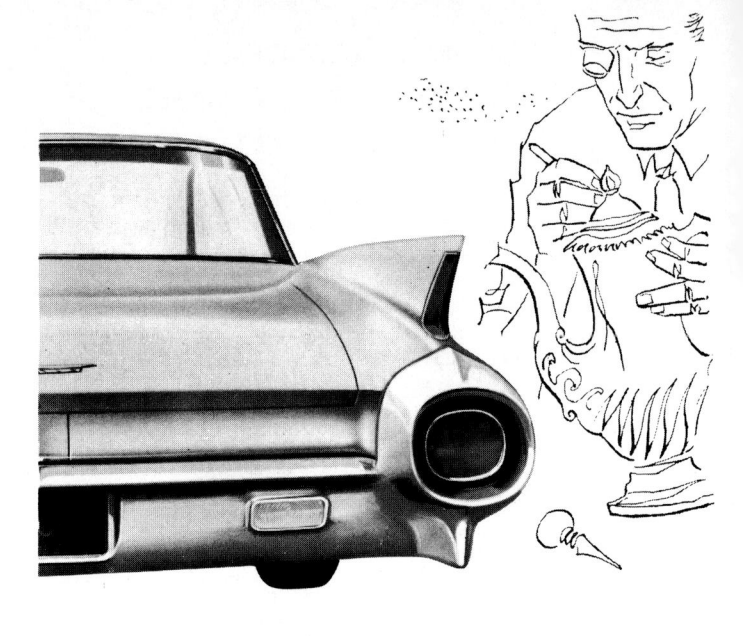

Distinctive to the Eldorado Brougham are the gracefully curved taillights recessed into the rear fender fins. Below, in the bumper extensions are circular tail-, stop-, and turn signal lights set within a red, outer, reflective ring. Twin rectangular back-up lights in the massive chromed rear bumper complete the rear lighting ensemble. At the vortex of the painted panel just above the rear bumper is a carefully fitted door concealing the gas tank filler cap. The entire luggage compartment, including the underside of the deck lid, is luxuriously carpeted throughout to match the interior elegance of the car itself.

Classically simple lines of the Eldorado Brougham's Fleetwood custom coachwork emphasize the exclusive character of this majestic motor car. The beauty of its sculptured glass and metal gives it an identity all its own. Thus there is only a single Brougham medallion of cloisonné enamel and chrome on each front fender side, a slim tapered goddess adorning the hood top and a tiny chromed crest on the headlamp visors.

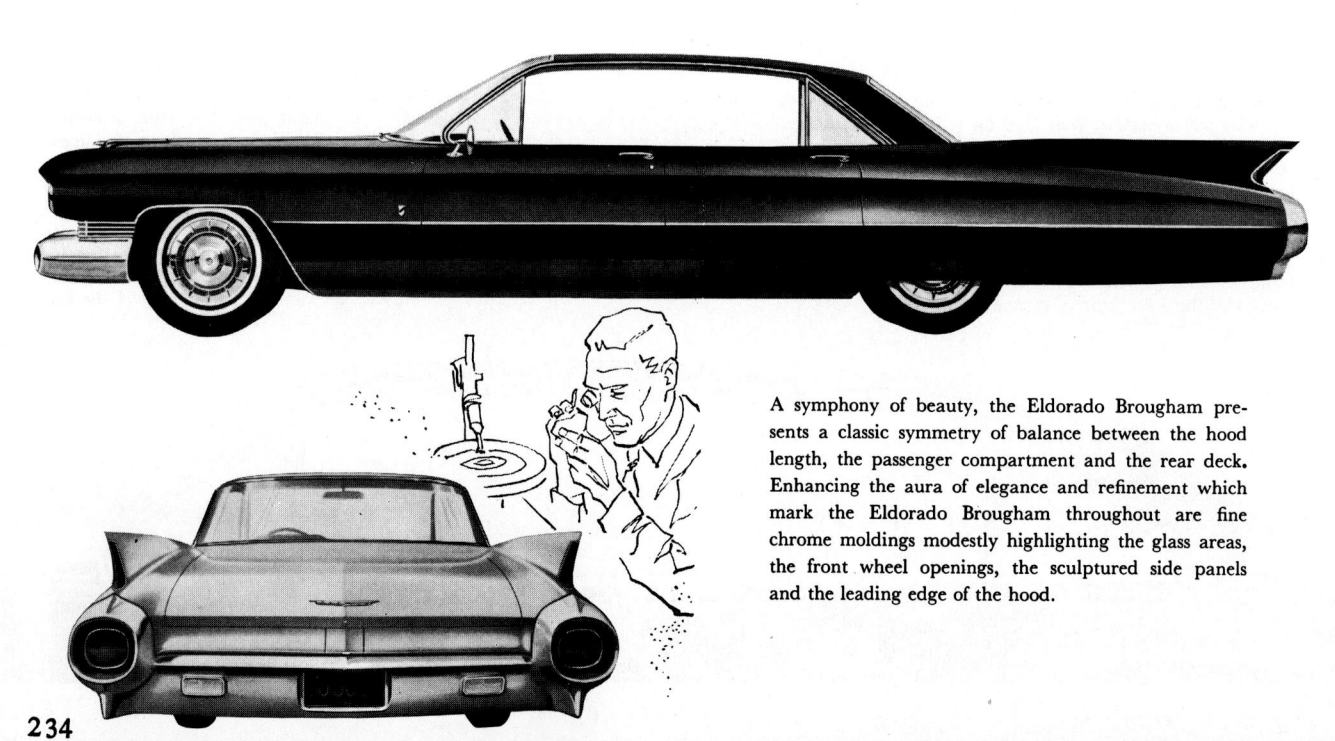

A symphony of beauty, the Eldorado Brougham presents a classic symmetry of balance between the hood length, the passenger compartment and the rear deck. Enhancing the aura of elegance and refinement which mark the Eldorado Brougham throughout are fine chrome moldings modestly highlighting the glass areas, the front wheel openings, the sculptured side panels and the leading edge of the hood.

ELDORADO BROUGHAM...
MOST COMPLETELY EQUIPPED
MOTOR CAR IN AMERICA!

In keeping with the custom design and craftsmanship of the Eldorado Brougham is the high degree of performance, comfort and convenience provided by its full complement of luxury equipment. While most of the features listed below are self-explanatory, comprehensive write-ups of such major items as the Eldorado "Q" engine, Cadillac Cruise Control, the Cadillac Air Conditioner and Heating System, Cadillac Hydra-Matic and Cadillac Air Suspension are available in the forward sections of this Data Book.

Armrest, center, front and rear
Cadillac Air Conditioner
Cadillac Air Suspension
Cadillac Cruise Control
Cadillac Power Brakes
Cadillac Power Steering
Cigarette Lighters, front (two)
Cigarette Lighters, rear (two)
Clock, electric, front and rear
Door Locks, electric
Fluted Wheel Discs (set of four)
Fog Lamps (pair)
Front Seat Adjustment (6-way), power operated
Headlight Dimmer (automatic)
Heater
Hydra-Matic Transmission
License Frames
Lights, front ash receivers
Lights, back-up (dual)
Lights, courtesy (automatic) each front and rear door
Lights, courtesy, front seat back
Lights, directional signal
Light, glove compartment (automatic)
Light, luggage compartment (automatic)
Outside Mirror, left side, remote-control
Outside Mirror, right side
Package compartments, locking, in rear package shelf
Parking Brake Warning Signal
Pocket, back of front seat
"Q" Engine (3 dual-barrel carburetors)
Radio with front and rear speakers
Rear quarter windows, power operated, automatic and manual
Rear-View Mirror, 3-way, E-Z-Eye
Remote-Control Luggage Compartment Lock
Shaded and/or Tinted Glass
Vent Window Regulators, power operated
Visor Vanity Mirror
Visors, dual sun, padded
Whitewall Tires, 8.40 x 15 Low Profile (set of five)
Window Regulators, power operated
Windshield Washer and Coordinator

Editor's Note: Although Cadillac never advertised the fact, the 1959 Brougham had an Italian-built Pinin Farina body. Chassis were pre-assembled and crated in Detroit then shipped to Italy where bodies were installed and interiors crafted. Then it was back to Detroit for finish painting, final touch-up, polishing and tune. According to legend, 100 Broughams were to have been completed during the 1959 model run, but one chassis was dropped in the harbor while being loaded thereby reducing the number to 99. The '59s with air-suspension had a control which allowed the body to remain in full-inflated position giving a much higher road clearance when needed. The 1957-1958 Broughams did not have this feature on their air-suspension systems.

Among the most distinctive features of the Eldorado Brougham is its flat roofline obliquely contoured along each side. The roof itself, with five concealed cross bars for strength and rigidity, is doubly insulated against heat, cold or sound with a cellulose deadener and foam insulator. The rear quarter window automatically recesses into the rear quarter panel, when a rear door is opened, for ease in entering or leaving the rear compartment. It then returns to its normal position when the door is closed. A switch on each rear door and two switches at the left of the steering column permit individual operation of rear quarter windows by the driver or rear compartment passengers.

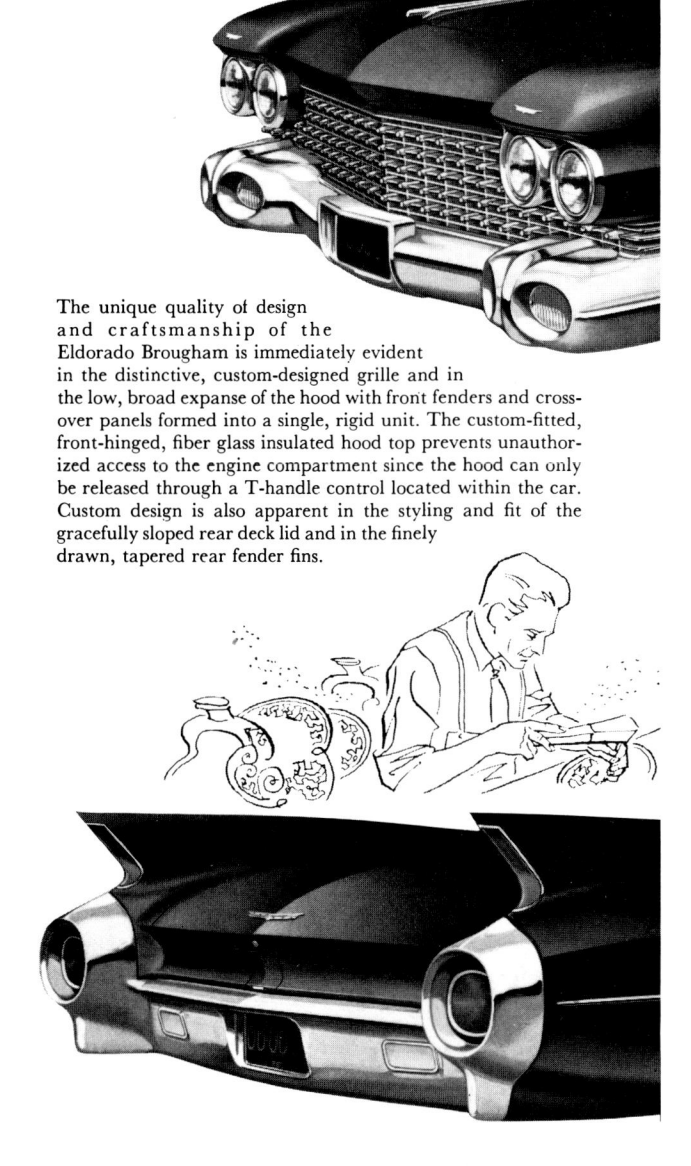

The unique quality of design and craftsmanship of the Eldorado Brougham is immediately evident in the distinctive, custom-designed grille and in the low, broad expanse of the hood with front fenders and cross-over panels formed into a single, rigid unit. The custom-fitted, front-hinged, fiber glass insulated hood top prevents unauthorized access to the engine compartment since the hood can only be released through a T-handle control located within the car. Custom design is also apparent in the styling and fit of the gracefully sloped rear deck lid and in the finely drawn, tapered rear fender fins.

All glass areas of the Eldorado Brougham are of tinted Safety Plate Glass providing an undistorted view with protection against the glare and heat of the sun. In addition, the upper portion of the curved windshield which extends well into the roofline is more deeply shaded for maximum comfort. Restrained treatment of chrome on the forward sloping windshield pillars and on window moldings furthers the air of elegance and refinement which marks the styling of this superb motor car. Door facings, exposed only when a door is open, are finished in the same lustrous acrylic paints as the exterior of the car.

POWER WINDOW REGULATORS

Power window regulators are optional at extra cost on the Sixty-Two sedans and coupe and provided as standard equipment on all other models. All four windows may be raised or lowered by the driver from controls on the left-hand instrument panel extension while single switches are provided for convenient individual window operation by passengers.

POWER VENTIPANE REGULATORS

Electrically operated front ventipanes are standard equipment on the Eldorados and the Fleetwood Sixty Special sedan and optional at extra cost on any other model when equipped with regular power windows (except on the Fleetwood 75 models). Two controls are provided on the driver's door panel with a single control on the opposite door for passenger use.

ELECTRIC DOOR LOCKS

Electric door locks are standard equipment on the Eldorados and available at extra cost on all other models except the Fleetwood 75 sedan and limousine. A master door locking switch is provided on each door of coupes, front doors of sedans. Pushing down on either switch locks all doors. Pushing up on either switch unlocks all doors. Individual doors may be unlocked simply by pulling up the individual door lock button.

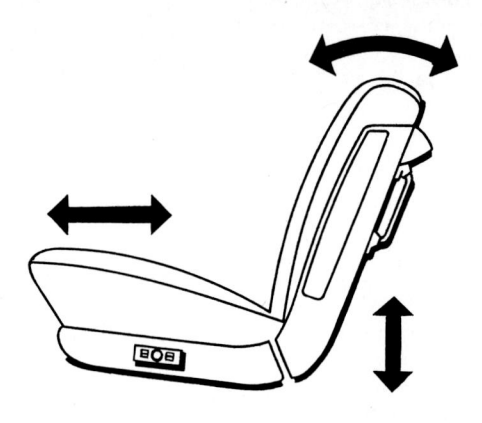

SIX-WAY POWER SEAT ADJUSTMENT

For all 1959 Cadillac cars equipped with the electrically powered fore-and-aft seat adjuster (except the Fleetwood 75 sedan and limousine) an electrically powered vertical and seat angle adjustment is also available as an extra-cost option. The complete six-way power seat is standard equipment on the Eldorados and optional at extra cost on all other models. Control switch is located on left side of front seat on the side panel. (Two-way power seat operative on driver's seat only is provided on Eldorados with bucket seat option.)

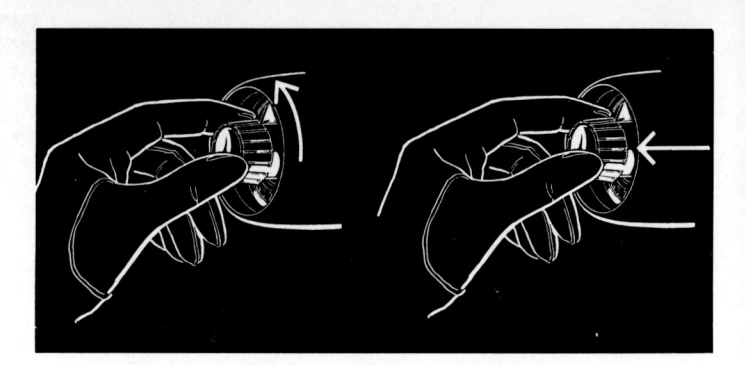

NEW CADILLAC CRUISE CONTROL

An additional convenience for owners of 1959 Cadillacs is the Cadillac Cruise Control. It permits the driver to maintain any speed at which he wishes to travel from approximately 25 to 80 m.p.h. without the necessity of keeping his foot on the accelerator. This is achieved by first setting the Cruise Control knob, located in the left-hand instrument panel nacelle, to a speed higher than that he wishes to travel. Then, when the driver has accelerated to the desired speed, the Cruise Control knob is turned slowly to the left until back pressure is felt on the accelerator pedal. Pulling the knob out now sets the Cruise Control to automatically maintain the selected speed uphill, downhill or on level ground.

If preferred, the driver may follow the foregoing procedure but omit pulling the knob. The accelerator will then react normally to his foot pressure until he tries to exceed the speed setting of the Cruise Control. At such time, a definite back pressure on the accelerator will be felt by the driver as a warning that he is about to pass his chosen speed. The accelerator pedal may be pushed past the pressure point to meet any emergency acceleration requirements.

Any application of the brakes, turning off the ignition or placing the Hydra-Matic lever in Park or Neutral releases the Cruise Control; however, back pressure will still be felt on the accelerator at the speed of the Cruise Control setting until Cruise Control knob is turned full right to the "OFF" position.

NEW FOG LAMPS

Cadillac Fog Lamps, standard on the Eldorados, optional at extra cost on all other models, are located in the outer extremities of the front bumper. Because of their low position they can illuminate the roadway ahead of the car while minimizing reflection against particles of moisture, snow or sleet.

CADILLAC POWER DECK LID LOCK

The Cadillac Power Deck Lid Lock permits releasing and slightly raising the deck lid by pushing a button located within the glove compartment. When the deck lid is again brought down to this position, the power lock automatically closes it the rest of the way and again locks it securely. (Standard on Eldorados.)

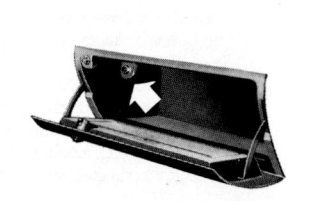

LICENSE PLATE FRAMES

Cadillac anodized, polished aluminum license plate frames with clear plastic windows add to the beauty of the car, cover the sharp edges of the plates and protect the plate numerals and letters from becoming chipped or defaced.

GROUP A . . . . $_____
   W—White Sidewall Tires   R—Radio
   H—Heater   E—E-Z-Eye Glass

GROUP B . . . . $_____
   K—Air Conditioner   R—Radio
   W—White Sidewall Tires   E—E-Z-Eye Glass
   H—Heater

GROUP 2 . . . . $_____
   F—Fog Lamps   D—Dor-Gards

GROUP 3 . . . . $_____
   U—Autronic Eye   D—Dor-Gards
   F—Fog Lamps

GROUP 4 . . . . $_____
   C—Cruise Control   F—Fog Lamps
   U—Autronic Eye   D—Dor-Gards

GROUP 5 . . . . $_____
   T—Air Suspension   F—Fog Lamps
   C—Cruise Control   D—Dor-Gards
   U—Autronic Eye

DO NOT ORDER ANY GROUP FOR ELDORADOS,
AS MOST OF THIS EQUIPMENT IS STANDARD.

SIGNAL SEEKING PRE-SELECTOR RADIO

The Cadillac signal seeking pre-selector radio offers three choices of tuning: manual, push-button for favorite stations, or selector bar which permits successive tuning in of each station across the dial. In addition, a three position switch permits setting the selector bar so that it will stop on only the strongest stations in the area or to reach out into two additional areas of weaker or more distant stations.

Cadillac radios, transistorized for 1959, also have printed circuits which eliminate many wires and soldered joints thus minimizing any possibility of shorts or loosened connections.

The left-hand knob turns the set on or off, adjusts the volume and has an outer ring for regulating base or treble tones. The right-hand knob is for manual tuning and for adjusting the antenna. Pushing in on the knob permits raising the antenna to any degree of its maximum height. Pulling out on the knob permits recessing the antenna fully into the right fender, a choice lacking in many competitive radios. An outer ring on the right-hand knob permits directing the sound through the front or rear speakers or through both speakers.

On the Fleetwood Seventy-Five sedan and limousine remote control tuning is available for rear compartment passengers.

ANTENNA IN RECESSED POSITION
IN RIGHT-FRONT FENDER.

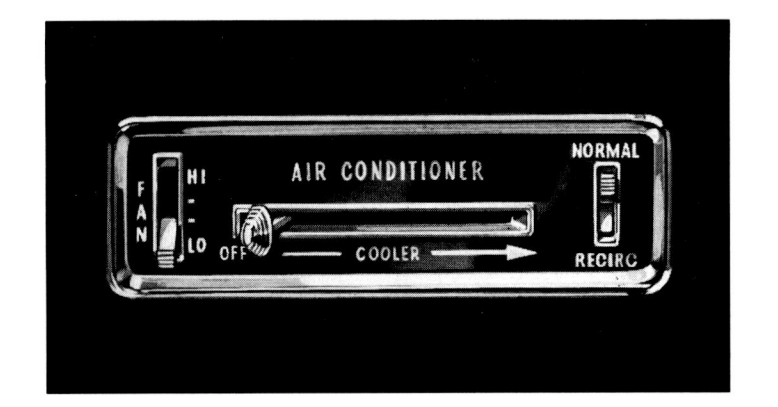

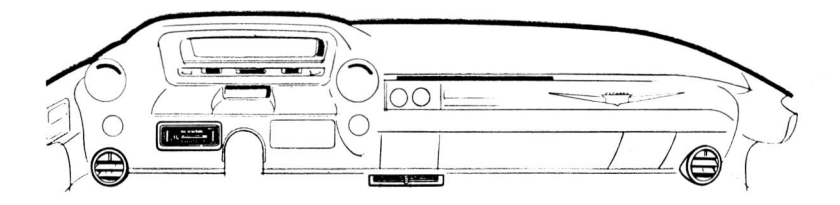

All Cadillac Air Conditioner equipped cars are provided with a 45-ampere, air-cooled, high capacity generator with adequate output, even at lower car speeds, to protect against excessive battery drain. In addition, a seven blade fan and full fan shroud assure efficient engine cooling even with all engine-driven accessories in use.

On the Fleetwood 75 sedan and limousine a completely independent cooling unit is provided in the rear compartment with the evaporator located in the trunk. Adjustable outlets are located overhead at each side of the rear compartment with controls located in the vanity compartment of the right armrest.

Rear Compartment Remote Control Radio . . $_____
Radio Foot-Control Switch . . . . $_____
Cadillac "Cushion Topper" . . . . $_____
Cadillac Transparent Plastic Seat Covers . . $_____
Cadillac Rubber Floor Mats
   Contour Front . . . . $_____
   Contour Rear . . . . $_____
   Rectangular . . . . $_____
Cadillac Seat Belts . . . . $_____
Cadillac Right-Hand Outside Rear-View Mirror . . . . $_____
Cadillac Dor-Gards . . . . $_____
Cadillac Spare Tire Cover . . . . $_____
Windshield Washer Solvent . . . . $_____
Cadillac Body Polish . . . . $_____
Cadillac Fabric Cleaner . . . . $_____
Cadillac Kar-Kleen Upholstery Cleaner . . . $_____
Cadillac Blue Coral . . . . $_____
Cadillac Blue Coral Sealer . . . . $_____
Cadillac Chrome Cleaner . . . . $_____
Cadillac Cooling System Inhibitor and Sealer . $_____
Cadillac Whitewall Tire Cleaner . . . . . $_____
Cadillac Tar and Road Oil Remover . . . . $_____

SPECIFICATIONS

ENGINE

Number of cylinders	8
Cylinder arrangement	90° V-type
Valve arrangement	Overhead
Bore and stroke	4″ x 3⅞″
Block and cylinder head material	Cast iron
Piston displacement	390 cu. in.
Taxable horsepower	51.2
Max. brake horsepower	325 @ 4800 r.p.m.
Eldorado engine	345 @ 4800 r.p.m.
Max. engine torque—lbs.-ft.	430 @ 3100 r.p.m.
Eldorado engine	435 @ 3400 r.p.m.
Compression ratio	10.5:1
Engine mounts	Vulcanized rubber
Number of points of suspension	3

PISTON AND RINGS

Make	Alcoa—Bohn—Sterling
Material	Aluminum alloy
Type	T-slot, cam ground
Weight	22.56 oz.
Clearance	.0015
Number of oil rings per piston	1
Number of comp. rings per piston	2
Top compression ring	Chrome-plated

RODS AND PINS

Wristpin length	3.093″
Wristpin material	Steel
Type	Locked in rod
Connecting rod length	6.500″
Material—connecting rod	Forged steel
Weight—connecting rod	22.56 oz.
Crankpin journal diameter	2¼″
Lower bearing material	Steel-back Moraine 400
Connecting rod bearing clearance	.0005″-.0021″
Connecting rod bearing end play	.008″-.014″ (total two rods)

CRANKSHAFT

Material	Forged alloy steel
Weight	71 pounds
Main bearing thrust	Rear main
Crankshaft end play	.002″ to .007″
Main bearing type	Slip-on
Main bearing removable	Yes
Main bearing material	Steel-back Durex
Main bearing clearance—rear	.0008″ to .0025″
Main bearing journal Diameter x Length:	
Number 1	2.625″ x .907″
Number 2	2.625″ x .907″
Number 3	2.625″ x .907″
Number 4	2.625″ x .907″
Number 5	2.625″ x 1.622″

CAMSHAFT

Drive	Chain
Camshaft sprocket material	Steel
Timing chain—make	Link Belt
Timing chain—no. of links	46
Timing chain—width	.6875″
Timing chain—pitch	.500″

VALVES

Valve arrangement	Overhead
Intake opens	39° B.T.C. at .001 lift
Intake closes	105° A.B.C. at .001 lift
Exhaust opens	85° B.B.C. at .001 lift
Exhaust closes	59° A.T.C. at .001 lift

INTAKE

Material	Alloy steel
Over-all length	4.794″
Diameter of head	1.875″
Angle of seat	44°
Lift	.451″

EXHAUST

Material	Alloy steel
Over-all length	4.815″
Diameter of head	1.500″
Angle of seat	44°
Lift	.451″
Hydraulic valve lifters	Yes
Valve inserts	None
Valve seats cooled by	Direct water circulation

LUBRICATION

Type	Full pressure
Oil under pressure to:	
Main bearings	Yes
Connecting rods	Yes
Wristpins	Splash
Camshaft bearings	Yes
Tappets	Yes
Oil pump type	Gear
Normal oil pressure	30 to 35 lbs. @ 30 m.p.h.
Capacity of oil reservoir	Dry, 6 qts.; Refill, 6 qts.
Type of oil level gauge	Dip stick
Make of pressure gauge	AC—Tell-Tale Lite
Oil filter	Standard
Type	Partial flow

FUEL

Gasoline tank capacity	21 gallons
Type of fuel feed	Camshaft pump
Carburetor—make	Rochester & Carter
Carburetor—type	Four-barrel downdraft*
Manifold heat control	Automatic
Type of air cleaner	Dry-pack
Dual tailpipe diameters	1.75″

*Three, Dual-barrel Carburetors on 345 h.p. engine, standard on Eldorados and optional on all other models.

COOLING

Water pump type	Centrifugal—dual outlet
Pressure relief valve	Yes
Choke for recirculation	Yes
Radiator core	Tube and center
Full-length cylinder water jacket	Yes
Water all around cylinders	Yes
Fan belt length	57″
Fan belt width	⅜″
Fan—no. of blades	4
Air-conditioned cars	7*
Cooling system capacity	18.5 qts.
With heater	19.2 qts. (Series 75, 20.75 qts.) Add .5 qt. for A/C

*Also on Series 75

GENERATOR

Make	Delco-Remy
Minimum charging speed	22 m.p.h. and up
Generator ventilation	Forced air
(Series 75 and air-conditioned cars)	Directed outside air

GENERATOR REGULATOR

Make	Delco-Remy
Voltage at cut-out closing	11.8—13.6 (adjust to 12.8)
(Series 75 and air-conditioned cars)	11.8—13.0 (adjust to 12.4)
Voltage regulator setting	14—15 (adjust to 14.5 at 90°)
(Series 75 and air-conditioned cars)	13.8—14.8 (adjust to 14.0 at 90°)
Generator max. charging rate	32—37 amp. (adjust to 35)
(Series 75 and air-conditioned cars)	42—47 amp. (adjust to 45)

STARTING MOTOR

Make	Delco-Remy
Flywheel teeth, integral or ring	Steel integral

IGNITION

Spark advance	Centrifugal and vacuum
Ignition unit: Make	Delco-Remy
Manual advance	None
Maximum centrifugal advance	Crankshaft (14°-18°), with "Q" engine (16.5°-20.5°)
Vacuum advance	Crankshaft (21.02°-24.0°), with "Q" engine (16.5°-19.5°)
Distributor breaker gap	.016″
Initial spark advance	5° B.T.C. (Nominal)
(on "Q" engine)	7.5° B.T.C. (Nominal)
Firing order	1-8-4-3-6-5-7-2
Ignition coil: Make	Delco-Remy
Spark Plugs:	
Make	AC
Model	44.0
Thread	14 mm.
Gap	.035″

BATTERY

Make	Delco 3EMR70-W
Number of plates	11
Capacity (amp. hrs.)	70
Terminal grounded	Negative
Location of battery	Under hood on tray at front right-hand side of radiator cradle.

LIGHTS AND HORN

Headlight—make	Guide sealed-beam (Dual)
Headlight cover glass, dia.	5¾″
Parking light—make	Guide
Taillight—make	Guide
Lighting switch—make	Delco-Remy
How are headlights dimmed?	Depressed beam—foot switch
Horn:	
Make	Delco-Remy
Type	Vibrator, seashell electric (2)*

*3 on Eldorados.

HYDRA-MATIC DRIVE

Type	Fully automatic step-gear type with controlled fluid coupling on forward gear set for smoother shifts.
Gearing	Planetary
No. of forward speeds	4
No. of forward speeds in "City" DR range	3
No. of forward speeds in "Country" DR range	4
No. of forward speeds in LO range	2
Transmission ratio, first	3.97:1
Transmission ratio, second	2.55:1
Transmission ratio, third	1.55:1
Transmission ratio, fourth	1:1
Transmission ratio, reverse	3.74:1
Oil capacity	11½ qts. dry (check dip stick)
Type of fluid	(*Automatic transmission fluid type "A"*)

SHIFT POINTS:

		With Rear Axle Ratio of: 2.94	3.21 or 3.36	3.77:1
Upshift DR-4 Range	**Throttle Opening**	**M.P.H.**	**M.P.H.**	**M.P.H.**
1st to 2nd	—Minimum	3-9	3-8	3-7
	—Maximum	18-21	16-19	16-18
2nd to 3rd	—Minimum	13-17	12-15	11-14
	—Maximum	40-43	37-39	35-37
3rd to 4th	—Minimum	22-25	20-23	19-21
	—Maximum	76-81	69-74	65-70
Downshift DR-4 Range				
4th to 3rd	—Minimum	17-14	16-13	15-12
	—Maximum	74-68	67-62	64-59
3rd to 2nd	—Minimum	12-8	11-7	10-7
	—Maximum	26-22	24-20	22-19
2nd to 1st	—Minimum	7-3	7-3	6-2
	—Maximum	13-9	12-8	11-6
DR-3 Range				
Same as DR-4 except upshifts from 3rd to 4th at:		76-81	69-74	65-70
downshifts from 4th to 3rd at		74-68	67-62	64-59
LO Range				
Same as DR-4 except upshifts to 3rd at		48-54	44-49	42-47
upshifts to 4th at		76-81	69-74	65-70
downshifts to 3rd at		74-68	67-62	64-59
downshifts to 2nd at		47-44	43-40	41-38

NOTE: Miles per hour at which shift is made is dependent on degree of throttle opening. Actually no gears shift. Term used for clarity of meaning.

FRAME

	Series 60-62-63-64	Series 75
Frame make	A. O. Smith	A. O. Smith
Frame depth, maximum	7″	7″
Frame thickness, maximum	$\frac{9}{64}$″	$\frac{5}{32}$″
Width of flange, maximum	$3\frac{17}{32}$″	$3\frac{17}{32}$″
Frame—Type	Tubular-center X frame	Tubular-center X frame

FRONT-END SUSPENSION

Front suspension, make	Own
Front suspension, type	Forked arms

1959

FRONT-END SUSPENSION—Continued

Forked arm bearings	Inner threaded
Knuckle support bearing	Spherical
Front wheel inner bearing, make and type	N.D. ball
Front wheel outer bearing, make and type	N.D. ball
Front spring, type	Helical coil*
Front spring, material	Spring steel
Shock absorber, type	Hydraulic direct-acting type
Front stabilizer	Torsion rod

*Air suspension standard on Eldorados, optional at extra cost on all other models.

REAR SUSPENSION

Type	Cadillac four-link
Springs	Helical coil*
Material	Spring steel
Spring bushings, type	Rubber
Shock absorbers	Hydraulic direct-acting, inverted "V" mounting

PROPELLER SHAFT

Number used	2
Type	Exposed

UNIVERSAL JOINTS

Make	Mechanics and Saginaw
Number used	3
Type	Cross and Trunnion
Bearing	Needle
Universal joints, lubricated	Permanently
Drive and torque taken through	Four-link rear suspension

STEERING

Steering	Hydraulic power
Type	Concentric gear
Make	Saginaw
Over-all steering ratio	18.9
Car turning radius (outside) bumper to bumper sweep	24'2" 27'0"

REAR AXLE

Rear axle, make	Own	
Rear axle, type	Semifloating	
Differential gear, make	Own	
Rear axle:		
Oil capacity	5 pints	
Grade recommended:		
S.A.E. viscosity	90 hypoid	

	Series 62-60-63-64	Series 75
Type of final gearing	Hypoid	
Gear ratio:		
Standard	2.94	3.36
Optional	3.21*	3.77
Pinion adjustment (except 75)	None	
Pinion bearing adjustment	None (preloaded)	
Are pinion bearings in sleeve?	No	
Backlash between pinion and ring gear	.003"-.010"	
Rear axle pinion shaft:		
Front bearing, type	Tapered roller	
Rear bearing, type	Tapered roller	

*Standard with 345-h.p. "Q" engine and on air-conditioned models. 2.94 optional with "Q" engine.

TIRES AND WHEELS

	Series 62-60-63-64	Series 75
Tires:		
Make	U. S. Royal, Firestone and Goodrich	
Type	Tubeless	
Size	8.00 x 15*	8.20 x 15
Ply rating	4	6
Inflation pressure:		
Front	24 lbs.	28 lbs.
Rear	24 lbs.	28 lbs.
Wheels:		
Type	Slotted disc	
Make	Kelsey-Hayes	
Rim, diameter	15"	
Rim, width	6.00"	
Tread:		
Front	61"	
Rear	61"	

*8.20 x 15 when whitewalls are ordered. Standard on Eldorados.

BRAKES

	Series 62-60-63-64	Series 75
Front and Rear:		
Brake drum diameter	12"	12"
Brake drum, internal or external	Internal	Internal
Brake lining, length per wheel:		
Forward shoe	10.05"	12.98"
Reverse shoe	12.98"	12.98"
Total	23.03"	25.96"
Brake lining width	2½"	2½"
Brake lining thickness	¼"	¼"
Brake lining effective area	210.32 sq. in.	233.72 sq. in.
Brake clearance	.010" top; .015" bottom	
Foot emergency brake location	Left side below dash	
Operates on	Rear service brakes	
Power brakes	Standard, all models	

MISCELLANEOUS SPECIFICATIONS

Car lifting device, jack	Bumper type, scissor type
Engine lubrication, type	Pressure
Chassis lubrication, type	High pressure
Axle lubrication, type	Splash

LUBRICANTS

Engine crankcase capacity	5 qts.
With oil filter (Std.)	6 qts.
Recommended viscosity	Min. anticipated temperature: +32°F. 20W or S.A.E. 20 +10°F. 20W −10°F. 10W Below −10°F. 5W
Drain	2000 miles (after initial 500-mile change)
Rear axle oil	5 pints
Recommended viscosity	90 hypoid
Auto trans. fluid type "A"	11½ qts. dry (check dip stick)
Gasoline	21 gals.

325-HORSEPOWER CADILLAC ENGINE

	Series 62 Sedans and Sedan de Villes (6-window)	Series 62 Coupe, Convertible and Coupe de Ville	Eldorado Biarritz and Eldorado Seville	Series 60 Special Sedan	Series 75 9-Passenger Sedan and Limousine
Wheelbase	130"	130"	130"	130"	149.8"
Over-all Length	225"	225"	225"	225"	244.8"
Over-all Width	80.2"	80.3"	80.3"	81.1"	80.2"
Over-all Height	56.2"***	54.1"****	54.8"†	56.2"	59.3"
Minimum Road Clearance	5.9"	5.9"	6.6"	5.9"	7.0"
Steering Ratio—Over-all	18.9	18.9	18.9	18.9	18.9
Turning Diameter	48.4"	48.4"	48.4"	48.4"	54.0"
Tread—Front	61"	61"	61"	61"	61"
Tread—Rear	61"	61"	61"	61"	61"
Tires, Tubeless—Size	8.00 x 15*	8.00 x 15*	8.20 x 15	8.00 x 15*	8.20 x 15
Tires—Ply Rating	4-ply	4-ply	4-ply	4-ply	6-ply

*8.20 x 15 supplied in whitewall tires (standard on Eldorado Biarritz and Seville). †54.4" on Biarritz.
**53.7" on 4-window sedans. ***53.7" on convertible.

	Series 62 Sedans and Sedan de Villes (6 window)	Series 62 Coupe, Convertible and Coupe de Ville	Eldorado Biarritz and Eldorado Seville	Series 60 Special Sedan	Series 75 9-Passenger Sedan and Limousine
Engine	325-horsepower Cadillac V-8	325-horsepower Cadillac V-8	345 horsepower Cadillac V-8	325-horsepower Cadillac V-8	325-horsepower Cadillac V-8
Compression Ratio	10.5:1	10.5:1	10.5:1	10.5:1	10.5:1
Piston Displacement	390 cu. in.	390 cu. in.	390 cu. in.	390 cu. in.	390 cu. in.
Valve Arrangement	Overhead	Overhead	Overhead	Overhead	Overhead
Carburetor	4-barrel	4-barrel	Three dual-barrel	4-barrel	4-barrel
Exhaust System	Dual	Dual	Dual	Dual	Dual
Transmission	Hydra-Matic	Hydra-Matic	Hydra-Matic	Hydra-Matic	Hydra-Matic
Steering	Hydraulic Power	Hydraulic Power	Hydraulic Power	Hydraulic Power	Hydraulic Power
Brakes	Power Brakes	Power Brakes	Power Brakes	Power Brakes	Power Brakes
Frame	Tubular-center X	Tubular-center X	Tubular-center X	Tubular-center X	Tubular-center X
Springs	Helical coil,* front and rear	Helical coil,* front and rear	Air Suspension front and rear	Helical coil,* front and rear	Helical coil,* front and rear
Drive	Cadillac Four-Link	Cadillac Four-Link	Cadillac Four-Link	Cadillac Four-Link	Cadillac Four-Link
Axle Ratio	2.94:1**	2.94:1**	3.21:1**	2.94:1**	3.36:1***

*Air Suspension optional at extra cost. **3.21 standard with "Q" engine and/or air-conditioned cars ... 2.94 optional with "Q" engine.
***3.77 optional on Series 75.

PRODUCTION DATA BY BODY TYPE

1950

Series 61 (V8-122") — 26,772
- 6137 Coupe — 11,839
- 6169 Sedan — 14,619
- 6169 Export Sedan, CKD — 312
- 61 Chassis — 2

Series 62 (V8-126") — 59,818
- 6219 Sedan — 41,890
- 6237 Coupe — 6,434
- 6237DX Coupe de Ville — 4,507
- 6267 Convertible Coupe — 6,986
- 62 Chassis — 1

Series 60 Special Fleetwood (V8-130")
- Sedan — 13,755

Series 75 Fleetwood (V8-146¾") — 3,512
- 7523L Business Sedan — 1
- 7523X Sedan — 716
- 7533X Imperial Sedan — 743
- 86 Commercial Chassis, 157" — 2,052

Total — 103,857

1951

Series 61 (V8-122") — 4,700
- 6137 Coupe — 2,400
- 6169 Sedan — 2,300

Series 62 (V8-126") — 81,844
- 6219 Sedan — 54,596
- 6219 Export Sedan, CKD — 756
- 6237 Coupe — 10,132
- 6237DX Coupe de Ville — 10,241
- 6267 Convertible Coupe — 6,117
- 62-126 Chassis — 2

Series 60 Special Fleetwood (V8-130")
- Sedan — 18,631

Series 75 Fleetwood (V8-146¾") — 5,165
- 7523L Business Sedan — 30
- 7523X Sedan — 1,090
- 7533X Imperial Sedan — 1,085
- 86 Commercial Chassis, 157" — 2,960

Total — 110,340

1952

Series 62 (V8-126") — 70,255
- 6219 Sedan — 42,625
- 6237 Coupe — 10,065
- 6237DX Coupe de Ville — 11,165
- 6267X Convertible Coupe — 6,400

Series 60 Special Fleetwood (V8-130")
- Sedan — 16,110

Series 75 Fleetwood (V8-146¾") Sedan — 1,400
Series 75 Fleetwood (V8-146¾") Imperial — 800
8680S Commercial Chassis, 157" — 1,694

Total — 90,259

1953

Series 62 (V8-126") — 85,446
- 6219 Sedan — 47,316
- 6219 Export Sedan, CKD — 324
- 6237 Coupe — 14,353
- 6237DX Coupe de Ville — 14,550
- 6267X Convertible Coupe — 8,367
- 6267SX Eldorado Convertible — 532
- 62 Chassis — 4

Series 60 Special Fleetwood (V8-130")
- Sedan — 20,000

Series 75 Fleetwood (V8-146¾") Sedan — 1,435
Series 75 Fleetwood (V8-146¾") Imperial — 765
8680S Commercial Chassis, 157" — 2,005

Total — 109,651

1954

Series 62 (V8-129") — 77,345
- 6219 Sedan — 33,845
- 6219 Export Sedan, CKD — 408
- 6219SX De Ville Sedan — 1
- 6237 Hardtop, 2-door — 17,460
- 6237DX Coupe de Ville — 17,170
- 6267X Convertible Coupe — 6,310
- 6267SX Eldorado Convertible — 2,150
- 62 Chassis — 1

Series 60 Special Fleetwood (V8-133") — 16,200
Series 75 Fleetwood (V8-149¾")
- Sedan — 889
Series 75 Fleetwood (V8-149¾")
- Imperial — 611
8680S Commercial Chassis, 158" — 1,635

Total — 96,680

1955

Series 62 (V8-129") — 118,586
- 6219 Sedan — 44,904
- 6219 Export Sedan, CKD — 396
- 6237 Hardtop, 2-door — 27,879
- 6237DX Coupe de Ville — 33,300
- 6267X Convertible Coupe — 8,150
- 6267SX Eldorado Convertible — 3,950
- 62 Chassis — 7

Series 60 Special Fleetwood (V8-133")
- Sedan — 18,300
Series 75 Fleetwood (V8-149¾")
- Sedan — 1,075
Series 75 Fleetwood (V8-149¾")
- Imperial — 841
8680S Commercial Chassis, 158" — 1,975

Total — 140,777

1956

Series 62 (V8-129") — 133,502
- 6219 Sedan — 26,222
- 6219 Export Sedan, CKD — 444
- 6237 Hardtop, 2-door — 26,649
- 6237DX Coupe de Ville — 24,086
- 6237SDX Eldorado Seville Coupe — 3,900
- 6239DX Sedan de Ville — 41,732
- 6267X Convertible Coupe — 8,300
- 6267SX Eldorado Biarritz conv. — 2,150
- 62 Chassis — 19

Series 60 Special Fleetwood (V8-133")
- Sedan — 17,000
Series 75 Fleetwood (V8-149¾")
- Sedan — 1,095
Series 75 Fleetwood (V8-149¾")
- Imperial — 955
8680S Commercial Chassis, 158" — 2,025

Total — 154,577

1957

Series 62 (V8-129½") — 118,372
- 6237 Hardtop, 2-door — 25,120
- 6237DX Coupe de Ville — 23,813
- 6237SDX Eldorado Coupe — 2,100
- 6239 Sedan — 32,342
- 6239DX Sedan de Ville — 23,808
- 6239SX Sedan Seville — 4
- 6267X Convertible Coupe — 9,000
- 6267SX Eldorado Biarritz conv. — 1,800
- 62 Export Sedan, CKD — 384
- 62 Chassis — 1

Series 60 Special Fleetwood (V8-133") — 24,000
Series 75 Fleetwood (V8-149.8") Sedan — 1,010
Series 75 Fleetwood (V8-149.8") Imperial — 890
Series 70 Eldorado Brougham (V8-126") — 400
8680S Commercial Chassis, 156" — 2,169

Total — 146,841

1958

Series 62 (V8-129.5") — 105,127
- 6237 Hardtop, 2-door — 18,736
- 6237DX Coupe de Ville — 18,414
- 6237SDX Eldorado Seville Coupe — 855
- 6239 Sedan, standard deck — 13,335
- 6239E Sedan, extended deck — 20,952
- 6239EDX Sedan de Ville — 23,989
- 6267X Convertible Coupe — 7,825
- 6267SX Eldorado Biarritz conv. — 815
- 6267SSX Special Eldorado Coupe — 1
- 62 Export Sedan, CKD — 204
- 62 Chassis — 1

Series 60 Special Fleetwood (V8-133") — 12,900
Series 75 Fleetwood (V8-149.8") Sedan — 802
Series 75 Fleetwood (V8-149.8") Imperial — 730
Series 70 Eldorado Brougham (V8-126") — 304
8680S Commercial Chassis — 1,915

Total — 121,778

1959

Series 62-63-64 (V8-130") — 126,421
- 6229 Sedan, 6-window — 23,461
- 6237 Hardtop, 2-door — 21,947
- 6239 Sedan, 4-window — 14,138
- 6267 Convertible Coupe — 11,130
- 62 Export Sedan, CKD — 60
- 6329 Sedan de Ville, 6-window — 19,158
- 6337 Coupe de Ville — 21,924
- 6339 Sedan de Ville, 4-window — 12,308
- 6437 Eldorado Seville Coupe — 975
- 6467 Eldorado Biarritz conv. — 1,320

Series 60 Special Fleetwood (V8-130") — 12,250
Series 67 Fleetwood (V8-149.8") Sedan — 710
Series 67 Fleetwood (V8-149.8")
- Limousine — 690
Series 69 Eldorado Brougham (V8-130") — 99
6890 Commercial Chassis, 156" — 2,102

Total — 142,272

For a complete listing of other books on CADILLAC published by Royco write to:
ROYCO
P.O. Box 7
Temple City, CA 91780

240